MW00471971

THE RISEN CHRIST CONQUERS MARS HILL

THE RISEN CHRIST
CONQUERS MARS HILL

Classic Discourses on Paul's Ministry in Athens

Thomas Manton, Thomas Watson, Jonathan Edwards,
Samuel Davies, John Dick, James Henley Thornwell,
John Eadie, John Charles Ryle, Benjamin B. Warfield,
Ned Stonehouse, Cornelius Van Til, Greg Bahnsen

SOLID GROUND CHRISTIAN BOOKS
BIRMINGHAM, ALABAMA USA

Solid Ground Christian Books
PO Box 660132
Vestavia Hills AL 35266
205-443-0311
mike.sgcb@gmail.com
www.solid-ground-books.com

THE RISEN CHRIST CONQUERS MARS HILL
Classic Discourses on Paul's Ministry in Athens

-Thomas Manton (1620-1677)
-Thomas Watson (1620-1686)
-Jonathan Edwards (1703-1758)
-Samuel Davies (1723-1761)
-John Dick (1764-1833)
-James H. Thornwell (1812-1862)
-John Eadie (1810-1876)
-J.C. Ryle (1816-1900)
-B.B. Warfield (1851-1921)
-Ned B. Stonehouse (1902-1962)
-Cornelius Van Til (1895-1987)
-Greg Bahnsen (1948-1995)

SPECIAL THANKS to David Bahnsen for his kind
permission to use his father's outstanding article.

First Solid Ground Edition – June 2013

Cover design by Borgo Design
Contact them at borgogirl@bellsouth.net

Cover image is a painting of Raphael (1483-1520)
titled *St. Paul Preaching at Athens*

ISBN- 978-159925-290-2

TABLE OF CONTENTS

Introduction: *Why This Book?* – Michael Gaydosh

Foreword by Sinclair Ferguson

CONTRIBUTORS IN THIS BOOK

Below is a list of the twelve articles that comprise this volume, and the places where these works were found. What an honor it is for us to present all of these gems under one cover for the first time ever.

(1) Thomas Manton (1620-1677) - *Sermon Upon Acts 17:30-31*, from Volume 16, published by Solid Ground Christian Books.

(2) Thomas Watson (1620-1686) - *The Day of Judgment Asserted*, from 'The Duty of Self-Denial' published by Soli Deo Gloria.

(3) Jonathan Edwards (1703-1758) - *The Final Judgment: or, The World Judged Righteously by Jesus Christ*, Vol. 2, by Banner of Truth Trust.

(4) Samuel Davies (1723-1761) - *The Universal Judgment*, Vol. 1 of 'The Sermons of Samuel Davies', published by Soli Deo Gloria.

(5) John Dick (1764-1833) - *Paul in Athens*, from 'Lectures on the Acts of the Apostles' published by Solid Ground Christian Books.

(6) James H. Thornwell (1812-1862) - *The Necessity and Nature of Christianity*, from Vol. 2, published by Solid Ground Christian Books.

(7) John Eadie (1810-1876) - *Paul at Athens*, from Chapter 10, 'Paul the Preacher' published by Solid Ground Christian Books.

(8) John Charles Ryle (1816-1900) - *Athens*, from 'The Upper Room' published by Banner of Truth Trust.

(9) Benjamin B. Warfield (1851-1921) - *False Religions and the True*, from 'Biblical, Theological Studies' by P & R Publishers.

(10) Ned B. Stonehouse: (1902-1962) - *The Areopagus Address*, from the Tyndale New Testament Lecture, 1949, by Tyndale Press, London.

(11) Cornelius Van Til (1895-1987) - *Paul at Athens*, a Booklet, distributed by Westminster Books.

(12) Greg Bahnsen (1948-1995) - *The Encounter of Jerusalem with Athens*, from 'Always Ready' published by Covenant Media Foundation.

INTRODUCTION
Why This Book?

This book was designed to bring together representatives of the last four centuries on a subject of perennial interest to the people of God: *How do we reach unbelievers with the timeless message of the Gospel?*

There is something of remarkable power in the ministry of the Apostle Paul in the great ancient city of Athens. Although he spent a brief period of time there, and did not have time to plant a church, he still left his mark in that barren center of philosophy and idolatry. Nearly 2000 years later the ministry of Paul continues to instruct, rebuke, correct and train in the ways of righteousness.

Solid Ground Christian Books has sought to gather one dozen messages from faithful ministers of the Gospel on this life-changing and ministry-transforming passage. Our desire is to follow the counsel found in Proverbs 13:23, "He who walks with wise men will be wise." The men found within the pages of this book were wise men because they feared God and sought to minister out of that fear which is "the beginning of wisdom." They were also men who loved God because of the great love with which they had been loved by God. Their love for God drove them to desire to know God and to make Him known to others.

If the Lord deems to smile upon our efforts, and the people of God appreciate this work, we plan to publish other books in this series. Plans are already underway for Classic Discourses on The Given Christ of John 3:16; Classic Discourses on The Smitten Christ; and Classic Discourses on the Incarnate Christ.

Be prepared for a treat. From the opening exposition by Thomas Manton, to the closing article by Greg Bahnsen, you will be carried over the same ground with a dozen trusted guides. They will not all point out the same things, but they will all unite to declare that the Gospel of the great Apostle is still the only hope for our broken world. Enjoy the ride.

Michael Gaydosh
Solid Ground Christian Books

FOREWORD

From the opening exposition of a seventeenth century Westminster Divine to the closing expositions of three twentieth century scholars associated with Westminster Seminary, *The Risen Christ Conquers Mars Hill* is a brilliantly conceived compilation of studies calculated both to educate and to stimulate.

Paul's great sermon to the intellectual elite of a declining Athens is one of the great moments in Church history. It well repays careful study for its foundational theology, its methodology as a presentation of the gospel of God to a pagan audience, and for the passion for Christ that lay behind it.

Here is careful theological exegesis, biblical doctrine, practical application, and sharp-edged apologetics all in one volume. The result? A book that cannot fail to instruct the mind, encourage confidence in the gospel's integrity, and challenge the church to a new boldness in witnessing to our paganism-restoring culture.

Sinclair Ferguson
First Presbyterian Church, Columbia SC

CHAPTER ONE

Expository Sermon on Acts 17:30,31

THOMAS MANTON

SERMON UPON ACTS XVII. 30, 31.

And the times of this ignorance God winked at ; but now commandeth all men everywhere to repent: because he hath appointed a day, in the which he will judge the world in righteousness by that man whom he hath ordained ; whereof he hath given assurance unto all men, in that he hath raised him from the dead.—ACTS xvii. 30, 31.

THE words are the conclusion of Paul's speech to the men of Athens, wherein, having disproved their idolatry, he cometh to show them the right way of returning from their sin and misery to their duty and happiness.

In them we have—(1.) An exhortation, ver. 30 ; (2.) An argument and motive to enforce it, ver. 31.

1. The exhortation, which consists of two parts—(1.) A censure of the past times ; (2.) The duty of the present time. Wherein, (1*st.*) The duty itself, repentance ; (2*d.*) The universality of its obligation, He 'commandeth all men everywhere to repent ;' that is, all without difference of nations, the call being now general.

2. The argument or motive to enforce it. The argument is—(1.) propounded ; (2.) confirmed.

[1.] Propounded, 'Because he hath appointed a day, in which he will judge the world in righteousness by that man whom he hath ordained.'

[2.] Confirmed, 'Whereof he hath given assurance unto all men, in that he hath raised him from the dead.'

To possess you with the full scope of this scripture, let me explain all these clauses.

I. I begin with the exhortation, which consists of two parts—(1.) The censure of the past times ; (2.) The duty of the present time.

First, In the censure of the past times two things are said of them— (1.) That they were times of ignorance ; and (2.) That God winked at them, or overlooked them.

1. That they were times of ignorance, and that easily leadeth into error. But now the light of the gospel was brought to them, God did more peremptorily insist upon his right, and commanded them to repent, and to turn from dead idols to the living God ; for the practices of ignorance will not become a time of knowledge : 1 Peter i. 14,

' As obedient children, not fashioning yourselves according to the former lusts in your ignorance.' There was a time when we knew neither the terror, nor the sweetness of the Lord, but securely lived in sin ; what we did then will misbecome us now. So Rom. xiii. 12, ' The night is far spent, the day is at hand ; let us therefore cast off the works of darkness, and let us put on the armour of light.' While they were heathens, they lived in ignorance of God and the way to true happiness, and in a profane godless course, and an utter carelessness and neglect of heavenly things. As in the night the wild and savage beasts go abroad foraging for their prey ; but, as the psalmist telleth us, Ps. civ. 22, 23, ' When the sun ariseth, they gather themselves together, and lay them down in their dens, and man goeth forth to his work ; ' so in this spiritual night of ignorance, sin reigneth, and brutish affections carry all before them, and a man is governed by sense and appetite, and not by reason and conscience ; but when the day dawneth, the man should show himself, and reason should be in dominion again ; and though before they neither minded God and their own souls, nor considered their danger, nor their remedy, yet now they should awake, and return and seek after God. Sins are more aggravated in times of more full gospel light ; for when light is come into the world, and men 'love darkness rather than light,' John iii. 19, then to our error there is added stubbornness and obstinacy ; and whatever connivance God used before, this will bring speedy ruin upon us.

2. The second thing which is said is that God winked at these times. There—(1.) We must open the meaning ; (2.) The necessity and use of this reflection.

[1.] The meaning. Certainly it is not meant of God's allowing of their idolatries ; that would entrench upon his honour, and hinder their repentance for former sins, and resolution of taking a new course for the future. What is the meaning then ? for some interpret the clause as speaking indulgence, others as intimating judgment, which though to appearance they seem contrary, yet both may stand together.

(1.) Some think it speaketh indulgence, as we translate it, ' winked at,' that is, looked not after them to punish or destroy them for their idolatries. Ignorance is sometimes made an excuse *a tanto*, though not *a toto*; as Acts iii. 17, ' I wot that through ignorance ye did it, as did also your rulers ;' and 1 Tim. i. 13, ' I was a blasphemer, and a persecutor, and injurious ; but I obtained mercy, because I did it ignorantly.' It somewhat mollified the sin.

(2.) Others think this clause speaketh a judgment. The vulgar readeth *neglexit*, God neglected those times, or regarded them not. As the Greeks complained, Acts vi. 1, ' That their widows were neglected,' παρεθεωροῦντο, overseen ; so here, ὑπεριδὼν, overlooked, or not regarded. So God is said elsewhere to deal with an apostate and sinning people : Heb. viii. 9, ' They continued not in my covenant, and I regarded them not ;' I took no notice of them to do them good. So God regarded not those times of ignorance, gave them not such helps and means as afterwards, or as now he did when he sent the gospel to them. To this sense I incline, partly because it is so explained in a parallel place : Acts xiv. 16, 17, ' Who in times past suffered all nations to walk in their own ways ; nevertheless he left not himself without a witness.' And partly because it agreeth with the thing itself: Ps. cxlvii. 19, 20, 'He hath showed his word unto Jacob, his statutes and his judgments unto Israel; he hath not dealt so with any nation: and as for his judgments, they have not known them.' The grace of external vocation is a great mercy, and the apostle would have them apprehensive of it; for when God sendeth the light of the gospel, he showeth the care that he hath of the lost nations: Eph. iii. 5, 'Which in other ages was not made known unto the sons of men, as it is now revealed unto his holy apostles and prophets by the Spirit.' Partly because God did punish the ignorance and error of the gentiles by giving them up to vile affections: Rom. i. 24, 'Wherefore God gave them up to uncleanness.' It is a severe judgment to be given up to our own lusts, and blindness and hardness of heart. But yet I do not exclude the former sense, because though the idolatry of the nations continued for many years, yet God continued many signal temporal mercies to them.

[2.] The necessity and use of this reflection.

(1.) It is an answer to their cavil, ver. 18, 'He seemeth to be a setter forth of strange gods.' Now the apostle replieth that the gods of their fathers were idols, and not gods. But how can it stand with the providence of the true God to permit it and forsake mankind so long? Those times of ignorance God overlooked, sent them no means nor messengers then, but now he doth; and so he teacheth them and us that it is not sufficient to follow the religion of our forefathers, unless they had followed the will of God. If God overlooked them, and vouchsafeth you more grace, you must not be prejudiced by the tradition, but improve the present advantage.

(2.) He, as much as in him lieth, taketh off the prejudice of the practice of former times by a prudent and soft censure. As also elsewhere: 1 Cor. ii. 8, 'Which none of the princes of this world knew; for had they known it they would not have crucified the Lord of glory.'

(3.) He insinuateth that ignorance doth not wholly excuse those that err, but rather commendeth the Lord's patience.

Secondly, The duty of the present time.

1. The duty pressed is repentance. The word is μετανοεῖν. Repentance is a returning to our wits again. We were sometimes ἀνόητοι, 'foolish,' Titus iii. 3. When the conversion of the nations is spoken of, it is said, Ps. xxii. 27, 'All the ends of the world shall remember and turn unto the Lord;' as if they were asleep, distracted, or out of their wits before the light of Christ's gospel shined into their hearts, not making use of common reason. We never act wisely nor with a condecency to our reasonable nature, till we return to the love and obedience of God.

2. This is here represented not as an indifferent and arbitrary thing, but as expressly and absolutely commanded. God's authority is absolute; if he hath commanded anything, contradiction must be silent, hesitation satisfied, all cavils laid aside, and we must address ourselves to the work speedily and seriously, without delaying, or disputing, or murmuring. God doth not advise or entreat only, but commandeth, or interposeth his authority. Now to break a known command, especially

of such weight and moment, is very dangerous : Luke xii. 47, 'That servant which knew his Lord's will, and prepared not himself, neither did according to his will, shall be beaten with many stripes ; ' James iv. 17, 'To him that knoweth to do good, and doth it not, to him it is sin.' A man in the dark may easily err and go astray ; but while we know better, and what is the express will of God concerning us, we must set ourselves to do it.

3. As universally required, 'All men everywhere ; ' not only Jews, but gentiles ; and not some sort of gentiles, but all ; you, Athenians, and all the world ; this universally bindeth. Some must turn from their idols, but all from their sinful ways, Whosoever will not repent when God calleth for repentance, they smart the more for it. Impenitency under the means is the worst sort of impenitency. I may say as Christ, Luke xiii. 5, 'Except ye repent, ye shall all likewise perish.'

II. The argument or motive. Which we consider—(1.) As propounded ; (2.) As confirmed.

First, As propounded. Where note—(1.) The time, 'He hath appointed a day wherein he will judge the world ; ' (2.) The manner, ' In righteousness ; ' (3.) The person, ' By that man whom he hath ordained.' These circumstances must be opened, and then we must consider how they make an argument.

For opening the circumstances.

1. The time appointed, but not revealed, 'He hath appointed a day.' The word *day* is not taken strictly for such a space of time as is usually signified by that notion, but it is put for a certain fixed space of time. The work cannot well be dispatched in twenty-four hours. There is *judicium discussionis*, and *judicium retributionis*, a judgment of search or trial, and a judgment of retribution. Though by the absolute power of God they may be commanded into their everlasting estate in an instant, yet the causes of the whole world cannot be discussed in an instant, especially when God designeth the full revelation of his justice in all his proceedings with men. Therefore, the apostle calleth that day, the day of 'the revelation of the righteous judgment of God,' Rom. ii. 5. When this time will be we cannot tell, for God hath not revealed it : Mat. xxiv. 36, 'But of that day and hour knoweth no man, no, not the angels in heaven, but my Father only ; ' and therefore it is curiosity to inquire, and rashness to determine : Acts i. 7, 'It is not for you to know the times or the seasons which the Father hath put in his own power.' It is enough for us to believe the thing, which is not strange to reason, that God should call his creatures to an account. Natural conscience is terrified with the hearing of it : Acts xxiv. 25, ' As Paul reasoned of righteousness, temperance, and judgment to come, Felix trembled.' And the same guilty fears are incident to all mankind : Rom. i. 32, ' Knowing the judgment of God ; ' they know also that they who have done such things as they have done are worthy of death. That we are God's subjects is evident to reason, because we depend upon him for life, being, and all things. That we have failed in our subjection to God, in denying the obedience due to him, is evident by the universal, daily, and sad experience of the whole world ; that error and sin will not take place to all eternity, but that there must be some time when the disorders of the world shall be rectified ; is a

truth that easily maketh its own way into the consciences of men, but is fully determined by the gospel.

2. For the manner, ' He will judge the world in righteousness ; ' that is, then the whole world shall receive the fruit of their doings, whether they be good or evil. But doth God ever judge the world otherwise than in righteousness ? I cannot say that, for ' far be it from the judge of all the earth not to do right,' Gen. xviii. 25. He never doth anything unjustly or unrighteously now, but then he will fully manifest his righteousness. He now judgeth the world in patience, but then in righteousness. There is a difference between a defect of justice and a transgression of the rules of justice. There is no injustice in God's dispensations of present providence, but yet there is a defect, or not a full measure or manifest demonstration of his justice showed now on the godly or the wicked. Therefore it is said, Eccles. viii. 14, ' There be just men to whom it happeneth according to the work of the wicked ; and again, there be wicked men to whom it happeneth according to the work of the righteous.' He doth not pass this censure upon the wise and righteous providence of God, but either speaketh according to the judgment of flesh and blood, which is apt to judge hardly of so strange a distribution, or according to the visible appearance of things, when evil things happen to good men, or good things to evil men. For outward things being not absolutely good and evil, are dispensed promiscuously, and in the day of trial God hath his end in these things, for humbling and exercising the good, and hardening the wicked : but in the day of recompense, then it shall be only ill with them that do evil, and well with them that do good, and the retributions of his justice shall be fully evidenced.

3. The person, ' By that man whom he hath ordained ; ' meaning thereby Christ. But why doth he call Christ *man*, rather than God ?

[1.] Partly with respect to the gentiles' incapacity to apprehend the mystery of the Trinity, or the incarnation of the Son of God ; and it concerneth us to dispense truths as people are able to bear them ; as Christ taught καθὼς ἠδύναντο ἀκούειν, ' As they were able to bear it,' Mark iv. 33. Therefore Paul would not offend them by doctrines which they could not yet understand.

You will say the resurrection was as offensive.

Ans. That was ἐν πρώτοις one of the first points of the apostolical catechism : Heb. vi. 1, 2, ' Therefore leaving the principles of the doctrine of Christ, let us go on unto perfection ; not laying again the foundation of repentance from dead works, and of faith towards God ; of the doctrine of baptism, and of laying on of hands, and of the resurrection of the dead, and of eternal judgment.' So that the apostle could not preach the very rudiments of christianity if he had not mentioned that.

[2.] Christ is to discharge this office in the visible appearance of man. As the judgment was to be visible, so the judge. The judgment is not to be acted by the Father or the Spirit, but by Christ in the human nature ; therefore his coming is called ' an appearance ; ' Titus ii. 13, ' Looking for that blessed hope, and the glorious appearing of the great God, and our Saviour Jesus Christ ; ' and 2 Tim. iv. 8, ' Henceforth there is laid up for me a crown of righteousness, which the Lord, the righteous judge, shall give me at that day, and not to me only, but to all them that love his appearance.' And when the judgment is spoken of, Christ is often designed by this expression, the Son of man: Mat. xxiv. 30, ' They shall see the Son of man coming in the clouds of heaven with power and great glory ;' and Mat. xvi. 27, ' For the Son of man shall come in the glory of his Father, with his angels ; and then he shall reward every man according to his works.' He is the visible actor in the judgment, sitting on a visible throne, that he may be seen and heard of all, and the godhead doth most gloriously manifest itself by the perfections of his human nature.

3. This power is given to Christ as a recompense of his humiliation. For therefore hath ' God highly exalted him, and given him a name above every name, that at the name of Jesus every knee shall bow, of things in heaven, and things in earth, and things under the earth,' Phil. ii. 9, 10, which is at the day of judgment : Rom. xiv. 10, 11, ' We shall all stand before the judgment-seat of Christ; for it is written, As I live, saith the Lord, every knee shall bow to me.' Then all creatures in heaven, earth, and hell are to own the sovereign power and empire of the crucified Saviour. Some do it willingly, as the elect angels, and men ; others do it by constraint, as the reprobate and evil angels, when they are forced to stand before the tribunal of Christ to receive their final doom and sentence. This is the last act of his kingly office, and the fruit and consequent of his humiliation. Therefore this Christ spake of when he stood before the tribunals of men : Mat. xxvi. 64, ' Hereafter ye shall see the Son of man sitting on the right hand of power, and coming in the clouds of heaven.' The despised man, who was before them as a criminal in their repute, summoneth them to answer before his tribunal at that day, when his shame shall be turned into glory, and the scandal of his first estate shall be fully taken off, and those that despised him as man shall be forced to acknowledge him as God.

Secondly, The subsequent proof : ' Whereof he hath given assurance to all men, in that he hath raised him from the dead.' That is a sufficient testimony to convince the whole world. The resurrection is a certain proof and argument of the dignity both of Christ's person and office. It is an attestation to his person : Rom. i. 4, ' Declared to be the Son of God with power, according to the Spirit of holiness, by the resurrection from the dead.' To his office and doctrine : John v. 27–29, ' And hath given him authority to execute judgment also, because he is the Son of man. Marvel not at this ; for the hour is coming in which all that are in the graves shall hear his voice, and shall come forth ; they that have done well, unto the resurrection of life ; and they that have done evil, unto the resurrection of damnation.' How doth this make faith to all the world ? for that is the word, $\pi i \sigma \tau \iota \nu \pi a \rho a \sigma \chi \grave{\omega} \nu$. *Ans.* God hath not given faith to all men, but he hath given an argument to all men that is a ground of faith, from whence faith may evidently conclude that Christ is our judge, for he hath raised him from the dead. Where is the force of this demonstration ? Others were raised from the dead, as Lazarus and the like, and yet they are not judges of the world. I answer—Christ died in the repute of men as a malefactor, but God justified him when he would not leave him under the power of death, but raised him up and assumed him into glory, thereby visibly declaring unto the world that the judgment passed upon him was not right, but that he was indeed what he gave out himself to be, the Son of God and the judge of the world, to whom power is given over all flesh, to save or destroy them. If he live with the Father in glory and majesty, it will necessarily follow that he was not a seducer, but that holy and righteous one by whom God will execute his judgment.

Secondly, What influence this hath upon repentance.

1. The very day appointed inferreth a necessity of change both of heart and life; for how else shall we stand in the judgment who have broken God's laws, and are obnoxious to his wrath and displeasure? If we should never be called to an account for what we have been and done here in the world, we might then freely indulge ourselves in all fleshly delights, and do what we please. But this is a principle of fear and restraint, that for all these things God will bring thee into the judgment: Eccles. xi. 9, ' Rejoice, O young man in thy youth and let the heart cheer thee in the days of thy youth ; and walk in the ways of thine heart, and in the sight of thine eyes : but know thou, that for all these things God will bring thee into judgment.' None of us can hide or withdraw ourselves from that great tribunal, before which we are to give an account of what we have done and received in the body. And therefore it is best, while we are in the way, to make our peace with God and break off our sins by repentance ; otherwise what quiet can we have in ourselves? or how can we keep ourselves when we are serious from trembling at wrath to come ? We may smother conscience, and baffle all convictions for the present; but, christians, you and I must be judged. Now when God riseth up to the judgment, what shall we answer him ? Job xxxi. 14, ' What then shall I do when God riseth up? and when he visiteth, what shall I answer him ? ' That must be thought on beforehand. If we have no answer which will satisfy now, much less then.

2. From the manner or strictness of that day's account, he will judge the world in righteousness: Eccles. xii. 14, ' God shall bring every work into judgment, with every secret thing, whether it be good, or whether it be evil.' Hypocrisy shall be disclosed, sincerity shall be rewarded, nothing shall be hidden from God's search ; no person shall be exempted, no work, either open or secret, but God will bring it into judgment. His infinite wisdom knoweth all, and his infinite justice will give due recompense to all. The businesses of all nations and persons shall be openly examined. What then is our duty but to exercise ourselves both in faith and repentance, that our judge may be our saviour, and it may go well with us when this search is made?

3. Chiefly from the person, sufficiently attested by the miracles of his life and resurrection from death. God hath determined and ordained the person by whom the whole world shall be judged. And from thence we may judge of the rule ; it is by his doctrine, and by our receiving or not receiving Christ. Surely it is our interest to be in with him who will cite us before his tribunal ; to accept his person as our Lord and Saviour : John i. 12, ' To as many as received him, to them gave he power to become the sons of God.' To believe and entertain his doctrine as the message of God: John v. 24, ' He that

heareth my word, and believeth on him that sent me, hath everlasting life, and shall not come into condemnation, but is passed from death to life.' To imitate his example : 1 John iv. 17, ' Herein is our love made perfect, that we may have boldness in the day of judgment; because as he is, so are we in this world.' To trust in his merit : Ps. ii. 12, ' Kiss the Son, lest he be angry, and ye perish from the way, when his wrath is kindled but a little : blessed are all they that put their trust in him.' To love him and live to him : 1 Cor. xvi. 22, ' If any man love not the Lord Jesus Christ, let him be anathema maranatha.' If he say, Come, ye blessed, or, Go, ye cursed, we must abide by it to all eternity. Woe to them that neglect his offers, contemn his ways, oppose his interest, oppress his servants. But blessed are they whose Redeemer is their judge ; he who shed his blood for them, must pass the sentence on them ; and one that is flesh of our flesh and bone of our bone is the final judge between us and God. Will he be harsh to his sincere disciples ? But to say all in a word, surely this consideration should do the work effectually, because his gospel and covenant is nothing else but a free promise of pardon upon condition of repentance: Luke xxiv. 47, ' That repentance and remission of sins should be preached in his name among all nations.' And to this end the apostles were to preach that Christ is judge : Acts x. 42, 43, ' He hath commanded us to preach unto the people, and to testify that it is he who was ordained of God to be the judge of quick and dead. To him give all the prophets witness, that through his name whosoever believeth in him, shall receive remission of sins.' Nothing showeth the necessity of remission of sins so much as the judgment, and the necessity of repentance to remission so much as the judge, who in his covenant hath made this condition. Nothing doth befriend the great discovery of the gospel, which is free pardon of sin by Christ upon repentance, so much as the sound belief of this truth, that Christ is judge.

Doct. That the great purpose and drift of the gospel where it is sent and preached is to invite men to repentance.

This appeareth abundantly by the scripture, that repentance is one of the first and chief lessons which the gospel teacheth. When the gospel kingdom was to be erected or set up, John the Baptist crieth, ' Repent ye, for the kingdom of heaven is at hand,' Mat. iii. 2. So when Jesus himself began to preach, his note is the same: Mat. iv. 17, ' He began to preach, and to say, Repent, for the kingdom of heaven is at hand.' His doctrine and the doctrine of the Baptist is all one in substance, and necessarily it must be so. The gospel findeth men under the tyranny of Satan, and offereth to bring them into the kingdom of God. So when he sent abroad his disciples first to the Jews, Mat. x. and afterwards to the world, Luke xxiv. 47, ' That repentance and remission of sins should be preached in his name.' The disciples were faithful to their commission : Acts ii. 38, ' Peter said unto them, ' Repent and be baptized every one of you in the name of Jesus Christ, for the remission of sins.' But to give you some reasons of it, I shall— (1.) Inquire what is repentance , (2.) What the gospel doth to promote it ; (3.) How convenient and necessary this is for all those that are willing to come out of the apostasy of mankind, and to return to their obedience to God.

First, What is repentance ? Sometimes it is taken largely for our whole conversion to God through the faith of Christ, as in the text: 'He commandeth all men to repent;' that is, to turn from their sins, and believe the gospel : 2 Tim. ii. 25, ' In meekness instructing those that oppose themselves, if peradventure God will give them repentance to the acknowledging of the truth ;' where the owning of the christian faith is called repentance. Sometimes strictly, as opposed to or rather distinguished from faith, as Acts xx. 21, ' Testifying both to the Jews, and also to the Greeks, repentance towards God, and faith toward our Lord Jesus Christ ;' where repentance is said to be towards God as the end, as faith is conversant about Christ as the means. And there it signifieth a return to the love and obedience of our Creator, which was our primitive duty before the fall, as faith implieth all the duties that belong to our recovery by Christ. In short, in the strict sense, there is not only a sorrow for what is past, which is a beginning and help to the other part ; for, 2 Cor. vii. 10, 'Godly sorrow working repentance unto salvation, not to be repented of ; ' but also a full purpose of heart to live unto God;' Gal. ii. 19, ' I through the law am dead to the law, that I might live unto God. Sometimes repentance is described by one term, called ' Repentance from dead works,' Heb. vi. 1 ; where by dead works are meant sins, which render us liable to death ; and often by the other, called a turning or returning to God : Zech. i. 3, 'Turn ye unto me, saith the Lord,' Acts xxvi. 18, ' To open their eyes, and to turn them from darkness to light, and from the power of Satan unto God.' From him we fell, to him we return ; and so it includeth an acknowledgment of our sins, with grief of heart, and a resolution to forsake them, that we may live unto God ; both of which, if they be hearty and sincere, will be evidenced by 'newness of life,' Rom. vi. 4, or doing works meet for repentance : Acts xxvi. 20, ' That they should repent and turn to God, and do works meet for repentance.' The sum of what he preached was reduced to three heads, the two first by way of foundation, the third by way of superstructure. The two first imply an internal change, the third the outward discovery of it. By ' repentance' is meant there a bethinking ourselves, or considering our ways, after we have gone wrong, with a broken-hearted sense and acknowledgment of the misery into which we have plunged ourselves by sin ; by ' turning to God,' our seeking happiness in God by Christ, and giving up ourselves to him to do his will ; and by ' works meet for repentance,' a suitable and thankful life. All practical divinity may be reduced to these three heads, a sense of our misery by nature, a flying to God by Christ for a remedy, and the life of love and praise, which becometh Christ's reconciled and redeemed ones. This is repentance.

Secondly, What the gospel doth to promote it.

1. It requireth it indispensably of all grown persons. In the text, ' He commandeth all men everywhere to repent.' And our Lord, telleth us that the great end of his commission was to call sinners to repentance : Mat. ix. 13, ' I am not come to call the righteous, but sinners to repentance.' The gospel findeth us not innocent, but in a lapsed estate, under the power of sin, entangled in the love of the world, and the snares of the devil, and obnoxious to the wrath of God. Now Christ

came to recover us from the devil, the world, and the flesh, unto God, that we may love him again, and be happy in his love ; so that they quite mistake the nature of our recovery who dream of a mere exemption from wrath, without an healing our natures, or restoring and putting poor creatures in joint again, which were disordered by the fall or that we can live in the love of God, before we are changed both in heart and life. No ; Christ took another course to call us, not only to pardon and eternal glory, but to repentance ; or strictly to enjoin this duty upon us, that by his grace we might recover a disposition of heart, which in some measure might incline and enable us to love, please, and obey God, and that under pain of his displeasure we might break off our sins, and live unto God ; for he came not to give liberty to any to live in sin.

2. By its promises, for it offereth pardon and life to the penitent believer, and to them only. None can enjoy the privileges of the new covenant but those that are willing to return to the duty which they owe to the Creator. This is gospel : Luke xxiv. 47, ' That repentance and remission of sins should be preached in his name ;' compared with Mark xvi. 16, ' He that believeth, and is baptized, shall be saved ; but he that believeth not shall be damned.' God and Christ are agreed that salvation should be dispensed upon these terms, and no other. We are not within the reach of the blessing and comfort of the promise till we repent.

3. By its ordinances, or the sacraments and seals of the covenant. As baptism, which serves for this use : Mat. iii. 11, ' I baptize you with water unto repentance ;' and Acts ii. 38, ' Repent and be baptized every one of you in the name of Jesus Christ, for the remission of sins.' This is the initial ordinance, which is our first covenanting with God ; and therein we bind ourselves to forsake all known sin, and to live unto God ; and from that time forward we must reckon ourselves as under such a vow, bond, debt and obligation : Rom. vi. 11, ' Reckon yourselves also to be dead indeed unto sin, but alive unto God through Jesus Christ our Lord.' What! doth our mortification or vivification depend on our esteem or conceit ? Will that kill sin or quicken holiness ? The meaning is, count yourselves obliged to die to sin and to persevere in holiness by your baptismal vow and covenant. In the Lord's supper, one great benefit offered and sealed to us is the remission of sins : Mat. xxvi. 28, ' For this is my blood of the new testament, which is shed for many, for the remission of sins ;' that is, supposing we make conscience of our baptismal vow, and renew our resolutions against sin, lest we grow cold and remiss in them.

Thirdly, How convenient and necessary this is for our recovery to God.

1. For the honour of God. Surely Christ communicateth the effects of his grace in a way becoming the wisdom of God as well as his justice. Now as the justice of God required that his wrath should be appeased, so his wisdom required that man should be converted and turned to God, because God, in dispensing pardon, will still preserve the honour of his law and government ; as he doth it in the impetration, so in the application ; as to the impetration that was not without satisfaction ; so to the application, that is not without repentance, or a consent to live according to the will of God. Now this would fall

to the ground if we should be pardoned without submission, without confession of past sin, or resolution of future obedience ; for till then we neither know our true misery, nor are we willing to come out of it ; for they that securely continue in their sins, they despise both the curse of the law, and the grace of the gospel.

2. The duty of the creature is secured when we are so solemnly bound to future obedience. Our first hearty consent to live in the love and service of our Creator, with a detestation of our former ways, is made in a solemn covenant manner, called therefore the bond of the covenant : Ezek. xx. 37, ' I will bring you into the bond of the covenant.' So Num. xxx. 2, ' If a man vow a vow unto the Lord, and swear an oath to bind his soul with a bond, he shall do according to all that proceedeth out of his mouth.' And besides, it is made in our anguish, when we drink of the bitter waters, and feel the smart of sin : Acts ix. 6, ' And he, trembling and astonished, said, Lord, what wilt thou have me to do ? ' And so the fittest time to induce an hatred of sin, and also love to God and holiness, as having then the sweetest and freshest sense of his love and mercy in providing a saviour for us, and offering pardon to us : Ps. cxxx. 4, ' There is forgiveness with thee, that thou mayst be feared.' Our thoughts are most conversant about these things : Rom. xii. 1, ' I beseech you therefore, brethren, by the mercies of God, that ye present your bodies a living sacrifice, holy, acceptable to God, which is your reasonable service.'

3. It is most for the comfort of the creature. There are some principles planted in the heart of man for the restraint of sin, which may be baffled for a time, but our fears will return upon us ; and till the soul be subject to God it can never be comfortable, nor at ease within itself ; and it is in vain to think we shall find rest for our souls till sin be more hated and God more loved : Mat. xi. 28, 29, ' Come unto me all ye that labour, and are heavy laden, and I will give you rest. Take my yoke upon you, and learn of me, for I am meek and lowly of heart, and ye shall find rest unto your souls.' The same reasons that enforce the necessity of a satisfaction to God's justice do also enforce the necessity of repentance, for else the heart of man is so constituted, that it will be a stranger to comfort. It is true God is not quick and severe upon every miscarriage, but yet the soul apprehendeth him an holy and just God, and therefore must be set to serve the ' living God,' or else the conscience is not ' purged from dead works,' Heb. ix. 12.

Use. Is to press us to mind this work of repentance. We put all upon faith, but overlook repentance ; yet the gospel aimeth at this, and without it the grace thereof is not rightly applied. It is a duty of great use, for God's glory, man's obedience, duty, and comfort dependeth on it. And it is indispensably necessary, by God's authority, *necessitate præcepti*, and by the new covenant constitution, *necessitate medii*. And dare we be slight in it ? The times of our ignorance show how necessary it is, and the light of the gospel doth more enforce it. Christ upbraided the cities where his mighty works were done, because they repented not : Mat. xi. 20–22, ' Then began he to upbraid the cities wherein most of his mighty works were done, because they repented not. Woe unto thee, Chorazin ! woe unto thee, Bethsaida ! for if the mighty works which were done in you had been done in Tyre and Sidon, they would have repented long ago in sackcloth and ashes. But I say unto you, It shall be more tolerable for Tyre and Sidon at the day of judgment than for you.' And there is a judgment will pass upon us: and if we repent not, who can stand in the judgment? Ps. cxxx. 3, 'If thou, Lord, shouldst mark iniquities, O Lord, who shall stand?'

What shall we do?

1. Expect not extraordinary dispensations. We have advantage enough by God's word: Luke xvi. 30, 'If one went to them from the dead they would repent.' There Christ impersonateth our natural thoughts, there is no need of that, conscience is awakened with the word. Christ is risen from the dead, and hath sent this message to us.

2. Rouse up yourselves: Ps. xxii. 47, 'All the ends of the world shall remember, and turn unto the Lord;' Ps. cxix. 59, 'I thought on my ways, and turned my feet unto thy testimonies.' Man is inconsiderate, and will not give conscience leave to work.

3. Observe God's checks. We are negligent, therefore God seeketh to awaken us: Prov. i. 23, 'Turn you at my reproof.' Smothering convictions breedeth atheism and hardness of heart.

4. Do what you can: Hosea v. 4, 'They will not frame their doings to return unto their God.' Then we are the more inexcusable in our impenitency when we will not so much as think and endeavour, or use the outward means which tend to repentance, or set about the work as well as we can. If we shut the door upon ourselves, who will pity us? God may do what he pleaseth, but we must do what he hath commanded, bend our course that way, for he has commanded us.

5. Ask it of God. Pray for it: Jer. xxxi. 19, 'Turn thou me, and I shall be turned.' Surely he is able to help you out of your difficulties: Mat. xix. 26, 'With God all things are possible.' He is willing, for he faileth not the serious soul: Acts v. 31, 'Him hath God exalted with his right hand to be a prince and a saviour, for to give repentance and forgiveness of sins.'

CHAPTER TWO

The Day of Judgment Asserted

THOMAS WATSON

THE DAY OF JUDGMENT ASSERTED

"Because He hath appointed a day, in the which He will judge the world in righteousness by that man whom He hath ordained; whereof he hath given assurance unto all men, in that He hath raised Him from the dead." Acts 17:31

When St. Paul perceived the idolatry at Athens, "his spirit was stirred in him," verse 16. His spirit was soured and embittered in him. Paul was a bitter man against sin; that anger is without sin which is against sin. Or, the word may signify, he was in a paroxysm, or burning fit of zeal. And zeal is such a passion as cannot be either dissembled or pent up; with this fire he discharged against their idolatry. "Ye men of Athens, I perceive that in all things ye are too superstitious. For as I passed by, and beheld your devotions, I found an altar with this description, 'To the Unknown God,' " verses 22-23. Nor does the Apostle only declaim against the false god, but declare to them the true God. And he does it from the effect: "That God who made the world and all things therein . . . is Lord of heaven and earth," verse 24. To create is the best demonstration of a Deity. And this God, being everywhere by way of repletion, cannot be locally confined. Acts 17:24: "He dwelleth not in temples made with hands." And though in former times, when the veil of ignorance was drawn over the face of the world, God seemed less severe—"The times of this ignorance God winked at"—though He did, as it were, "overlook" them, not taking the extremity of the law, yet "now He commandeth all men everywhere to repent," verse 30. And if it is asked, "Why *now* repent? Why may we not take our full sleep?" the reason is because *now* is the broad daylight of the gospel, which, as it reveals sin more clearly, so it more clearly reveals judgment upon sinners: "He hath appointed a day in which He will judge the world."

These words are God's alarm to the world to awaken it out of security. This is a sweet yet dreadful point. When St. Paul discoursed of judgment to come, Felix trembled, Acts 24:25. He who is not affected with this truth has a heart of stone.

For the illustration of this, there are six things I shall discuss:

1. There shall be a day of judgment.
2. Why there must be a day of judgment.
3. When the day of judgment shall be.
4. Who shall be the Judge.
5. The order and the method of the trial.
6. The effect or consequence of it.

1. I begin with the first: *There shall be a day of judgment.* There is a twofold day of judgment:

(1) A particular judgment. At the day of death, immediately upon the soul's dissolution from the body, it has a judgment passed upon it, Hebrews 9:27. "Then shall the dust return to the earth as it was: and the spirit shall return unto God that gave it," Ecclesiastes 12:7. As soon as the breath expires, the soul receives its

particular sentence and knows how it shall be with it to all eternity.

(2) There is a general day of judgment, which is the great judgment, when the world shall be gathered together. And of this the text is to be understood: "He hath appointed a day in the which He will judge the world." I might give you a whole jury of Scriptures giving their verdict to this, but in the mouth of two or three witnesses the truth will be confirmed. "God shall bring every work into judgment, with every secret thing, whether it be good, or whether it be evil," Ecclesiastes 12:14. "Every idle word that men shall speak, they shall give account thereof in the day of judgment," Matthew 12:36. *Now* is the day of arrears; *then* will be the day of account. "For He cometh, for He cometh to judge the earth," Psalm 96:13. The repetition denotes the certainty and infallibility of His coming.

2. *Why there must be a day of judgment.*

(1) That God may execute justice on the wicked. Things seem to be carried here in the world with an unequal balance. The "candle of God shines upon" the wicked, Job 29:3. "They that tempt God are even delivered," Malachi 3:15. Diogenes, seeing Harpalus, a thief, go on prosperously, said that surely God had cast off the government of the world, and did not mind how things went here below. "There shall come in the last days scoffers, saying, Where is the promise of His coming?" 2 Peter 3:3-4. Therefore, God will have a day of judgment to vindicate His justice. He will let sinners know that long forbearance is no forgiveness.

(2) That God may exercise mercy to the godly.

Here piety was the white which was shot at. They who prayed and wept had the hardest measure. Those Christians whose zeal flamed most met with the fiery trial. "For Thy sake we are killed all the day long; we are accounted as sheep for the slaughter," Romans 8:36. "The saints," said Cyprian, "are put in the wine-press, and oft the blood of these grapes is pressed out." God will therefore have a day of judgment that He may reward all the tears and sufferings of His people. They shall have their crown and throne and white robes, Revelation 7:9; though they may be losers *for* Him, they shall lose nothing *by* Him.

3. *When the day of judgment shall be.*

It is certain there shall be a judgment; it is uncertain when. The angels do not know the day, nor does Christ either as He was man (Matthew 24:36; Mark 13:32). And the reason why the time is not known is:

(1) That we may not be curious. There are some things which God would have us be ignorant of. "It is not for you to know the times or the seasons, which the Father hath put in His own power," Acts 1:7. We must not pry into God's ark or meddle with his secrets of government. As Salvian said, "It is a kind of sacrilege for any man to break into the Holy of Holies and enter into God's secrets."

(2) God has concealed the time of judgment that we may not be careless. We are always to keep sentinel, having our loins girded and our lamps burning, not knowing how soon that day may overtake us. Austin said, "God would have us live every day as if the last day were approaching."

Believe that every morning's ray
Hath lighted up thy latest day.

This is the genuine use which our Savior makes of it. Mark 13:32-33: "Of that day and hour knoweth no man, no, not the angels which are in heaven. Take ye heed, watch and pray: for ye know not when the time is."

But though we cannot know precisely when this day of the Lord shall be, yet in probability the time cannot be far off. Hebrews 10:37: "He that shall come will come, and will not tarry." Chrysostom had a simile: "When we see an old man going on crutches, his joints weak, his radical moisture dried up; though we do not know the just time when he will die, yet it is sure he cannot live long because nature's stock is spent. So the world is decrepit and goes, as it were, upon crutches. Therefore it cannot be long before the world's funerals, and the birthday of judgment."

The age which St. John wrote in was "the last time," 1 John 2:18. In the Greek it is "the last hour." Then surely the time we now live in may be called "the last minute." Psalm 96:13: "For He cometh to judge the earth." It is not "He shall come," but "He cometh," to show how near the time is. It is almost daybreak and the court is ready to sit. James 5:9: "The Judge standeth at the door."

Verily, if security, apostasy, decay of love, inundation of sin, and revelation of Antichrist are made in Scripture the symptoms and prognostications of the last day, we, having these gray hairs among us, know that the day of judgment cannot be far off.

4. *Who shall be the Judge?*

I answer, the Lord Jesus Christ. Thus it is in the text: "He will judge the world by that man whom He hath ordained," that man who is God-man. We must take heed of judging others; this is Christ's work. John 5:22: "The Father hath committed all judgment unto the Son." He who once had a reed put into His hand, His Father will now put a scepter into His hand. He who had a purple robe put upon Him in derision shall come in His Judge's robes. He who hung upon the cross shall sit upon the bench. There are two things in Christ which eminently qualify Him to be a Judge:

(1) Prudence and intelligence to understand all causes that are brought before Him. He is described with seven eyes in Zechariah 3:9, to note His omniscience. He is like Ezekiel's wheels, full of eyes, Ezekiel 10:12. Christ is a heart-searcher. He not only judges the fact but the heart, which no angel can do.

(2) Strength whereby He is able to be avenged upon His enemies. Christ is armed with sovereignty; therefore the seven stones are said to be upon one stone, Zechariah 3:9, to denote the infinite strength of Christ. And He is described with seven horns, Revelation 5:6. As Christ has an eye to see, so He has a horn to push; as He has His balance, so He has His sword; as He has His fan and His sieve, so He has His lake of fire, Revelation 20:10.

5. *The order and method of the trial.*

Observe: (1) the summons; (2) the Judge's coming to the bench; and (3) the process and trial itself.

(1) The summons to the court, and that is by the sounding of the trumpet. 1 Thessalonians 4:16: "The

Lord Himself shall descend from heaven with a shout, with the voice of the archangel, and with the trump of God." St. Jerome said that whatever he was doing he thought he heard the noise of the trumpet sounding in his ears. "Arise, ye dead, and come to judgment." Note:

The shrillness of the trumpet. It shall sound so loud that the dead shall hear it.

The efficacy of the trumpet. It shall not only startle the dead, but raise them out of their graves, Matthew 24:31. They who will not hear the trumpet of the ministry sounding but lie dead in sin shall be sure to hear the trumpet of the archangel sounding.

(2) The manner of the Judge's coming to the bench. Christ's coming to judgment will be glorious yet dreadful.

It will be glorious to the godly. The Apostle calls it, Titus 2:13: "the glorious appearing of the great God and our Savior Jesus Christ."

Christ's person shall be glorious. At His first coming in the flesh His glory was veiled over, Isaiah 53:2-3; all who saw the man did not see the Messiah. But His second coming will be very illustrious and resplendent. He shall "come in the glory of His Father," Mark 8:38. That is, He shall wear the same embroidered robes of majesty as His Father.

Christ's attendants shall be glorious. He "shall come with all His holy angels," Matthew 25:31. These sublime, seraphic spirits, who for their luster are compared to lightning, Matthew 28:3, are Christ's satellites, part of Christ's train and retinue. He who was led to the cross with a band of soldiers shall be attended to the bench with a guard of angels.

Christ's coming to judgment will be dreadful to the

wicked. At the coming of this Judge, there will be a fire
burning round about Him. He "shall be revealed from
heaven with His mighty angels, in flaming fire, taking
vengeance on them that know not God, and that obey
not the gospel of our Lord Jesus Christ," 2 Thessalonians 1:7-8. When God gave His law upon the mount,
"there were thunders and lightnings; and Mount Sinai
was altogether on a smoke, because the Lord descended upon it in fire," Exodus 19:16-18. "If God was
so terrible at the giving of the law, O how terrible will
He be when He shall come to require His law?" said
Augustine.

(3) The process or the trial itself, where observe the
universality, the formality, and the circumstances of
the trial.

The universality of the trial. It will be a very great as-
size; never was the like seen. "For we must all appear
before the judgment seat of Christ," 2 Corinthians
5:10. Kings and nobles, councils and armies, those who
were above all trial here, have no charter of exemption
granted them. They must appear before Christ's tribunal and be tried for their lives. Neither power nor
policy can be a subterfuge. They who refused to come
to the throne of grace shall be forced to come to the
bar of justice. And the dead as well as the living must
make their appearance. Revelation 20:12: "I saw the
dead, both small and great, stand before God." We do
not usually cite men in our courts when they are dead,
but at that day the dead are called to the bar; and not
only men but angels. Jude 6: "The angels which kept
not their first estate, but left their own habitation, He
hath reserved in everlasting chains under darkness
unto the judgment of the great day."

The formality of the trial, which consists in the opening of the books. Daniel 7:10 and Revelation 20:12: "The judgment was set, and the books were opened." There are two books that will be opened:

First, the book of God's omniscience. God not only observes, but registers all our actions. Job 14:16: "Thou numberest my steps." The word there "to number" signifies to put a thing into a book. It is as if Job had said, "Lord, Thou keepest Thy daybook and enterest down all my actions into the book." We read of God's book of remembrance, Malachi 3:16. This book will be produced at the last day.

Second, the book of conscience. Let there never be so much written in a book, yet, if it is clasped, it is not seen. Men have their sins written in their conscience, but the book is clasped (the searing of the conscience is the clasping of the book); but when this book of conscience shall be unclasped at the great day, then all their hypocrisy, treason, and atheism shall appear to the view of men and angels, Luke 12:3. The sins of men shall be written upon their forehead as with a pen of iron.

The circumstances of the trial. Where consider four things: the impartiality, the exactness, the perspicuity, and the supremacy.

• The impartiality of the trial. Jesus Christ will do every man justice. He will, as the text says, "judge the world in righteousness." It will be a day of equitable judgment; justice holds the scales. The Thebans pictured their judges as being blind and without hands—blind, that they might not respect persons, and without hands, that they might take no bribes. Christ's scepter is a scepter of righteousness, Hebrews 1:8. He is no respecter of persons, Acts 10:34. It is not nearness of blood that prevails; many of Christ's kindred shall be condemned. It is not gloriousness of profession; many shall go to hell with Christ in their mouths. Matthew 7:22: "Many will say to Me in that day, Lord, Lord, have we not prophesied in Thy name? And in Thy name cast out devils? And in Thy name done many wonderful works?" Yet, though they cast out devils, they are cast out to the devil. It is not the varnish of a picture that a judicious eye is taken with, but the curiousness of the work. It is not the most shining profession which Christ is taken with, unless he sees the curious workmanship of grace in the heart drawn by the pencil of the Holy Ghost. Things are not carried there by parties "but in a most just balance." Christ has true weights for false hearts. There are no fees taken in that court. The judge will not be bribed with a hypocritical tear or a Judas kiss.

• The exactness of the trial. It will be very critical. Then will Christ thoroughly purge His floor, Matthew 3:12. Not a grace or a sin but His fan will discover. Christ will, at the day of judgment, make a heart anatomy, as the surgeon makes a dissection in the body and evaluates several body parts, or as the goldsmith brings his gold to the balance and touchstone and pierces his gold through to see if it is right and genuine, and whether there is not a baser metal within. Thus the Lord Jesus, whose eyes are as a flame of fire, Revelation 1:14, will pierce through the hearts of men and see if there is the right metal within, having the image and superscription of God upon it. Paint falls off in the fire. The hypocrite's paint will fall off at the fiery trial. Nothing then will stand us in stead but sincerity.

• The perspicuity of the trial. Sinners shall be so clearly convicted that they shall hold up their hand at the bar and cry, "Guilty." Those words of David may be fitly applied here: "That Thou mightest be clear when Thou judgest," Psalm 51:4. The sinner himself shall clear God of injustice. The Greek word for vengeance signifies "justice." God's taking vengeance is doing justice. Sin makes God angry, but it cannot make Him unrighteous. The wicked shall drink a sea of wrath, but not sip one drop of injustice. Christ will say, "Sinner, what apology can you make for yourself? Are not your sins written in the book of conscience? Did you not have that book in your own keeping? Who could have inserted anything into it?" Now the sinner, being self-condemned, shall clear his Judge: "Lord, though I am damned, yet I have no wrong done me. Thou art clear when Thou judgest."

• The supremacy of the court. This is the highest court of judicature, from whence is no appeal. Men can remove their causes from one place to another, from the Common Law to the Court of Chancery, but from Christ's court there is no appeal. He who is once doomed here finds his condition irreversible.

6. *The sixth and last particular is the effect or consequence of the trial, which consists in three things:*

(1) Segregation. Christ will separate the godly and the wicked. Matthew 25:32: "He shall separate them from one another, as a shepherd divideth his sheep from the goats." Then will be the great day of separation. It is a great grief to the godly in this life that they live among the wicked. Psalm 120:5: "Woe is me, that I sojourn in Mesech, that I dwell in the tents of Kedar."

Wicked men blaspheme God, Psalm 74:18, and persecute the saints, 2 Timothy 3:12. They are compared to
dogs, Psalm 22:16; to bulls, Psalm 68:30; and to lions,
Psalm 57:4. They roar upon the godly and tear them as
their prey. Cain kills, Ishmael mocks, Shimei rails. The
godly and the wicked are now promiscuously mingled
together, Matthew 13:30, and this is as offensive as ty-
ing a dead man to a living. But Christ will ere long
make a separation, as the fan separates the wheat from
the chaff, as a furnace separates the gold from the
dross, or as a fine sieve strains the spirit from the dregs.
Christ will put the sheep by themselves who have the
earmark of election upon them, and the goats by
themselves, after which separation there follows:

(2) The sentence, which is twofold:

First, the sentence of absolution pronounced upon
the godly. "Come, ye blessed of My Father, inherit the
kingdom prepared for you from the foundation of the
world," Matthew 25:34. After the pronouncing of this
blessed sentence, the godly shall go from the bar and
sit on the bench with Christ. 1 Corinthians 6:2: "Know
ye not that the saints shall judge the world?" The saints
shall be with Christ's assessors; they shall sit with Him
in judicature as the justices of peace sit with the judge.
They shall vote with Christ and applaud Him in all His
judicial proceedings. Here the world judges the saints,
but there the saints shall judge the world.

Second, the sentence of condemnation pronounced upon the wicked. "Depart from Me, ye
cursed, into everlasting fire, prepared for the devil and
his angels," Matthew 25:41. I may allude to James 3:10:
"Out of the same mouth proceedeth blessing and cursing." Out of the same mouth of Christ proceeds bless-

ing to the godly and cursing to the wicked." The same wind which brings one ship to the haven blows another ship upon the rock.

"Depart from Me." The wicked once said to God, "Depart." Job 21:14: "They say unto God, Depart from us." And now God will say to them, "Depart from Me." This will be a heart-rending word. Chrysostom said, "This word 'depart!' is worse than the fire." Psalm 16:11: "Depart from Me, in whose presence is fullness of joy."

Third, after this sentence follows the execution. Matthew 13:30: "Bind the tares in bundles to burn them." Christ will say, "Bundle up these sinners. Here are a bundle of hypocrites, there a bundle of apostates, there a bundle of profane persons. Bind them up and throw them in the fire." And no cries or entreaties will prevail with the Judge. The sinner and the fire must keep one another company. He who would not weep for his sins must burn for them.

It is "everlasting fire." The three children were thrown into the fire, but they did not stay in long. Daniel 3:26: "Nebuchadnezzar came near to the mouth of the burning fiery furnace, and spake, and said, Shadrach, Meshach, and Abednego, ye servants of the most high God, come forth, and come hither. Then Shadrach, Meshach, and Abednego came forth of the midst of the fire." But the fire of the damned is everlasting fire. This word "ever" breaks the heart. Length of time cannot terminate it; a sea of tears cannot quench it. The wrath of God is the fire and the breath of God the bellows to blow it up to all eternity. Oh, how dreadfully tormenting will this fire be! To endure it will be intolerable; to avoid it will be impossible.

USE 1. OF PERSUASION.

Let me persuade all Christians to believe this truth that there shall be a day of judgment. "Rejoice, O young man, in thy youth; and let thy heart cheer thee in the days of thy youth, and walk in the ways of thine heart, and in the sight of thine eyes: but know thou, that for all these things God will bring thee into judgment," Ecclesiastes 11:9. This is a great article of our faith, that Christ shall come to judge the quick and the dead. Yet how many live as if this article were blotted out of their creed! We have too many epicures and atheists who drown themselves in sensual delights and live as if they did not believe either in God or the day of judgment. The Lucianists and Platonists deny the immortality of the soul; the Photinians hold there is no hell. I have read of the Duke of Silesia who was so infatuated that he did not believe either God or the devil. I wish there were not too many of this duke's opinion. Would men dare swear, be unchaste, or live in malice if they believed in a day of judgment? Oh, mingle this text with faith. "The Lord hath appointed a day in which He will judge the world." There must be such a day. Not only does Scripture assert it, but reason confirms it. There is no kingdom or nation in the world but has its sessions and courts of judicature; and shall not God, who sets up all other courts, be allowed His? That there shall be a day of judgment is engrafted by nature in the consciences of men. Peter Martyr tells us that some of the heathen poets have written that there are certain judges appointed (Minos, Rhadamanthus, and others) to examine and punish offenders after this life.

USE 2. OF INFORMATION.

See here the sad and deplorable estate of wicked men. This text is as the handwriting on the wall which may make their "knees to smite one against another," Daniel 5:6. The wicked shall come to judgment, but they "shall not stand in the judgment," Psalm 1:5. In the Hebrew it is "they shall not rise up." God shall be decked with glory and majesty, His face as the appearance of lightning, His eyes as lamps of fire, and a sword of justice in His hand, and shall call the sinner by name and say, "Stand forth. Answer to the charge that is brought against you. What can you say for your pride, oaths, drunkenness? These sins you have been told of by My ministers whom I sent rising up early and going to bed late; but you persisted in your wickedness with a neck of iron, a brow of brass, and a heart of stone. All the tools which I wrought with were broken and worn out upon your rocky spirit. What can you say for yourself that the sentence should not be passed?"

Oh, how amazed and confused will the sinner be! He will be found speechless; he will not be able to look his Judge in the face. Job 31:14: "What then shall I do when God riseth up? And when He visiteth, what shall I answer Him?" Oh, wretch, you who can now outface your minister and your godly parents, when they tell you of sin—you shall not be able to outface your Judge. When God rises up, the sinner's countenance will be fallen.

Not many years ago, the bishops used to visit in their diocese, and call several persons before them as criminal. All the world is God's diocese, and shortly He is coming on His visitation and will call men to account. Now, when God shall visit, how shall the impure soul be able to answer Him? 1 Peter 4:18: "Where shall the ungodly and the sinner appear?" You who die in your sin are sure to be cast at the bar. John 3:18: "He that believeth not is condemned already." That is, he is as sure to be condemned as if he were condemned already. And once the sentence of damnation is passed, miserable man, what will you do? Where will you go? Will you seek help from God? He is a consuming fire. Will you seek help from the world? It will be all on fire about you. From the saints? Those you derided on earth. From the good angels? They defy you as God's enemy. From the bad angels? They are your executioners. From your conscience? There is the worm that gnaws. From mercy? The lease is run out. Oh, the horror and hellish despair which will seize upon sinners at that day! Oh, the sad convulsions! Their heads shall hang down, their cheeks blush, their lips quiver, their hands shake, their conscience roar, and their heart tremble. What stupefying medicine has the devil given to men that they are insensible of the danger they are in? The cares of the world have so filled their head, and the profits of it have so bewitched their heart, that they mind neither death nor judgment.

USE 3. OF EXHORTATION.

BRANCH 1. Possess yourselves with the thoughts of the day of judgment. Think of the solemnity and impartiality of this court. Feathers swim upon the water; gold sinks into it. Light, feathery spirits float in vanity, but serious Christians sink deep in the thoughts of judgment. Many people are like quicksilver; they cannot be made to fix. If the ship is not well ballasted, it will soon overturn. The reason why so many are over-

turned with the vanities of the world is that they are
not well ballasted with the thoughts of the day of judgment. Were a man to be tried for his life, he would
think to himself of all the arguments he could to plead
in his own defense. We are all shortly to be tried for
our souls. While others are thinking how they may
grow rich, let us think to ourselves how we may abide
the day of Christ's coming. The serious thoughts of
judgment would be:

First, a curbing bit to sin. "Am I stealing the forbidden fruit and the judgment so near?"

Second, a spur to holiness. 2 Peter 3:10-11: "But the
day of the Lord will come as a thief in the night; in the
which the heavens shall pass away with a great noise,
and the elements shall melt with fervent heat, the
earth also and the works that are therein shall be
burned up. Seeing then that all these things shall be
dissolved, what manner of persons ought ye to be in all
holy conversation and godliness?"

BRANCH 2. Let us solemnly prepare ourselves for
this last and great trial. That is, by setting up a judgment seat in our own souls, let us begin a private session before the assizes. It is wisdom to bring our souls
first to trial. Lamentations 3:40: "Let us search and try
our ways." Let us judge ourselves according to the rule
of the Word and let conscience bring in the verdict.
The Word of God gives several characters of a man
who shall be absolved at the day of judgment and is
sure to go to heaven:

Character 1. The first character is humility. Job
22:29: "The Lord shall save the humble person." Now,
let conscience bring in the verdict. Christian, are you
humble? Not only humbled, but humble? Do you es-

teem others better than thyself? Philippians 2:3. Do you cover your duties with the veil of humility, as Moses put a veil on his face when it shone? If conscience brings in this verdict, you are sure to be acquitted at the last day.

Character 2. Love to the saints. 1 John 3:14: "We know that we have passed from death unto life, because we love the brethren." Love makes us like God; it is the root of all the graces. Does conscience witness this for you? Are you perfumed with this sweet spice of love? Do you delight in those who have the image of God? Do you reverence their graces? Do you bear with their infirmities? Do you love to see Christ's picture in a saint, though hung in never so poor a frame? This is a good sign that you shall pass for currency at the day of judgment.

Character 3. A penitential frame of heart. Acts 11:18: "Repentance unto life." Repentance unravels sin and makes it not to be. Jeremiah 50:20: "In those days the iniquity of Israel shall be sought for, and there shall be none." A great ball of snow is melted and washed away with the rain; great sins are washed away by holy tears. Now, can conscience bring in the evidence for you? Do you tune the penitential string? Ambrose asked, "You who have sinned with Peter, do you weep with Peter?" And do your tears drop from the eye of faith? This is a blessed sign that you are judgment-proof, and that when your iniquities shall be sought at the last day they shall not be found.

Character 4. Equity in our dealings. "Who shall ascend into the hill of the Lord? Or who shall stand in His holy place?" Psalm 24:3-4. "He that hath clean hands." Injustice sullies and defiles the hand. What does conscience say? Is your hand clean? It is a vain thing to hold the Bible in one hand and false weights in the other.

Beloved, if conscience, upon a Scripture trial, gives in the verdict for us, it is a blessed sign that we shall lift up our heads with boldness at the last day. Conscience is God's echo in the soul. The voice of conscience is the voice of God, and if conscience, upon an impartial trial, acquits us, God will acquit us. 1 John 3:21: "If our heart condemns us not, then have we confidence toward God." If we are absolved in the lower court of conscience, we are sure to be absolved at the last day in the high court of justice. It would be a sweet thing for a Christian thus to bring himself to a trial. Seneca tells us of a Roman who every day called himself to account: "What infirmity is healed? How have you grown better?" Then he would lie down at night with these words: "Oh, how sweet and refreshing is my sleep to me!"

USE 4. OF CONSOLATION.

Here is a fountain of consolation opened to a believer, and that in three cases: 1. Discouraging fear; 2. Weakness of grace; and 3. Censures of the world.

Case 1. Here is comfort in case of discouraging fear. "Oh," said a believer, "I fear my grace is not invincible armor. I fear the cause will go against me at the last day." Indeed, so it would if you were out of Christ. But, as in our law courts the client has his attorney or advocate to plead for him, so every believer, by virtue of the interest he has in Christ, has Christ to plead his cause for him. 1 John 2:1: "If any man sin, we have an Advocate with the Father, Jesus Christ the righteous."

What if Satan is the accuser if Christ is the Advocate? Christ never lost any cause that He pleaded. Nay, His very pleading alters the nature of the cause. Christ will show the debt book crossed with His own blood. And it is no matter what is charged if all is discharged. Here is a believer's comfort—his Judge will be his Advocate.

Case 2. Here is comfort with regard to weakness of grace. A Christian, seeing his grace is so defective, is ready to be discouraged. But at the day of judgment, if Christ finds but a small coin of sincerity, it shall be accepted. If yours is true gold, though it may be light, Christ will put His merits into the scales and make it sufficient. He who has no sin of allowance shall have grains of allowance. I may allude to that verse in Amos 9:9, "Yet shall not the least grain fall to the earth." He who has but a grain of grace, not the least grain shall fall to hell.

Case 3. It is comfort in case of censures and slanders. The saints go here through strange reports, "through evil report and a good report," 2 Corinthians 6:8. John the Baptist's head on a platter is a common dish nowadays. It is ordinary to bring in a saint beheaded of his good name. But at the day of judgment Christ will unload His people of all their injuries. He will vindicate them from all their calumnies. Christ will be the saint's character witness. He, at that day, will present His Church "not having spot or wrinkle," Ephesians 5:27.

CHAPTER THREE

The Final Judgment: or,
The World Judged Righteously by Jesus Christ

JONATHAN EDWARDS

THE FINAL JUDGMENT

INTRODUCTION

"God hath appointed a day in which he will judge the world in righteousness by Jesus Christ." – Acts 17:31

These words are a part of the speech which Paul made in Mars' hill, a place of concourse of the judges and learned men of Athens. Athens was the principal city of that part of Greece which was formerly a commonwealth by itself, and was the most noted place in the whole world for learning, philosophy, and human wisdom, And it continued so for many ages, till at length the Romans having conquered Greece, its renown from that time began to diminish. And Rome having borrowed learning of it, began to rival it in science, and in the polite and civil arts. However, it was still very famous in the days of Christ and the apostles, and was a place of concourse for wise and learned men.

Therefore, when Paul came thither, and began to preach concerning Jesus Christ, a man who had lately been crucified at Jerusalem (as in Acts 17:18), the philosophers thronged about him, to hear what he had to say. The strangeness of his doctrine excited their curiosity, for they spent their time in endeavoring to find out new things, and valued themselves greatly upon their being the authors of new discoveries, as we are informed in Acts 17:21. They despised his doctrine in their hearts, and esteemed it very ridiculous, calling the apostle a babbler. For the preaching of Christ crucified was to the Greeks foolishness, 1 Cor. 1:23, yet the Epicurean and Stoic philosophers, two different sects, had a mind to hear what the babbler had to say.

Upon this Paul rises up in the midst of them, and makes a speech. And as he speaks to philosophers and men of learning, he speaks quite differently from his common mode of address. There is evidently, in his discourse, a greater depth of thought, more philosophical reasoning, and a more elevated style, than are to be found in his ordinary discourses to common men. His speech is such as was likely to draw the attention and gain the assent of philosophers. He shows himself to be no babbler, but a man who could offer such reason, as they, however they valued themselves upon their wisdom, were not able to gainsay. His practice here is agreeable to what he saith of himself, 1 Cor. 9:22, "that he became all things to all men, that he might by all means save some." He not only to the weak became as weak, that he might gain the weak, but to the wise he became as wise, that he might gain the wise.

In the first place, he reasons with them concerning their worship of idols. He declares to them the true God, and points out how unreasonable it is to suppose, that he delights in such superstitious worship. He begins with this, because they were most likely to hearken to it, as being so evidently agreeable to the natural light of human reason, and also agreeable to what some of their own poets and philosophers had said (Acts 17:28). He begins not immediately to tell them about Jesus Christ, his dying for sinners, and his resurrection from the dead. But first draws their attention with that to which they were more likely to hearken. And then, having thus introduced himself, he proceeds to speak concerning Jesus Christ.

He tells them, the times of this ignorance concerning the true God, in which they had hitherto been, God winked at. He suffered the world to lie in heathenish darkness. But now the appointed time was come, when he expected *men should everywhere repent,* "because he had appointed a day, in the which he will judge the world in righteousness by that man whom he hath ordained." As an enforcement to the duty of turning to God from their ignorance, superstition, and idolatry, the apostle brings in this, that God had appointed such a Day of Judgment. And as a proof of this, he brings the resurrection of Christ from the dead.

Concerning the words of the text, we may observe,

That in them the apostle speaks of the general judgment: *He will judge the* World.—The time when this shall be, on the appointed day: *He hath appointed a day.*—How the world is to be judged: *In righteousness.*— The man by whom it is to be judged: *Christ Jesus whom God raised from the dead.*

DOCTRINE

There is a day coming in which there will be a general righteous judgment of the whole world by Jesus Christ.

In speaking upon this subject, I shall show, That God is the Supreme Judge of the world. That there is a time coming, when God will, in the most public and solemn manner, judge the whole world. That the person by whom he will judge it is Jesus Christ. That the transactions of that day will be greatly interesting and truly awful. That all shall be done in righteousness. And finally, I shall take notice of those things which shall be immediately consequent upon the judgment.

SECTION I - *God is the supreme judge of the world.*

I. God is so by *right.* He is by right the supreme and absolute ruler and disposer of all things, both in the natural and moral world. The rational understanding part of the creation is indeed subject to a different sort of government from that to which irrational creatures are subject. God governs the sun, moon, and stars. He governs even the motes of dust which fly in the air. Not a hair of our heads falleth to the ground without our heavenly Father. God also governs the brute creatures. By his providence, he orders, according to his own decrees, all events concerning those creatures. And rational creatures are subject to the same sort of government. All their actions, and all events relating to them, being ordered by superior providence, according to absolute decrees so that no event that relates to them ever happens without the disposal of God, according to his own decrees. The rule of this government is God's wise decree, and nothing else.

But rational creatures, because they are intelligent and voluntary agents, are the subjects of another kind of government. They are so only with respect to those of their actions, in which they are *causes by counsel,* or with respect to their voluntary actions. The government of which I now speak is called *moral* government, and consists in two things, in giving laws, and in judging.

God is, with respect to this sort of government, by right the sovereign *ruler* of the world. He is possessed of this right by reason of his infinite greatness and excellency, by which he merits, and is perfectly and solely fit for, the office of supreme ruler. He that is so excellent as to be infinitely worthy of the highest respect of the creature, has thereby a right to that respect. He deserves it by a merit of condignity, so that it is injustice to deny it to him. And he that is perfectly wise and true, and is only so regarded, has a right in everything to be regarded, and to have his determinations attended to and obeyed.

God has also a right to the character of supreme ruler, by reason of the absolute dependence of every creature on him. All creatures, and rational creatures no less than others, are wholly derived from him, and every moment are wholly dependent upon him for being, and for all good, so that they are properly his possession. And as, by virtue of this, he has a right to give his creatures whatever rules of conduct he pleases, or whatever rules are agreeable to his own wisdom. So the mind and will of the creature ought to be entirely conformed to the nature and will of the Creator, and to the rules he gives, that are expressive of it.

For the same reason, he has a right to *judge* their actions and conduct, and to fulfill the sanction of his law. He who has an absolute and independent right to give laws, has evermore the same right to judge those to whom the laws are given. It is absolutely necessary that there should be a judge of reasonable creatures. And sanctions, or rewards and punishments, annexed to rules of conduct are necessary to the being of laws. A person may instruct another without sanctions, but not give laws. However, these sanctions themselves are vain, are as good as none, without a judge to determine the execution of them. As God has a right to be Judge, so has he a right to be the *supreme* Judge. And none has a right to reverse his judgments, to receive appeals from him, or to say to him, Why judgest thou thus?

II. God is, *in fact,* the supreme Judge of the world. He has power sufficient to vindicate his own right. As he has a right which cannot be disputed, so he has power which cannot be controlled. He is possessed of omnipotence, wherewith to maintain his dominion over the world. And he does maintain his dominion in the moral as well as the natural world. Men may refuse subjection to God as a lawgiver. They may shake off the yoke of his laws by rebellion. Yet they cannot withdraw themselves from his judgment. Although they will not have God for their lawgiver, yet they shall have him for their Judge. The strongest of creatures can do nothing to control God, or to avoid him while acting in his judicial capacity. He is able to bring them to his judgment-seat, and is also able to execute the sentence which he shall pronounce.

There was once a notable attempt made by opposition of power entirely to shake off the yoke of the moral government of God, both as lawgiver, and as Judge. This attempt was made by the angels, the most mighty of creatures. But they miserably failed in it. God notwithstanding acted as their Judge in casting those proud spirits out of heaven, and binding them in chains of darkness unto a further judgment, and a further execution. "God is wise in heart and mighty in strength; who hath hardened himself against him, and hath prospered?" Job 9:4. Wherein the enemies of God deal proudly, he is above them. He ever has acted as Judge in bestowing what rewards, and inflicting what punishments, he pleased on the children of men. And so he does still. He is daily fulfilling the promises and threatenings of the law, in disposing of the souls of the children of men, and so he evermore will act.

God acts as Judge towards the children of men more especially,

First, in man's particular judgment at death. Then the sentence is executed, and the reward bestowed *in part;* which is not done without a judgment. The soul, when it departs from the body, appears before God to be disposed of by him, according to his law. But by this appearing before God, to be judged at death, we need understand no more than this, that the soul is made immediately sensible of the presence of God, God manifesting himself immediately to the soul, with the glory and majesty of a Judge, that the sins of the wicked and the righteousness of the saints are brought by God to the view of their consciences, so that they know the reason of the sentence given, and their consciences are made to testify to the justice of it. And that thus the will of God for the fulfillment of the law, in their reward or punishment, is made known to them and executed. This is undoubtedly done at every man's death.

Second, in the great and general judgment, when all men shall together appear before the judgment-seat to be judged, and which judgment will be much more solemn, and the sanctions of the law will to a further degree be fulfilled.—But this brings me to another branch of the subject.

SECTION II - *That there is a time coming when God will, in the most public and solemn manner, judge the whole world of mankind.*

The doctrine of a general judgment is not sufficiently discoverable by the light of nature. Indeed some of the heathens had some obscure notions concerning a future judgment. But the light of nature, or mere unassisted reason, was not sufficient to instruct the world of fallen men in this doctrine. It is one of the peculiar doctrines of revelation, a doctrine of the gospel of Jesus Christ. There were indeed some hints of it in the Old Testament, as in Psa. 96:13, "The Lord cometh to judge the world with righteousness, and his people with his truth." And Eccles. 12:14, "For God will bring every work into judgment, with every secret thing, whether it be good, or whether it be evil." And in some other such like passages. But this doctrine is with abundantly the greatest clearness revealed in the New Testament. There we have it frequently and particularly declared and described with its circumstances.

However, although it be a doctrine of revelation, and be brought to light by the gospel, the brightest and most glorious revelation that God has given to the world; yet it is a doctrine which is entirely agreeable to reason, and of which reason gives great confirmation. That there will be a time before the dissolution of the world, when the inhabitants of it shall stand before God and give an account of their conduct; and that God will in a public manner, by a general and just judgment, set all things to rights respecting their moral behavior, is a doctrine entirely agreeable to reason. Which I shall now endeavor to make appear. But I would premise that what we would inquire into is not whether all mankind shall be judged by God. For that is a thing that the light of nature clearly teaches, and we have already spoken something of it. But whether it be rational to think that there will be a *public* judgment of all mankind *together*. This I think will appear very rational from the following considerations.

I. Such a judgment will be a more glorious display of God's majesty and dominion. It will be more glorious because it will be more open, public, and solemn.—Although God now actually exercises the most sovereign dominion over the earth, although he reigns and does all things according to his own will, ordering all events as seemeth to himself good, and although he is actually Judge in the earth, continually disposing of men's souls according to their works; yet he rules after a more hidden and secret manner, insomuch that it is common among the proud sons of men to refuse acknowledging his dominion. Wicked men question the very existence of a God, who taketh care of the world, who ordereth the affairs of it, and judgeth in it. And therefore they cast off the fear of him. Many of the kings and great men of the earth do not suitably acknowledge the God who is above them, but seem to look upon themselves as supreme, and therefore tyrannize over mankind, as if they were in no wise accountable for their conduct. There have been, and now are, many atheistical persons, who acknowledge not God's moral dominion over mankind. And therefore they throw off the yoke of his laws and government. And how great a part of the world is there now, and has there always been, that has not acknowledged that the government of the world belongs to the God of Israel, or to the God of Christians, but has paid homage to other imaginary deities, as though they were their sovereign lords and supreme judges. Over how great a part of the world has Satan usurped the dominion, and set up himself for God, in opposition to the true God!

Now, how agreeable to reason is it, that God, in the winding up of things, when the present state of mankind shall come to a conclusion, should in the most open and public manner, manifest his dominion over the inhabitants of the earth, by bringing them all, high and low, rich and poor, kings and subjects, together before him to be judged with respect to all that they ever did in the world! That he should thus openly discover his dominion in this world, where his authority has been so much questioned, denied, and proudly opposed! That however God be not now visibly present upon earth, disposing and judging in that visible manner that earthly kings do. Yet at the conclusion of the world he should make his dominion visible to all, and with respect to all mankind, so that every eye shall see him, and even they who have denied him shall find, that God is supreme Lord of them, and of the whole world!

II. The end of judgment will be more fully answered by a public and general, than only by a particular and private, judgment. The end for which there is any judgment at all is to display and glorify the righteousness of God; which end is more fully accomplished by calling men to an account, bringing their actions to the trial, and determining their state according to them, the whole world, both angels and men, being present to behold, than if the same things should be done in a more private way. At the Day of Judgment there will be the most glorious display of the justice of God that ever was made. Then God will appear to be entirely righteous towards everyone. The justice of all his moral government will on that day be at once discovered. Then all objections will be removed. The conscience of every man shall be satisfied. The blasphemies of the ungodly will be forever put to silence, and argument will be given for the saints and angels to praise God forever: Rev. 19:1,2, "And after these things I heard a great voice of much people in heaven, saying, Alleluia; salvation, and glory, and honor, and power be to the Lord our God: for true and righteous are his judgments."

III. It is very agreeable to reason, that the irregularities which are so open and manifest in the world, should, when the world comes to an end, be publicly rectified by the supreme governor. The infinitely wise God, who made this world to be a habitation for men, and placed mankind to dwell here, and has appointed man his end and work, must take care of the order and good government for the world, which he has thus made. He is not regardless how things proceed here on earth. It would be a reproach to his wisdom, and to the perfect rectitude of his nature, to suppose so. This world is a world of confusion. It has been filled with irregularity and confusion ever since the fall. And the irregularities of it are not only private, relating to the actions of particular persons, but states, kingdoms, nations, churches, cities, and all societies of men in all ages, have been full of public irregularities. The affairs of the world, so far as they are in the hands of men, are carried on in the most irregular and confused manner.

Though justice sometimes takes place, yet how often do injustice, cruelty, and oppression prevail! How often are the righteous condemned, and the wicked acquitted and rewarded! How common is it for the virtuous and pious to be depressed, and the wicked to be advanced! How many thousands of the best men have suffered intolerable cruelties, merely for their virtue and piety, and in this world have had no help, no refuge to fly to! The world is very much ruled by the pride, covetousness, and passions of men. Solomon takes much notice of such like irregularities in the present state (in his book of Ecclesiastes), hereby he shows the vanity of the world.

Now, how reasonable is it to suppose, that God, when he shall come and put an end to the present state of mankind, will in an open, public manner, the whole world being present, rectify all these disorders! And that he will bring all things to a trial by a general judgment, in order that those who have been oppressed may be delivered; that the righteous cause may be pleaded and vindicated, and wickedness, which has been approved, honored, and rewarded, may receive its due disgrace and punishment; that the proceedings of kings and earthly judges may be inquired into by him, whose eyes are as a flame of fire; and that the public actions of men may be publicly examined and recompensed according to their desert! How agreeable is it to divine wisdom thus to order things, and how worthy of the supreme governor of the world!

IV. By a public and general judgment, God more fully accomplishes the reward he designs for the godly, and punishment he designs for the wicked. One part of the reward which God intends for his saints, is the honor which he intends to bestow upon them. He will honor them in the most public and open manner, before the angels, before all mankind, and before them that hated them. And it is most suitable that it should be so. It is suitable that those holy, humble souls, that have been hated by wicked men, have been cruelly treated and put to shame by them, and who have been haughtily domineered over, should be openly acquitted, commended, and crowned, before all the world.

So one part of the punishment of the ungodly will be the open shame and disgrace which they shall suffer. Although many of them have proudly lifted up their heads in this world, have had a very high thought of themselves, and have obtained outward honor among men; yet God will put them to open shame, by showing all their wickedness and moral filthiness before the whole assembly of angels and men, by manifesting his abhorrence of them, in placing them upon his left hand, among devils and foul spirits, and by turning them away into the most loathsome, as well as most dreadful, pit of hell, to dwell there forever.—Which ends may be much more fully accomplished in a general, than in a particular judgment.

SECTION III - *The world will be judged by Jesus Christ.*

The person by whom God will judge the world is Jesus Christ, the God-man. The second person in the Trinity, that same person of whom we read in our Bibles, who was born of the Virgin Mary, lived in Galilee and Judea, and was at last crucified without the gates of Jerusalem, will come to judge the world both in his divine and human nature, in the same human body that was crucified, and rose again, and ascended up into heaven. Acts 1:11, "This same Jesus that is taken up from you into heaven, shall come in like manner, as ye have seen him go into heaven." It will be his human nature which will then be seen by the bodily eyes of men. However, his divine nature, which is united to the human, will then also be present. And it will be by the wisdom of that divine nature that Christ will see and judge.

Here naturally arises an inquiry, Why is Christ appointed to judge the world rather than the Father or the Holy Ghost? We cannot pretend to know all the reasons of the divine dispensations. God is not obliged to give us an account of them. But so much may we learn by divine revelation, as to discover marvelous wisdom in what he determines and orders with respect to this matter. We learn,

I. That God seeth fit, that he who is in the *human nature*, should be the Judge of those who are of the human nature. John 5:27, "And hath given him authority to execute judgment also, because he is the Son of man." Seeing there is one of the persons of the Trinity united to the human nature, God chooses, in all his transactions with mankind, to transact by him. He did so of old, in his discoveries of himself to the patriarchs, in giving the law, in leading the children of Israel through the wilderness, and in the manifestations he made of himself in the tabernacle and temple. When, although Christ was not actually incarnate, yet he was so in design, it was ordained and agreed in the covenant of redemption, that he should become incarnate. And since the incarnation of Christ, God governs both the church and the world by Christ. So he will also at the end *judge* the world by him. All men shall be judged by God, and yet at the same time by one invested with their own nature,

God seeth fit, that those who have bodies, as all mankind will have at the Day of Judgment, should see their Judge with their bodily eyes, and hear him with their bodily ears. If one of the other persons of the Trinity had been appointed to be Judge, there must have been some extraordinary outward appearance made on purpose to be a token of the divine presence, as it was of old, before Christ was incarnate. But now there is no necessity of that. Now one of the persons of the Trinity is actually incarnate, so that God by him may appear to bodily eyes without any miraculous visionary appearance.

II. Christ has this honor of being the Judge of the world given him, as a *suitable reward* for his sufferings. This is a part of Christ's exaltation. The exaltation of Christ is given him in reward for his humiliation and sufferings. This was stipulated in the covenant of redemption. And we are expressly told, it was given him in reward for his sufferings, Phil. 2:8-11, "And being found in fashion as a man, he humbled himself, and became obedient unto death, even the death of the cross. Wherefore God also hath highly exalted him, and given him a name which is above every name: that at the name of Jesus every knee should bow, of things in heaven, and things in earth, and things under the earth; and that every tongue should confess, that Jesus Christ is Lord, to the glory of God the Father."

God seeth meet, that he who appeared in such a low estate amongst mankind, without form or comeliness, having his divine glory veiled, should appear amongst men a second time, in his own proper majesty and glory, without a veil. To the end that those who saw him here at the first, as a poor, frail man, not having where to lay his head, subject to much hardship and affliction, may see him the second time in power and great glory, invested with the glory and dignity of the absolute Lord of heaven and earth. And that he who once tabernacled with men, and was despised and rejected of them, may have the honor of arraigning all men before his throne, and judging them with respect to their eternal state! John 5:21-24.

God seeth meet that he who was once arraigned before the judgment-seat of men, and was there most vilely treated, being mocked, spitted upon, and condemned, and who was at last crucified, should be rewarded, by having those very persons brought to his tribunal, that they may see him in glory, and be confounded. And that he may have the disposal of them for all eternity. As Christ said to the high priest while arraigned before him, Matt. 26:64, "Hereafter ye shall see the Son of man sitting on the right hand of power, and coming in the clouds of heaven."

III. It is needful that Christ should be the Judge of the world, in order that he may *finish* the work of redemption. It is the will of God, that he who is the redeemer of the world should be a *complete* redeemer; and that therefore he should have the whole work of redemption left in his hands. Now, the redemption of fallen man consists not merely in the impetration of redemption, by obeying the divine law, and making atonement for sinners, or in preparing the way for their salvation, but it consists in a great measure, and is actually fulfilled, in converting sinners to the knowledge and love of the truth, in carrying them on in the way of grace and true holiness through life, and in finally raising their bodies to life, in glorifying them, in pronouncing the blessed sentence upon them, in crowning them with honor and glory in the sight of men and angels, and in completing and perfecting their reward. Now, it is necessary that Christ should do this, in order to his finishing the work which he has begun. Raising the saints from the dead, judging them, and fulfilling the sentence is part of their salvation. And therefore it was necessary that Christ should be appointed Judge of the world, in order that he might *finish* his work (John 6:39,40, chap. 5:25-31). The redemption of the bodies of the saints is part of the work of redemption; the resurrection to life is called a redemption of their bodies (Rom. 8:23).

It is the will of God, that Christ himself should have the fulfilling of that for which he died, and for which he suffered so much. Now, the end for which he suffered and died was the complete salvation of his people.

And this shall be obtained at the last judgment, and not before. Therefore it was necessary that Christ be appointed Judge, in order that he himself might fully accomplish the end for which he had both suffered and died. When Christ had finished his appointed sufferings, God did, as it were, put the purchased inheritance into his hands, to be kept for believers, and be bestowed upon them at the Day of Judgment.

IV. It was proper that he who is appointed king of the church should rule till he should have put all his enemies under his feet. In order to which, he must be the Judge of his *enemies,* as well as of his people. One of the offices of Christ, as redeemer, is that of a king. He is appointed king of the church and head over all things to the church. And in order that his kingdom be complete, and design of his reign be accomplished, he must *conquer* all his enemies, and then he will deliver up the kingdom to the Father. 1 Cor. 15:24,25, "Then cometh the end, when he shall have delivered up the kingdom to God, even the Father; when he shall have put down all rule, and all authority and power. For he must reign till he hath put all enemies under his feet." Now, when Christ shall have brought his enemies, who had denied, opposed, and rebelled against him, to his judgment-seat, and shall have passed and executed sentence upon them, this will be a final and complete *victory* over them, a victory which shall put an end to the war. And it is proper that he who at present reigns and is carrying on the war against those who are of the opposite kingdom, should have the honor of obtaining the victory, and finishing the war.

V. It is for the abundant *comfort of the saints* that Christ is appointed to be their Judge. The covenant of grace, with all its circumstances, and all those events to which it has relation, is every way so contrived of God, as to give strong consolation to believers: for God designed the gospel for a glorious manifestation of his grace to them. And therefore everything in it is so ordered, as to manifest the most grace and mercy.

Now, it is for the abundant consolation of the saints, that their own Redeemer is appointed to be their Judge. That the same person who spilled his blood for them has the determination of their state left with him, so that they need not doubt but that they shall have what he was at so much cost to procure.

What matter of joy to them will it be at the last day, to lift up their eyes, and behold the person in whom they have trusted for salvation, to whom they have fled for refuge, upon whom they have built as their foundation for eternity, and whose voice they have often heard, inviting them to himself for protection and safety, coming to judge them.

VI. That Christ is appointed to be the Judge of the world will be for the more abundant *conviction of the ungodly*. It will be for their conviction that they are judged and condemned by that very person whom they have rejected, by whom they might have been saved, who shed his blood to give them an *opportunity* to be saved, who was wont to offer his righteousness to them, when they were in their state of trial, and who many a time called and invited them to come to him, that they might be saved. How justly will they be condemned by him whose salvation they have rejected, whose blood they have despised, whose many calls they have refused, and whom they have pierced by their sins!

How much will it be for their conviction, when they shall hear the sentence of condemnation pronounced, to reflect with themselves, how often has this same person, who now passes sentence of condemnation upon me, called me, in his word, and by his messengers, to accept of him, and to give myself to him! How often has he knocked at the door of my heart! and had it not been for my own folly and obstinacy, how might I have had him for my *Savior*, who is now my incensed *Judge!*

SECTION IV - *Christ's coming, the resurrection, the judgment prepared, the books opened, the sentence pronounced and executed.*

I. Christ Jesus will, in a most magnificent manner, descend from heaven with all the holy angels. The man Christ Jesus is now in the heaven of heavens, or, as the apostle expresses it, *far above all heavens,* Eph. 4:10. And there he has been ever since his ascension, being there enthroned in glory, in the midst of millions of angels and blessed spirits. But when the time appointed for the Day of Judgment shall have come, notice of it will be given in those happy regions, and Christ will descend to the earth, attended with all those heavenly hosts, in a most solemn, awful, and glorious manner. Christ will come with divine majesty; he will come in the glory of the Father, Matt. 16:27, "For the Son of man shall come in the glory of his Father, with his angels."

We can now conceive but little of the holy and awful magnificence in which Christ will appear, as he shall come in the clouds of heaven, or of the glory of his retinue. How mean and despicable, in comparison with it, is the most splendid appearance that earthly princes can make! A glorious visible light will shine round about him, and the earth, with all nature, will tremble at his presence. How vast and innumerable will that host be which will appear with him! Heaven will be for the time deserted of its inhabitants.

We may argue the glory of Christ's appearance, from his appearance at other times. When he appeared in transfiguration, his face did shine as the sun, and his raiment was white as the light. The apostle Peter long after spoke of this appearance in magnificent terms, 2 Pet. 1:16,17, "We were eye-witnesses of his majesty; for he received from God the Father honor and glory, when there came such a voice to him from the excellent glory." And his appearance to St. Paul at his conversion, and to St. John, as related in Rev. 1:13 etc. were very grand and magnificent. But we may conclude, that his appearance at the Day of Judgment will be vastly more so than either of these, as the occasion will be so much greater. We have good reason to think, that our nature, in the present frail state, could not bear the appearance of the majesty in which he will then be seen.

We may argue the glory of his appearance, from the appearances of some of the angels to men, as of the angel that appeared at Christ's sepulcher, after his resurrection, Matt. 28:3, "His countenance was like lightning, and his raiment white as snow." The angels will doubtless all of them make as glorious an appearance at the Day of Judgment, as ever any of them have made on former occasions. How glorious, then, will be the retinue of Christ, made up of so many thousands of such angels! And how much more glorious will Christ, the Judge himself, appear, than those his attendants! Doubtless their God will appear immensely more glorious than they.

Christ will thus descend into our air, to such a distance from the surface of the earth, that everyone, when all shall be gathered together, shall see him, Rev. 1:7, "Behold, he cometh with clouds, and every eye shall see him."

Christ will make this appearance suddenly, and to the great surprise of the inhabitants of the earth. It is therefore compared to a cry at midnight, by which men are wakened in a great surprise.

II. At the sound of the last trumpet, the dead shall rise, and the living shall be changed. As soon as Christ is descended, the last trumpet shall sound, as a notification to all mankind to appear. At which mighty sound shall the dead be immediately raised, and the living changed. 1 Cor. 15:52, "For the trumpet shall sound, and the dead shall be raised incorruptible, and we shall be changed." Matt. 24:31, "And he shall send his angels with a great sound of a trumpet." 1 Thess. 4:16, "For the Lord himself shall descend from heaven with a shout, with the voice of the archangel, and with the trump of God." There will be some great and remarkable signal given for the rising of the dead, which it seems will be some mighty sound, caused by the angels of God, who shall attend on Christ.

Upon this all the dead shall rise from their graves. All, both small and great, who shall have lived upon earth since the foundation of the world, those who died before the flood, and those who were drowned in the flood, all that have died since that time, and that shall die to the end of the world. There will be a great moving upon the face of the earth, and in the water, in bringing bone to his bone, in opening graves, and bringing together all the scattered particles of dead bodies. The earth shall give up the dead that are in it, and the sea shall give up the dead that are in it.

However the parts of the bodies of many are divided and scattered; however many have been burnt, and their bodies have been turned to ashes and smoke, and driven to the four winds; however many have been eaten of wild beasts, of the fowls of heaven, and the fishes of the sea; however many have consumed away upon the face of the earth, and great part of their bodies have ascended in exhalations; yet the all-wise and all-powerful God can immediately bring every part to his part again.

Of this vast multitude some shall rise to life, and others to condemnation. John 5:28,29, "All that are in the graves shall hear his voice, and shall come forth, they that have done good, unto the resurrection of life; and they that have done evil, unto the resurrection of damnation."

When the bodies are prepared, the departed souls shall again enter into their bodies, and be re-united to them, never more to be separated. The souls of the wicked shall be brought up out of hell, though not out of misery, and shall very unwillingly enter into their bodies, which will be but eternal prisons to them. Rev. 20:13, "And death and hell delivered up the dead that were in them." They shall lift their eyes full of the utmost amazement and horror to see their awful Judge. And perhaps the bodies with which they shall be raised will be most filthy and loathsome, thus properly corresponding to the inward, moral turpitude of their souls.

The souls of the righteous shall descend from heaven together with Christ and his angels: 1 Thess. 4:14, "Them also which sleep in Jesus will God bring with him." They also shall be re-united to their bodies, that they may be glorified with them. They shall receive their bodies prepared by God to be mansions of pleasure to all eternity. They shall be every way fitted for the uses, the exercises, and delights of perfectly holy and glorified souls. They shall be clothed with a superlative beauty, similar to that of Christ's glorious body. Phil. 3:21, "Who shall change our vile body, that it may be fashioned like unto his glorious body." Their bodies shall rise incorruptible, no more liable to pain or disease, and with an extraordinary vigor and vivacity, like that of those spirits that are as a flame of fire. 1 Cor. 15:43,44, "It is sown in dishonor, it is raised in glory: it is sown in weakness, it is raised in power: it is sown a natural body, it is raised a spiritual body." With what joy will the souls and bodies of the saints meet, and with what joy will they lift their heads out of their graves to behold the glorious sight of the appearing of Christ! And it will be a glorious sight to see those saints arising out of their graves, putting off their corruption, and putting on incorruption and glory.

At the same time, those that shall then be alive upon the earth shall be changed. Their bodies shall pass through a great change, in a moment, in the twinkling of an eye. 1 Cor. 15:51,52, "Behold, I show you a great mystery; We shall not all sleep, but we shall all be changed, in a moment, in the twinkling of an eye, at the last trump." The bodies of the wicked then living will be changed into such hideous things, as shall be answerable to the loathsome souls that dwell in them, and such as shall be prepared to receive and administer eternal torments without dissolution. But the bodies of the righteous shall be changed into the same glorious and immortal form in which those that shall be raised will appear.

III. They shall all be brought to appear before Christ, the godly being placed on the right hand, the wicked on the left; Matt. 25:31, 32,33. The wicked, however unwilling, however full of fear and horror, shall be brought or driven before the judgment-seat. However they may try to hide themselves, and for this purpose creep into dens caves of the mountains, and cry to the mountains to fall on them, and hide them from the face of him that sitteth on the throne, and from the wrath of the Lamb; Rev. 6:15,16. Yet there shall not one escape. To the Judge they must come, and stand on the left hand with devils. On the contrary, the righteous will be joyfully conducted to Jesus Christ, probably by the angels. Their joy will, as it were, give them wings to carry them thither. They will with ecstasies and raptures of delight meet their friend and Savior, come into his presence, and stand at his right hand.

Besides the one standing on the right hand and the other on the left, there seems to be this difference between them that when the dead in Christ shall be raised, they will all be caught up into the air, where Christ shall be, and shall be there at his right hand during the judgment, never more to set their feet on this earth. Whereas the wicked shall be left standing on the earth, there to abide the judgment. 1 Thess. 4:16,17, "The dead in Christ shall rise first; then we which are alive and remain, shall be caught up together with them in the clouds to meet the Lord in the air: and so shall we ever be with the Lord."

And what a vast congregation will there be of all the men, women, and children that shall have lived upon earth from the beginning to the end of the world! Rev. 20:12, "And I saw the dead, small and great, stand before God."

IV. The next thing will be that the books shall be opened. Rev. 20:12, "I saw the dead, great and small, stand before God; and the books were opened." Which books seem to be these two, the book of God's remembrance, and the book of Scripture. The former as the evidence of their deeds which are to be judged, the latter as the rule of judgment. The works both of the righteous and of the wicked will be brought forth that they may be judged according to them, and those works will be tried according to the appointed and written rule.

First, the works of both righteous and wicked will be rehearsed. The book of God's remembrance will be first opened. The various works of the children of men are, as it were, written by God in a book of remembrance. Mal. 3:16, "A book of remembrance was written before him." However ready ungodly men may be to make light of their own sins, and to forget them; yet God never forgets any of them. Neither does God forget any of the good works of the saints. If they give but a cup of cold water with a spirit of charity, God remembers it.

The evil works of the wicked shall then be brought forth to light. They must then hear of all their profaneness, their impenitence, their obstinate unbelief, their abuse of ordinances, and various other sins. The various aggravations of their sins will also be brought to view, as how this man sinned after such and such warnings, that after the receipt of such and such mercies; one after being so and so favored with outward light, another after having been the subject of inward conviction, excited by the immediate agency of God. Concerning these sins, they shall be called to account to see what answer they can make for themselves. Matt. 12:36, "But I say unto you, that every idle word that men shall speak, they shall give account thereof in the Day of Judgment." Rom.14:12, "So then every one of us shall give account of himself to God."

The good works of the saints will also be brought forth as evidences of their sincerity, and of their interest in the righteousness of Christ. As to their evil works, they will not be brought forth against them on that day. For the guilt of them will not lie upon them, they being clothed with the righteousness of Jesus Christ. The Judge himself will have taken the guilt of their sins upon him. Therefore their sins will not stand against them in the book of God's remembrance. The account of them will appear to have been canceled before that time. The account that will be found in God's book will not be of debt, but of credit. God cancels their debts, and sets down their good works, and is pleased, as it were, to make himself a debtor for them, by his own gracious act.

Both good and bad will be judged according to their works. Rev. 20:12, "And the dead were judged out of those things that were found written in the books, according to their works." And verse 13, "And they were judged every man according to their works." Though the righteous are justified by faith, and not by their works, yet they shall be judged *according to* their works: then works shall be brought forth as the evidence of their faith. Their faith on that great day shall be tried by its fruits. If the works of any man shall have been bad, if his life shall appear to have been unchristian, that will condemn him, without any further inquiry. But if his works, when they shall be examined, prove good and of the right sort, he shall surely be justified. They will be declared as a sure evidence of his having believed in Jesus Christ, and of his being clothed with his righteousness.

But by works we are to understand all voluntary exercises of the faculties of the soul. As for instance, the words and conversation of men, as well as what is done with their hands. Matt. 12:37, "By thy words thou shalt be justified, and by thy words thou shalt be condemned." Nor are we to understand only outward acts, or the thoughts outwardly expressed, but also the thoughts themselves, and all the inward workings of the heart. Man judgeth according to the outward appearance, but God judgeth the heart. Rev. 2:23, "I am he that searcheth the heart and the reins, and I will give unto every one of you according to his works." Nor will only positive sins be brought into judgment, but also omissions of duty, as is manifest by Matt. 25:42, etc. "For I was an hungred, and ye gave me no meat; I was thirsty, and ye gave me no drink," etc.

On that day secret and hidden *wickedness* will be brought to light. All the uncleanness, injustice, and violence, of which men have been guilty in secret, shall be manifest both to angels and men. Then it will be made to appear, how this and that man have indulged themselves in wicked imaginations, in lascivious, covetous, malicious, or impious desires and wishes. And how others have harbored in their hearts enmity against God and his law; also impenitency and unbelief, notwithstanding all the means used with them, and motives set before them, to induce them to repent, return, and live.

The *good works* of the saints also, which were done in secret, shall then be made public, and even the pious and benevolent affections and designs of their hearts, so that the real and secret characters of both saints and sinners shall then be most clearly and publicly displayed.

Second, the book of Scripture will be opened, and the works of men will be tried by that touchstone. Their works will be compared with the Word of God. That which God gave men for the rule of their action while in this life, shall then be made the rule of their judgment. God has told us beforehand, what will be the rule of judgment. We are told in the Scriptures upon what terms we shall be justified, and upon what terms we shall be condemned. That which God has given us to be our rule in our lives, he will make his own rule in judgment.

The rule of judgment will be twofold. The *primary* rule of judgment will be the law. The law ever has stood, and ever will stand in force, as a rule of judgment, for those to whom the law was given. Matt. 5:18, "For verily I say unto you, Till heaven and earth pass, one jot or one tittle shall in no wise pass from the law, till all be fulfilled." The law will so far be made the rule of judgment, that not one person at that day shall by any means be justified or condemned, in a way inconsistent with that which is established by the law. As to the wicked, the law will be so far the rule of judgment respecting them, that the sentence denounced against them will be the sentence of the law. The righteous will be so far judged by the law, that although their sentence will not be the sentence of the law, yet it will by no means be such a sentence as shall be inconsistent with the law, but such as it allows. For it will be by the righteousness of the law that they shall be justified.

It will be inquired concerning everyone, both righteous and wicked, whether the law stands against him, or whether he has a fulfillment of the law to show. As to the *righteous,* they will have fulfillment to show. They will have it to plead, that the Judge himself has fulfilled the law for them. That he has both satisfied for their sins, and fulfilled the righteousness of the law for them. Rom. 10:4, "Christ is the end of the law for righteousness to everyone that believeth." But as to the wicked, when it shall be found, by the book of God's remembrance, that they have broken the law, and have no fulfillment of it to plead, the sentence of the law shall be pronounced upon them.

A *secondary* rule of judgment will be the gospel, or the covenant of grace, wherein it is said, "He that believeth shall be saved, and he that believeth not shall be damned:" Mark 16:16. "In the day when God shall judge the secrets of men by Jesus Christ according to my gospel" Rom. 2:16. By the gospel, or covenant of grace, eternal blessedness will be adjudged to believers. When it shall be found that the law hinders not, and that the curse and condemnation of the law stands not against them, the reward of eternal life shall be given them, according to the glorious gospel of Jesus Christ.

V. The sentence will be pronounced. Christ will say to the wicked on the left hand, "Depart, ye cursed, into everlasting fire, prepared for the devil and his angels." How dreadful will these words of the Judge be to the poor, miserable, despairing wretches on the left hand! How amazing will every syllable of them be! How will they pierce them to the soul! These words show the greatest wrath and abhorrence. Christ will bid them *depart.* He will send them away from his presence, will remove them forever far out of his sight, into an everlasting separation from God, as being most loathsome, and unfit to dwell in his presence, and enjoy communion with him.

Christ will call them *cursed. Depart, ye cursed,* to whom everlasting wrath and ruin belong, who are by your own wickedness prepared for nothing else, but to be firebrands of hell, who are the fit objects and vessels of the vengeance and fury of the Almighty. *Into fire.* He will not send them away merely into a loathsome prison, the receptacle of the filth and rubbish of the universe. But into a furnace of fire. That must be their dwelling-place, there they must be tormented with the most racking pain and anguish. It is *everlasting* fire. There is eternity in the sentence, which infinitely aggravates the doom, and will make every word of it immensely more dreadful, sinking, and amazing to the souls that receive it. *Prepared for the devil and his angels.* This sets forth the greatness and intenseness of the torments, as the preceding part of the sentence does the duration. It shows the dreadfulness of that fire to which they shall be condemned, that it is the same that is prepared for the devils, those foul spirits and great enemies of God. Their condition will be the same as that of the devils, in many respects; particularly as they must burn in the fire forever.

This sentence will doubtless be pronounced in such an awful manner as shall be a terrible manifestation of the wrath of the Judge. There will be divine, holy, and almighty wrath manifested in the countenance and voice of the Judge. And we know not what other manifestations of anger will accompany the sentence. Perhaps it will be accompanied with thunders and lightnings, far more dreadful than were on Mount Sinai at the giving of the law. Correspondent to these exhibitions of divine wrath, will be the appearances of terror and most horrible amazement in the condemned. How will all their faces look pale! How will death sit upon their countenances, when those words shall be heard! What dolorous cries, shrieks, and groans! What trembling, and wringing of hands, and gnashing of teeth, will there then be!

But with the most benign aspect, in the most endearing manner, and with the sweetest expressions of love, will Christ invite his saints on his right hand to glory; saying, "Come, ye blessed of my Father, inherit the kingdom prepared for you from the foundation of the world" Matt. 25:34. He will not bid them to go from him, but *to come with him;* to go where he goes; to dwell where he dwells; to enjoy him, and to partake with him. He will call them *blessed,* blessed of *his Father,* blessed by him whose blessing is infinitely the most desirable, namely, God. *Inherit the kingdom.* They are not only invited to go with Christ, and to dwell with him, but to inherit a kingdom with him, to sit down with him on his throne, and to receive the honor and happiness of a heavenly kingdom. "Prepared for you from the foundation of the world." This denotes the sovereign and eternal love of God, as the source of their blessedness. He puts them in mind, that God was pleased to set his love upon them, long before they had a being, even from eternity. That therefore God made heaven on purpose for them, and fitted it for their delight and happiness.

VI. Immediately after this, the sentence will be executed, as we are informed, Matt. 25:46, "These shall go away into everlasting punishment; but the righteous into life eternal." When the words of the sentence shall have once proceeded out of the mouth of the Judge, then that vast and innumerable throng of ungodly men shall go away, shall be driven away, shall be necessitated to go away with devils, and shall with dismal cries and shrieks be cast into the great furnace of fire prepared for the punishment of devils, the perpetual thunders and lightnings of the wrath of God following them. Into this furnace they must in both soul and body enter, never more to come out. Here they must spend eternal ages in wrestling with the most excruciating torments, and in crying out in the midst of the most dreadful flames, and under the most insupportable wrath.

On the other hand, the righteous shall ascend to heaven with their glorified bodies, in company with Christ, his angels, and all that host which descended with him. They shall ascend in the most joyful and triumphant manner, and shall enter with Christ into that glorious and blessed world, which had for the time been empty of its creature inhabitants. Christ having given his church that perfect beauty, and crowned it with that glory, honor, and happiness, which were stipulated in the covenant of redemption before the world was, and which he died to procure for them; and having made it a truly glorious church, every way complete, will present it before the Father, without spot, or wrinkle, or any such thing. Thus shall the saints be instated in everlasting glory, to dwell there with Christ, who shall feed them, and lead them to living fountains of water, to the full enjoyment of God, and to an eternity of the most holy, glorious, and joyful employments.

SECTION V - *All will be done in righteousness.*

Christ will give to every man his due, according to most righteous rule. Those who shall be condemned, will be most justly condemned, will be condemned to that punishment which they shall most justly deserve, and the justice of God in condemning them will be made most evident. Now the justice of God in punishing wicked men, and especially in the degree of their punishment, is often blasphemously called in question. But it will be made clear and apparent to all. Their own consciences will tell them that the sentence is just, and all cavils will be put to silence.

So those that shall be justified, shall be most justly adjudged to eternal life. Although they also were great sinners, and deserved eternal death; yet it will not be against justice or the law, to justify them, they will be in Christ. But the acquitting of them will be but giving the reward merited by Christ's righteousness, Rom. 3:26, "That God may be just, and the justifier of him that believeth in Jesus."

Christ will judge the world in righteousness, particularly as he will give to everyone a *due proportion* either of reward or punishment, according to the various characters of those who shall be judged. The punishments shall be duly proportioned to the number and aggravations of the sins of the wicked. And the rewards of the righteous shall be duly proportioned to the number of their holy acts and affections, and also to the degree of virtue implied in them.—I would observe further,

I. That Christ cannot fail of being just in judging through *mistake*. He cannot take some to be sincere and godly, who are not so, nor others to be hypocrites, who are really sincere. His eyes are as a flame of fire, and he searcheth the hearts and trieth the reins of the children of men. He can never err in determining what is justice in particular cases, as human judges often do. Nor can he be blinded by prejudices, as human judges are very liable to be. Deut. 10:17, "He regardeth not persons, nor taketh reward." It is impossible he should be deceived by the excuse, and false colors, and pleas of the wicked, as human judges very commonly are. It is equally impossible that he should err, in assigning to everyone his proper proportion of reward or punishment, according to his wickedness or good works. His knowledge being infinite, will effectually guard him against all these, and other such errors.

II. He cannot fail of judging righteously through an *unrighteous* disposition. For he is infinitely just and holy in his nature. Deut. 32:4, "He is the rock, his work is perfect; for all his ways are judgment: a God of truth, and without iniquity, just and right is he." It is not possible that an infinitely powerful, self-sufficient being should be under any temptation to injustice. Nor is it possible that an infinitely wise being, who knoweth all things, should not choose justice. For he who perfectly knows all things perfectly knows how much more amiable justice is than injustice. And therefore must choose it.

SECTION VI - *Those things which will immediately follow the Day of Judgment.*

I. After the sentence shall have been pronounced, and the saints shall have ascended with Christ into glory, this world will be dissolved by fire. The conflagration will immediately succeed the judgment. When an end shall have been put to the present state of mankind, this world, which was the place of their habitation during that state, will be destroyed, there being no further use for it. This earth which had been the stage upon which so many scenes had been acted, upon which there had been so many great and famous kingdoms and large cities, where there had been so many wars, so much trade and business carried on for so many ages, shall then be destroyed. These continents, these islands, these seas and rivers, these mountains and valleys, shall be seen no more at all. All shall be destroyed by devouring flames. This we are plainly taught in the Word of God. 2 Pet. 3:7, "But the heavens and the earth which are now, by the same word are kept in store, reserved unto fire against the Day of Judgment, and perdition of ungodly men." Verse 10, "But the day of the Lord will come as a thief in the night; in the which the heavens shall pass away with a great noise, and the elements shall melt with fervent heat, the earth also and the works that are therein shall be burnt up." 2 Pet. 3:12, "Looking for and hasting unto the coming of the day of God, wherein the heavens being on fire shall be dissolved, and the elements shall melt with fervent heat."

II. Both the misery of the wicked and the happiness of the saints will be increased beyond what shall be before the judgment. The misery of the wicked will be increased, as they will be tormented not only in their souls, but also in their bodies, which will be prepared both to receive and administer torment to their souls. There will doubtless then be the like connection between soul and body, as there is now. And therefore the pains and torments of the one will affect the other. And why may we not suppose that their torments will be increased as well as those of the devils? Concerning them we are informed (Jam. 2:19) that they believe there is one God, and tremble in the belief; expecting no doubt that he will inflict upon them, in due time more severe torments than even those which they now suffer. We are also informed that they are bound "in chains of darkness, to be reserved unto judgment; *and* unto the judgment of the great day," (2 Pet. 2:4, and Jude 6) which implies that their full punishment is not yet executed upon them, but that they are now reserved as prisoners in hell, to receive their just recompense on the Day of Judgment. Hence it was that they thought Christ was *come to torment them before the time.* Matt. 8:29. Thus the punishment neither of wicked men nor devils will be complete before the final judgment.

No more will the happiness of the saints be complete before that time. Therefore we are in the New Testament so often encouraged with promises of the resurrection of the dead, and of the day when Christ shall come the second time. These things are spoken of as the great objects of the expectation and hope of Christians. A state of separation of soul and body is to men an unnatural state. Therefore when the bodies of the saints shall be raised from the dead, and their souls shall be again united to them, as their state will be more natural, so doubtless it will be more happy. Their bodies will be *glorious* bodies, and prepared to administer as much to their happiness, as the bodies of the wicked will be to administer to their misery.

We may with good reason suppose the accession of happiness to the souls of the saints will be great, since the occasion is represented as the marriage of the church, and the Lamb. Rev. 19:7, "The marriage of the Lamb is come, and his wife hath made herself ready." Their joy will then be increased because they will have new arguments of joy. The body of Christ will then be perfect, the church will be complete. All the parts of it will have come into existence, which will not be the case before the end of the world. No parts of it will be under sin or affliction. All the members of it will be in a perfect state. And they shall all be together by themselves, none being mixed with ungodly men. Then the church will be as a bride adorned for her husband, and therefore she will exceedingly rejoice.

Then also the Mediator will have fully accomplished his work. He will then have destroyed, and will triumph over, all his enemies. Then Christ will have fully obtained his reward, and fully accomplished the design which was in his heart from all eternity. For these reasons Christ himself will greatly rejoice with him. Then God will have obtained the end of all the great works which he has been doing from the beginning of the world. All the designs of God will be unfolded in their events. Then his marvelous contrivance in his hidden, intricate, and inexplicable works will appear, the ends being obtained. Then the works of God being perfected, the divine glory will more abundantly appear. These things will cause a great accession of happiness to the saints, who shall behold them. Then God will have fully glorified himself, his Son, and his elect. Then he will see that all is very good, and will entirely rejoice in his own works. At the same time the saints also, viewing the works of God brought thus to perfection, will rejoice in the view, and receive from it a large accession of happiness.

Then God will make more abundant manifestations of his glory, and of the glory of his Son. Then he will more plentifully pour out his Spirit, and make answerable additions to the glory of the saints, and by means of all these will so increase the happiness of the saints, as shall be suitable to the commencement of the ultimate and most perfect state of things, and to such a joyful occasion, the completion of all things. In this glory and happiness will the saints remain forever and ever.

SECTION VII - *The uses to which this doctrine is applicable.*

I. The *first use* proper to be made of this doctrine is of *instruction.* Hence many of the mysteries of Divine Providence may be unfolded. There are many things in the dealings of God towards the children of men, which appear very mysterious, if we view them without having an eye to this last judgment, which yet, if we consider this judgment, have no difficulty in them. As,

First, that God suffers the wicked to live and prosper in the world. The infinitely holy and wise Creator and Governor of the world must necessarily hate wickedness. Yet we see many wicked men spreading themselves as a green bay-tree. They live with impunity; things seem to go well with them, and the world smiles upon them. Many who have not been fit to live, who have held God and religion in the greatest contempt, who have been open enemies to all that is good, who by their wickedness have been the pests of mankind. Many cruel tyrants, whose barbarities have been such as would even fill one with horror to hear or read of them; yet have lived in great wealth and outward glory, have reigned over great and mighty kingdoms and empires, and have been honored as a sort of earthly gods.

Now, it is very mysterious, that the holy and righteous Governor of the world, whose eye beholds all the children of men, should suffer it so to be, unless we look forward to the Day of Judgment. And then the mystery is unraveled. For although God for the present keeps silence, and seems to let them alone; yet then he will give suitable manifestations of his displeasure against their wickedness. They shall then receive condign punishment. The saints under the Old Testament were much stumbled at these dispensations of Providence, as you may see in Job 21, and Psa. 73, and Jer. 12. The difficulty to them was so great, because then a future state and a Day of Judgment were not revealed with that clearness with which they are now.

Second, God sometimes suffers some of the best of men to be in great affliction, poverty, and persecution. The *wicked* rule, while *they* are subject. The wicked are the head, and they are the tail. The wicked domineer, while they serve, and are oppressed, yea are trampled under their feet, as the mire of the streets. These things are very common, yet they seem to imply great confusion. When the wicked are exalted to power and authority, and the godly are oppressed by them, things are quite out of joint. Prov. 25:26, "A righteous man falling down before the wicked, is as a troubled fountain, and a corrupt spring." Sometimes one wicked man makes many hundreds, yea thousands, of precious saints a sacrifice to his lust and cruelty, or to his enmity against virtue and the truth, and puts them to death for no other reason but that for which they are especially to be esteemed and commended.

Now, if we look no further than the present state, these things appear strange and unaccountable. But we ought not to confine our views within such narrow limits. When God shall have put an end to the present state, these things shall all be brought to rights. Though God suffers things to be so for the present, yet they shall not proceed in this course always. Comparatively speaking, the present state of things is *but for a moment*. When all shall be settled and fixed by a divine judgment, the righteous shall be exalted, honored, and rewarded, and the wicked shall be depressed and put under their feet. However the wicked now prevail against the righteous, yet the righteous shall at last have the ascendant, shall come off conquerors, and shall see the just vengeance of God executed upon those who now hate and persecute them.

Third, it is another mystery of providence, that God suffers so much public injustice to take place in the world. There are not only private wrongs, which in this state pass unsettled, but many public wrongs, wrongs done by men acting in a public character, and wrongs which affect nations, kingdoms, and other public bodies of men. Many suffer by men in public offices, from whom there is no refuge, from whose decisions there is no appeal. Now it seems a mystery that these things are tolerated, when he that is rightfully the Supreme Judge and Governor of the world is perfectly just. But at the final judgment all these wrongs shall be adjusted, as well as those of a more private nature.

II. Our *second use* of this subject shall be to apply it to the *awakening* of sinners. You that have not the fear of God before your eyes, that are not afraid to sin against him, consider seriously what you have heard concerning the Day of Judgment. Although these things be now future and unseen, yet they are real and certain. If you now be left to yourselves, if God keep silence, and judgment be not speedily executed, it is not because God is regardless how you live, and how you behave yourselves. Now indeed God is invisible to you, and his wrath is invisible. But at the Day of Judgment, you yourselves shall see him with your bodily eyes. You shall not then be able to keep out of his sight, or to avoid seeing him. Rev. 1:7, "Behold he cometh with clouds; and every eye shall see him, and they also which pierced him: and all kindreds of the earth shall wail because of him." You shall see him coming in the clouds of heaven. Your ears shall hear the last trumpet, that dreadful sound, the voice of the archangel. Your eyes shall see your Judge sitting on the throne, they shall see those manifestations of wrath which there will be in his countenance. Your ears shall hear him pronounce the sentence.

Seriously consider, if you live in the ways of sin, and appear at that day with the guilt of it upon you, how you will be able to endure the sight or the hearing of these things, and whether horror and amazement will not be likely to seize you, when you shall see the Judge descending, and hear the trump of God. What account will you be able to give, when it shall be inquired of you, why you led such a sinful, wicked life? What will you be able to say for yourselves, when it shall be asked, why you neglected such and such particular duties, as the duty of secret prayer, for instance? Or why you have habitually practiced such and such particular sins or lusts? Although you be so careless of your conduct and manner of life, make so light of sin, and proceed in it so freely, with little or no dread or remorse; yet you must give an account of every sin that you commit, of every idle word that you speak, and of every sinful thought of your hearts. Every time you deviate from the rules of justice, of temperance, or of charity; every time you indulge any lust, whether secretly or openly, you must give an account of it. It will never be forgotten, it stands written in that book which will be opened on that day.

Consider the rule you will be judged by. It is the perfect rule of the divine law, which is exceeding strict, and exceeding broad. And how will you ever be able to answer the demands of this law?—Consider also,

First, that the Judge will be *supreme* Judge. You will have no opportunity to appeal from his decision. This is often the case in this world. When we are dissatisfied with the decisions of a judge, we often may appeal to a higher, a more knowing, or a more just judicatory. But no such appeal can be made from our Divine Judge. No such indulgence will be allowed. Or if it were allowed, there is no superior judge to whom the appeal should be made. By his decision, therefore, you must abide.

Second, the Judge will be *omnipotent.* Were he a mere man, like yourselves, however he might judge and determine, you might resist, and by the help of others, if not by your own strength, prevent or elude the execution of the judgment. But the Judge being omnipotent, this is utterly impossible. In vain is all resistance, either by yourselves, or by whatever help you can obtain. "Though hand join in hand, the wicked shall not be unpunished," Prov. 11:21. As well might you "set the briers and thorns in battle against God," Isa. 27:4.

Third, the Judge will be *inexorable.* Human judges may be prevailed upon to reverse their sentence, or at least to remit something of its severity. But in vain will be all your entreaties, all your cries and tears to this effect, with the great Judge of the world. Now indeed he inclines his ear, and is ready to hear the prayers, cries, and entreaties of all mankind. But then the day of grace will be past, and the door of mercy be shut. Then although ye spread forth your hands, yet the Judge will hide his eyes from you. Yea, though ye make many prayers, he will not hear. Isa. 1:15. Then the Judge will deal in fury. His eye shall not spare, neither will he have pity. And though ye cry in his ears with a loud voice, yet will he not hear you. Eze. 8:18. And you will find no place of repentance in God, though you seek it carefully with tears.

Fourth, the Judge at that day will not mix mercy with justice. The time for mercy to be shown to sinners will then be past. Christ will then appear in another character than that of the merciful Savior. Having laid aside the inviting attributes of grace and mercy, he will clothe himself with justice and vengeance. He will not only, in general, exact of sinners the demands of the law, but he will exact the whole, without any abatement. He will exact the very uttermost farthing, Matt. 5:26. Then Christ will come to fulfill that in Rev. 14:10, "The same shall drink of the wine of the wrath of God, which is poured out without mixture, into the cup of his indignation." The punishment threatened to ungodly men is *without any pity.* See Eze. 5:11, "Neither shall mine eye spare; neither will I have any pity." Here all judgments have a mixture of mercy. But the wrath of God will be poured out upon the wicked without mixture, and vengeance will have its full weight.

III. I shall apply myself, *thirdly,* to several *different characters* of men.

First, to those who live in secret wickedness. Let such consider that for all these things God will bring them into judgment. Secrecy is your temptation. Promising yourselves this, you practice many things, you indulge many lusts, under the covert of darkness, and in secret corners, which you would be ashamed to do in the light of the sun, and before the world. But this temptation is entirely groundless. All your secret abominations are even now perfectly known to God, and will also hereafter be made known both to angels and men. Luke 12:2,3, "For there is nothing covered, that shall not be revealed; neither hid, that shall not be known. Therefore whatsoever ye have spoken in darkness, shall be heard in the light: and that which ye have spoken in the ear in closets, shall be proclaimed upon the house-tops."

Before human judges are brought only those things which are known. But before this Judge shall be brought the most "hidden things of darkness, and even the counsels of the heart," 1 Cor. 4:5. All your secret uncleanness, all your secret fraud and injustice, all your lascivious desires, wishes, and designs, all your inward covetousness, which is idolatry, all your malicious, envious, and revengeful thoughts and purposes, whether brought forth into practice or not, shall then be made manifest, and you shall be judged according to them. Of these things, however secret, there will be need of no other evidence than the testimony of God and of your own consciences.

Second, to such as are not just and upright in their dealings with their fellow-men. Consider, that all your dealings with men must be tried, must be brought forth into judgment, and there compared with the rules of the Word of God. All your actions must be judged according to those things which are found written in the book of the Word of God. If your ways of dealing with men shall not agree with those rules of righteousness, they will be condemned. Now, the Word of God directs us to practice entire justice. "That which is altogether just shalt thou follow," Deut. 16:20, and to do to others as we would they would do to us. But how many are there, whose dealings with their fellow-men, if strictly tried by these rules, would not stand the test!

God has, in his word, forbidden all deceit and fraud in our dealings one with another, Lev. 11:13. He has forbidden us to oppress one another, Lev. 25:14. But how frequent are practices contrary to those rules, and which will not bear to be tried by them! How common are fraud and trickishness in trade! How will men endeavor to lead on those with whom they trade in the dark, that so they may make their advantage! Yea, lying in trading is too common a thing among us. How common are such things as that mentioned, Prov. 20:14, "It is nought, it is nought, saith the buyer; but when he is gone his way, then he boasteth."

Many men will take the advantage of another's ignorance to advance their own gain, to his wrong. Yea, they seem not to scruple such practices. Beside downright lying, men have many ways of blinding and deceiving one another in trade, which are by no means right in the sight of God, and will appear to be very unjust, when they shall be tried by the rule of God's Word at the Day of Judgment. And how common a thing is oppression or extortion, in taking any advantage that men can by any means obtain, to get the utmost possible of their neighbor for what they have to dispose of, and their neighbor needs!

Let such consider, that there is a God in heaven, who beholds them, and sees how they conduct themselves in their daily traffic with one another, and that he will try their works another day. Justice shall assuredly take place at last. The righteous Governor of the world will not suffer injustice without control. He will control and rectify it by returning the injury upon the head of the injurer. Matt. 7:2, "With what measure ye mete, it shall be measured to you again."

Third, to those who plead for the lawfulness of practices generally condemned by God's people. You who do this, consider that your practices must be tried at the Day of Judgment. Consider, whether or no they are likely to be approved by the most holy Judge at that day. Prov. 5:21, "The ways of man are before the eyes of the Lord; and he pondereth all his goings." However, by your carnal reasonings, you may deceive your own hearts, yet you will not be able to deceive the Judge, he will not hearken to your excuses, but will try your ways by the rule. He will know whether they be straight or crooked.

When you plead for these and those liberties which you take, let it be considered, whether they be likely to be allowed of by the Judge at the last great day. Will they bear to be tried by his eyes, which are purer than to behold evil, and cannot look on iniquity?

Fourth, to those who are wont to excuse their wickedness. Will the excuses which you make for yourselves be accepted at the Day of Judgment? If you excuse yourselves to your own consciences, by saying that you were under such and such temptations which you could not withstand, that corrupt nature prevailed, and you could not overcome it, that it would have been so and so to your damage if you had done otherwise, that if you had done such a duty, you would have brought yourselves into difficulty, would have incurred the displeasure of such and such friends, or would have been despised and laughed at. Or if you say, you did no more than it was the common custom to do, no more than many godly men have done, no more than certain persons of good reputation now practice, that if you had done otherwise, you would have been singular. If these be your excuses for the sins which you commit, or for the duties which you neglect, let me ask you, will they appear sufficient when they shall be examined at the Day of Judgment?

Fifth, to those who live in impenitence and unbelief. There are some persons who live in no open vice, and perhaps conscientiously avoid secret immorality, who yet live in impenitence and unbelief. They are indeed called upon *to repent and believe the gospel,* to forsake their evil ways and *thoughts,* and to return to God, that he may have mercy on them; to come unto Christ, *laboring,* and *heavy-laden with sin,* that they may obtain *rest* of him; and are assured, that if they *believe, they shall be saved;* and that if they *believe not, they shall be damned;* and all the most powerful motives are set before them, to induce them to comply with these exhortations, especially those drawn from the eternal world. Yet they persist in sin, they remain impenitent and unhumbled. They will not come unto Christ that they may have life.

Now such men shall be brought into judgment for their conduct, as well as more gross sinners. Nor will they be any more able to stand in the judgment than the other. They resist the most powerful means of grace, go on in sin against the clear light of the gospel, refuse to hearken to the kindest calls and invitations, reject the most amiable Savior, the Judge himself, and despise the free offers of eternal life, glory, and felicity. And how will they be able to answer for these things at the tribunal of Christ?

IV. If there be a Day of Judgment appointed, then let all be very strict in trying their own sincerity. God on that day will discover the secrets of all hearts. The judgment of that day will be like the fire, which burns up whatsoever is not true gold. Wood, hay, stubble, and dross, shall be all consumed by the scorching fire of that day. The Judge will be like a refiner's fire, and fuller's soap, which will cleanse away all filthiness, however it may be colored over. Mal. 3:2, "Who may abide the day of his coming? and who shall stand when he appeareth? for he is like a refiner's fire, and like fuller's soap." And Mal. 4:1, "For behold the day cometh that shall burn as an oven, and all the proud, yea, and all that do wickedly, shall be stubble, and the day that cometh shall burn them up, saith the Lord of hosts."

There are multitudes of men that wear the guise of saints, appear like saints, and their state, both in their own eyes and in the eyes of their neighbors, is good. They have sheep's clothing. But no disguise can hide them from the eyes of the Judge of the world. His eyes are as a flame of fire. They search the hearts and try the reins of the children of men. He will see whether they be sound at heart. He will see from what principles they have acted. A fair show will in no degree deceive him, as it does men in the present state. It will signify nothing to say, "Lord, we have eaten and drunk in thy presence; and in thy name have we cast out devils, and in thy name have done many wonderful works." It will signify nothing to pretend to a great deal of comfort and joy, and to the experience of great religious affections, and to your having done many things in religion and morality, unless you have some greater evidences of sincerity.

Wherefore let everyone take heed that he be not deceived concerning himself. And that he depend not on that which will not bear examination at the Day of Judgment. Be not contented with this, that you have the judgment of men, the judgment of godly men, or that of ministers, in your favor. Consider that they are not to be your judges at last. Take occasion frequently to compare your hearts with the Word of God. That is the rule by which you are to be finally tried and judged. And try yourselves by your works, by which also you must be tried at last. Inquire whether you lead holy Christian lives, whether you perform universal and unconditional obedience to all God's commands, and whether you do it from a truly gracious respect to God.

Also frequently beg of God, the Judge, that he would search you, try you now, and discover you to yourselves, that you may see if you be insincere in religion. And that he would lead you in the way everlasting. Beg of God, that if you be not upon a good foundation, he would unsettle you, and fix you upon the sure foundation. The example of the psalmist in this is worthy of imitation. Psa. 26:1,2, "Judge me, O Lord, examine me, and prove me; try my reins and mine heart." And Psa. 139:23,24, "Search me, O God, and know my heart: try me, and know my thoughts.

And see if there be any wicked way in me, and lead me in the way everlasting." God will search us hereafter, and discover what we are, both to ourselves and to all the world. Let us pray that he would search us, and discover our hearts to us now. We have need of divine help in this matter; for the heart is deceitful above all things.

V. If God has appointed a day to judge the world, let us judge and condemn ourselves for our sins. This we must do, if we would not be judged and condemned for them on that day. If we would escape condemnation, we must see that we justly may be condemned. We must be so sensible of our vileness and guilt, as to see that we deserve all that condemnation and punishment which are threatened. And that we are in the hands of God, who is the sovereign disposer of us, and will do with us as seemeth to himself good. Let us therefore often reflect on our sins, confess them before God, condemn and abhor ourselves, be truly humbled, and repent in dust and ashes.

VI. If these things be so, let us by no means be forward to judge others. Some are forward to judge others, to judge their hearts both in general and upon particular occasions, to determine as to the principles, motives, and ends of their actions. But this is to assume the province of God, and to set up ourselves as lords and judges. Rom. 14:4, "Who art thou, that thou judgest another man's servant?" Jam. 4:11, "Speak not evil one of another, brethren. He that speaketh evil of his brother, and judgeth his brother, speaketh evil of the law, and judgeth the law." To be thus disposed to judge and act censoriously towards others, is the way to be judged and condemned ourselves. Matt. 7:1,2, "Judge not, that ye be not judged. For with what judgment ye judge, ye shall be judged: and with what measure ye mete, it shall be measured to you again."

VII. This doctrine affords matter of great consolation to the godly. This Day of Judgment, which is so terrible to ungodly men, affords no ground of terror to you, but abundant ground of joy and satisfaction. For though you now meet with more affliction and trouble than most wicked men, yet on that day you shall be delivered from all afflictions, and from all trouble. If you be unjustly treated by wicked men, and abused by them, what a comfort is it to the injured, that they may appeal to God, who judgeth righteously. The psalmist used often to comfort himself with this.

Upon these accounts the saints have reason to love the appearing of Jesus Christ. 2 Tim. 4:8, "Henceforth there is laid up for me a crown of righteousness, which the Lord, the righteous Judge, shall give me at that day: and not to me only, but to all those that love his appearing." This is to the saints a blessed hope. Titus 2:13, "Looking for that blessed hope, and the glorious appearing of the great God, and our Savior Jesus Christ. This day may well be the object of their eager desire, and when they hear of Christ's coming to judgment, they may well say, "Even so come, Lord Jesus," Rev. 22:20. It will be the most glorious day that ever the saints saw. It will be so both to those who shall die, and whose souls shall go to heaven, and to those who shall then be found alive on earth. It will be the wedding-day of the church. Surely then in the consideration of the approach of this day, there is ground of great consolation to the saints.

CHAPTER FOUR

The Universal Judgment

SAMUEL DAVIES

THE UNIVERSAL JUDGMENT.

ACTS XVII. 30, 31.—*And the times of this ignorance God winked at ; but now commandeth all men everywhere to repent : because he hath appointed a day, in the which he will judge the world in righteousness, by that man whom he hath ordained ; whereof he hath given assurance unto all men, in that he hath raised him from the dead.*

THE present state is the infancy of human nature; and all the events of time, even those that make such noise, and determine the fate of kingdoms, are but the little affairs of children. But if we look forward and trace human nature to maturity, we meet with events vast, interesting, and majestic; and such as nothing but divine authority can render credible to us who are so apt to judge of things by what we see. To one of those scenes I would direct your attention this day; I mean the solemn, tremendous, and glorious scene of the universal judgment.

You have sometimes seen a stately building in ruins; come now and view the ruins of a demolished world. You have often seen a feeble mortal struggling in the agonies of death, and his shattered frame dissolved; come now and view universal nature severely labouring and agonizing in her last convulsions and her well-compacted system dissolved. You have heard of earthquakes here and there that have laid Lisbon, Palermo, and a few other cities in ruins; come now and feel the tremors and convulsions of the whole globe, that blend cities and countries, oceans and continents, mountains, plains, and valleys, in one promiscuous heap. You have a thousand times beheld the moon walking in brightness, and the sun shining in his strength; now look and see the sun turned into darkness, and the moon into blood.

It is our lot to live in an age of confusion, blood, and slaughter; an age in which our attention is engaged by the clash of arms, the clangor of trumpets, the roar of artillery, and the dubious fate of kingdoms; but draw off your thoughts from these objects for an hour, and fix them on objects more solemn and interesting: come view

> " A scene that yields
> A louder trumpet, and more dreadful fields ;
> The world alarmed, both earth and heaven o'erthrown,
> And gasping nature's last tremendous groan ;
> Death's ancient sceptre broke, the teeming tomb,
> The Righteous Judge, and man's eternal doom.''

Such a scene there certainly is before us; for St. Paul tells us that " God hath given assurance to all men that he will judge the world in righteousness by that man whom he hath ordained;" and that his resurrection, the resurrection of him who is God and man, is a demonstrative proof of it.

My text is the conclusion of St. Paul's defence or sermon before the famous court of Areopagus, in the learned and philosophical city of Athens. In this august and polite assembly he speaks with the boldness, and in the evangelical strain, of an apostle of Christ. He first inculcates upon them the great truths of natural religion, and labours faithfully, though in a very gentle and inoffensive manner, to reform them from that stupid idolatry and superstition into which even this learned philosophical city was sunk, though a Socrates, a Plato, and the most celebrated sages and moralists of pagan antiquity had lived and taught in it. Afterwards, in the close of his discourse, he introduces the glorious peculiarities of Christianity, particularly the great duty of repentance, from evangelical motives, the resurrection of the dead, and the final judgment. But no sooner has he entered upon this subject than he is interrupted, and seems to have broken off abruptly; for when he had just hinted at the then unpopular doctrine of the resurrection of the dead, we are told, *some mocked*, and others put it off to another hearing : *We will hear thee again of this matter*.

In these dark times of ignorance which preceded the publication of the gospel, God seemed to wink or connive at the idolatry and various forms of wickedness that had overspread the world ; that is, he seemed to overlook* or to take no notice of them, so as either to punish them, or to give the nations explicit calls to repentance. But now, says St. Paul, the case is altered. Now the gospel is published through the world, and therefore God will no longer seem to connive at the wickedness and impenitence of mankind, but publishes his great mandate to a rebel world, explicitly and loudly, *commanding all men every where to repent ;* and he now gives them particular motives and encouragements to this duty.

One motive of the greatest weight, which was never so clearly or extensively published before, is the doctrine of the universal judgment. This the connection implies: "He now commandeth all men to repent, because he hath appointed a day for judging all men." And surely the pros-

* ὑπεριδων.

pect of a judgment must be a strong motive to sinners to repent:—this, if anything, will rouse them from their thoughtless security, and bring them to repentance. Repentance should, and one would think must, be as extensive as this reason for it. This St. Paul intimates. "He now commandeth all men to repent, because he hath given assurance to all men" that he has "appointed a day to judge the world." Wherever the gospel publishes the doctrine of future judgment, there it requires all men to repent; and wherever it requires repentance, there it enforces the command of this alarming doctrine.

God has *given assurance to all men;* that is, to all that hear the gospel, that he has appointed a day for this great purpose, and that Jesus Christ, God-man, is to preside in person in this majestic solemnity. He has given assurance of this; that is, sufficient ground of faith; and the assurance consists in this, that *he hath raised him from the dead.*

The resurrection of Christ gives assurance of this in several respects. It is a specimen and a pledge of a general resurrection, that grand preparative for the judgment: it is an incontestible proof of his divine mission; for God will never work so unprecedented a miracle in favour of an impostor: it is also an authentic attestation of all our Lord's claims; and he expressly claimed the authority of supreme Judge as delegated to him by the Father; "the Father judgeth no man, but hath committed all judgment to the Son." John v. 22.

There is a peculiar fitness and propriety in this constitution. It is fit that a world placed under the administration of a Mediator should have a mediatorial Judge. It is fit this high office should be conferred upon him as an honourary reward for his important services and extreme abasement. Because he humbled himself, therefore

God hath highly exalted him. Phil. ii. 8, 9. It is fit that creatures clothed with bodies should be judged by a man clothed in a body like themselves. Hence it is said that "God hath given him authority to execute judgment, because he is the Son of man." John v. 27. This would seem a strange reason, did we not understand it in this light. Indeed, was Jesus Christ man only, he would be infinitely unequal to the office of universal Judge; but he is God and man, *Immanuel, God with us;* and is the fittest person in the universe for the work. It is also fit that Christ should be the supreme Judge, as it will be a great encouragement to his people for their Mediator to execute this office: and it may be added, that hereby the condemnation of the wicked will be rendered more conspicuously just; for, if a Mediator, a Saviour, the Friend of sinners, condemns them, they must be worthy of condemnation indeed.

Let us now enter upon the majestic scene. But alas! what images shall I use to represent it? Nothing that we have seen, nothing that we have heard, nothing that has ever happened on the stage of time, can furnish us with proper illustrations. All is low and grovelling, all is faint and obscure that ever the sun shone upon, when compared with the grand phenomena of that day; and we are so accustomed to low and little objects, that it is impossible we should ever raise our thoughts to a suitable pitch of elevation. Ere long we shall be amazed spectators of these majestic wonders, and our eyes and our ears will be our instructors. But now it is necessary we should have such ideas of them as may affect our hearts, and prepare us for them. Let us therefore present to our view those representations which divine revelation, our only guide in this case, gives us of the person of the Judge, and the manner of his appearance; of the resurrection of the dead, and the transformation of the living; of the universal convention of all the sons of men before the supreme tribunal; of their separation to the right and left hand of the Judge, according to their characters; of the judicial process itself; of the decisive sentence; of its execution, and of the conflagration of the world.

As to the person of the Judge, the psalmist tells you, *God is Judge himself*. Psalm l. 6. Yet Christ tells us, "the Father judgeth no man, but hath committed all judgment unto the Son; and hath given him authority to execute judgment also, because he is the Son of man." John v. 22, 27. It is therefore Christ Jesus, God-man, as I observed, who shall sustain this high character; and for the reasons already alleged, it is most fit it should be devolved upon him. Being God and man, all the advantages of divinity and humanity centre in him, and render him more fit for this office than if he were God only, or man only. This is the august Judge before whom we must stand; and the prospect may inspiré us with reverence, joy, and terror.

As for the manner of his appearance, it will be such as becomes the dignity of his person and office. He will shine in all the uncreated glories of the Godhead, and in all the gentler glories of a perfect man. His attendants will add a dignity to the grand appearance, and the sympathy of nature will increase the solemnity and terror of the day. Let his own word describe him. "The Son of man shall come in the glory of his Father, with his angels." Matt. xvi. 27. "The Son of man shall come in his glory, and all the holy angels with him; then shall he sit upon the throne of his glory." Matt. xxv. 31: "The Lord Jesus shall be revealed from heaven with his mighty angels, in flaming fire taking vengeance on them that know not God, and that obey not the gospel of our Lord Jesus

Christ." 2 Thess. i. 7, 8. And not only will the angels, those illustrious ministers of the court of heaven, attend upon that solemn occasion, but also all the saints who had left the world from Adam to that day; for *those that sleep in Jesus*, says St. Paul, *will God bring with him.* 1 Thess. iv. 14. The grand imagery in Daniel's vision is applicable to this day: and perhaps to this it primarily refers: "I beheld till the thrones were cast down," or rather set up,* "and the Ancient of days did sit, whose garment was white as snow, and the hair of his head like the pure wool: his throne was like the fiery flame, and his wheels as burning fire. A fiery stream issued and came forth from before him: thousand thousands ministered unto him, and ten thousand times ten thousand stood before him." Dan. vii. 9, 10. Perhaps our Lord may exhibit himself to the whole world upon this most grand occasion, in the same glorious form in which he was seen by his favourite John, "clothed with a garment down to the foot, and girt about the breasts with a golden girdle: his head and his hairs white like wool, as white as snow; his eyes as a flame of fire: his feet like unto fine brass, as if they burned in a furnace; his voice as the sound of many waters, and his countenance as the sun shining in his strength." Rev. i. 13, &c. Another image of inimitable majesty and terror the same writer gives us, when he says, "I saw a great white throne, and him that sat on it, from whose face the earth and the heaven fled away, and there was found no place for them." Astonishing! what an image is this! the stable earth and heaven cannot bear the majesty and terror of his look; they fly away affrighted, and seek a place to hide themselves, but no place is found to shelter them; every region

---

* This sense is more agreeable to the connection, and the original word will bear it ; which signifies *to pitch down* or *place*, as well as *to throw down* or *demolish*. And the LXX translate it, *the thrones were put up*, or *fixed*.

through the immensity of space lies open before him.*
Rev. xx. 11.

This is the Judge before whom we must stand; and this
is the manner of his appearance.   But is this the babe of
Bethlehem that lay and wept in the manger?   Is this the
supposed son of the carpenter, the despised Galilean?   Is
this the man of sorrows?   Is this he that was arrested,
was condemned, was buffeted, was spit upon, was crowned
with thorns, was executed as a slave and a criminal, upon
the cross?   Yes, it is he; the very same Jesus of Nazareth.
But oh how changed! how deservedly exalted!   Let
heaven and earth congratulate his advancement.   Now let
his enemies appear and show their usual contempt and
malignity.   Now, Pilate, condemn the King of the Jews
as an usurper.   Now, ye Jews, raise the clamour, *Crucify
him, crucify him !*

> " Now bow the knee in scorn, present the reed ;
> Now tell the scourg'd Impostor he must bleed."—YOUNG.

Now, ye Deists and Infidels, dispute his divinity and
the truth of his religion if you can.   Now, ye hypocritical

---

* This is the picture drawn by the pencil of inspiration.   We may now
contemplate the imagery of a fine human pen.

> ————————From his great abode
> Full on a whirlwind rides the dreadful God :
> The tempest's rattling winds, the fiery car,
> Ten thousand hosts his ministers of war,
> The flaming Cherubim, attend his flight.
> And heaven's foundations groan beneath the weight.
> Thro' all the skies the forky lightnings play,
> And radiant splendours round his head display.
> From his bright eyes affrighted worlds retire :
> He speaks in thunder and he breathes in fire.
> Garments of heavenly light array the God ;
> His throne a bright consolidated cloud—
> Support me, heaven, I shudder with affright;
> I quake, I sink with terror at the sight.
> *The Day of Judgment, a Poem, a little varied.*

Christians, try to impose upon him with your idle pretences. Now despise his grace, laugh at his threatenings, and make light of his displeasure if you are able. Ah! now their courage fails, and terror surrounds them like armed men. Now they hide themselves in the dens, and in the rocks of the mountains; and say to the mountains and rocks, Fall on us, and hide us from the face of him that sitteth on the throne, and from the wrath of the Lamb; for the Lamb that once bled as a sacrifice for sin now appears in all the terrors of a lion; and the great day of his wrath is come, and who shall be able to stand? Rev. vi. 15. Oh! could they hide themselves in the bottom of the ocean, or in some rock that bears the weight of the mountains, how happy would they think themselves. But, alas!

> "Seas cast the monsters forth to meet their doom,
> And rocks but prison up for wrath to come.—YOUNG.

While the Judge is descending, the parties to be judged will be summoned to appear. But where are they? They are all asleep in their dusty beds, except the then generation. And how shall they be roused from their long sleep of thousands of years? Why, "the Lord himself shall descend from heaven with a shout, with the voice of the archangel, and with the trump of God." 1 Thess. iv. 16. *The trumpet shall sound,* and they that are then alive shall not pass into eternity through the beaten road of death, but *at the last trumpet they shall be changed,* changed into immortals, *in a moment, in the twinkliug of an eye.* 1 Cor. xv. 51, 52. Now all the millions of mankind, of whatever country and nation, whether they expect this tremendous day or not, all feel a shock through their whole frames, while they are instantaneously metamorphosed in every limb, and the pulse of immortality begins to beat strong in every part. Now also the slumberers under ground begin to stir, to rouse, and spring to life. Now see graves opening, tombs bursting, charnel-houses rattling, the earth heaving, and all alive, while these subterranean armies are bursting their way through. See clouds of human dust and broken bones darkening the air, and flying from country to country over intervening continents and oceans to meet their kindred fragments, and repair the shattered frame with pieces collected from a thousand different quarters, whither they were blown away by winds, or washed by waters. See what millions start up in company in the spots where Ninevah, Babylon, Jerusalem, Rome, and London once stood! Whole armies spring to life in fields where they once lost their lives in battle, and were left unburied; in fields which fattened with their blood, produced a thousand harvests, and now produce a crop of men. See a succession of thousands of years rising in crowds from grave-yards round the places where they once attended, in order to prepare for this decisive day. Nay, graves yawn, and swarms burst into life under palaces and buildings of pride and pleasure, in fields and forests, in thousands of places where graves were never suspected. How are the living surprised to find men starting into life under their feet, or just beside them; some begining to stir and heave the ground; others half-risen, and others quite disengaged from the incumbrance of earth, and standing upright before them! What vast multitudes that had slept in a watery grave, now emerge from rivers, and seas, and oceans, and throw them into a tumult! Now appear to the view of all the world the Goliahs, the Anakims, and the other giants of ancient times; and now the millions of infants, those little particles of life, start up at once, perhaps in full maturity, or perhaps in the lowest class of mankind, dwarfs of immortality. *The dead, small and great, will arise to stand before God; and the sea* shall *give up the dead which were in it.* Rev. xx. 12, 13. Now the *many that sleep in the dust of the earth shall awake, some to everlasting life, and some to shame and everlasting contempt.* Dan. xii. 2. *Now the hour is come when all that are in the grave shall hear the voice of the Son of God, and shall come forth; they that have done good, to the resurrection of life; and they that have done evil, to the resurrection of damnation.* John v. 28. *Though after our skin, worms destroy this body, yet in our flesh shall we see God, whom we shall see for ourselves; and* these *eyes shall behold him, and not another.* Job. xix. 26, 27. Then *this corruptible* [body] *shall put on incorruption, and this mortal shall put on immortality.* 1 Cor. xv. 23.

As the characters, and consequently the doom of mankind, will be very different, so we may reasonably suppose they will rise in very different forms of glory or dishonour, of beauty or deformity. Their bodies indeed will all be improved to the highest degree, and all made vigorous, capacious, and immortal. But here lies the difference: the bodies of the righteous will be strengthened to bear *an exceeding great and eternal weight of glory,* but those of the wicked will be strengthened to sustain a heavier load of misery; their strength will be but mere strength to suffer a horrid capacity of greater pain. The immortality of the righteous will be the duration of their happiness, but that of the wicked of their misery; their immortality, the highest privilege of their nature, will be their heaviest curse: and they would willingly exchange their duration with an insect of a day, or a fading flower. The bodies of the righteous will " shine as the sun, and as the stars in the firmament for ever and ever;" but those of the wicked will be grim, and shocking, and ugly, and hateful as hell. The bodies of the righteous will be fit mansions for their heavenly spirits to inhabit, and every feature will speak the delightful passions that agreeably work within; but the wicked will be but spirits of hell clothed in the material bodies; and malice, rage, despair, and all the infernal passions, will lower in their countenances, and cast a dismal gloom around them! Oh! they will then be nothing else but shapes of deformity and terror! they will look like the natives of hell, and spread horror around them with every look.*

With what reluctance may we suppose will the souls of the wicked enter again into a state of union with these shocking forms, that will be everlasting engines of torture to them, as they once were instruments of sin! But oh! with what joy will the souls of the righteous return to their old habitations, in which they once served their God with honest though feeble endeavours, now so gloriously repaired and improved! How will they congratulate the resurrection of their old companions from their long sleep in death, now made fit to share with them in the sublime employments and fruitions of heaven? Every organ will be an instrument of service and an inlet of pleasure, and the soul shall no longer be encumbered but assisted by this union to the body. Oh what surprising creatures can Omnipotence raise from the dust! To what a high degree of beauty can the Almighty refine the offspring of the earth! and into what miracles of glory and blessedness can he form them! †

---

* How weak, how pale, how haggard, how obscene,
  What more than death in every face and mien !
  With what distress, and glarings of affright
  They shock the heart, and turn away the sight!
  In gloomy orbs their trembling eye-balls roll,
  And tell the horrid secrets of the soul.
  Each gesture mourns, each look is black with care ;
  And every groan is loaden with despair.—YOUNG.

† Mark. on the right, how amiable a grace !
  Their Maker's image fresh in every face!

Now the Judge is come, the Judgment-seat is erected, the dead are raised. And what follows? Why, the universal convention of all the sons of men before the Judgment-seat. The place of judgment will probably be the extensive region of the air, the most capacious for the reception of such a multitude; for St. Paul tells us the saint shall "be caught up together in the clouds to meet the Lord in the air." 1 Thess. iv. 17. And that the air will be the place of judicature, perhaps, may be intimated when our Lord is represented as coming in the clouds, and sitting upon a cloudy throne. These expressions can hardly be understood literally, for clouds which consisted of vapours and rarified particles of water, seem very improper materials for a chariot of state, or a throne of judgment but they may very properly intimate that Christ will make his appearance, and hold his court in the region of the clouds; that is, in the air; and perhaps that the rays of light and majestic darkness shall be so blended around him as to form the appearance of a cloud to the view of the wondering and gazing world.

To this upper region, from whence our globe will lie open to view far and wide, will all the sons of men be convened. And they will be gathered together by the ministry of angels, the officers of this grand court. The Son of man, when he comes in the clouds of heaven with power and great glory, "shall send forth his angels with a great sound of the trumpet, and they shall gather together his elect from the four winds, and from one end of heaven to the other." Matt. xxiv. 30, 31. Their ministry also extends to the wicked, whom they will drag away to

What purple bloom my ravish'd soul admires,
And their eyes sparkling with immortal fires!
Triumphant beauty! charms that rise above
This world, and in blest angels kindle love!—
Oh! the transcendent glories of the Just!—YOUNG.

judgment and execution, and separate from the righteous. For "in the end of the world," says Christ, "the Son of man shall send forth his angels, and they shall gather out of his kingdom all things that offend, and them which do iniquity: and shall cast them into a furnace of fire: there shall be wailing and gnashing of teeth." Matt. xiii. 40, 41, 42.

What an august convocation, what a vast assembly is this! See flights of angels darting round the globe from east to west, from pole to pole, gathering up here and there the scattered saints, choosing them out from among the crowd of the ungodly, and bearing them aloft on their wings *to meet the Lord in the air!* while the wretched crowd look and gaze, and stretch their hands, and would mount up along with them; but, alas! they must be left behind, and wait for another kind of convoy; a convoy of cruel, unrelenting devils, who shall snatch them up as their prey with malignant joy, and place them before the flaming tribunal. Now all the sons of men meet in one immense assembly. Adam beholds the long line of his posterity, and they behold their common father. Now Europeans and Asiatics, the swarthy sons of Africa and the savages of America, mingle together. Christians, Jews, Mahometans, and Pagans, the learned and the ignorant, kings and subjects, rich and poor, free and bond, form one promiscuous crowd. Now all the vast armies that conquered or fell under Xerxes, Darius, Alexander, Cæsar, Scipio, Tamerlane, Marlborough, and other illustrious warriors, unite in one vast army. There, in short, all the successive inhabitants of the earth for thousands of years appear in one assembly. And how inconceivably great must the number be! When the inhabitants of but one county are met together, you are struck with the survey. Were all the inhabitants of a kingdom convened in one place, how much more striking would be the sight! Were all the inhabitants of the kingdoms of the earth convened in one general rendezvous, how astonishing and vast would be the multitude! But what is even this vast multitude compared with the long succession of generations that have peopled the globe, in all ages, and in all countries, from the first commencement of time to the last day! Here numbers fail, and our thoughts are lost in the immense survey. The extensive region of the air is very properly chosen as the place of judgment; for this globe would not be sufficient for such a multitude to stand upon. In that prodigious assembly, my brethren, you and I must mingle. And we shall not be lost in the crowd, nor escape the notice of our Judge; but his eye will be as particulary fixed on every one of us as though there were but one before him.

To increase the number, and add a majesty and terror to the assembly, the fallen angels also make their appearance at the bar. This they have long expected with horror, as the period when their consummate misery is to commence. When Christ, in the form of a servant, exercised a god-like power over them in the days of his residence upon earth, they almost mistook his first coming as a Saviour for his second coming as their Judge; and therefore they expostulated, *Art thou come to torment us before the time?* Matt. viii. 29. That is to say, We expect thou wilt at last appear to torment us, but we did not expect thy coming so soon. Agreeable to this, St. Peter tells us, " God spared not the angels that sinned, but cast them down to hell, and delivered them into chains of darkness, to be reserved unto judgment." 2 Peter ii. 4. To the same purpose St. Jude speaks: "The angels which kept not their first estate, but left their own habitation, he hath reserved in everlasting chains under darkness, unto the judgment of the great day." Jude 6. What horribly majestic figures will these be! and what a dreadful appearance will they make at the bar! angels and archangels, thrones, and dominions, and principalities, and powers blasted, stripped of their primeval glories, and lying in ruins; yet majestic even in ruins, gigantic forms of terror and deformity; great though degraded, horribly illustrious, angels fallen, gods undeified and deposed.*

Now the Judge is seated, and anxious millions stand before him waiting for their doom. As yet there is no separation made between them; but men and devils, saints and sinners, are promiscuously blended together. But see! at the order of the Judge, the crowd is all in motion! they part, they sort together according to their character, and divide to the right and left. When all nations are gathered before the Son of man, *himself has told us,* "He shall separate them one from another, as a shepherd divideth his sheep from the goats; and he shall set the sheep on his right hand, but the goats on the left." Matt. xxv. 32, 33. And, oh! what strange separations are now made! what multitudes that once ranked themselves among the saints, and were highly esteemed for their piety, by others as well as themselves, are now banished from among them, and placed with the trembling criminals on the left hand! and how many poor, honest-hearted, doubting, desponding souls, whose foreboding fears had often placed them there, now find themselves, to their agreeable sur-

---

*————————The foe of God and man
From his dark den, blaspheming, drags his chain,
And rears his blazing front, with thunder scarred;
Receives his sentence, and begins his hell.
All vengeance past, now seems abundant grace;
Like meteors in a stormy sky, how roll
His baleful eyes! he curses whom he dreads,
And deems it the first moment of his fall.—YOUNG.

prise, stationed on the right hand of their Judge, who smiles upon them! What connections are now broken! what hearts torn assunder! what intimate companions, what dear relations parted for ever! neighbour from neighbour, masters from servants, friend from friend, parents from children, husband from wife; those who were but one flesh, and who lay in one another's bosoms, must part for ever. Those that lived in the same country, who sustained the same denomination, who worshipped in the same place, who lived under one roof, who lay in the same womb, and sucked the same breasts, must now part for ever. And is there no separation likely to be made then in our families or in our congregation? Is it likely we shall all be placed in a body upon the right hand? Are all the members of our families prepared for that glorious station? Alas! are there not some families among us who, it is to be feared, shall all be sent off to the left hand, without so much as one exception? for who are those miserable multitudes on the left hand? There, through the medium of revelation, I see the drunkard, the swearer, the whoremonger, the liar, the defrauder, and the various classes of profane, profligate sinners. There I see the unbeliever, the impenitent, the lukewarm formalist, and the various classes of hypocrites, and half-Christians. There I see the *families that call not upon God's name*, and whole nations that forget him. And, oh! what vast multitudes, what millions of millions of millions do all these make! And do not some, alas! do not many of you belong to one or other of these classes of sinners whom God, and Christ, and Scripture, and conscience conspire to condemn? If so, to the left hand you must depart among devils and trembling criminals, whose guilty minds forbode their doom before the jndicial process begins. But who are those glorious immortals upon the right hand? They are those who have surrendered themselves entirely to God, through Jesus Christ, who have heartily complied with the method of salvation revealed in the gospel; who have been formed new creatures by the almighty power of God; who make it the most earnest, persevering endeavour of their lives to work out their own salvation, and to live righteously, soberly, and godly in the world. These are some of the principal lineaments of their character who shall have their safe and honourable station at the right hand of the sovereign Judge. And is not this the prevailing character of some of you? I hope and believe it is. Through the medium of Scripture revelation then I see you in that blessed station. And, oh! I would make an appointment with you this day to meet you there. Yes, let us this day appoint the time and place where we shall meet after the separation and dispersion that death will make among us; and let it be at the right hand of the Judge at the last day. If I be so happy as to obtain some humble place there, I shall look out for you, my dear people. There I shall expect your company, that we may ascend together to join in the more exalted services and enjoyments of heaven, as we have frequently in the humbler forms of worship in the church on earth. But, oh! when I think what unexpected separations will then be made, I tremble lest I should miss some of you there. Are you not afraid lest you should miss some of your friends, or some of your families there? or that you should then see them move off to the left hand, and looking back with eagerness upon you, as if they would say, " This is my doom through your carelessness; had you but acted a faithful part towards me, while conversant with you or under your care, I might now have had my place among the saints." Oh! how could you bear such significant piercing looks from a child, a servant, or a friend! Therefore now do all in your power to "convert sinners from the error of their way, and to save their souls from death."

When we entered upon this practical digression, we left all things ready for the judicial process. And now the trial begins. Now "God judges the secrets of men by Jesus Christ." Rom. ii. 16. All the works of all the sons of men will then be tried; "For," says St. Paul, "we must all appear before the judgment-seat of Christ, that every one may receive the things done in his body, according to that he hath done, whether it be good or bad." 2 Cor. v. 10. St. John in his vision "saw the dead judged according to their works." Rev. xx. 12, 13. These works immediately refer to the actions of the life, but they may also include the inward temper, and thoughts of the soul, and the words of the lips; for all these shall be brought into judgment. "God," says Solmon, "shall bring every work into judgment, and every secret thing, whether it be good, or whether it be evil." Eccl. xii. 14. And though we are too apt to think our words are free, he that is to be our Judge has told us that "for every idle word which men speak, they shall give an account in the day of judgment; for by thy words," as well as thy actions, "thou shalt be justified; and by thy words thou shalt be condemned." Matt. xii. 36, 37.

What strange discoveries will this trial make? what noble dispositions that never shone in full beauty to mortal eyes; what generous purposes crushed in embryo for want of power to execute them; what pious and noble actions concealed under the veil of modesty, or misconstrued by ignorance and prejudice; what affectionate aspirations, what devout exercises of heart, which lay open only to the eyes of Omniscience, are now brought to full light, and receive the approbation of the Supreme Judge before the assembled universe? But on the other hand, what works of shame and darkness, what hidden things of dishonesty, what dire secrets of treachery, hypocrisy, lewdness, and various forms of wickedness artfully and industriously concealed from human sight, what horrid exploits of sin now burst to light in all their hellish colours, to the confusion of the guilty, and the astonishment and horror of the universe! Sure the history of mankind must then appear like the annals of hell, or the biography of devils! Then the mask of dissimulation will be torn off. Clouded characters will clear up, and men as well as things will appear in their true light. Their hearts will be, as it were, turned outwards, and all their secrets exposed to full view. The design of the judicial inquiry will not be to inform the omniscient Judge, but to convince all worlds of the justice of his proceedings; and this design renders it necessary that all these things should be laid open to their sight, that they may see the grounds upon which he passes sentence. And may not the prospect of such a discovery fill some of you with horror? for many of your actions, and especially of your thoughts, will not bear the light. How would it confound you, if they were now all published, even in the small circle of your acquaintance? How then can you bear to have them all fully exposed before God, angels, and men! Will it not confound you with shame, and make you objects of everlasting contempt to all worlds?

These are the facts to be tried. But by what rule shall they be tried? From the goodness and justice of God we may conclude that men will be judged by some rule known to them, or which at least it was in their power to know. Now the light of reason, the law of nature, or conscience, is a universal rule, and universally known, or at least knowable by all the sons of men, heathens and

Mahometans, as well as Jews and Christians: and therefore all mankind shall be judged by this rule. This the consciences of all now forebodes; " for when the Gentiles which have not the law, do by nature the things contained in the law, these, not having the law, are a law unto themselves, which show the works of the law written in their hearts, their conscience also bearing witness, and their thoughts, the meanwhile, accusing or else excusing one another." Rom. ii. 14, 15. By this rule their consciences now acquit or condemn them, because they know that by this rule they shall then be judged: this seems to be a kind of innate presentiment of human nature. As the heathens were invincibly ignorant of every rule but this, they shall be judged by this only. But as to those parts of the world that enjoyed, or might enjoy the advantages of revelation, whether by tradition with the Anti-Mosaic world, or in the writings of Moses and the prophets with the Jews, or in the clearer dispensation of the gospel with the Christian world, they shall be judged by this revealed law. And by how much the more perfect the rule, by so much the stricter will their account be. That which would be an excusable infirmity in an African or an American Indian, may be an aggravated crime in us who enjoy such superior advantages. This is evident from the repeated declarations of sacred writ. " As many as have sinned without law, (that is, without the written law,) shall also perish without law; and as many as have sinned in the law shall be judged by the law, in the day when God shall judge the secrets of men according to my gospel." Rom. ii. 12, 16. " If I had not come and spoken unto them," says the blessed Jesus, " they had not had sin ;" that is, they would not have had sin so aggravated, or they would not have had the particular sin of unbelief in rejecting the Messiah: *but now they have no cloak for their sin,*

John xv. 22; that is, now when they have had such abundant conviction, they are utterly inexcusable. "This," says he, "is the condemnation;" that is, this is the occasion of the most aggravated condemnation; "that light is come into the world, and men loved darkness rather than light, because their deeds were evil." John iii. 19. "That servant which knew his Lord's will, and prepared not himself, neither did according to his will, shall be beaten with many stripes; but he that knew not, and did commit things worthy of stripes, (observe, ignorance is no sufficient excuse, except when invincible,) shall be beaten with few stripes; for unto whomsoever much is given, of him shall be much required." Luke xii. 47, 48. Upon these maxims of eternal righteousness, the Judge will proceed in pronouncing the doom of the world; and it was upon these principles he declared, in the days of his flesh, "that it should be more tolerable in the day of judgment for Sodom and Gomorrah, for Tyre and Sidon," than for those places that enjoyed the advantages of his ministry, and misimproved it. Matt. xi. 21, 24. Whether upon these principles sinners among us have not reason to expect they will obtain a horrid precedence among the million of sinners in that day, I leave you to judge, and to tremble at the thought.

There is another representation of this proceeding, which we often meet with in the sacred writings, in allusion to the forms of proceedings in human courts. In courts of law, law-books are referred to, opened, and read for the direction of the judges, and sentence is passed according to them. In allusion to this custom, Daniel, in vision, saw *the judgment was set, and the books were opened :* Dan. vii. 10. And St. John had the same representation made to him : "I saw the dead," says he, "small and great, stand before God, and the books were opened; and another book was opened, which is the book of life; and the dead were judged out of the things which were written in the books, according to their works: Rev. xx. 12.

Should we pursue this significant allusion, we may say, then will be opened the book of the law of nature; and mankind will be tried according to its precepts, and doomed according to its sentence. This is a plain and vast volume, opened and legible now to all that can read their own hearts; that have eyes to look round upon the works of God, which show his glory and their duty; and who have ears to hear the lectures which the sun and moon, and all the works of creation, read to them night and day. Then, too, will be opened the book of Scripture-revelation, in all its parts, both the law of Moses and the gospel of Christ; and according to it will those be judged who lived under one or other of these dispensations. Then it will appear that *that* neglected, old-fashioned book called the Bible is not a romance, or a system of trifling truths, but the standard of life and death to all who had access to it. Then will also be opened the book of God's remembrance. In that are recorded all the thoughts, words, actions, both good and bad, of all the sons of men: and now the immense account shall be publicly read before the assembled universe. Then, likewise, as a counterpart to this, will be opened the book of conscience; conscience which, though unnoticed, writes our whole history as with an iron pen and the point of a diamond.*

---

* O treacherous Conscience! while she seems to sleep
 On rose and myrtle, lull'd with Syren song;
 While she seems, nodding o'er her charge, to drop
 On headlong appetite the slacken'd reign,
 And give us up to license unrecall'd,
 Unmark'd—as from behind her secret stand
 The sly informer minutes every fault,

Then, also, we are expressly told, will be opened the book of life : Rev. xx. 12, in which are contained all the names of all the heirs of heaven.   This seems to be an allusion to those registers which are kept in cities or corporations, of the names of all the citizens or members who have a right to all the privileges of the society.   And I know not what we can understand by it so properly as the perfect knowledge which the omniscient God has, and always had from eternity, of those on whom he purposed to bestow eternal life, and whom he has from eternity, as it were, registered as members of the general assembly and church of the first-born, who are written in heaven, or as denizens of that blessed city.   These, having been all prepared by his grace in time, shall be admitted into the New Jerusalem in that day of the Lord.

Farther, the representation which the Scripture gives us of the proceedings of that day leads us to conceive of witnesses being produced to prove the facts.   The omniscient Judge will be a witness against the guilty.   " I will come near to you to judgment, and I will be a swift witness against the sorcerers, and against the adulterers, and against false swearers, and against those that oppress, and hear not me, saith the Lord of Hosts :" Mal. iii. 5.   And he will, no doubt, be a witness for his people, and attest their sincere piety, their interest in Christ, and those good dispositions or actions which were known only to him.

> And her dread diary with horror fills—
> Unnoted notes each moment misapply'd,
> In leaves more durable than leaves of brass,
> Writes our whole history ; which Death shall read
> In every pale offender's private ear ;
> And Judgment publish, publish to more worlds
> Than this and endless age in groans resound.
> Such, sinner, is that sleeper in thy breast ;
> Such is her slumber ; and her vengeance such
> For slighted counsel. —————   YOUNG.

Angels, also, that ministered to the heirs of salvation, and no doubt inspected the affairs of mankind, will be witnesses. Devils too, who once tempted, will now become accusers. Conscience within will also be a witness! it shall acquit the righteous of many unjust imputations, and attest the sincerity of their hearts and their many good actions. But oh! it will be the most terrible witness against the ungodly! They will be witnesses against themselves, (Josh. xxiv. 22,) and this will render them self-tormentors. Conscience will re-echo to the voice of the Judge, and cry, Guilty, guilty, to all his accusations. And who can make the wicked happy when they torment themselves? Who can acquit them when they are self-condemned? Conscience, whose evidence is now so often suppressed will then have full scope, and shall be regarded. Whom conscience condemns the righteous Judge will also condemn; for, "if our hearts condemn us, God is greater than our hearts, and knoweth all things," 1 John iii. 20, knoweth many more grounds for condemning us than we, and therefore much more will he condemn us. In short, so full will be the evidence against the sinner, that the Scripture which is full of striking imagery to affect human nature, gives life to inanimated things upon this occasion, and represents them as speaking. Stones and dust shall witness against the ungodly. The dust under the feet of their ministers shall witness against them: Matt. x. 14. " The stone shall cry out of the wall, and the beam out of the timber shall answer it." Heb. ii. 11. The rust of their gold and silver shall be a witness against them, and shall eat their flesh as it were fire. James v. 3. Nay, the heavens shall reveal their iniquity, and the earth shall rise up against them. Job xx. 27. Heaven and earth were called to witness that life and death were set before them, Deut. xxx. 19, and now they will give in their evidence that they chose death. Thus God and all his creatures, heaven, earth, and hell, rise up against them, accuse and condemn them. And will not sinners accuse and witness against one another? Undoubtedly they will. They who lived or conversed together upon earth, and were spectators of each other's conduct, will then turn mutual witnesses against each other. Oh, tremendous thought! that friend should inform and witness against friend; parents against children, and children against parents; ministers against their people, and people against their ministers; alas! what a confounding testimony against each other must those give in who are now sinning together!

Thus the way is prepared for the passing sentence. The case was always clear to the omniscient Judge, but now it is so fully discussed and attested by so many evidences, that it is quite plain to the whole world of creatures, who can judge only by such evidence, and for whose conviction the formality of a judicial process is appointed. How long a time this grand court will sit, we cannot determine, nor has God thought fit to inform us; but when we consider how particular the trial will be, and the innumerable multitude to be tried, it seems reasonable to suppose it will be a long session. It is indeed often called a day; but it is evident a day in such cases does not signify a natural day, but the space of time allotted for transacting a business, though it be a hundred or even a thousand years. Creatures are incapable of viewing all things at once, and therefore, since the trial, as I observed, is intended to convince them of the equity of the divine proceedings, it is proper the proceedings should be particular and leisurely, that they may have time to observe them.

We are now come to the grand crisis, upon which the eternal states of all mankind turn; I mean the passing the great decisive sentence. Heaven and earth are all silence and attention, while the Judge, with smiles in his face, and a voice sweeter than heavenly music, turns to the glorious company on his right hand, and pours all the joys of heaven into their souls, in that transporting sentence, of which he has graciously left us a copy; *Come, ye blessed of my Father, inherit the kingdom prepared for you from the foundation of the world.* Every word is full of emphasis, full of heaven, and exactly agreeable to the desires of those to whom it is addressed. They desired, and longed, and languished to be near their Lord; and now their Lord invites them, Come near me, and dwell with me for ever. There was nothing they desired so much as the blessing of God, nothing they feared so much as his curse, and now their fears are entirely removed, and their designs fully accomplished, for the supreme Judge pronounces them blessed of his Father. They were all poor in spirit, most of them poor in this world, and all sensible of their unworthiness. How agreeably then are they surprised, to hear themselves invited to a kingdom, invited to inherit a kingdom, as princes of the blood-royal, born to thrones and crowns! How will they be lost in wonder, joy, and praise, to find that the great God entertained thoughts of love towards them, before they had a being, or the world in which they dwelt had its foundation laid, and that he was preparing a kingdom for them while they were nothing, unknown even in idea, except to himself? O brethren! dare any of us expect this sentence will be passed upon us? Methinks the very thought overwhelms us. Methinks our feeble frames must be unable to bear up under the extatic hope of so sweetly oppressive a blessedness. Oh! if this be our sentence in that day, it is no matter what we suffer in the intermediate space; that sentence would compensate for all, and annihilate the sufferings of ten thousand years.

But hark! another sentence breaks from the mouth of the angry Judge, like vengeful thunder. Nature gives a deep tremendous groan; the heavens lower and gather blackness, the earth trembles, and guilty millions sink with horror at the sound! And see, he whose words are works, whose fiat produces worlds out of nothing; he who could remand ten thousand worlds into nothing at a frown; he whose thunder quelled the insurrection of rebel angels in heaven, and hurled them headlong down, down, down, to the dungeon of hell; see, he turns to the guilty crowd on his left hand; his angry countenance discovers the righteous indignation that glows in his breast. His countenance bespeaks him inexorable, and that there is now no room for prayers and tears. Now, the sweet, mild, mediatorial hour is past, and nothing appears but the majesty and terror of the judge. Horror and darkness frown upon his brow, and vindictive lightnings flash from his eyes. And now, (Oh! who can bear the sound!) he speaks, " Depart from me, ye cursed, into everlasting fire prepared for the devil and his angels!" Oh! the cutting emphasis of every word! Depart! depart from me; from me, the Author of all good, the Fountain of all good, the Fountain of all happiness. Depart, with all my heavy, all-consuming curse upon you! Depart into fire, into everlasting, fire, prepared, furnished with fuel, and blown up into rage, prepared for the devil and his angels, once your companions in sin, and now the companions and executioners of your punishment!

Now the grand period is arrived in which the final, everlasting states of mankind are unchangeably settled. From this all-important era their happiness or misery runs on in one uniform, uninterrupted tenor; no change, no gradation, but from glory to glory, in the scale of perfection, or from gulf to gulf in hell. This is the day in which all the schemes of Providence, carried on for thousands of years, terminate.

> " Great day ! for which all other days were made :
> For which earth rose from chaos : man from earth :
> And an eternity, the date of gods,
> Descended on poor earth-created man !"—YOUNG.

Time was; but it is no more! Now all the sons of men enter upon a duration not to be measured by the revolutions of the sun, nor by days, and months, and years. Now eternity dawns, a day that shall never see an evening. And this terribly illustrious morning is solemnized with the execution of the sentence. No sooner is it passed than immediately the wicked "go away into everlasting punishment, but the righteous into life eternal." Matt. xxv. 46. See the astonished, thunder-struck multitude on the left hand, with sullen horror, and grief, and despair in their looks, writhing with agony, crying and wringing their hands, and glancing a wishful eye towards that heaven which they lost : dragged away by devils to the place of execution! See, hell expands her voracious jaws, and swallows them up! and now an eternal farewell to earth and all its enjoyments! Farewell to the cheerful light of heaven! Farewell to hope, that sweet relief of affliction!

> ———" Farewell, happy fields,
> Where joy for ever dwells ! Hail, horrors ! hail,
> Infernal world ! and thou, profoundest hell,
> Receive thy new possessors !"—MILTON.

Heaven frowns upon them from above, the horrors of hell spread far and wide around them, and conscience within preys upon their hearts. Conscience! O thou abused, exasperated power, that now sleepest in so many breasts! what severe ample revenge wilt thou then take upon those that now dare to do thee violence! Oh the dire reflections which memory will then suggest! the remembrance of mercies abused! of a Saviour slighted! of means and opportunities of salvation neglected and lost! this remembrance will sting the heart like a scorpion. But O eternity! eternity! with what horror will thy name circulate through the vaults of hell! eternity in misery! no end to pain! no hope of an end! Oh this is the hell of hell! this is the parent of despair! despair the direst ingredient of misery, the most tormenting passion which devils feel. But let us view a more delightful and illustrious scene.

See the bright and triumphant army marching up to their eternal home, under the conduct of the Captain of their salvation, where they *shall ever be with the Lord*, 1 Thess. iv. 17, as happy as their nature in its highest improvements is capable of being made. With what shouts of joy and triumph do they ascend! with what sublime hallelujahs do they crown their Deliverer! with what wonder and joy, with what pleasing horror, like one that has narrowly escaped some tremendous precipice, do they look back upon what they once were! once mean, guilty, depraved, condemned sinners! afterward imperfect, broken-hearted, sighing, weeping saints! but now innocent, holy, happy, glorious immortals!

> " Are these the forms that mouldered in the dust?
> Oh the transcendent glories of the just!"—Young.

Now with what pleasure and rapture do they look forward through the long, long prospect of immortality, and call it their own! the duration not only of their existence, but of their happiness and glory! Oh shall any of us share in this immensely valuable privilege! how immensely transporting the thought!

"Shall we, who some few years ago were less
Than worm, or mite, or shadow can express;
Were nothing; shall we live, when every fire
Of every star shall languish or expire?
When earth's no more, shall we survive above,
And through the shining ranks of angels move?
Or, as before the throne of God we stand,
See new worlds rolling from his mighty hand?—
All that has being in full concert join,
And celebrate the depths of love divine!"—YOUNG.

Oh what exploits, what miracles of power and grace, are these! But why do I darken such splendours with words without knowledge? the language of mortals was formed for lower descriptions. "Eye hath not seen, nor ear heard, neither have entered into the heart of man, the things which God hath prepared for them that love him." 1 Cor. ii. 9.

And now when the inhabitants of our world, for whose sake it was formed, are all removed to other regions, and it is left a wide extended desert, what remains, but that it also meet its fate? It is fit so guilty a globe, that had been the stage of sin for so many thousands of years, and which even supported the cross on which its Maker expired, should be made a monument of the divine displeasure, and either be laid in ruins, or refined by fire. And see! the universal blaze begins! the heavens pass away with a great noise; the elements melt with fervent heat; the earth also and the works that are therein are burnt up. 2 Pet. iii. 10. Now stars rush from their orbits; comets glare; the earth trembles with convulsions; the Alps, the Andes, and all the lofty peaks or long extended ridges of mountains burst out into so many burning Ætnas, or thunder, and lighten, and smoke, and flame, and quake like Sinai, when God descended upon it to publish his fiery law! Rocks melt and run down in torrents of flame; rivers, lakes, and oceans boil and evaporate. Sheets of fire and pillars of smoke, outrageous and insufferable thunders and lightnings burst, and bellow, and blaze, and involve the atmosphere from pole to pole.* The whole globe is now dissolved into a shoreless ocean of liquid fire. And where now shall we find the places where cities stood, where armies fought, where mountains stretched their ridges, and reared their heads on high? Alas! they are all lost, and have left no trace behind them where they once stood. Where art thou, oh my country? Sunk with the rest as a drop into the burning ocean. Where now are your houses, your lands, and those earthly possessions you were once so fond of? They are nowhere to be found. How sorry a portion for an immortal mind is such a dying world as this! And, oh!

> " How rich that God who can such charge defray,
> And bear to fling ten thousand worlds away!"—Young.

Thus, my brethren, I have given you a view of the solemnities of the last day which our world shall see. The view has indeed been but very faint and obscure : and such will be all our views and descriptions of it, till our eyes and our ears teach us better. Through these avenues you will at length receive your instructions. Yes, brethren, those ears that now hear my voice shall hear the all-alarming clangor of the last trumpet, the decisive sentence from the mouth of the universal Judge, and the horrid crash of falling worlds. These very eyes with which you now see one another, shall yet see the descending Judge, the assembled multitudes, and all the majestic phenomena of that day. And we shall not see

---

> * " See all the formidable sons of fire,
> Eruptions, earthquakes, comets, lightnings play
> Their various engines ; all at once discharge
> Their blazing magazines ; and take by storm
> This poor terrestrial citadel of man."—Young.

them as indifferent spectators; no, we are as much concerned in this great transaction as any of the children of men. We must all appear before the judgment-seat, and receive our sentence according to the deeds done in the body. And if so, what are we doing that we are not more diligently preparing? Why does not the prospect affect us more? Why does it not transport the righteous with *joy unspeakable, and full of glory?* 1 Peter i. 8. And why are not the *sinners in Zion afraid? Why does not fearfulness surprise the hypocrites?* Isa. xxxiii. 14. Can one of you be careless from this hour till you are in readiness for that tremendous day?

What! do the sinners among you now think of repentance? Repentance is the grand preparative for this awful day; and the apostle, as I observed, mentions the final judgment in my text as a powerful motive to repentance. And what will criminals think of repentance when they see the Judge ascend his throne? Come, sinners, look forward and see the flaming tribunal erected, your crimes exposed, your doom pronounced, and your hell begun; see a whole world demolished, and ravaged by boundless conflagration for your sins! With these objects before you, I call you to repent! I call you! I retract the words: God, the great God, whom heaven and earth obey, commands you to repent. Whatever be your characters, whether rich or poor, old or young, white or black, wherever you sit or stand, this command reaches you; *for God now commandeth all men everywhere to repent.* You are this day firmly bound to this duty by his authority. And dare you disobey with the prospect of all the awful solemnities of judgment before you in so near a view? Oh! methinks I have now brought you into such a situation, that the often-repeated but hitherto neglected call to repentance will be regarded by you. Repent you

must, either upon earth or in hell.   You must either spend
your time or your eternity in repentance.   It is absolutely
unavoidable.   Putting it off now does not remove the
necessity, but will only render it the more bitter and severe
hereafter.   Which then do you choose? the tolerable,
hopeful medicinal repentance of the present life, or the
intolerable, unprofitable, despairing repentance of hell?
Will you choose to spend time or eternity in this melancholy exercise?   Oh! make the choice which God, which
reason, which self-interest, which common sense recom-
mend to you.   Now repent at the command of God, *because
he hath appointed a day in which he will judge the world
in righteousness, by that Man whom he hath ordained, of
which he hath given you all full assurance in that he
raised him from the dead.*   AMEN.

CHAPTER FIVE

Paul in Athens

JOHN DICK

CHAP. xvii. 15—34.

THE obstacles to the success of the gospel, when it was first published, were of too formidable a nature, to have been surmounted
by human courage and prudence.   It was encountered by the prejudices and bigotry of the Jews; by prejudices the more obstinate,
as they were founded in reverence for the religion which their an-
cestors had received from God himself; by bigotry originating in
the distinction which had long subsisted between them and the
Gentiles, and anxious to secure the perpetual monopoly of the
blessings of the covenant.   But, it was not in the moral state of the
Jews alone, that Christianity met with opposition, which no impos-
ture, however dexterously managed, could have overcome.   The
age in which it appeared, was an age of learning and science.
The boundaries of knowledge were extended; the human mind
was highly cultivated; and the mythological tales of antiquity
were despised, and openly derided.   A new system of falsehood
had no chance of eluding the test of severe examination, and could
not have defended itself, against the arguments and the scorn of
philosophical inquirers.   We have already seen the gospel triumph-
ing over the hostility of the Jews, many of whom embraced it as
the completion of their law, and became the disciples of Him, whom
their rulers had rejected and crucified.   We are now to observe the
issue of its conflicts with the philosophy of Greece.   By some men,
whose minds the pride of wisdom had elated, Paul was treated
with great contempt ; but even in Athens, the school of science
and refinement, Christianity could boast of its success; and we
know, that before three centuries had elapsed, it trampled in the
dust the sophistry and eloquence of the heathen world.

The Apostle having been compelled, by the arts of the Jews, to leave Berea, was conducted to Athens, where he remained for some time' expecting the arrival of Silas and Timotheus. Athens was the most celebrated city of Greece. Originally the capital of a small and barren principality, it rose to distinction, not only by the number of its inhabitants, and the magnificence of its buildings, but by the influence which it acquired over the counsels and affairs of the Greeks, by its extensive commerce, its numerous and flourishing colonies and dependencies, the wars in which it was engaged, and the exploits of its statesmen and generals; but, above all, by the unrivalled eminence which it attained, in the arts and sciences. In this city, genius, taste, and skill in the elegant and ornamental studies, seemed to be assembled, as in their favourite residence. Here, philosophy carried on its profound and subtile researches into the nature of man, and the constitution of the universe; here, eloquence rose to a degree of excellence, which has seldom been equalled, and never surpassed; here, architecture and statuary displayed those exquisite productions, the remains of which are beheld with admiration, and present the finest models to modern artists. But, while we fondly cherish the memory of the polite and ingenious Athenians, how mortifying is it to reflect, that when Paul visited the city, it was " wholly given to idolatry!" We perceive the strength of our faculties contrasted with their weakness; and the melancholy conviction is forced upon us, that the highest cultivation of reason, unassisted by revelation, is insufficient to preserve us from the utmost extravagance and folly in religion. The most enlightened city in the heathen world, was full of idols. It was crowded with images, and temples, and altars. The Athenians were more addicted to idolatry, and had multiplied the objects of it more than any of their neighbours. " In this city," says an ancient writer, " It is easier to find a God than a man." How just is the account given by Paul of the Gentile philosophers! "Professing themselves to be wise, they became fools: and changed the glory of the incorruptible God into an image made like to corruptible man, and to birds, and four-footed beasts, and creeping things."

" The spirit of Paul was stirred in him," by the idolatry of the Athenians. The indignity offered to the true God, by the worship of his unworthy rivals, roused his zeal, and he felt the most lively pity for a people, who, notwithstanding their distinguished attainments, were, in the language of the Scriptures, " sitting in dark ness, and in the region and shadow of death." "He therefore disputed in the synagogue with the Jews, and with the devout persons, and in the market daily, with them that met with him." In the synagogue, he had no occasion to dispute upon the subject of idolatry, because it was abhorred by the Jews, and the devout persons, or proselytes, had renounced it ; but agreeably to his usual practice, he addressed himself first to his countrymen, proving that Jesus of Nazareth whom he preached, was the Messiah. His labours, however, were not confined to the synagogue. In the market, the place of public resort, he entered into conversation with the Gentiles ; and although the subject is not particularly mentioned, yet it is evident, from what follows, that he endeavoured to convince them of the folly and impiety of their religion, and declared to them the living God, and his Son the only Mediator.

The attention of the Athenians was excited by this new system, so different from their own religion, and from all the modifications of polytheism, with which they were acquainted. The philosophers were surprised and displeased, that a barbarian, for such they accounted Paul, should presume to appear in Athens, and publish doctrines contrary both to the established faith, and to their peculiar dogmas. We are informed, that "certain philosophers of the Epicureans, and of the Stoics encountered him." It was natural that these should be the first to contend with him, because among all the sects of philosophy, there was none, to whose tenets Christianity was more adverse. The Epicureans were Atheists. According to them the world was formed by chance, out of materials which had existed from eternity. Acknowledging from complaisance, the Gods, who were publicly worshipped, they excluded them from any concern in human affairs, and affirmed, that regardless of the prayers and actions of men, they contented themselves with the enjoyment of indolent felicity. They pronounced pleasure to be the chief good, and the business of a wise man to consist, in devising the means of spending life in ease and tranquillity. All the genuine motives to the practice of virtue, and all just ideas of virtue itself, were banished from the philosophy of the Epicureans, which made self love the sole spring of our actions, and gave loose reins to the sensual appetites. The system of the Stoics was of a different character. They believed the existence of God, his government of the universe, and the subsistence of the soul after the death of the body. But they confounded the Deity with his own works, and supposed him to be the soul of the world. If on the subject of providence they expressed many just and sublime sentiments, they connected with it the doctrine of fate, or of an inexplicable necessity, the immutable decrees of which God, as well as man, was compelled to obey. Their notions respecting the soul were very different from the Christian doctrine of immortality; for they imagined, that in the future state it should lose all separate consciousness, and be resolved into the divine essence. Unlike the herd of Epicureans, they placed the happiness of man in the practice of virtue, and inculcated a comparatively pure and exalted morality; but the praise to which this part of their system entitled them, was forfeited by a spirit of pride, strained to the most audacious impiety. "Between God and the good man," they said, "there is only this difference, that the one lives longer than the other." They proceeded still farther, and dared to maintain, "that there was one respect in which the wise or good man excelled God; the latter was wise by nature, but the former, from choice." It is not easy to determine, whether the self-sufficient Stoics, or the profligate disciples of Epicurus, were less disposed to lend a favourable ear to the gospel. On the one hand, it commanded the lovers of pleasure to renounce the impure gratifications of sense, and to seek happiness in the favour of God and the cultivation of holiness; and, on the other, it humbled the proud moralists, by mortifying descriptions of human depravity, by referring them not to their own merit, but to the divine mercy, for the hope of immortality, and by the unwelcome information, that they must be indebted for true virtue, and should ascribe all the praise of it, to supernatural assistance.

"The Stoics and Epicureans, therefore, encountered him: and some said, what will this babbler say?" It is unnecessary to detail the criticisms of learned men upon the word rendered "babbler."* The term employed in our translation, probably conveys with sufficient accuracy the idea which was entertained of Paul, by those haughty philosophers. They considered him as a contemptible prating fool; a man who would speak, and at the same time, had nothing to bring forward, but the extravagant and incoherent fancies of an ignorant mind. To the learned Greeks, the doctrine of Christ crucified appeared to be foolishness. In Christian countries, where

---

* Wits. in vita Pauli. sect. vi.

better opportunities of perceiving its truth and excellence are enjoyed, the sentiments of the learned and the unlearned, prior to the supernatural illumination of their minds, are not more favourable, although, in consequence of their education and their habits, they may speak of it in terms of respect. In their eyes, it is folly, and those who preach it, are babblers. " The natural man receiveth not the things of the Spirit of God ; for they are foolishness unto him : neither can he know them, because they are spiritually discerned." " Others said, He seemeth to be a setter forth of strange Gods : because he preached unto them Jesus, and the resurrection." When Paul affirmed that Jesus was the Son of God, and that having been exalted to the right hand of the Father, and invested with authority over all persons and things, he was entitled to the religious homage and obedience of mankind, he proclaimed a God, of whom the Athenians had never before heard even the name. The idea of a resurrection was not absolutely new to the Gentiles, but it was the object neither of their belief nor of their hopes. Some are of opinion, that those hearers of Paul were guilty of a gross mistake, and supposed, that the resurrection was the name of a person, or a female Divinity, to whom, in conjunction with Jesus Christ, religious honours should be paid. Paul seemed to them to be a setter forth of strange "Gods,' of more than one new object of adoration. And, indeed, as some of the heathens had erected temples to Honour, Piety, Hope, and Concord, or to abstract ideas and qualities, which fancy had deified, we can conceive them to have imagined, that there might be a goddess called Resurrection. By the laws of the Athenians, and of other ancient nations, all attempts by private persons, to make any innovation in the religion of the state, were strictly prohibited. It was one of the charges against Socrates, " that he did not acknowledge the Gods whom the city acknowledged, and that he introduced new Gods."*

" And they took him, and brought him unto Areopagus." The Areopagus was a court of great authority, which derived its name from the place where its meetings were held, a hill in the city sacred to Mars. It was composed of a considerable number of judges, who were persons of experience, integrity, and blameless reputation, and had power to superintend the manners of the people, and to punish offences against religion and the state. Paul does not seem to have

---

* Xenoph. Apolog. Socrat.

been brought into this court in the character of a criminal, but for the purpose of explaining his doctrine in the presence of men, who were deemed capable to judge of it, and could publicly admit or reject the new religion which he published.   The Athenians were influenced, on this occasion, more by curiosity, than by zeal for their own religion, or by a disposition candidly to examine the claims of Christianity.   When Paul came before the court, they said, " May we know what this new doctrine, whereof thou speakest, is ?"   They did not expect, and they were not disposed to receive, instruction from a person, whom they reputed a babbler; but they hoped to be entertained with his novel and extravagant opinions.   Novelty, indeed, had irresistible charms in the eyes of that people, in whose character there seems to have been a mixture of lightness and fickleness.   " For all the Athenians, and strangers which were there, spent their time in nothing else, but either to tell or to hear some new thing."   This unfavourable account of the inhabitants of Athens, was not dictated by partiality, on the part of the sacred historian, or by resentment at their usage of Paul.   The same account is given by other writers; and their celebrated orator, Demosthenes, has reproached them with idle curiosity at a time, when the danger which threatened their country, demanded serious deliberation, and active exertions for the public safety.*

Having been requested to explain the nature of his doctrine, Paul addressed the Court of Areopagus in a speech, which consisted of two parts, in one of which he exposed the folly of heathen idolatry, and, in the other, announced the most important articles of the Christian faith.   " Then Paul stood in the midst of Mars hill," or Areopagus, " and said, Ye men of Athens, I perceive, that in all things ye are too superstitious."   There is an inaccuracy in the translation of this verse.   Superstition conveys the idea of something wrong in religion.   It originates in misconceptions of the object of worship, which give rise to a multiplicity of arbitrary and fanciful observances, with a view to appease his anger, and conciliate his favour.   The Apostle might have justly accused the Athenians of superstition, or rather of idolatry; but it may be doubted, whether, at this time, he intended to bring forward either the one charge or the other.   To call a man too superstitious implies, that he might, without a fault, be superstitious in a moderate degree.   It

---

* Demosth. Philip. I.

is not the thing itself, but its excess, which is blamed. But, in the opinion of Paul, the religious system of the Athenians was essentially erroneous. The Greek word rendered, superstitious, denotes a fearer or worshipper of demons, who were conceived to be a class of intermediate beings between the Gods and men, but sometimes in Scripture signify the Gods themselves, who were adored by the heathens. By the Athenians, it was used to describe a devout or religious person. It is probable, that it is employed by the Apostle in the same sense, and that this is his meaning; "I perceive, that in all things ye are more devout than the inhabitants of other cities." He gave them this character, because he had observed that their city was "wholly given to idolatry." The objects of worship were more numerous in Athens, than in any other place which he had visited; and the people displayed peculiar zeal and assiduity, in performing the rites of their religion.

In proof of their uncommon devotion, Paul appeals to an altar, which he had seen in the city, with this inscription, "To the unknown God;" and which afforded decisive evidence of the extraordinary piety of the Athenians. It discovered so anxious a desire to leave no Divine Being without his due honours, and to secure the favour of all who might have influence over human affairs, that rather than be guilty of an omission, they would pay homage to a Deity, with whose name and attributes they were not acquainted. Different accounts have been given of the occasion on which this altar was erected. We are told, that during a pestilence, which desolated the city, the Athenians having in vain applied for relief to their national Gods, were directed, by the philosopher Epimenides, to offer sacrifices to the unknown God, as alone able to remove the calamity.* There is another opinion, which is the more probable, because the words of Paul seem to import, that this altar was dedicated to the God of the Jews. In consequence of the dispersion of that people, the Gentiles had obtained some notices of him, but still he was to them an unknown God, because their information respecting him was very limited and indistinct. Among the Jews themselves, he dwelt in thick darkness, and was sometimes addressed as a God that "hid himself;" the symbols of his presence were confined to the recesses of the sanctuary, into which, none but the high-priest, once a year, was permitted to enter; and they carefully

---

* Diog. Laert. in vita Epimenidis.

concealed his name, Jehovah, from the Gentiles, and superstitiously avoided pronouncing it in common conversation. It was called the ineffable name. It is no wonder that a God, who withdrew from the sight of his own worshippers, should have been characterized by strangers as The Unknown. An obscure rumour of his divinity had reached the ears of the Athenians; and that devout people, dreading his power, and eager to gain his patronage, had consecrated an altar to his honour, and performed such rites as they supposed would be pleasing to him. But they worshipped him ignorantly, having no knowledge of his real character, nor of his sacred institutions. In answer to the question, " May we know what this new doctrine, whereof thou speakest, is ?" Paul informed the Areopagites, that he had come to declare this unknown God, and to teach them to worship Him, in an intelligent and acceptable manner. " Whom ye ignorantly worship, him declare I unto you." This is the design of the subsequent part of his speech, in illustrating which, I shall point out the several particulars contained in it, without exactly attending to the order, in which they are delivered.

The Apostle begins with informing his audience, that the unknown God was the Creator of the world, and of all the orders of beings which inhabit it. " God made the world, and all things therein." In particular, he asserts that he was the Maker of man. " He hath made of one blood all nations of men, for to dwell on all the face of the earth." Concerning the origin of the universe, different opinions were entertained by the Gentile philosophers. The Epicureans taught, that it was formed by chance, or by a fortuitous concourse of atoms, and pretended to account for the production of men and other animals, without the interposition of the Gods, in a manner not more creditable to their understandings than to their piety. Others believed the world to be eternal; or holding the pre-existence of matter, assigned to the Deity merely the office of giving it its present form and arrangement. By all the philosophers, the idea of a proper creation was rejected, as being contrary to their established maxim, that out of nothing, nothing could be made.* In opposition to this fundamental principle of Heathenism, Paul declared that God had called the heavens and the earth into existence by his almighty word.

---

* Ocell. Lucan. de Universi Natura, cap. i. Sallust. de Diis et Mundo, cap. xvii.

He proceeds to lay down, in the next place, the doctrine of providence. God who made the world is " the Lord of heaven and earth : He giveth to all life, and breath, and all things : He hath determined the times before appointed, and the bounds of our habitation." The Apostle adds, " In Him we live, and move, and have our being ;" and quotes the saying of the poet Aratus, " For we are also his offspring." The doctrine of providence was not new to the Gentiles, like that of creation. It was, indeed, denied by the followers of Epicurus, who represented the Gods as indifferent spectators of what was passing on the earth, and the Stoics, notwithstanding their fine sayings on the subject, may be charged with having virtually overthrown it, by their notions of fate ; but other philosophers, and the common people, believed, that the Divine government extended to this world, and regulated the affairs of individuals, and nations. Hence, the supplications, thanksgivings, and sacrifices, which were offered up on public and private occasions. Our views of providence have been enlarged and corrected by revelation, which informs us, that God is constantly present with his works ; that he cares for all his creatures, and for the individual, as well as the species ; that our situation in life, and the changes in our condition, are determined and disposed by his wisdom ; and that the laws of nature are the operations of his power, by which the order of the universe is maintained. " All things," said a heathen poet, " are full of God." The enlightened eye perceives him, not only in that majestic orb of light, which blazes in the heavens, but in the meanest reptile, and in the humblest weed which springs from the earth. We feel him stirring within us. It is by his secret influence, that our blood circulates, our stomach digests its food, and our lungs perform their important functions ; it is by him, that our spirit thinks, and wills, animates our bodies, and receives impressions from the organs of sense. The universal Parent sustains and nourishes every being, to whom he has imparted life, and exercises a particular care towards men, " for we are also his offspring."

From these principles Paul draws the following inferences.

First, God is not confined to a particular place. " Seeing that he is Lord of heaven and earth, he dwelleth not in temples made with hands." The Gentiles believed, that, by the performance of certain ceremonies, the Gods were induced to descend into the temples which had been erected to their honour, and that they resided in the images by which they were represented. Their deluded worshippers, therefore, resorted to the temples, in the persuasion, that their devotions would be more acceptable there than in any other place; and sometimes, they contended who should sit nearest the images, that their prayers might be better heard.   In opposition to these gross conceptions, Paul declared, that the Most High is not a local Deity, but a great and incomprehensible Being, whose essence fills heaven and earth.   Once, indeed, there was a temple, in which he dwelt by a glorious symbol, and received the oblations and prayers of the Israelites; but they were too well instructed to suppose, that Jehovah himself was confined within the walls of a house. The whole earth exhibited signs of his presence; and his gracious aid was obtained in every place, where his name was devoutly invocated.

Secondly, He is independent and self-sufficient.   "Neither is he worshipped with men's hands, as though he needed any thing." Although the more enlightened Heathens were convinced, that the Gods were not in want of any thing, which it was in the power of men to bestow, yet the common people believed, that in presenting costly oblations, they conferred a favour upon them which they were bound to repay; and, hence, they reproached them with ingratitude, and treated them with indignity, when they were disappointed of the blessings which they expected to obtain.   Some were even so gross as to imagine, that their Deities were gratified with the smell of the incense and the sacrifices which were burnt upon the altars.*   But, to what want can he be subject, who "giveth to all life, and breath, and all things?"   The bounty of his providence is a proof, that his stores are inexhaustible.   He who sustains from day to day, and from year to year, millions of creatures, can stand in no need of foreign supply.   It is the duty of men to adore him with reverence and gratitude, and by performing this reasonable and delightful service, their own happiness will be promoted; but the praises, the obedience, and the gifts of all orders of beings in the universe, would make no addition to his infinite and immutable felicity.

Thirdly, He is a spiritual and invisible being.   "Forasmuch then, as we are the offspring of God, we ought not to think that the Godhead is like unto gold, or silver, or stone graven by art and man's device."   The Heathen Deities were supposed, by their votaries, to

---

* Arnobii adv. Gentes. Lib. vii.

have bodies, which, although immortal, were, like ours, nourished with food and drink, might suffer weariness and pain, and needed to be refreshed by rest and sleep. The images which they formed of gold, silver, and stone, were conceived to be true representations of them. But, more exalted conceptions of the Father of their spirits, should have been entertained by his rational offspring. A corporeal being is necessarily limited in his essence, and in all his perfections. How could such a being, circumscribed in place and in power, have given existence to the immense system of creation; and how could he superintend its affairs! The living soul in man is the more excellent part of his compound nature; and the heathens themselves regarded the body as its prison. Why did they admit the thought, that what they felt to be an incumbrance, constituted a part of the nature of the Gods, who were so much exalted above them? Man, indeed, is prone to believe, that the object of his worship is such a one as himself. But, when we elevate our minds to the Greatest and Best of all beings, it is surely more consonant to reason, to remove from the idea of him all the imperfections of creatures; to attribute to him every possible excellence in the highest degree; to conceive of him as independent upon time and place, and comprehending in his mysterious existence all space, and all duration. This sublime conception accords only with a spiritual being. The pure spirituality of the divine essence, however, is a discovery which we owe solely to revelation. When our Saviour said, "God is a spirit," he expressed a truth, unknown to the wise men of the ancient world.

With these reasonings, Paul intermixes an observation upon the duty of men in reference to their Maker, the knowledge of whom they should have exerted the utmost diligence to acquire; for he had revealed himself in the works of creation and providence, with a design, "that they should seek the Lord, if haply they might feel after him, and find him, though he be not far from every one of us." Reason, the distinguishing attribute of man, finds its noblest employment, in tracing the power, and goodness, and wisdom of its Author, in the frame and constitution of the Universe. Before the eyes of all nations the book of nature is unfolded, in which the existence and attributes of God are written in legible characters. His works were the only means of knowing him, which the Gentiles possessed. The Apostle represents those means as not the most favourable to the success of their inquiries, because the information which they communicated was imperfect, and the conclusion to which they led was uncertain. He compares the Gentiles to a blind man, or to a person in the dark, groping for an object, which he does not well know where to find. The description is just and striking. How many have been their mistakes, and how gross their errors, in both ancient and modern times! Unable to determine, whether there is one God or a thousand, whether he governs the world, or neglects it, what is the nature of his government, what homage he demands from his creatures, and what expectations they should entertain in reference to a future state, do they not present the melancholy spectacle of men, whose spark of reason was insufficient to dispel the gloom, in which they were enveloped? The cause, however, of their ignorance is to be found, not so much in the obscurity of nature, as in the weakness and depravity of the human understanding. Our intellectual powers were enfeebled by the fall; our minds are perverted by prejudice, and misled by the imagination and the passions. The characters in the book of nature are as distinct as ever, but our mental sight is impaired, so that we read with difficulty, and commit many errors, till Jesus Christ, by the gospel, restore clearness and vigour to our eyes.

Although it was the will of God, that men should seek after him, yet the Gentiles had not found him. They had embraced the illusions of fancy for truth, and had adored the creature in the room of the Creator. God had left them to the wanderings of their vain minds, and had not interposed to check the progress of error. "The times of this ignorance he winked at." This is an allusion to a person who intending not to intermeddle with what is transacting around him, closes his eyes, that he may seem not to observe it. God gave no revelation of his will to the Gentiles; he sent no inspired messenger to reclaim them from idolatry. Does it appear strange, that he should have neglected so great a portion of his rational offspring, although he beheld them engaged in pernicious errors, and departing farther and farther from his ways? Let it be considered, that he was under no obligation to interpose in favour of persons, who had already disregarded the voice of nature, and had voluntarily permitted their reason to be warped and blinded by their passions. Besides, it seems to have been his intention in leaving men to multiply follies and crimes from age to age, till religion and virtue were utterly lost, to demonstrate the necessity of revelation, and to prepare the world for gratefully receiving that discovery of his will, which he purposed to make in the fullness of time. " For after that, in the wisdom of God, the world by wisdom knew not God, it pleased God by the foolishness of preaching to save them that believe."

But the season of dereliction was past. God had remembered his forlorn creatures, and mercifully provided means for reclaiming them from ignorance and impiety. " But now he commandeth all men every where to repent." These words do not imply, that the former idolatry of the Gentiles was innocent, and that now only it was their duty to forsake it; but they obviously signify, that the plan of the divine procedure towards them was changed. God had sent forth his ministers to convince them of their wickedness, in apostatising from their Maker and Benefactor, and to command them to return to his service. This command was enforced by one of the most awful doctrines of our religion, that of the future judgment, in its circumstances more solemn than the judgment which the Gentiles expected ; not a private inquiry into the actions of each individual at his death, but a public trial of the human race, assembled together to hear the sentence, which will consign them to everlasting happiness, or misery. " Because he hath appointed a day in the which he will judge the world in righteousness, by that man whom he hath ordained ; whereof he hath given assurance unto all men, in that he hath raised him from the dead." The mention of the judgment, led the Apostle, by a natural transition, to the grand subject of his mission. It does not appear, whether he was permitted to illustrate the topics, introduced in the conclusion of his speech ; but it is not improbable that the Athenians, from curiosity, would listen for some time, to his account of Jesus and the resurrection.

The curiosity of a part of the audience was soon satisfied ; and the doctrine of Paul seemed to them to be less deserving of patient attention, than of ridicule. " When they heard of the resurrection of the dead, some mocked." By the Gentiles, a resurrection was accounted neither credible nor desirable. They believed that at death, the body mingled for ever with its native earth ; and that, if the soul was not extinguished with the breath, it subsisted in an unembodied state, or was clothed with a new and purer vehicle. They laughed, therefore, when Paul assured them, that, at some distant period, the dust lying in the grave should resume its original form, and be again endowed with life and sensation. " And others said, We will hear thee again of this matter." They were neither prepared to assent to what he had told them, nor disposed to reject it, without examination. Although strange, it might be true ; and it was therefore entitled to another hearing. Their language indicated a state of mind, which, upon reflection, and more ample information, would probably terminate in conviction.

There were a few, however, to whom his doctrine seemed not only curious and probable, but true. Among these, were Dionysius, a member of the court of Areopagus, and a woman called Damaris, and some others, whose names are not mentioned. The number of converts was small, but they were the first-fruits of an abundant harvest. The philosophical pride of Athens ere long humbled itself before the cross of Christ ; and Jehovah reigned alone, amidst its deserted temples, and its idols laid prostrate in the dust.

Let the boast of reason cease. Let infidels no longer dare to decry revelation as unnecessary, and to extol the powers of the human mind as a sufficient guide in religion. The strength of reason has been tried ; and the experiment was made in the most favourable circumstances. You have not been hearing of barbarous tribes, among whom intellect had received no cultivation, and we perceive rather the instincts of the lower animals, than the nobler faculties of man. You have been introduced to the Athenians, the most enlightened and refined people of antiquity. And what were the achievements of reason, in the seat of elegance and philosophy ? Did it discover the unity of God, and present to him a pure and rational worshp ? Do we find in the writings of those polished Greeks, a complete system of natural religion? Alas ! we see in Athens, not only the common idolatry of heathen cities, but its utmost extravagance, as if unassisted reason, the more it was improved, had served the more, by its false lights, to lead mankind astray. Let us learn from this memorable example, that we stand in need of a surer and a more perfect guide ; let us rejoice, that the gospel, like " the day-spring from on high," has arisen upon us, to conduct us in the way of truth and peace. Infidels themselves are indebted to it, although they disdain to acknowledge the obligation. By its aid, they see farther and more distinctly than the greatest philosophers of ancient times, whom they do not surpass in intellectual vigour, nor equal in diligence of research. Yet, with base ingratitude, they turn the benefit which they have derived from revelation, into an argument against it; and exclaim, that the glorious luminary, from which they have stolen their light, is useless, and should be blotted out of the heavens.

Let us remember, that great privileges infer high responsibility. "The times of this ignorance God winked at; but now commandeth all men every where to repent." At no time, indeed, did he tolerate idolatry, for it was impossible, that he should have ever approved of those who worshipped and served the creature, instead of the Creator. In the Epistle to the Romans, Paul asserts, that the Gentiles were " without excuse." But, our Saviour has shown, that the punishment inflicted upon sinners in the future state, will bear an exact proportion to their means of information, and their excitements to duty.

Speaking of the city, by the inhabitants of which his Apostles should be rejected, he says, " It shall be more tolerable for the land of Sodom and Gomorrah in the day of judgment than for that city." He selects the worst of the heathens, and declares, that their doom shall be less severe than that of the despisers of the gospel. Our privileges are greater than even those of the hearers of Christ, during his ministry upon earth. Revelation is completed; it is confirmed by ample and luminous evidence; and the Holy Ghost is sent forth to enlighten our minds. If, after all, we remain ignorant of the true God, or form false and dishonourable conceptions of his attributes and dispensations; if we neglect to worship him, or content ourselves with offering to him only bodily service; if we give that obedience to the world and the flesh, to which he alone is entitled, what apology can we plead for our conduct?. Are we not the most ungrateful and perverse of men? What then can we expect, but that in the day of retribution, our privileges, of which we vainly boast, shall each of them have a voice to accuse us, and shall demand our condemnation, for the glory of divine justice? Happy are they who live in a Christian land, if they only prize and improve their advantages. But as for those by whom they are neglected, it would have been better for them, that they had lived and died among heathens. They should have perished by a milder doom. "For this is the condemnation, that light is come into the world, and men loved darkness rather than light, because their deeds were evil."

CHAPTER SIX

The Necessity and Nature of Christianity, Being an Exposition of Acts 17

JAMES H. THORNWELL

THE NECESSITY

AND

NATURE OF CHRISTIANITY.

THE first public conflict, as Milman properly remarks,[1] betwixt Christianity and Paganism took place at Athens. The champion on the one side was Paul, the distinguished Apostle of the Gentiles, who had himself been a relentless persecutor of the Gospel, and who had been graciously honoured with supernatural evidence of its truth. He was prepared to speak what he knew and to testify what he had seen. On the other side were certain philosophers of the Epicureans and Stoics, impelled partly by curiosity and partly by vanity of contest to encounter one whom their philosophic pride prompted them to stigmatize as a babbler, and their settled indifference to truth to receive as a setter-forth of strange gods.

The loss of Athenian independence had removed the checks which, in ancient times, political considerations had arbitrarily imposed upon freedom of debate and liberty of discussion in regard to the popular religion; and though this renowned city was still the headquarters of the reigning superstitions of the world, no philosopher was likely, for the sake of his opinions, however apparently licentious or heretical, to be exposed to the fate of Socrates, Stilpo or Diagoras. In the schools of Athens, no subjects were too sacred for discussion, too profound for inquiry, or too sublime and mysterious to awe the efforts of vain curiosity. The stubborn doctrines of the Stoics, the polite, accommodating

---

[1] History of Christianity, Book II., chap. iii., p. 178. Amer. Ed.

principles of the Epicureans, the sentimental refinements of Plato and the practical methods of the illustrious Stagirite, the claims of the popular worship, the superstitions of the mass, and the hidden mysteries disclosed to a chosen few,—were matters of free, open, unrebuked debate. In such a city, the long-chosen abode of philosophy, science and the arts, the literary metropolis of the world, rendered holy to a freeman by the mute memorials of Independence eloquent in ruins,—in such a city, and among such a people, the Apostle of the Gentiles appears the champion of the Gospel, against philosophy, science, idolatry, superstition—all the wisdom of this world arrayed in enmity to God. To the eye of sense the odds were fearfully against him. His name and country were identified, among the Pagan nations around him, with all that was little, contracted and mean. A Jew by birth, exclusive in his religion, and a reputed bigot in his opinions, he presented, in his national associations, those features of disgust which provoked the satire of Juvenal, the contempt of Gallio and the raillery of Martial. It is true Paul was a scholar skilled in Grecian models; but all his pretensions to refinement and elegance were sunk in the fact that he was a *Jew,* as the valour and courtly influence of Naaman were nothing to the damning consideration that after all he was a leper. But curiosity was too strong for either prejudice or contempt. His disputes in the synagogue with his own brethren, his instructions to those whom he found seriously intent upon the duties of religion, and his public discussions in the market-place with all whom the providence of God threw in his way, had made him the object of attention to the leading sects of philosophy. *Then certain philosophers of the Epicureans and of the Stoics encountered him.*[1]

We may here pause to contemplate the contrast in their motives and aims and those of the servant of Jesus. He had come to Athens as a stranger. Driven from Thessalonica by a popular tumult excited by religious bigotry, he

[1] Acts xvii. 18.

sought safety and quiet in this mart of learning, elegance and Paganism; and while tarrying for his brethren, his spirit was stirred in him when he saw the city wholly given to idolatry. He looked not upon its statues and temples, its altars and sacrifices, with the eye of poetry or taste. These ornaments of art, these imposing monuments of genius and skill, however they might adorn the names and perpetuate the memories of Phidias and Praxiteles, were an insult to God; and, like Elijah, the prophet of another dispensation, he was very jealous for the Lord God of Hosts. His imagination could not expatiate in rapture upon scenes which proclaimed too plainly to the ear of faith that the curse of the Almighty was there. What signified the beauty of the work when the end was death? While he mused and saw, the fire burned; the love of Christ, an emotion felt for the first time, perhaps, upon that classic soil—zeal for the glory of God, intense desires for the salvation of the lost, the terrific sanctions of the law,—all pressed upon him and roused his noble spirit to lift up his voice like a trumpet, to cry aloud and spare not. He was a man of God, and the word of the Lord was like fire in his bones. His position was indeed sublime, and though the object of contempt, ridicule or idle curiosity to others, he was raised by the grandeur of his mission and a Tenant in his heart whom the world knew not yet, above all the petty desires which vanity, pride or ambition could suggest, and like his Divine Master prayed in spirit for those who despised him. He had no doubtful disputations to propose, but a message to proclaim in the name of God. He was no dialectician from the Schools, but an ambassador of the skies; he preached not the wisdom of men, but the wisdom of God in a mystery. He spake with the confidence of one whose feet rested upon the rock of eternal truth, and with the persuasiveness of one who was not a lord of the faith, but a helper of the joy of his hearers. The zeal, devotion and deep convictions which glowed in his soul made him earnest, but neither an enthusiast nor fanatic. His discourse is managed with consummate skill, and while the Word of the Lord is plainly declared, it is studiously framed with a reference to the state, prejudices and opinions of the assembly. Paul had seen, among the monuments of Athens, an altar to the Unknown God. This furnishes the Apostle with a text. He begins with the statement of a general fact, true of all men, but pre-eminently true of the Athenians, that the interests of religion, in some form or other, must and will exact attention. Man is essentially a religious animal. His nature calls for religious worship. He must have a God to pray to, as well as a God to swear by, and while the true God is unknown the heart will be filled with idols in His place. All idolatry consists essentially in the false worship of the true, or a superstitious worship of the unknown, God. Having paved his way to the favourable attention of his hearers, Paul proceeds to recapitulate the leading doctrines of Natural Religion, to some of which, with more or less modification, the Stoics might assent, and to others the Epicureans.[1] The doctrines of providence, of human responsibility, of a moral government, are not only announced, but are pressed as formal arguments against a false worship, and urged as motives for seeking to be ascertained of the truth. The obvious dictates of nature, if properly heeded, are sufficient to condemn idolatry. The fall of man, his present depravity, and the necessity of repentance, are briefly and compendiously stated, and then the peculiar doctrines of the Gospel are summarily discussed under the heads of Jesus and the resurrection.

The effects of this sermon are briefly detailed by the historian.[2] Some of them treated the matter with downright scorn ; others were afraid that it might be true, but were not prepared to make the sacrifices which a full assent would obviously require. Still there were a few, a select and noble band, consisting alike of plebeians and philosophers, who clave to the Apostle and believed his doctrines. It is re-

[1] Milman's History of Christ, Book II., chap. iii., p. 179. Amer. Ed.
[2] Acts xvii. 32–34.

markable that these effects were produced, not by Paul's dissertations upon natural religion, upon the being and providence of God, the accountability of man, and the strict moral government which has been established in the world. He seems to have been heard with patience as long as he insisted upon these and kindred topics. Even his denunciations of idolatry, though a direct rebuke of their practice, and a tacit imputation upon their understanding or integrity, awakened no visible displeasure. But the very moment that the Apostle entered upon the territory of grace, and proceeded to expound those mysteries of the Gospel which eye had not seen nor ear heard, neither had it entered into the heart of man to conceive, the effect was striking and characteristic; some mocked, others said, We will hear thee again of this matter, and only here and there an auditor received the engrafted Word and lived.

This sermon of Paul at Athens deserves our serious attention, as it sets forth, in brief and pregnant heads, the whole contents of revelation, and the essential doctrines in particular of what is properly and exclusively Christianity. Revelation and Christianity are not convertible terms. Everything that even the Bible contains is not a part of Christianity. There have been at least three dispensations of this religion, distinguished from each other by outward form and accidental circumstances; and each of these is described in the Bible, and the peculiarities of each throw light upon the general scheme to which they all pertain.

Everything in revelation is subsidiary to Christianity, but is not necessarily part and parcel of its being. Some things are presupposed in it—their truth is essential to its arrangements; and other things belong to the age, people and country of its first introduction. All these subsidiary and incidental circumstances are to us the subjects of revelation, and therefore to be received with undoubting faith, but much may be received and the Gospel in its essence not be embraced, and many revealed facts may be unknown and yet the salvation of the Gospel imparted. It is, therefore,

a profoundly interesting question, What is Christianity?
What are the essential features of that system which Jesus
introduced into the world, and which without His interposition would not only have been unknown, but would not
and could not have been true? What are those peculiarities which, wherever they have been proclaimed, whether
on the Areopagus of Athens, in the seats of modern learning, the halls of science, the church, the market-place or
meeting-house, have uniformly made some mock, and stag-
gered others, until God by His Spirit gave them a lodg-
ment in the heart? The solution of this question is of fundamental importance. Our lives depend upon it. True,
the Gospel is a simple system; but notwithstanding its simplicity multitudes perish with a lie in their right hands,
fondly dreaming that they are in the ark, when they are
only sheltered by bulrushes. Thousands mistake what
Christianity is and die; they kindle a fire and walk in its
light, and receive the punishment at God's hand that they
shall lie down in sorrow. Let us, therefore, address ourselves to this question with the solemnity and earnestness
the nature of the subject demands.

The course of thought pursued by the Apostle in this celebrated sermon, the disposition and arrangement of his topics,
and the obvious relations which they sustain to each other,
will correct many prevalent errors, and conduct us by an
easy process to the precise views which ought to be entertained. Paul first insists upon the *necessity* of the Gospel,
and then announces its doctrines in their adaptation to the
wants they were designed to relieve.

1. First, then, what is the *necessity* of Christianity? What
is the call for it in the circumstances of our race? And
what end, consequently, was it designed to answer? The
necessity of *revelation* is a point upon which Christian
apologists are accustomed to insist as establishing the antecedent credibility of the fact; and though their arguments
are, for the most part, conclusive, as showing the likelihood
of some interposition to mitigate our ignorance, they fail to

present the peculiar need of such a dispensation as that of
the Gospel.   It is too frequently taken for granted that " the
supposition of sin does not bring in any new religion, but
only makes new circumstances and names of old things, and
requires new helps and advantages to improve our powers,
and to encourage our endeavours ; and thus the law of grace
is nothing but a restitution of the law of nature."[1]   The
ground ordinarily assumed is the ignorance of man and the
goodness of God ; and this ignorance, which seems to be regarded as the principal injury of the fall, has reference to
the great facts of natural religion, which, if known, would
have sufficient efficacy to secure amendment of life and everlasting happiness.   The controversy has been, in many instances, so conducted with the Deists as to convey the impression that the doctrines of nature were sufficient to constitute the complete religion of a sinner ; the sole point in
dispute being the competency of reason to discover these
doctrines without supernatural aid.[2]   We are represented as
creatures destined for another life, and needing information
in reference to its character and its connection with the
present, which cannot be derived from the light of nature.
In this view Christianity is no new religion ; it is only a
new publication of that which subsisted from the beginning
of our race.   It is a *revelation*, strictly and properly so called,
and nothing more ; and its whole relation to us is exhausted
when we receive and submit to it as a Divine teacher.[3]   We

[1] This extraordinary statement is quoted by Halyburton from one who,
he says, "wore a mitre."—Nat. Rel. Insuf., chap. 1, p. 279—Works in
one volume.

[2] This is the impression left by Paley ; and it is clearly the doctrine
of Mr. Locke.   His Christianity is nothing but *Revealed Deism*.

[3] It is very unfortunate that the distinctions between Christianity and
natural religion have been expressed by the terms natural and revealed
religion.   The idea obviously suggested by this phraseology is that their
difference lies in the sources whence we derive our knowledge of them.
Nothing, however, has been more clearly proved by Christian writers—
among whom we may especially refer to Halyburton and to Norris—
than that we are as much indebted to revelation for any adequate knowledge of natural religion as for the mysteries of the Gospel.   They are

are ignorant, for example, of a future life; or if we have, from the operations of conscience or the spontaneous desires of the soul, vague convictions or indistinct impressions of continued existence in another state or among other scenes, the evidence is too feeble and shadowy to furnish the grounds of a steady belief. Christianity, accordingly, relieves our blindness and brings life and immortality to light. The apprehensions of nature it reduces to realities; its vague impressions to the certainty of facts. So, again, without revelation we are represented as uncertain whether our conduct here shall affect our destinies hereafter, or what is the nature of the connection which subsists between the present and the future. Christianity comes to our assistance and teaches us that this present world is a school for eternity; and that according to our characters and conduct here will be our destiny hereafter. This is the method in which the apologists for Christianity have too often conducted the argument with the Deists. There has been no dispute between them as to *what* religion is sufficient to secure the happiness of a sinner. They are, for the most part, agreed in its nature and principles; but it has been keenly debated whether reason, since the fall, is capable of discovering this religion without supernatural assistance, or of authenticating it with sufficient evidence to make it of practical importance. We may admit that the argument is conclusive as conducted by the friends of revelation. Natural religion is certainly not the offspring of natural light. In the present condition of our race, whatever may be the evidences which exist within us and around us of the being, perfection and character of God, of the condition of man, and the relation he sustains to his Creator, his darkened faculties are incompetent to gather from them the conceptions which make up the

---

both *revealed*. The difference between them is radical and essential, and not accidental or contingent. They are different *religions*. One is the religion of our nature before the fall; the other the religion of grace after the fall. The one contemplates God simply as a moral Governor; the other as a Saviour and Redeemer.

fabric of natural religion, however he may prove its truth from these sources after the ideas have been suggested to the mind. We confidently believe that if natural religion were the *sole* religion of a sinner, revelation would still be necessary to teach us what it is, to republish it with light and power, to free it from corruption, superstition and abuse, and present it in the symmetry of its parts and the integrity of its combination. But then this, although a *revelation*, would not be Christianity. It might remove the veil from the eye of ignorance, and unfold realities of tremendous power to alarm the guilty and stimulate the righteous; but all its truths would be independent of the mission of the Saviour, except in so far as he was the instrument in the hands of Providence to unfold them. That this whole theory is fundamentally wrong—though sustained by the splendid names of Locke and Paley, though the favourite and cherished hypothesis, during the dynasty of the Stuarts, defended alike by mitred prelates and humble curates—that Christianity is something more, immeasurably more than a *revelation* of truths, which in themselves were independent of the mission of Christ, may be inferred from the order and connection in which Paul has here introduced the mysteries of the Gospel. It is not a little remarkable that every solitary element of the system which those who take this view of the subject make it the object of Jesus to communicate, was insisted on by the Apostle before he gets to the Gospel. The great doctrines of natural religion which constituted the faith and the worship of man before the fall, are treated as preliminary to the distinctive peculiarities of Christianity. The creed of Herbert—the most liberal of the Deists, as good a Christian as many who have defended miracles and prophecy—so far as this creed is natural religion, is recapitulated by the Apostle as introductory to the Gospel. The unity of God; His absolute independence and universal sovereignty; the relation in which He stands to men; the necessity of religious worship, and the guilt and folly of idolatry; the perfection of His moral government, and the essential, unchangeable distinctions of right and wrong,—these are all eloquently enforced, but these are not the Gospel.   We do not say that they are not revealed truths—we do not say that any religion is the offspring of mere natural light; but we do say, and the method of the Apostle justifies us in saying it, that although these are truths of revelation, and truths which must be recognized in order to understand the Gospel, yet they are not Christianity.   We will go a step farther and assert that the natural religion which Paul preached on Mars' Hill contained propositions which unassisted reason is utterly, under any circumstances, incompetent to discover; and which yet, from the beginning, must have been parts of the primitive religion of the race.   He insists upon the Federal Headship of Adam.   This is the fundamental truth in nature's system.   We are of *one* blood. There is a mysterious unity in our race, indicated by a common descent and a common nature, in consequence of which we sustain different relations to each other from those which we would have sustained if we had been separate, independent, isolated beings.   In our world there is not only *society*, but *kindred*—not only similarity, but identity of nature; and our religion proceeds upon a principle which recognizes this unity, and in its great charter of hope treated with the race in one man.   So, also, the doctrine of the Trinity is a doctrine of natural religion.   But there might have been imparted to us a knowledge of the object of worship, the great federal dispensation under which our race was created, and the consequent condemnation and ruin of mankind in the first man, who was of the earth, earthy,—and yet not a single doctrine of the Gospel, as connected with the mission of Jesus, be known.   Nay, all these things, whether known or not, would have been true had Jesus never been born or never died.   Paul's Christianity, therefore, was something more than a republication of natural religion, even in its true form and perfect proportions, as adoring the Trinity and binding the race in a federal compact with a common head.   The Apostle virtually admits that in our present state we cannot discover the true system under which we were born, and which attaches to our natures as moral and as human. There was a season of ignorance in which all who had no revelation were permitted to walk. But the removal of this ignorance is not all that the Gospel proposes; it is a new dispensation, out of which new duties and new relations to God spontaneously grow. God *now* commandeth all men everywhere to repent, because He hath appointed a day in the which He will judge the world in righteousness by that Man whom He hath ordained; whereof He hath given assurance unto all men, in that He hath raised Him from the dead. It is plain that Paul regarded Jesus as introducing a religion whose distinctive law, so far as it respected human conduct and obedience, was the law of repentance. We shall not stop to inquire whether repentance is a duty of nature; but as here unfolded by the Apostle it depends upon principles supernatural and Divine. But the argument which we would frame from this passage, against the supposition that the prime necessity of our nature arises from our ignorance, and is therefore to be relieved simply by revelation, is drawn from the importance which the Apostle attaches to the resurrection of Jesus and the consequent resurrection of the dead. The religion which Paul preached at Athens, and which the necessities of all men require, is a religion into which this fact must enter. We must bear in mind that the resurrection, neither of Jesus nor His followers, is ever treated in the Christian Scriptures as a *proof* of Christianity; it is always made a *part* of it—an essential, indispensable element of the scheme. It is not presented to us simply as a *miracle*, authenticating the Divine mission of Christ, though of course this must be an incidental result, but it is treated as being as really, and truly, and necessarily a component part of the Gospel as the death or incarnation of the Saviour. Paul[1] sums up the whole of Christianity in Jesus and the resurrection: For I delivered unto you, first of all, that which I also received; how that

[1] Acts xvii. 18; 1 Cor. xv. 3.

Christ died for our sins according to the Scriptures, and that He was buried, and that He rose again the third day, according to the Scriptures. The death, burial, resurrection of Christ,—these were the facts upon which the Gospel depended that Paul preached at Athens and Corinth. To represent the resurrection as a mere proof of Christianity, resting upon the same footing with the other miracles of the New Testament, and authenticating Christ's supernatural commission in the same way, is without sanction from the Scriptures. It is never treated simply as a credential—a motive to belief, but not the thing to be believed. On the contrary, Paul affirms that if Jesus be not risen our preaching is vain, and your faith is also vain—the Gospel is absolutely worthless. This cannot be said of any single miracle of the Saviour or His apostles. They might have wrought more, they might have wrought fewer; the Gospel would have been the same. But if Jesus had not *risen*, there would have been no Gospel, and we should *have been in our sins*.

The passage in Romans which seems to make the resurrection a proof of the Sonship of Christ has a much wider sweep than interpreters have been accustomed to give to it. The ordinary view is, that as Christ before His death had declared Himself to be the Son of God, and as He was condemned by the Jewish courts upon the ground of His supernatural pretensions to a Divine generation alone, His resurrection from the dead was the endorsement by the Father of the veracity of His own testimony. But, according to this view, any other miracle would have answered the same purpose. The darkened heavens, the yawning earth, the cleaving rocks and the rising dead had already proclaimed His Sonship as truly as the resurrection—proclaimed it so loudly and powerfully that the centurion confessed the stupendous truth, while all the people that came together to that sight, beholding the things which were done, smote their breasts and returned.[1] The impressions of that scene were as awful and convincing as any mere miracles could

[1] Luke xxiii. 47–49.

possibly have made. Every previous miracle had as much authenticated the Divine mission of Jesus, and, of course, the Divine truth of all that He had uttered, as this final one of His resurrection from the dead. And that God never intended it as a *mere proof* is evident from the fact that He did not show Himself openly to all the people, but to witnesses chosen beforehand.

The whole reasoning of the Apostle goes upon the supposition that His resurrection *directly* declared His Sonship; it did not simply declare that he spoke the truth when he affirmed it, but it attested the fact independently of any such connection. The Psalmist, looking to this great event, represents the Almighty as proclaiming by it, Thou art my Son, this day have I begotten Thee;[1] and when He ascended into heaven the joyful acclamation was heard, "God is gone up with a shout, Jehovah with the sound of a trumpet."[2]

It is, therefore, evident that both the Old Testament and the New represent the resurrection not only as an integral part of Christianity, but as a pregnant proof of the eternal Sonship of Christ, and consequently every scheme must be false in which this great fact is not obviously possessed of this distinction. Whatever the Gospel is, it must be something into which the resurrection essentially enters, and so enters as to establish the Sonship of Jesus; and as neither the one nor the other can be affirmed of His office as a Prophet, it is very certain that the necessity which Paul contemplated must lie much deeper than the natural ignorance of man in regard to truths which are independent of the mission of Jesus. It is obvious that whatever the Gospel is, its truths must have been *created* by the mission of Jesus. They would not have existed at all if He had not been born, crucified, buried, and if He had not risen from the dead.

Enough has been said to show that Paul contemplated Christianity as something more than a *revelation*. This proposition may strike our readers as hardly worth the

[1] Ps. ii. 7; Acts xiii. 33.   [2] Ps. xlvii. 5.

labour we have expended upon it, but those who have been brought most in contact with the educated minds of the country must be sensible that the difficulties which they experience in Christianity are largely owing to this low view.

The principles of natural religion seem so reasonable, when once they are fairly proposed, that it is hard to get quit of the conviction that what so obviously commends itself to the understandings and consciences of men might have been discovered without supernatural light.   The presumption against *revelation* is increased by confining its scope to a department of truths which were certainly the original furniture of reason, and which, when once they are announced, reason, apart from the influence of prejudice and passion, does not hesitate to recognize.   To tell us that nature and Christianity embrace exactly the same religion, that Christianity is distinguished by nothing but the source from which it springs, that its sole object is to publish with clearness and enforce with authority the doctrines of nature, is to put its necessity on a footing which, however successfully it may be maintained, will seldom produce that deep and earnest conviction of need which hails the Gospel with joy, and detects in its provisions an adequate reason for the interposition of God.   This low view of the subject has not only to encounter the supposed presumption against revelation in general, but an additional presumption against that species of revelation which, with an immense apparatus of means, does little more than enlarge the territory of knowledge and .dispel a few floating clouds from the atmosphere of truth.   The great bell of the universe is rung to preach a sermon of which nature was previously in possession of the heads.

Lord Herbert's difficulties with Christianity arose, for the most part, from an utter misconception of its principal design.   The question could never be raised concerning the sufficiency of reason if the proper end of the Gospel were kept steadily in view.   Deism was comparatively unknown in England until a style of preaching was adopted which confounded morality with holiness, habits with the Spirit of God, and faith with a general conviction of truth—which discarding all its distinctive doctrines, reduced Christianity to a frozen system of heathenism, and made the ministers of Jesus little better than the " miserable apes of Epictetus." When the prelate and the curate were equally anxious to have the world believe that their Gospel had exploded the antiquated notions of spirituality and grace, that such uncouth phrases as justification, adoption, regeneration and redemption were stripped of their repulsiveness, and adjusted as well to the notions as the dialect of fashionable life, it is not to be wondered at that men should stare at the pomp of preparation with which *such* a religion had been announced to the world. The affluence of means and the poverty of result were so conspicuously in contrast that the question seems to have been naturally suggested, whether, if *this* were all, reason might not have been left to itself. We can sympathize with such difficulties ; and though we are far from asserting—for we by no means believe—that unassisted reason since the fall would ever have discovered the whole system of natural religion, yet we are as far from asserting that Christianity is the form in which a revelation designed chiefly to assist reason would have been given. To this inadequate conception of its office, as a mere handmaid to nature, is owing in some degree the fact that the whole current of modern philosophy, under the pretext of great veneration for religion, is fatal in its tendencies to the claim of inspiration. The sufficiency of reason has been defended, not on historical but psychological grounds, and the excellency of Christianity is represented as consisting in the distinctness and fullness with which it echoes the voice of nature. This is to betray the Saviour with a kiss. These insidious assaults may indeed be repelled by direct arguments, but we can only reach the source of the evil by placing the necessity of the Gospel on its true basis. The change which sin has introduced in the relations of our race to God, and the glorious provisions of the new covenant, must be set in the light in which the Scriptures uniformly put them, if we would not judge of Divine revelation by a false standard.   To show that ignorance is not the great evil which Christ came to dispel, that the scheme of redemption is a vast and mighty dispensation of grace, a stupendous work which our exigencies demanded and God was glorious in doing, is to remove one of the leading difficulties which press upon educated men when they first turn their attention to the subject.   They often hesitate because they do not understand the case.

2. Others, unable to escape from the pervading testimony of Scripture that the mission of Jesus contemplated a work to be done as well as truths to be revealed—that Christianity is a grand dispensation of providence and grace, involving a series of supernatural acts directed to the salvation of the sinner, the history of which in their origin, relations and results is the principal instruction it imparts—while they discard the low conceptions of an earth-born philosophy which can detect in the Gospel nothing but a republication of natural religion, fail yet to rise to an adequate apprehension of the real nature of Christ's mediation.   Whether it be owing to a fastidious modesty which perverts a just dread of presumption and a becoming sense of ignorance into a refusal to be wise up to what is written, or whether there be a lurking dislike of the principle upon which a consistent explanation can be given of the method of redemption— whatever be the cause, there are men who admit an apparent necessity of the interposition of the Mediator, and yet fail to present in their account of His work any correspondence discoverable by us to the necessity they acknowledge. They very justly represent natural religion as unsuited to the condition of a sinner; it makes no provision for the pardon of the guilty; it knows nothing of mercy, nothing of restoration to the favour of God.   Conducted upon the principle of distributive justice, it promises life to the obedient, denounces death to transgressors, but opens no door of hope to the wretch who has incurred its curse.   It *must*

render to every man according to his works—" to them who by patient continuance in well-doing seek for glory and honour and immortality, eternal life; but unto them that are contentious and do not obey the truth, but obey unrighteousness, indignation and wrath, tribulation and anguish upon every soul of man that doeth evil, of the Jew first and also of the Gentile." With these representations—not so strongly and emphatically made, we confess, as the nature of the case seems to us to warrant—of the necessity of justification to the salvation of a sinner and the hopelessness of any justification by personal obedience, it is not a little remarkable that the persons we have in view should miss of the precise nature of redemption in its relations to man, and make it the great purpose of the Saviour to introduce a new principle of government or a new method of administration, which has the effect of mitigating the severity of law, putting the guilty in a capacity of salvation, and furnishing them with facilities for turning to account the advantages of their new condition. This principle is the pardon of sin upon repentance. Jesus has made it possible that God should receive penitent transgressors into favour, and has rendered penitence itself less difficult and arduous than it is found to be under the regular and ordinary course of nature. How this capacity of salvation has been introduced by Him the advocates of the system do not pretend to explain; it is due, in some way mysterious to us and unrevealed in Scriptures, to His humiliation, sufferings and death. It is enough for us to know the fact that repentance has the efficacy ascribed to it, without presuming to inquire how it came to be possessed of it.[1]

[1] "Some have endeavoured to explain the efficacy of what Christ has done and suffered for us beyond what the Scripture hath authorized; others, probably because they could not explain it, have been for taking it away, and confining His office as Redeemer of the world to His instruction, example and government of the Church; whereas, the doctrine of the Gospel appears to be, not only that He taught the efficacy of repentance, but rendered it of the efficacy which it is by what He did and suffered for us; that He obtained for us the benefit of having our

None can censure more severely than ourselves that arrogance of understanding which refuses to recognize any dispensation as Divine which cannot be adjusted to the measures of human probability. We are too sensible of the ignorance of man and the greatness of God to dream for a moment of making our finite reason the standard of the counsels of infinite wisdom ; and we sympathize profoundly with the humility of mind, always characteristic of exalted attainments, that shrinks in reverence from the clouds and darkness which surround the throne of the Eternal. It is the glory of God to conceal a thing.; and where He has drawn a veil over the operations of His hand it is presumption in us to pry into His secrets or speculate with confidence on the mysteries He has not thought fit to reveal. But it is neither piety nor modesty—it is unbelief, however speciously disguised—which makes darkness where God has given light ; mystery, where all things are plain. To say that we are left in ignorance as to the method by which the mediation of Christ achieves the salvation of a sinner, is to contradict all those passages of Scripture which directly teach, as well as indirectly imply, that the wisdom of God is conspicuously displayed in the scheme of redemption, and in which it is made the duty of the saints to admire it. " We preach Christ crucified," says the Apostle, " unto the Jews a stumbling-block and unto the Greeks foolishness ; but unto them which are called, both Jews and Greeks, Christ the power of God and the wisdom of God." " Howbeit we speak wisdom among them that are perfect." The lowest conception of wisdom involves the idea that the means should be adapted to the end, and it is displayed only in so far as the correspondence betwixt them is capable of

repentance accepted unto eternal life, not only that He revealed to sinners that they were in a capacity of salvation, and how they might obtain it, but, moreover, that He put them in this capacity of salvation by what He did and suffered for them—put us into a capacity of escaping future punishments and obtaining future happiness. And it is our wisdom thankfully to accept the benefit by performing conditions upon which it is offered on our part without disputing how it was procured on His."— *Butler's Analogy*, Pt. ii., chap. v., § 6.

being discerned. Where the adaptation of means to an end is not perceived, wisdom may indeed exist, but it is absurd to say that it can be an object of admiration. That emotion can be elicited only by an actual contemplation of the fitness upon which the wisdom depends. It is, accordingly, impossible that believers should be expected to glorify that attribute of God to which, as much as to His power and grace, we are indebted for the economy of redemption, if they are not permitted to see how the mediation of Christ is adapted to effect their salvation. They can no more be filled with admiration at the contemplation of a wisdom which is concealed from their understandings than they can be filled with love at the contemplation of a beauty which is hidden from their eyes. We are very far from asserting that we, or any other finite intelligence, can comprehend the whole mystery of godliness : there are facts in redemption, such as the incarnation, and the subsistence of two natures in one person, and there may be designs in reference to other worlds, and perhaps also in relation to our own, proposed by it in the infinite counsels of God, which shall for ever transcend the capacities of creatures. We do not pretend to know the whole case. We hardly presume that we ever shall know it. Throughout the countless cycles of eternity we expect to occupy the anxious position of the angels, who, previous to the advent, are represented as earnestly inquiring into these things. The glories of redemption are as boundless, the depths of its wisdom as fathomless, as the infinite perfections of the Godhead. But, though there be heights which the loftiest genius cannot climb, and depths which no finite line can sound, still we maintain that there *is* a wisdom which we can discover and a wisdom we are required to adore. In so far as our own personal acceptance is involved we can see the fitness of Jesus for His work and the fitness of His work to the necessities of man. If we cannot comprehend all the fullness of meaning in which Christ crucified is the wisdom of God, we can at least receive that portion of light which irradiates our own *salvation ;* and we dare not brand as delusion all that joy in Him which flows not simply from the faith that He is a Saviour, but from the felt conviction that He is a Saviour peculiarly adapted to our wants. We must therefore protest against any hypothesis which discards as presumptuous all efforts to explain how the sacrifice of Christ contributes to our pardon. Whatever other mysteries surround the cross, this point is not left to the hazard of conjecture or the uncertainty of speculation. It is *revealed*, or words have lost their meaning, and the Bible is a book of riddles.

But the most serious objection to the theory in question is, that it represents Christ as introducing by His work a new principle in the moral government of God, or a new method of administration, which cannot be conceived without confusion of ideas nor expressed without a contradiction in terms. The patrons of the scheme, studious to put in its true light the inadequacy of natural religion, are not wanting in proofs that whatever intimations the facts of experience may give of the possibility of mercy under the general government of God, they all point to mediation as the channel of compassion, and furnish no ground to suppose that any arbitrary purpose on the part of our Judge, or any penitence or amendment on our part, could have arrested the execution of the curse. Between penitence and pardon they are unable to trace any natural or necessary connection; but a mediator may cause to be instituted, and in the case of Christ has caused to be instituted, a dispensation of leniency under which repentance may be followed by forgiveness. The defect of natural religion to which Christianity is a remedy is not that nature admits of no repentance, but that repentance is incapable of securing pardon. The design of mediation is to establish a connection between them; not to make one or the other possible or certain, but, supposing them to exist or to be capable of existing, to bind them in a new relation unknown to nature.

Now we take leave to say that Christianity has instituted no connection between penitence and pardon which is not founded in the very nature of things. Their relation to each other is not contingent, but necessary; not derived from the interposition of a Mediator, but from their essential relations to God. There never was a case, and there never will be a case in all the history of the universe, of a penitent sinner's being damned. What is repentance in its full development but a restoration to that state of integrity and holiness, of knowledge, righteousness and communion with God, from which Adam by transgression fell? And can we entertain the thought, without horror, that He whose nature is in sympathy with the righteous should banish into outer darkness those who are devoted to His law, who love His name and rejoice in His glory? A penitent sinner is one who has been a transgressor, but is now just; the laws of God are now put within his mind and written on his heart, and his moral condition is evidently one which renders the supposition of punishment incongruous and contradictory. Such a man is as unfit for the atmosphere of hell as an impenitent transgressor is unfit for the atmosphere of heaven. There is obviously, therefore, no principle of reason or nature, as there is unquestionably none of revelation, which teaches that a man may be penitent and perish—that he may be driven into final banishment with the love of God in his heart and the praise of God upon his tongue. On the contrary, we are expressly taught that " if the wicked will turn from all his sins that he hath committed, and keep all my statutes, and do that which is lawful and right, he shall surely live, he shall not die; all his transgressions that he hath committed, they shall not be mentioned unto him: in his righteousness that he hath done he shall live."[1] This seems to be the dictate of right reason. The incongruity is so palpable and revolting of dooming to destruction one who at the time is possessed of every element of character that puts him in harmony with the perfections of God, that writers[2] are by no means wanting who

[1] Ezek. xviii. 21, 22.

[2] Locke and Warburton may be particularly mentioned. Of course.

are as confident in asserting a natural, as those whom we
have more immediately in view an instituted, connection betwixt penitence and pardon.   The difficulty of natural religion is, not that it excludes the penitent from hope, but
that it precludes the possibility of repentance itself.   Upon
the hypothesis that the thorough and radical change of heart
and character implied in the Scripture doctrine of sanctification could take place under its administration—that a man
could be delivered from his moral degradation and reinstated
into that condition of righteousness to which its promises of
life are directed—we see no harm in asserting that in his
righteousness that he hath done he shall live.   The question
under the law of nature in regard to such a case is precisely
analogous to the question under the law of grace whether an
apostate saint can be damned.   The true answer is that the
case can never occur.   Nature shuts us up in despair because
it shuts us up in *impenitence*.   The least transgression con-
tracts guilt; guilt calls for punishment; and this punishment
consists in that banishment from God which is attended, in
every dependent being, with spiritual death and the unbroken
dominion of sin.   To be a sinner therefore once, is to be a
sinner for ever, unless some agency should be interposed to
arrest the natural and ordinary course of justice and law.
Hence the office of a Mediator must be, not to make repentance efficacious of pardon, but to make repentance possible.
It is, accordingly, the great blessing which is promised, as
well as the paramount duty enjoined under the dispensation
of the Gospel.   In other words, it is the great end of Christianity to restore and secure to man the holiness he has lost.

   The first step, it is obvious, which must be taken in this

however, what they mean by *repentance* is no real repentance at all.
That is a change of heart effected by the power which originally formed
it, and a man thus renewed is evidently in a state of salvation already.
Holiness is salvation, or there is nothing which deserves the name.   But
the case is very different in relation to those changes which are wrought
in our characters by the law of habit under the influence of convictions
and of fear.   Such repentance is no preparation for heaven, and such
penitents are worthy of death.

work of renovation is the removal of guilt. In the only sense in which it can be conceived that repentance is likely to be acceptable to God, all its appropriate exercises are the results of His favour and of the communication of His grace. If the least degree of sin entails spiritual death, if death must continue as long as guilt abides, and repentance is a resurrection from this state, the guilt, in some way or other, must be effaced before life can be imparted. There must be pardon before there can be that union with God which is the foundation of all holiness as contradistinguished from morality. It is guilt which seals the soul in impotence, and that guilt must cease to be imputed before a renovation of the nature can be effected. To say that an unpardoned sinner can repent, is to affirm that he may be under the curse and in the favour of God at one and the same time—that he is both dead and alive, active and senseless, free and a slave, at the same moment and in the same relations. There is no method of escaping from these palpable contradictions but by making pardon prior in the order of nature to repentance, and resolving both into a state of reconciliation, for which we are indebted to the gracious interference of a Mediator. The same work, whatever it may be, which removes our guilt and propitiates the favour of the Father of our spirits, entitles us to those communications of love which render us meet to enjoy the blessedness of His smile. We must be pardoned that we may live; and we must live in order to repent; so that repentance and pardon are indeed indissolubly connected; not, however, as cause and effect, nor in the order in which they are too commonly presented, but as the joint results of a common grace arranged in the relation of means to an end, pardon being in order to repentance.[1]

[1] In what we have said about the priority of pardon to repentance, we do not mean that the sense of pardon is experienced, or that the thing itself formally takes place, antecedently to regeneration. In the actual communication of grace, the heart must be changed before faith can exist, and faith must be exerted before justification can be had. But the *grounds* of pardon in the work and intercession of Christ are presupposed in any provisions for the renewal and the sanctification of the

That these were the doctrines which Paul preached on the Areopagus at Athens cannot of course be directly collected from the brief record of his sermon which has come down to us; but that he could not have taught any different theory seems to us plain from the nature of the arguments he employed: " And the times of this ignorance God winked at, but now commandeth all men everywhere to repent, because He hath appointed a day in the which He will judge the world in righteousness by that Man whom He hath ordained; whereof He hath given assurance unto all men, in that He hath raised Him from the dead." The Apostle here makes it the great design of the Gospel, in contradistinction from the law of nature, to inculcate the duty of repentance. As long as men were left to the light of their own eyes, without any adequate revelations of the method of redemption, the doctrine of repentance was not promulgated, because the grace of it was not yet to be imparted. The dead were not commanded to live, because He had not arrived whose voice could penetrate their graves and quicken the pulse of immortality. It is only in connection with the kingdom of heaven that the Scriptures ever insist upon repentance, because it is in that kingdom alone that repentance can possibly exist. Had not Jesus appeared, no eye would ever have wept a tear, no heart ever heaved a sigh of godly sorrow for sin. When we attend to the steps by which Paul reaches the conclusion that God now commandeth all men everywhere to repent—that the generation of holiness and the destruction of sin are the characteristic ends of the Gospel—the inference is inevitable that his views of repentance must have been very different from that which makes it the

sinner, and the mission of the Spirit through which he is made a partaker of Christ is in consequence of that mediation which could effect nothing if it did not remove guilt. We mean nothing more in what we have said than the absolution in heaven and the imputation of Christ, of which Owen speaks in his Death of Christ and Vindiciæ Evangelicæ. See also Witsius, Dissert. Ireni. and Halyburton's Inquiry into the Nature of Regeneration, etc. But see particularly chaps. xi. and xii. of Owen on the Death of Christ.

condition of pardon.   It will be recollected that the general judgment is not presented as a *motive* to amendment, but as a proof that it is commanded.   He does not say that men *ought* to repent because they will be judged, but that they are *commanded* to do it.   He first collects the command from a general judgment in righteousness, and then proves, not that there will be a judgment, but that it will be in righteousness, because Jesus has been raised from the dead.   The sum of his reasoning is briefly this : Men are required to be holy, because God will hereafter deal with them upon the principle of distributive justice ; and that this is the method of His government is put beyond doubt by the resurrection of His Son from the dead.

There are two aspects in which this inspired argument is inconsistent with the doctrines we have been combatting. In the first place, if we are ignorant of the nature of the Saviour's mediation, and know not the principles on which it contributes to our pardon, it is impossible to detect any logical connection betwixt His resurrection and ascension and the final judgment of the world in righteousness.   If we know not what relations to the law He sustained in His death, we must be incompetent to perceive how His resurrection secures its supremacy.   Paul does not adduce the resurrection as a proof of His Divine mission, and through it a proof of what He had asserted in regard to the proceedings of the last day, but he appeals to it as a fact, which in itself contained an infallible assurance from God that the world should be judged in righteousness.   It is a fact which, as soon as it is understood, proclaims this awful truth.

In the next place, if repentance is the appointed precursor of pardon, then it is either a principle of natural justice that the penitent should be pardoned, or under the mediation of Christ the government of God is not one of distributive justice.   To assert that repentance and pardon are connected as antecedent and consequent, under the dispensation of nature, is to set aside all those arguments by which the divines of this school are accustomed to establish the

necessity of mediation.   To say that under the mediation
of Christ the government of God is not strictly and properly just, is to contradict the Apostle, who affirms a general
judgment in righteousness, of which this very mediation is
the clearest and most convincing proof.   Hence, they must
be either inconsistent with themselves or inconsistent with
the apostle in making it the end of Christianity to put men
in a capacity of salvation, by dissolving, through the work
of Christ, the natural connection between guilt and punishment when a moral change has taken place in ourselves.

3.   There is another class of divines possessing many points
of resemblance to the one whose opinions we have just been
considering.   They differ, however, in the circumstance that
they profess to understand the principle on which the efficacy of what they denominate *atonement* depends.   They are
unwilling to assert the absolute necessity of the death of
Christ, not from the modesty which shrinks from the presumption of pronouncing with confidence upon what the
Almighty might or might not do, but from the principle,
plainly avowed and elaborately defended, that public policy
is the only necessity to be admitted.   Those very considerations of expediency by which others have been accustomed
to repel objections, and which are in felt disproportion to the
importance and magnitude of the event, are received by
them as a complete explanation of the case.   The great
problem to be solved by the death of the Redeemer was
the consistency of pardon with the honour of the Divine
Name, and the dignity of the Divine administration, and
the general prosperity of the universe.   It was a terrible
tragedy enacted before the eyes of all creatures to display
the holiness of God and illustrate the transcendent enormity
of sin.   It was intended to give emphasis and depth of
impression to truths which might have been obscured or
undervalued if sin had been absolutely pardoned, or pardoned upon mere repentance.   The divines of this school
do not hesitate to assert that, according to their scheme, the
method of salvation involves an inversion of the principles

of strict retribution. "Neither Christ nor the sinner"—we use the very words of Dr. Wardlaw—"neither Christ nor the sinner has his own due. The guilty who, according to these principles, should suffer, escapes, and the innocent, who should escape, suffers. In no strict and proper sense, then, can distributive justice be *satisfied* by substitution, when its demands, instead of being adhered to and fulfilled, are, for a special purpose and by an act of Divine sovereignty, suspended, superseded, overruled." These men, whatever they may affirm to the contrary, regard the distinctions betwixt right and wrong, not as final and ultimate, but as means to an end. The great purpose of God in the government of His creatures is the production of the largest amount of happiness, and His laws are nothing but the expedients of His prudence and wisdom to accomplish the ends of His benevolence. When, accordingly, the public good can be promoted without these laws, there is nothing in the nature of rectitude, the perfections of the Deity, or the relations of man to his Creator which prevents them from being suspended, superseded or overruled. They are binding because they are necessary to the well-being of the universe; and when a larger amount of happiness can be produced without them, the same reason which induced the Deity to prescribe them induces Him to set them aside. Policy is superior to right, or rather right is nothing but policy under another name. Experience, however, and the obvious fitness of things concur to demonstrate that the principles of morality are, for the most part, the highest expediency; that truth, justice, benevolence are the surest means of private felicity and public prosperity, and that the interests of the universe accordingly require that all the Divine proceedings should be distinguished by the tendency to impress an awful sense of them upon the minds of intelligent creatures. When, therefore, the Divine administration in any degree departs from them, the general result should be a stronger commendation of them than if they had been faithfully and punctiliously observed. Whenever God, in other words,

breaks His own law, the design should be to make that law
more sacredly and solemnly impressive upon the minds of
His subjects.   It is seen to be "more honoured in the
breach than in the observance."

That we have not misrepresented the theory in question,
nor the reasoning by which it is supported, however inconsistent that reasoning appears in our account of it, will be
obvious to any one who will take the trouble to analyze and
compare the following statements from a work of confessed
ability : " *Distributive,* or, as others designate it, *retributive*
justice, according to its strict requirements, admits not of
substitution.   It issues a righteous law with a righteous
sanction.   It passes its sentence of condemnation against
the transgressor of that law.   It makes no mention of any
possible satisfaction but the punishment of the guilty themselves, the endurance by them of the penal sanction in their
own persons.   It is only by the death of the sinner himself that the proper demand of the law can be fulfilled, that
the principles of distributive justice can have their due application, and that under this aspect of it, consequently,
justice, can be satisfied.   According to the requisition of
justice in its distributive sense, every man personally must
have *his own due.*   But in substitution it is otherwise.
There is an inversion of the principles of strict retribution.
Neither Christ nor the sinner has his own due.   The guilty
who, according to those principles, should suffer, escapes, and
the innocent, who should escape, suffers.   In no strict and
proper sense, then, can distributive justice be *satisfied* by
substitution, when its demands, instead of being adhered to
and fulfilled, are for a special purpose and by an act of Divine
sovereignty suspended, superseded, overruled.   It is well to
remark, however, that in another sense it was satisfied, all
its ends being virtually and to the full effected by other
means.   And this leads me to the true end of atonement.
It is to *public justice,* as we have before defined it, that in
substitution and propitiation the satisfaction is made.   The
grand design is to preserve unsullied the glory of the great

principles of eternal rectitude; to show the impossibility of the claims of equity founded in these principles and essential to the government of the universe being dispensed with; to settle in the minds of God's intelligent creatures, as the subjects of His moral administration, the paramount obligation and immutable permanence of their claims; to give such a manifestation of the Divine regard to these elements of His immaculate administration as to preclude the possibility of any the remotest surmise that in the pardon of sin they have been at all overlooked or placed in abeyance, and thus to render it consistent with Divine propriety, or, in other words, honourable to the whole character as well as to the law and the government of Jehovah, to extend pardoning mercy to the guilty, and to reinstate them in His favour according to the provisions of the Gospel. It is thus that, in so pardoning, His regard to righteousness is as conspicuous as His delight in mercy, and, in the minds of the pardoned, the impression of the claims of the one as deep as that of their obligations to the other. In this view of it the scheme possesses a Divine grandeur. The glory of God and the good of His universal empire, the two great ends of *public justice*, are with 'all wisdom and prudence' admirably combined in it. It is as essential to the latter of these ends as it is to the former (they can never indeed be separated) that the authority of the Divine government be maintained in its awful and inviolable sacredness; that the demands of the law be upheld without one jot or tittle of abatement; that no sin appear as venial; and that if any sinner is pardoned, the mercy shown to the offender be shown in such way, on such a ground, through such a medium, as shall at once manifest the Divine reprobation of his offences, and, at the same time, secure the restitution of the guilty perpetrator of them to the principles, affections and practice of holy allegiance. Such are the purposes and such the effects of the Christian atonement."[1]

The plain meaning of all this smooth and beautiful decla-

[1] Wardlaw on Atonement, pp. 58–60.

mation is, that God may do evil that good may come. He may do a thing which confessedly is not just. He may invert the principles of strict retribution, suspend, supersede, overrule the operation of His own law, provided in so doing He make His creatures feel the paramount obligation and immutable permanence of the claims that are set aside. Rectitude is essentially eternal and unchangeable,[1] but God need not observe it if by occasional departures from its rules He can make the universe more scrupulous and punctilious. The death of Christ was, accordingly, a grand expedient by which the Deity in all wisdom and prudence has successfully contrived to impress with commanding emphasis the eternal principles of truth and justice upon the minds of every other intelligent being, while He Himself, in this awful dispensation, confessedly disregards them. Such is the theory as expounded by one of its ablest advocates.

Our business at present is not with the merits of it, but simply with the question whether the historian has not furnished reasons for believing that, whether true or false, this was not the scheme of atonement which Paul preached in the metropolis of Paganism. Paul's gospel is compendiously expressed in Jesus and the *resurrection*. But so far as we can discover, the resurrection is no necessary part of the Gospel upon this scheme, which resolves the death of Christ into considerations of expediency, and explains its efficacy by the moral impression against sin it is suited to produce. The two great ends of public justice, we are told in the passage just quoted, are the glory of God and the good of His universal empire, and these ends, according to the patrons of the scheme, are adequately secured by a dispensation which shows that God *hates* while He pardons iniquity. All that would seem to be essential, therefore, is the sufferings and death of the Redeemer. The resurrection is not an element of the work of redemption; it is simply a necessary fact springing from the divinity of the sufferer,

---

[1] Upon this subject Dr. Wardlaw has expressed himself very strongly, both in his Christian Ethics and his work on Atonement.

and no more conducive to the expiation of our guilt than
the eating and drinking which pertained to His humanity,
or the alternations of activity and repose which were inseparable from His sublunary state.   As Jesus was God, it was
certain that He could not be holden of the bands of death.
He had power to lay down His life, He had power to take
it up again ; but if we could conceive the possibility of His
permanent subjection to the dominion of the grave, the impression, for aught that appears, of the transcendent enormity of sin, would have been more awful than is likely to
be produced by temporary suffering followed by unutter-
able glory.   To say that such a doom would have been a
revolting exhibition of cruelty is either to deny that the
principle on which His sufferings were inflicted was just, and
then any degree of them would have been a measure of
cruelty, or to affirm that there is a point beyond which justice cannot push the punishment of sin, and then it ceases
to be the mighty evil they represent it.   Upon any view of
the case, therefore, the resurrection is an immaterial circumstance in this scheme of redemption.   Suffering, the visible
and palpable endurance of it, this is what is required to the
manifestation of the righteousness of God—this is what is
needed for the purpose of salutary impression.[1]

It deserves further to be remarked that according to this
scheme the resurrection of Christ furnishes no proof that
God will judge the world in righteousness.   If by righteousness we are to understand the principle of distributive jus-

---

[1] "Meanwhile it is enough to remind you how the idea of *manifestation*
is associated with the atonement.   There is not only a provision for the
exercise of the Divine righteousness in man's salvation, but there is the
declaration of that righteousness.   Now, in order to this, there is required
not suffering merely, but the palpable and visible endurance of it.   It
would not otherwise have the necessary impression and effect. . . . And
without vain and presumptuous speculations we are, every one of us, sensible that the spectacle of a Saviour *thus* dignified, *thus* suffering, is enough
for the purpose of salutary impression—impression deep, solemn, awful,
of the Divine righteousness, and impression amply and delightfully en-
couraging of the Divine mercy."— *Wardlaw on Atonement*, Dis. II., pp.
45, 46.

tice—and such, in all similar connections, seems to be its meaning—*that*, according to this hypothesis, is inverted. Neither man nor the Saviour receives his due. If we are to understand the Public Justice to which so much importance is attached, *that* may be illustrated by the *death*, but we cannot perceive its relation to the *resurrection*, of Christ, which becomes, upon this hypothesis, a necessary adjunct of the *person*, but no part of the *work*, of the Redeemer.

There is another objection to this theory suggested by the sermon at Athens, which, if we can make it as clear to our readers as it is to ourselves, will, we apprehend, be conclusive against it. The whole discourse seems to have been conducted on the principle that the Gospel is its own witness—that the facts of redemption authenticate themselves; that we can reason from its phenomena as effects to their origin in the mind of God, as we ascend from nature up to nature's Cause. Paul has evidently taken it for granted—for there is no allusion to any external proofs of the Divine mission of Jesus, and no intimation that he himself wrought any miracles at Athens—that as the heavens proclaim the glory of God and the firmament showeth His handiwork, so the death and resurrection of Jesus, when properly apprehended, are their own proofs that He is the power of God to salvation to every one that believeth. The work itself proves its divinity. That work cannot be acknowledged without prompting the confession of Peter, Thou hast the words of eternal life, and we believe and are sure that Thou art the Christ, the Son of the living God. Now there is one branch of this *a posteriori* argument which is absolutely impossible upon the theory of Public Justice. The resurrection furnishes no direct proof of the Deity and Sonship of Christ. There is nothing in the nature of the sufferings which He underwent which requires that the sufferer should be a Divine Person. As to their amount, for aught that appears, they might have been endured by a creature; and as to their design, we could not have pronounced beforehand that a very solemn and awful display of the holiness of God and the malignity of sin, fitted to inspire with a salutary fear the minds of the guilty, might not have been made by one who was less than Jehovah's fellow.[1]   Hence the mere fact that He died the death which He died, and triumphed over it in His resurrection from the grave, is no necessary proof of what Paul affirms it to demonstrate with power—that He was the true and proper Son of God.   He died—He rose. These are the facts.   Now, if there be not something in the nature of His death which imperatively demanded that the sufferer should be Divine, there can be nothing in the nature of the resurrection to declare His Deity.   If we know beforehand that He was God, we can account for His resurrection upon that hypothesis, but there is nothing in the circumstance itself which, independently of any other proofs, demonstrates His eternal Sonship as well as His kindred to man.   It deserves further to be remarked that, according to this hypothesis, the connection between the death of Christ and the salvation of His people is a matter of arbitrary appointment, and the entire efficacy of His work is resolved into the dignity of His person.   In the Epistle to the Corinthians the Apostle teaches us that there is a species of death which if *any one* endures in the name and for the sake of others, they shall be acquitted, renewed and sanctified. Because we thus judge, says he, that if one died for all, then all died.   The death of the substitute is, in law and justice, the death of the principal; it delivers him from guilt.   The effect depends not upon the *person* dying, but upon the nature and relations of the death itself.   If any other being could have been found who was capable of dying the death which Christ died, the same glorious results would have followed.   His Deity was essential, not to establish the connection between His death and the salvation of His people, but to create the possibility of the death itself.   There was

---

[1] Dr. Wardlaw admits as much in attempting to prove the necessity of Christ's death from the fact that He *did* die, which, no doubt, is very sound reasoning from cause to effect, but it cannot be reversed.—P. 14. Cf. p. 46.

a peculiarity about it which absolutely demanded the strength of Omnipotence to undergo it. None but God could have shed the blood which Jesus poured out. When it is said that the value of Christ's sufferings depends upon His person, it is not intended that a fictitious importance is to be attached to something inherently and essentially worthless, in consequence of its association with a Divine being—which is the only sense of the terms consistent with the theory of Public Justice. The meaning is that they were fully and completely the *death* which the exigencies of the case required, and which they could not possibly have been if the sufferer had been less than Divine. Redemption is glorious, not because God achieves it, but because none but God *could* achieve it. The death of Jesus was glorious, not because it was His death, but because it *could* be the death of no other. A creature might as well have undertaken to *create* as to *save* a world. The work itself demands the interposition of God; and any theory which fails to represent the death of Christ as an event which, in its own nature, as clearly proclaims His Divinity as His superintending care and preservation of all things, cannot be the Gospel which Paul preached at Rome, at Corinth, at Athens, and which extorted from Thomas, upon beholding the risen Saviour, the memorable confession, My Lord and my God!

4. If the necessity of the Gospel is not founded in the ignorance of man, nor the want of a natural connection between penitence and pardon, nor the policy of government, the question recurs, What is the *nature* of it and what peculiarities must distinguish the provisions that are intended to relieve it? It is obvious that Paul, in his recapitulation of the great principles of natural religion, designed to produce in the minds of his hearers a deep and pungent conviction that sin had occasioned an emergency in the government of God which rendered salvation, independently of Jesus and the resurrection, hopelessly impossible. These very principles created the difficulty. They represent God as a just judge and a righteous governor; dispensing rewards and

punishments according to the rule of distributive justice; dealing with every man according to his works. The first great necessity of man, therefore, as a sinner, arises from his guilt—an obligation to punishment which, according to the eternal principles of rectitude, cannot be set aside. The government of the world is not prudential, but moral; and under a strict and proper moral government the wicked cannot be received into favour; they *must* be punished. There can consequently be no hope to a sinner until the problem is solved how God can be *just;* not simply wise, discreet or prudent—this is not the difficulty which a sense of guilt presses upon the conscience of a sinner, but how God can be *just;* can maintain the principle upon which His administration is conducted, and yet receive transgressors into favour. There appears to be an impossibility in the pardon of sin under the law of nature. This first and paramount necessity, springing from guilt under a righteous government, it is the design of Christianity to relieve. It is accordingly an amazing dispensation of Providence and Grace which proposes to reconcile the pardon of the guilty with the strictest principles of justice; which, while it opens a door of hope to the guilty and removes the apprehensions which conscience awakens in the breast of transgressors, demonstrates, at the same time, in the clearest and brightest light, that God will judge the world in righteousness by that man whom He hath ordained. The more clearly the doctrines of natural religion are understood, the more hopeless becomes the condition of a sinner. The imperfect knowledge of them which can be gathered from the dictates of our own consciousness, the crude and mouldering remains which may yet be detected of the law originally written on the heart, are enough to arouse our fears and fill the mind with anxiety and suspense as to the possibility of final acceptance upon any terms. As the light increases, and revelation pours in upon us its discoveries of our former state, of our present ruin, of God's immutable holiness and inflexible justice, despair thickens upon us. Our hearts condemn us, and God is

greater than our hearts and knoweth all things. The
anxious question is wrung from us, "Wherewith shall I
come before the Lord and bow before the High God?
Shall I come before Him with burnt-offerings, with calves
of a year old? Will the Lord be pleased with thousands
of rams, or with ten thousands of rivers of oil? Shall I
give my first-born for my transgression, the fruit of my
body for the sin of my soul?" Now, guilt is only another
name for a conviction of *ill desert*. It is the response of the
human soul to the justice of punishment, and is utterly independent, as all human experience testifies, of all calcula-
tions of expediency. The burden upon the conscience is not
simply that we shall suffer, for suffering may be a calamity
as well as a punishment; not that the interests of the universe and the safety of God's throne demand our misery;
these are considerations which never enter into the bitterness
of remorse. The burden which presses with intolerable
weight upon the soul is the terrible conviction, wrung from
the depths of our moral nature, that we have done wrong
and *deserve* to die. It is this feeling that we *deserve* our
doom which kindles the hell within us. If we could strip
ourselves of the burning consciousness of this fact, no
amount of evil could ever be regarded in the light of punishment. Whatever was inflicted for the general good we
might nerve ourselves to bear, from lofty considerations of
benevolence and self-sacrifice; and to whatever was inevitable we might bow with patience, if not with resignation.
But energy and resolution avail nothing against a sense of
guilt; the feeling of ill desert drinks up the spirits, and
"conscience makes cowards of us all." This, then, is the
peculiarity which distinguishes guilt—it is a conviction that
punishment is due, that it ought to be inflicted, and that
under a righteous government, sooner or later, it *will* be inflicted; and it is precisely this sense of guilt which the
truths of natural religion are adapted to produce within us.
It is the echo of our own hearts to the fearful condemnation
of a holy God.

If guilt is the response of the soul to the justice of punishment, the only way in which its sting can be extracted is
by an arrangement which shall make the punishment cease
to be just, and give the sinner a right to escape from the
evils which conscience forecasts. By no other conceivable
method can peace and tranquillity, in conformity with the
principles of eternal rectitude, be imparted to the mind.
The source of all its fear is the conviction that it *ought* to
die, and unless a contrary conviction can be produced that
the same justice which doomed to death now exempts from
the curse, guilt will continue to agitate the heart with dismal forebodings which cannot be dismissed as phantoms,
because they are founded in the very nature of the soul.
This *obligation* to punishment, this *righteousness* of condemnation, must cease to press, or the need which guilt creates
cannot be relieved. The sinner feels, in other words, that
the justice which calls for his blood must be satisfied, or
that blood be yielded to its demand. It is, accordingly,
the glory of the Gospel that the blood of Christ who, through
the eternal Spirit, offered Himself without spot to God,
purges the conscience, dispels all its distracting fears, and
imparts peace and serenity where despair and guilt had held
their troubled reign. Availing itself of a principle which
in every dispensation of religion has been fundamental in
the Divine dealings with our race, which belongs to natural
as well as supernatural religion, and which, in some form
or other, has always commended itself to the moral judgments of mankind, it reveals to us a work in consequence
of which the pardon of sin on the part of God becomes
not merely a dictate of mercy, but a matter of right. Jesus,
in the name of His people and as their federal head and
representative, has endured the curse, and the justice of
God is now solemnly pledged to Him to exempt them from
personal subjection to its woes. He has died the death of
the law, and, upon an obvious principle of justice from the
relations in which they stand to Him, His death · is their
death. If one died for all, then all died. We are baptized

into His death. I am crucified with Christ, nevertheless I live; yet not I, but Christ liveth in me.

No scheme of atonement that fails to represent Christ as submitting to the proper penalty of the law which the sins of His people had provoked, and in such relations to them that His sufferings can be justly charged as their own, can be regarded as adapted to the exigencies of *guilt*. It does not relieve that condition of the conscience which apprehends punishment as a matter of right. It does not meet the prime necessity of the sinner. He is still left *guilty*,[1] under *obligation* to punishment; and if his iniquities are pardoned, law and justice are defrauded of their due. Hence, if the principles of natural religion are immutable, there can be no peace to the transgressor until he is placed in a position in which it is no longer *right* to remember his offences against him. When God can be just and faithful in blotting out his transgressions, then, and not till then, is his conscience sprinkled with clean water and purged from dead works. Christianity must take away our *guilt*, or it leaves us under the curse of nature. This, we maintain, is precisely what the Gospel achieves. The Lamb of God bore away our guilt. He became a curse for us, sin for us, though He Himself knew no sin, that we might be made the righteousness of God in Him. He was wounded for our transgressions, He was bruised for our iniquities, the chastisement of our peace was upon Him, and with His stripes we are healed. All we like sheep have gone astray, but the Lord hath laid on Him the iniquities of us all. It is in reference to this aspect of the work of Christ as expiating guilt that the eternal covenant which He came to ratify and seal is styled The counsel of peace. The kingdom which He came to establish consists in joy and peace, and the great blessing which He communicates to all who are sprinkled with His blood is that peace which passeth all understanding, and which abides unshaken amid the agitations and tumults, the glooms and convulsions of the world. Through

[1] This is admitted by Dr. Wardlaw and divines of the same school.

Him God becomes the God of peace, the Gospel the message of peace, preachers of righteousness the heralds of peace, and the two great results of His work, according to the rapturous song of the angels, are glory to God in the highest and peace on earth. We see no alternative, but an open denial that the Gospel is the religion of a sinner, adapted to those moral necessities of his nature which spring from the immutable principles of natural religion, or a cordial admission of the fact that Christ by His sufferings and death completely satisfied the justice of God in regard to the sins of His people. They, through Him, either cease to be guilty or they must die; their consciences are either purged by His blood or they have no peace. They are still under the law and its curse, or they are delivered from its condemnation. It is idle to speak of the ends of punishment being answered by anything but punishment itself, of costly and imposing expedients by which a salutary impression is made on the universe, and the righteousness of God illustriously displayed and the malignity of sin unfolded; this may be true, but all this does not reach the malady within, the plague of the sinner's conscience. That is seized by the strong hand of justice, and until its iron grasp is relaxed, until right as well as policy ceases to demand his blood, he cannot be at ease. Hence it is, and must be, an indispensable element in anything which deserves the name of *atonement* that it satisfies the justice of God, or lays the foundation of a claim of right to exemption from punishment.[1]

But guilt is not the only need a sense of which is awakened by those truths of nature which Paul proclaimed at Athens. To be delivered from guilt is to be put in the moral position of the innocent without obstructions to the

---

[1] "Even the commender and publisher of Grotius' Book of 'Satisfaction,' the learned Vossius himself, affirmeth, that Christ by His death purchased for us a double right: First, a right of escaping punishment, and then a right of obtaining the reward."—*Owen's Death of Christ*, chap. x.

free communication of Divine favour, and without a right to any good but the exemption from ill.[1] Such persons might be made alive to God, but they could have no claims to His favour, and no security for whatever integrity might be graciously imparted. It is only to the *just* that the confirmed state of blessedness which the Scriptures mean by *life* is infallibly promised. Obedience to the law, *righteousness*, is the indispensable condition of God's everlasting favour. If, therefore, the scheme of redemption had done nothing more than deliver us from the curse of the law, though it would have conferred an incalculable benefit upon us, an unutterably great salvation, it would not have done all, that the necessities of the case required, to secure the perfection and blessedness of our nature. If it had gone so far as to remove spiritual death and re-establish the communion of the soul with God, the life which it imparted might still have been contingent. It might be forfeited by disobedience; and in the actual circumstances of our race, surrounded with temptations, encompassed with infirmities, ensnared alike by the world and the Devil, if our first father under much greater advantages failed when left to himself, it is morally certain that all of us would have come short of the glory of God. A contingent life would have been a cruel mockery of our hopes. Hence, the Gospel proposes not merely to deliver us from the condemnation

---

[1] " The satisfaction of Christ tends, in all that it is, to the honour and reparation of the justice of God. This, then, in its utmost extent and efficacy, cannot give ground to build such a right upon. The ultimate effect of satisfaction may be accomplished, and yet not the least right to any good thing communicated to them for whom this satisfaction is made. The good things attending the death of Christ may be referred unto two heads, the amotion of evil and the collation of good. For the first, the amotion of evil, the taking that from us that it may not grieve us, and subducting us from the power and presence thereof, it is immediately aimed at by satisfaction. That the curse of the law be not executed, that the wrath to come be not poured out, is the utmost reach of the death of Christ considered as satisfactory. . . . For positive good things in grace and glory, by satisfaction alone, they are not at all respected."—*Owen's Death of Christ*, chap. xi.

of sin, to put us into a state in which it is no longer right to damn us, but to introduce us into a state in which it is right to *bless* us. It proposes to give us a title to life—a title founded on the same eternal principle of rectitude which would have confirmed Adam in holiness and bliss for ever if he had fulfilled the condition of his trial. The Gospel, in other words, proposes to justify, and upon the broad principle of righteousness to open the kingdom of heaven to all believers. This righteousness secures our holiness, secures life, because it secures God's favour and gives a right, under the constitution of His own government, to the enjoyment of Him as the supreme portion of the soul. They who are justified must be glorified. The very end of justification is to take away the contingency of holiness. If Adam had maintained his integrity during the term of his probation, his justification would have imparted to him no element of character which he did not previously possess—the image of God was not half drawn upon him ; but it would have put him in a *state* in which he could never lose his holiness nor be exposed to the risk of condemnation. And so the justification of a sinner introduces him into a state in which he can no more be left to the dominion of sin and the possibility of the curse than Christ can lose His glory or God be unfaithful to His promises and oath. " For whom He did foreknow He also did predestinate to be conformed to the image of His Son, that He might be the first-born among many brethren ; moreover, whom He did predestinate them He also called, and whom He called them He also justified, and whom He justified them He also glorified."

Such, we apprehend, is the substance of that doctrine which Paul preached in his first open conflict with Paganism. The religion he proclaimed was pre-eminently that of a sinner— adapted, in all its provisions, to the spiritual necessities of a fallen being under the righteous government of God. The altars around him were dumb, yet pregnant, witnesses that the wants which the Gospel undertook to relieve were not the fictions of fancy nor the creatures of superstition, but the urgent demands of the soul.   Under the imperfect light of heathenism there were still cases in which conscience asserted its supremacy, and summoned the guilty to the tribunal of the unknown God.   The uncertainty which invested the doctrine of a future life was suited to quicken the apprehensions of guilt, while the utter darkness, into which the spirit seemed to retire, invited a disturbed imagination to people its ˙shades with ministers of vengeance and executioners of justice.   Amid all the ignorance of God and vagueness of conjecture which pertained to the condition of a thoughtful Pagan, the terrible impression would cleave to him that he was under a curse.   It would haunt his dreams like the ghost of the murdered, embitter his waking hours, turn life itself into a burden, and make him long, yet dread, to die.   He might endeavour to lay the flattering unction to his soul that the great Unknown in whose hands he was, and to whom he was responsible, was good and kind, and would be tender to his infirmities and failures; but the scenes of wretchedness around him, the frightful ravages of disease, pestilence and death ; the stern and relentless judgments which scourge entire generations and in their progress sweep away nations; the cry of weeping, lamentation and woe which bursts from the smitten bosoms of the whole family of man ; the portentous fact, written in blazing characters around him, stamped upon the cheek of the dying, the brow of the living, and even upon inanimate nature itself, that God has a controversy with men, and that though He is good He yet deals out to the trembling tribes of earth the vials of a fierce indignation,—considerations like these would thicken the blackness with which conscience had covered the future, and shroud the soul in the deepest night of despair.   If the siren voice of hope should attempt to whisper that there yet might be peace, the monitor of God within would proclaim, in tones of thunder, There is no peace to the wicked.   If there should still be an effort to prop the sinking spirit upon the mercy of its Author, Nature would cry aloud from her thousand chambers of suffering and anguish, Woe, woe, woe to the inhabitants of earth! Where could comfort be found? Where could peace be sought, except in that desperate hardihood of spirit which would sternly banish thought, and, like the beasts that perish, catch only the passing moment as it flies? And what is the religion which such a sinner, grappling with despair, burdened with life and afraid to die,—what is the religion which the necessities of his soul demand? Is it more of light in relation to God, His law, His justice and the stern retributions of eternity, when what he knows already presses on his conscience like a night-mare, and peoples the land of darkness with all that is awful in mysterious power, with all that is dreadful in insulted justice? Ah, no! He needs not light, but life—not philosophy and science, not new discoveries in heaven and earth, but a Saviour—a Saviour who can pluck him from the wrath to come, arrest the avenger of blood, seize the sword of justice, put it up into its scabbard, bid it rest and be still. The glory of Christianity is its Saviour, and His power to save is in the blood by which he extinguished the fires of the curse, and the righteousness by which He bought life for all His followers. Jesus made our curse, Jesus made our righteousness, this, this is the Gospel! All else is philosophy and vain deceit. This it is which gives Christianity its power. By this, and this alone, it subdues the ferocity of passion, disarms temptation of its violence, disrobes the world of its charms, changes the tiger into the lamb, and makes the lion eat straw like the ox. This constitutes the grand difference between the religion of Mohammed and the religion of Jesus, between the Koran and the Bible.

Upon this scheme, and this scheme alone, as it seems to us, the preaching of Paul at Athens can be reduced to consistency and method. It accounts for the importance which he attached to the doctrines of nature. He would acquaint the patient with his malady before he explained the character and application of the remedy, especially when it was likely to be sought just in the degree in which it was felt to be needed.

In the next place, it makes the resurrection an integral part of Christianity. That resurrection was the justification of Jesus as the Head of the Church, the discharge of the prisoner upon the satisfaction of the debt, as well as the passage of our great High Priest into the holiest of all. If Christ had remained under the power of death, the curse of the law could not have been removed from us; we should have died in our sins. He was delivered for our offences, and was raised again for our justification.

Upon this view we may add, further, that the resurrection of Christ becomes what Paul affirms it to be, a signal proof of His eternal Sonship, if by His eternal Sonship we understand that spirit of holiness according to which He is truly and properly God. None but Jehovah's fellow could have received the stroke of Jehovah's justice in His bosom and survived the blow. The penalty of the law was no vulgar ill, to be appeased by a few groans and tears, by agony, sweat and blood. It was the wrath of the infinite God, which, when it falls upon a creature, crushes him under the burden of eternal death. It is a blackness of darkness through which no ray of light or hope can ever penetrate the soul of a finite being; to all such it must be the blackness of darkness *for ever*. But Jesus endured it, Jesus satisfied it, Jesus bowed beneath that death which the law demanded, and which sinks angels and men to everlasting ruin, and came victorious from the conflict. If He had been a creature, He would have been crushed, sunk, lost; if He had been less than God, the bitterness of death could not have been passed; never, never could He have emerged from that thick darkness into which He entered when He made His soul an offering for sin. The morning of the third day—and a more glorious morn never dawned upon our earth—for ever settled, to all who understood the event, the Deity of Jesus. It was the crisis of all human hope. When our great Substitute had given up the ghost for us and descended into hell, the possibility of His return to us depended on His ability to meet the infinite wrath of the Infinite God. When the terrific cup was administered and He drank it and died, His slumbers in Joseph's tomb could never have been broken unless He could thunder with a voice like God, and bear the burden of infinite woe. The third day, which proclaimed His triumph, declared Him to be the Son of God with power, according to the spirit of holiness, by His resurrection from the dead. He had died a death which none could die but one who was Almighty.

But Paul teaches us that the resurrection is not only a proof of the Deity of Christ, but a proof, at the same time, that God will judge the world in righteousness by that Man whom He hath ordained; that His government, in other words, is conducted on the principle of distributive justice. This is an obvious inference from that representation of Christianity which makes the sufferings of Jesus a full and perfect satisfaction of the penalty of the law, and His life of spotless obedience the ground to all claim of everlasting bliss. No other scheme harmonizes the salvation of a sinner with the immutable principles of natural religion. This is its characteristic excellence; it rears the fabric of grace, not upon the ruins, but the fulfilment, of the law. God is never seen to be more gloriously just, nor the law more awfully sacred, than when He spared not His own Son, but delivered Him up for us all. The impression which this event makes is indeed solemn, awful, sublime. It was a wonder in heaven, a terror in hell, and is the grand instrument through which the rebellion of earth is subdued and the stout-hearted made to melt at the remembrance of sin. Upon the cross it is written in characters of blood that none can ever be pardoned who have not died, in their substitute, the death of the law—that none can ever be admitted into heaven who cannot present that obedience to which life is promised. Justice has its full demands upon the representative of the sinner, while grace abounds to the sinner himself. It may be said, however, that the admission of a substitute is itself a compromise of the strictness of justice. Without entering into the abstract question, it is sufficient for our present purpose to observe that God never contemplated any other justification of our race than through the obedience of a federal head. This was the fundamental principle of the covenant which contains the substance of natural religion. If Adam had stood, we should all have been justified by his obedience; as having fallen, we sinned in him, and fell with him in his first transgression. No promise of life has ever been made to man upon any other basis than that of imputed righteousness. It is nature's method, as well as the method of grace, and as natural law is admitted to be just, there is no concession nor compromise of the eternal principles of right in laying upon Christ the iniquities of us all.

From the exposition given of this noble monument of eloquence which inspiration has transmitted to us, it may be seen what constitutes the essence of the Gospel. It is Jesus and the resurrection—Jesus dying for our sins and raised again for our justification. Where these elements are wanting, whatever else may be found, there is no Christianity. A penal death and a perfect righteousness imputed, the one for pardon and the other for acceptance—these are things which make the Gospel glad tidings of great joy. To deny these is to deny Christ.

We may here see also that the most successful method of preaching is that which aims at thorough and radical *convictions* of sin. The law must be applied with power to the conscience, or the preciousness of grace will be very inadequately known. The superficial piety of the present day is owing, in a large degree, to feeble impressions of the malignity of sin. That complete breaking up of the fallow ground of the heart, that groaning under bondage, that deep sense of weakness and nothingness, which characterized the experience of the past generation, are unsuited to the haste and bustle of this stirring age. The transition from absolute indifference to cordial reliance upon

Christ must now be made in an instant. One gush of
sorrow, one leap of joy, and the work must be done.
Such converts can know little of the law, little of Christ,
and less of themselves. Men must be soundly instructed
by Moses if they would know the sweetness of the liberty
in Christ.

CHAPTER SEVEN

Paul at Athens

JOHN EADIE

PAUL AT ATHENS.

Acts xvii. 15—34; 1 Thess. iii. 1.

It was by night that Paul and Silas were sent away from Thessalonica. There had been tumult and violence, and a cry of treason and disloyalty had been raised. At such a time it would have been easy to throw the city into a commotion, and in the midst of it to assassinate the objects of popular dislike. Besides, Jason had given bail, probably to send away the so-called disturbers of the peace, and it was therefore deemed advisable that Paul and Silas should leave quietly and unobserved by the infuriated rabble and their malignant instigators. The missionaries travelled to Berea, fifty-seven miles south-west, and commencing their evangelical labours, found the Jews in that city more docile and less under the influence of prejudice than those in Thessalonica. They "received the word with all readiness;" and were *more noble*—in candour and frankness; more ingenuous, for, instead of scorning the truth and reviling its preachers, they did what really was their duty—" they searched the scriptures daily whether those things were so "—whether the statements made by Paul corresponded with the Hebrew oracles. The inference then is, that he preached in the Berean synagogue the same truths, and in much the same form, as he had done in the previous cities which he had visited. The result was, as indeed always happens when there is openness of mind and study of the Bible, that "many believed," *honourable women which were Greeks*—proselytes of high rank—and " of men not a few."

But Jewish rancour never slept. It had failed in its object so far, but no thanks to it—the apostle still lived. Yet it pursued him with the staunchness of a blood-hound, and go where he pleased, it soon tracked his steps and came up with him. For we are told—" But when the Jews of Thessalonica had knowledge that the word of God was preached of Paul at Berea, they came thither also and stirred up the people." Paul must therefore take leave of the noble Bereans, and still pursue his southward journey; this time without his colleagues. There was work before him, and Jewish spite gave him no rest till he overtook it. Though he had been invited across the Ægean by a man of Macedonia, he must now depart from that province. They "immediately sent away Paul to go as it were to the sea;" Silas and Timothy being left behind. The words— " as it were to the sea," do not mean as they seem to do in English, that his journey sea-ward was a mere feint to elude his enemies, though some have held this notion, but merely that he travelled designedly toward the sea. Probably he might not intend to embark at once—at least for Athens—but might wish to revisit Philippi and Thessalonica. It is not formally stated, but the inference is, that Paul went by sea to Athens. The journey by land would have been one of two hundred and fifty-one miles, and there is no record of it or of any place visited on the way; whereas the voyage, if he took shipping at the mouth of the Haliacmon, might be accomplished in three days. The apostle, after sailing past shores, islands, mountains, head-lands, and scenes of imperishable fame—Olympus, Mara-thon, Salamis, and Sunium—landed at Phalerum, or rather at the Piræus, and wending his way between the long walls built by Themistocles, but now partly in ruins, entered the city—"mother of arts and eloquence"—the intellec-tual metropolis of the world.

The splendour of Greece had waned, and it had passed under Roman sway. But what had survived the ravages of time and conquerors attested its ancient grandeur. In that region of south-eastern Europe, genius had dwelt incarnate. It had built the loftiest epics, recited the happiest histories, argued in the stateliest dialogues, wept in the saddest tragedies, laughed in the wittiest comedies, harangued in the mightiest orations, discoursed in the subtlest metaphysics, erected the noblest temples, carved the truest statues, painted the divinest pictures, wrestled in the greatest games, spoken the finest language, sung the gayest songs, and fought the bravest battles—that the world ever saw. The studies of the apostle, not at Jerusalem certainly, and least of all at the feet of Gamaliel, but in his native Tarsus, renowned for its cultivation of Grecian literature, must have made him acquainted with these glories of Athens. He had enjoyed the grace and euphony of Xenophon, and been charmed with the simple dignity of Herodotus. He had thrilled under Æschylus, and glowed with Demosthenes, whose intense logic and barbed interrogations he sometimes reproduces. He could be no stranger to the imagery and music of Homer, the depth and beauty of Plato, the arms, oratory,

and magnificence of Pericles, or the terse compacted style
of Thucydides which he occasionally resembles; and he
must have often pictured to himself the groves of the Ilissus,
the proportions of the Parthenon, and the keen discussions
of the Porch, the Academy, the Lyceum, and the Garden.

The city which he entered was "built nobly, pure the
air, and light the soil." The limestone rock on which
Athens stands, supplied the ordinary material for its
buildings, and also from many of its quarries the marble
for its nobler structures. The plain is bounded by ranges
of hills—on the north-west by Mount Parnes, on the
south-east by Mount Hymettus, and on the north-east by
Mount Pentelicus, out of which rises the higher pinnacles
of Lycabettus, looking upon the city as Arthur's seat upon
Edinburgh. About a mile south-west from it, and in the
city, there rose the Acropolis, not unlike Stirling castle in the
upper valley of the Forth. West of it was a smaller rock,
the Areopagus or scene of judgment—the council meeting
in the open air on its south-eastern summit, and sitting on
benches hewn out in the rock, which form three sides of a
quadrangle. To the south-west, and about a quarter of a
mile from it, there was another and lower eminence, the
Pnyx, the place of the great popular assemblies—also held
in the open air under the deep blue of a Grecian sky—
with its *bema* or stone block on which the orator stood
and addressed the crowd, which gathered in a semicircular
area of twelve thousand square yards before him, and
where Solon, Demosthenes, and Pericles often spoke to the
assembled "men of Athens."

The apostle is now in this city, not ignorant of its

ancient renown, of its history and literature. And he was alone, having sent word by those who conducted him to Athens, to Timothy and Silas to rejoin him "with all speed." Timothy soon came, but was soon sent off again to Thessalonica, as we learn from 1 Thess. iii. 1, 2. In fact, it would seem as if Paul had originally intended to make Athens only a rendezvous, and not a scene of labour, till he found from Timothy that Macedonia was still shut against him. As he waited, he wandered through its streets with inquisitive and sorrowing gaze, it was so unlike Jerusalem, the city of God. His spirit was *stirred within him*—roused and excited to profound grief and indignation, as he surveyed its glories, not with the eye of an artist, but that of a Christian. The statues and temples were not looked on by him as the creations of genius, but the means and results of debasing superstitions. Intellect, taste, and beauty were alike profaned, for the one God was dethroned. Wherever the solitary stranger gazed, he saw the manifestations of polytheism—nature deified, humanity depicted as superhuman, and virtues, nay, even vices, exalted into divinities. It was an unwonted sight which greeted him. The city was *wholly given to idolatry* —idol-full; crammed, as one might say, with idols—one idolatrous mass. Its public buildings were consecrated as temples, and its streets and forums thickly peopled with statues of the gods. Never had he seen the second commandment so wantonly and systematically violated; never had he beheld so much art and wealth lavished on a wretched idolatry. There had never met his gaze such artistic beauty of appearance with such spiritual deformity of purpose, such symmetry of form and structure with such miserable misconception of the Divine unity and infinity. The epithet "idol-full" given by Luke to Athens, is fully verified by ancient writers both of satire and history. One of the former affirms that it was easier to find a god than a man in it; and one of the latter, that it was one whole altar, one entire sacrifice and offering to the gods. Another tells us how a person could scarce find his way through its streets for the troops of idol-mongers. In the crowds of gods which, turn as you will, your eye gazed upon, were Minerva and Neptune, Jupiter and Ceres, Apollo and Bacchus, Hercules and Theseus, the Muses and the Furies, Venus and the Graces, Diana and the Nymphs of the Dêmos or civic assembly. Altars or temples were erected to Fame, Modesty, Energy, Mercy, Persuasion, Victory, and Oblivion.

But the apostle was no vulgar iconoclast; he did not lift his arm, and in the name of the Lord of Hosts "break down the carved work." He sought to reach the hearts of men, and therefore he first spoke to his countrymen and to the proselytes, and then turned to the Athenian population. These last he met in the *market-place*—forum—which was usually crowded with loungers. This market-place of Athens, surrounded by stately porticoes and colonnades, served not only the purpose of an exchange and news-room, was not only a scene of pleasure as well as business, but philosophers and poets traversed it, and the sharp wit of the people was whetted by a perpetual war of words and exchange of raillery. It was, in short, the heart of Athens, sending forth its vital currents on all sides. Every variety of population was there, and the apostle easily found numbers to listen to his preaching, to batter him with question upon question, to turn his earnestness into ridicule, and toss aside with satiric levity or gay invective the point of his argument and appeals. A man of his experience and practical wisdom could easily secure such admissions and extort such assents from an opponent, as that he should be led, step by step and unconsciously, to an untenable conclusion or one in utter contrast to his original statement, and thus the onlookers would be reminded of the humour and shrewdness of the old Socratic dialogue.

Close upon the agora or forum was a porch or arcade, painted with frescos from the battle of Marathon; there Zeno had taught, and there the Stoics, his followers, still congregated. The audacity of a Hebrew foreigner in daring to ascribe ignorance to the sages of Athens, and in affirming that he was the vehicle of a new and superior philosophy, must have created a sensation which not only surged through the populace, but reached the schools of philosophy. The Epicureans and Stoics, therefore, assailed him, and some of them set him down as a *babbler*—one that fluently retails meaningless scraps, and others as a preacher of new divinities. The last conclusion was nearest the truth, though the expression proved how grievously they misinterpreted the apostle's message. Other some said—" He seemeth to be a setter forth of strange gods." The plural " gods " may be used for the singular, the reference being to Jesus, and to the resurrection as proving his Godhead; but it is a very natural inference from the subjoined explanation, because he preached unto them " Jesus and the resurrection," that the Greek term *anastasis*—resurrection,

was taken for a female deity, as if Paul had brought to
Athens a new pair of divinities. His preaching opposed
the Epicurean theory of creation and the Stoical notion of
providence; proclaimed a personal presiding God, who has
created all things, whose worship must be spiritual, and on
whom man depends for being and well-being; who takes an
interest in every creature, and orders all things wisely and
well; who has perfect freedom of action, ruling as He wills;
whose heart is as tender as His arm is powerful; whose
pure and righteous law commands obedience; whose image
seeks conformity from man as his highest dignity and perfection, and whose presence and glory in another sphere are
the crown of that immortal blessedness which His genuine
worshippers are assured of possessing. Such novelties
excited both the philosophers and the volatile population,
whose passion for news was proverbial. Paul was, therefore,
brought out of the noise and bustle of the forum up those sixteen steps cut in the rock to Mars-hill—Areopagus—not to
be tried, but to address the assembly on that convenient and
hallowed spot. He was not arraigned or put on his defence,
but was taken to Mars-hill, only to gratify the inquisitive
population, who said, with a tinge of polite irony—"May
we," or can we, "know what this new doctrine whereof
thou speakest is?" The historian, to explain the cause of
this eager procedure, which the apostle met with nowhere
else, adds a trait of Athenian character—"For all the
Athenians, and strangers which were there, spent their
time in nothing else, but either to tell or to hear some *new
thing*"—some newer thing than the last news they had
gathered. Demosthenes himself cries in his first Philippic

—"Do ye like walking about and asking one another, is there any news? Why, could there be greater news than a man of Macedon conquering the Athenians and directing the policy of Greece?"

On these stone benches had sat the judges so renowned for equity in former times, and there many a solemn appeal and stirring oration had been delivered for and against the culprit. The associations connected with the scene might indeed have overpowered him. There had Socrates, at seventy years of age, been judged and condemned as "a setter forth of strange gods," and he was about to declaim against the prevalent idolatry, standing in the midst of its artistic and architectural glories. Well might his heart be stilled for a moment when he remembered his position where many a brave man had quailed, and when he thought of the fastidious and prejudiced audience before him, and of the solemn and unwelcome truths he was about to announce to them. Yet he stands unmoved, while mighty thoughts are stirring within him. He rises to the occasion, and as his eye takes in the scene, he begins as easily, quietly, and pointedly, as if he had been wont to stand there before—"Ye men of Athens, I perceive that in every point of view ye carry your reverence for the gods farther than most: for, as I was passing along and inspecting the objects of your devotion, I found also an altar on which had been inscribed—"To an Unknown God;" what, therefore, without knowing it, ye worship, that I proclaim to you. The God who made the world and all that is in it, as being Himself Lord of heaven and earth, dwelleth not in hand-made temples, neither is He ministered to with men's hands as if He were in want of anything, seeing Himself is giving to all life, breath, and all things, and did make every nation of men sprung of one blood to dwell on the whole face of the earth, having appointed the times and the limits of their habitation, so as that they should seek God, if by any chance they might feel after and find Him. And, indeed, He is not far from every one of us, for in Him we live, and move, and have our being, as also some of your own poets have said—'For His offspring also are we.' Therefore, being the offspring of God, we ought not to think that the divine nature is like gold, or silver, or stone, the sculpture of man's art and device. The past periods of this ignorance God having indeed overlooked, does now command all men in all places to repent; because He has appointed a day in which He will judge the world in righteousness by that man whom He has ordained, having afforded assurance to all men, in that He has raised Him from the dead."—The address, for the sake of illustration, may be divided into three parts.

Part I.

The apostle thus commences—"Ye men of Athens, I perceive that in all things ye are *too superstitious*"—or, rather, "ye carry your reverence for the gods farther than most." The phrase, "too superstitious," as implying blame, is an unfortunate translation. The apostle appeals simply to the fact, and not to its character. He only uttered a commonplace, for the Athenians were noted among the other Grecian peoples for this propensity. They had preeminence in the scrupulous and unlimited attention paid by them to the national worship. The inspired orator alludes simply to this notorious circumstance, but neither smiles at it in compliment, nor frowns upon it in censure. The implication is, that he came to guide and rectify this tendency of the Athenian mind. It had outcropped in every possible way, and given a multiform expression to itself in sculpture and masonry; but his mission was to turn it into the true course, and lead it to the knowledge of the one, pure, invisible, infinite, eternal, and loving Spirit.

Standing where the apostle did, he saw his words verified all around him. Above him was a temple of Mars from whom the hill took its name; and near him was the subterranean sanctuary of the Eumenides or Furies, but usually called by the first title, from the same feeling which led the old Scottish people to name the fairies the "good folk," though they were a waspish and capricious race. The forum he had left was studded with statues, the altar of the twelve gods being in its centre and the temple of Venus at its eastern end, while on all sides of it were deified heroes of the old mythology. Behind him was the Pnyx sacred to Jove, and before him was the Acropolis, its sides and summit covered with religious monuments, every available ledge laden with its shrine or image, its platforms filled with sculptured groups of gods in various forms and attitudes; on its northern extremity the Erectheum, with its inclosures and its presiding deities; the cave of Pan and Apollo with its sacred fountain not far from its base, and adjoining it the sanctuary of Aglaurus; and the Parthenon crowning the whole, the central glory of the scene; while opposite the magnificent Propylæa, and formed out of the trophies of Marathon, was the gigantic bronze statue of the goddess herself, with spear and shield—the name-mother of the city, and its great protector. In the north-west quarter was the temple of Theseus, and in the opposite direction was that of Jupiter Olympius. A temple of Ceres was close to the Pompeium, in which were kept the robes and vases for the religious processions; and a temple of the divine Mother was near to the great council-house in which also were shrines and altars. There were shrines, too, at the principal gates. The altar of Prometheus was within the groves of the Academy; and the Lyceum, with its tall plane-trees, was dedicated to Apollo. There were also the Pythium and the Delphinium, characteristic names of temples, with those of Euclea, of Castor and Pollux, and of Serapis. Every street, in short, had some object or scene of devotion; every view was bounded and fringed with fanes and idols. Paul had now visited many towns, had been at Antioch, Paphos, and Philippi, but he had seen nothing to compare with Athens in its excessive idolatry.

The apostle then gives the plain reason why he concluded that the Athenians were careful beyond others in this worship—" For as I passed by and beheld your devotions "—rather, "as I was passing along and surveying the objects of your devotion, I found an altar with this inscription—' To the Unknown God' "—more correctly, " to an Unknown God." This is the apostle's proof of his previous statement, and he bases it on his own personal observation. He tells them that what he saw was evidence of their great scrupulosity in matters of worship. Not only did they worship gods whose titles and attributes they knew, but they had built an altar to a foreign god, whose name even they were not acquainted with, and offered homage to an anonymous divinity. They were not contented with their own gods, but they had introduced a nameless stranger, and erected an altar to him. Were they not then, as he had named them, lavish in their worship—so sweepingly attentive in their religion as to recognize in their extravagant devotions the existence of an undiscovered divinity? Ancient writers verify the apostle's statement. Philostratus, in his life of Apollonius, that strange wanderer, says—" It is safe to speak well of all the gods, especially at Athens, where are erected also altars of unknown gods." Pausanias, who visited Athens about a hundred years after the apostle, and has left a full account of the city, speaks of such an altar at Phalerum, one of the ports of the city. How the custom originated, we know not. It is said, that during a plague, when it was not

ascertained which of the gods had sent it, an altar was
built to the appropriate divinity whoever he was—and they
did not identify him for fear of mistake—was built to him
who had sent it, and who could alone remove it, though his
name was unknown. But, in reality, this impulse was the
natural result of polytheism. Amidst the multiplicity of
gods, there was great anxiety lest any one should be forgotten, for the neglected deity might be affronted at such an
omission, and be provoked to punish it. The worshipper
therefore offered homage to all the gods he knew—and to
all others, if any existed, though he did not know them.
He dreaded the vengeance of some power unrecognized by
him; and to secure that every deity was invoked, he might
erect an altar to an unknown god. Miserable uncertainty!
when the devotee on the one hand feared the revenge of
some god, if he did homage to his rival, and, on the other
hand, incurred an awful retribution if, in his haste or
ignorance, any of the hosts of deities should be unackow-
ledged and slighted by him! Amidst the crowds of known
and shrined divinities at Athens, there was one with an
altar, but without a name—an unknown god. On the
statement of this fact, so patent to his audience, and which
probably they accepted as a tribute to their catholic piety,
the apostle skilfully and suddenly founds his defence and
introduction. In the synagogue he had selected his theme
from Moses, but on the Areopagus he takes his text from
a heathen altar. To the children of Abraham he proclaimed the Christ, but to the citizens of Athens he
"preached Jesus." Nor did he declaim, like an excited
Jew, against pagan idolatry, but he penetrated to the

feeling which lies beneath it—to that inner necessity under which man must worship; and thus he adds—

" Whom, therefore, ye ignorantly worship, Him declare I unto you;" or " What, therefore, not knowing it, ye worship, that I proclaim unto you." The neuter form makes the declaration more emphatic from its very vagueness. The apostle admits that they worshipped, for a feeling of instinctive devotion underlies polytheism. True, indeed, he argues—" What say I then? that the idol is anything? or that which is offered in sacrifice to idols is anything? But I say, that the things which the Gentiles sacrifice, they sacrifice to devils, and not to God: and I would not that ye should have fellowship with devils." In this passage, addressed to the neighbouring city of Corinth, the apostle dwells on the result or actual character of idolatry. Being such a violation of the divine law, it is a sphere of the devil's operation so contrived that he is adored. It is not Jupiter that is worshipped, since there is no such being or power. Evil spirits lurk behind the idolatrous framework, and make it subservient to their purposes, prey upon man's worshipping instincts, and really receive the homage. Yet there is worship offered on the part of man; his ignorant and fallen spirit knows that there is something above it, something which can and does shape its destiny, with which it is indissolubly connected, and to which it, therefore, erects temples and consecrates altars. It would be rash to affirm that the apostle expressly identifies the " unknown God " with the true God. The unknown God was some being over and beyond their conventional divinities, and there is no proof that the mysterious God of the Jews was intended. But such an altar was a confession that their catalogue did not comprehend all the powers and essences of the universe; that there was or might be some Being beyond the circuit of their recognition, who might be chagrined or angry if Athens should overlook him. This admission the speaker seizes on, and says—There is such a God, unknown, indeed, to you, and Him I proclaim. He thus replies that, in one sense, he is not "a setter forth of strange gods;" but he does not say that the very god who owned the anonymous altar was Jehovah, for the god of that altar must have been really an idol, so far as Athenian imagination pictured him. But he took the idea which the inscription implied, and expanded it. There is a God unknown to you—a being not found in your lists—who has no statue among these numerous groups, and no temple on that eminence; Him so dimly and scantily acknowledged, the one true God, I proclaim. By this very thought he takes Him out of the category of the Greek divinities. He is not one of them, nor yet another of similar nature who claims admission among them. O, no. He is—

"God that made the world, and all things therein, seeing that He is Lord of heaven and earth, dwelleth not in temples made with hands." He is God, the one Creator—of earth, and all in it and on it; its furniture and its population; its botanical productions and its living creatures. The one God made the world—its hills with their crowns of snow, and its valleys with their fields and flowers; its rivers, lakes, and seas; its mines and minerals; its grasses and herbs; its rock and soils; its climates and physical influences; every nation upon it, and all that supports them and gives them occupation or pleasure. Tokens of His existence are on every side—alike in the atom of sand and the strata of majestic mountains; in the lordly eagle and in the insect that sports away its existence during the brief sunset; as well in the instinct which rules the lower creation, as in the reason which dignifies man. The air around, and the breeze which freshens into a hurricane— the tide which lifts the water of the gulf and harbour with such periodical uniformity; the freshness of spring and the life of summer — all are brought into being by the one God on high. Nothing is self-produced. He is the one Maker. Trees may propagate themselves, but their veins and vessels, their secret chemical elaborations, their life and organism, the fruit of the fig and the oil of the Athenian olive, are from Him. The sculptor does not originate his materials, nor the painter his colours; each finding them as made by the great Artist only recombines and applies them. Demosthenes did not invent the language in which he spoke, any more than the nightingale had taught herself the melody which gushes from her throat. The Creator's inspiration gives not only the love of art and the endow- ments of genius, but He has also supplied what art and genius had wrought upon—the metal out of which the sword of Miltiades had been forged, the parchment on which the laws of Solon had been inscribed, and the ivory and gold out of which the queenly statue of the city- goddess had been constructed. Nor does nature only prove that there is an original vital force, but also that this force, as guided by wisdom and prompted by love, resides in a living personal Intelligence. The world is not eternal, nor is it the result of an eternal series of causes, or the wondrous product of chance. Nay, the more we explore the causes in operation around us, and the farther and higher we carry our analysis of them, the more do we feel them relieved of complexity and converging into unity, and the more clearly do we discern that all causes are themselves but the effects of the First Great Cause, Himself uncaused —the "God that made the world and all things therein."

This conception strikes at the root of polytheism. The Athenians had their gods which they specially claimed, and the nations around them rejoiced in similar property. The gods of the one were not the gods of the other, nor was any alliance recognized among them. Each race had its own tutelar divinity, to whose mythic powers it owed its existence, and sometimes its name. The hill on which Paul stood had its title from one god, and the city had its name from the guardian goddess Minerva—Pallas Athené. But the apostle vindicates the unity of God as sole Creator. He made and filled the earth—"The earth is the Lord's, and the fulness thereof, the world, and they that dwell therein." The Athenians spent their time in continuous inquiries after something new; surely their passion for novelty was now gratified. Creation was a new idea to them. Plato had not dreamed of it; Aristotle had taken it out of the range of possibilities. The relation of matter to mind was not understood among them, nor could they speculate successfully on the origin of the universe. But the apostle's simple statement laid down the truth, that the earth took its being from God's creative power, was not, on the one hand, a fortuitous concourse of atoms, nor, on the other, the result of some necessary law which controlled divinity itself, or acted without the superintendence of a personal governing God. The forms of creation, as shown by modern science, prove it to have been a voluntary act, and not the product of what a French philosopher calls " a necessary force." Nor has the Creator been obliged to repeat Himself. The fossils of the earlier rocks have no analogues among the beds of the tertiaries. Successive acts of creation, and the introduction of a thousand new species, did not exhaust His styles of work. "The Lord God, the Creator of the ends of the earth, fainteth not, neither is weary." He is not, as those Epicureans dreamed, some dim phantom far above the stars in idle and voluptuous indifference; nor is He, as the Stoic argued, the soul of the world, which

> " Lives through all life, extends through all extent,
> Spreads undivided, operates unspent."

God made the earth, and He is above it and apart from it, but yet its active Lord and untiring benefactor; and it is in no sense the complement of His being, or a necessary evolution of His essence. The one Creator is enthroned upon the work of His hands.

Creation is thus ascribed by the apostle to God, and though we cannot comprehend the act or process, we never can doubt it. For, if there has been no creation, then all is eternal, and all is God or an evolution of God. On such a hypothesis there can be no law, no freedom, no personality, and no moral distinctions; for what we term sin would be as really thought or done by God as what we term virtue, since He would be the only thinker and agent in the universe. But, though we cannot understand creation as either the making of something out of nothing, or the eduction of result from latent almighty power, or the image of what is real in the archetypal Mind, we can know it in some of its properties. We can picture a portion of space unfurnished, and then picture it as peopled with worlds. Nor will it avail as an argument against the idea of creation, that it implies change in an unchangeable God; for the purpose to create is eternal, and omnipotence is not changed in essence when it puts forth an effort. The relation of the finite to the infinite is of all things indeed the most perplexing. That the one and that the other exists our consciousness assures us in every act of cognition. To deny the infinite and sink into atheism, or to deny the finite and dream ourselves into pantheism, is a revolt against reason, a vain attempt to burst those limits which are necessarily imposed upon human thought. We enter not on the question as to man's knowledge of the infinite, or as to the form and foundation of his constitutional beliefs. Only it is evident to consciousness that ideas of eternity and infinity surround all our thoughts; for to whatever point of time or of space we reach forth in fancy, we are forced to believe in time and space still stretching beyond. It is true that we can neither grasp infinitude nor span eternity, but we do have a notion of either without a comprehension of them—such a notion as suffices for faith and worship. So feeble is reason out of its sphere, and so true, in fine, is the declaration of the apostle—"Through faith we understand that the worlds were framed by the word of God; so that things which are seen were not made of things which do appear."

And as the sole originator He has the indefeasible right of being sole governor. He is "Lord of heaven and earth," proprietor and ruler of the universe—not earth only, but heaven and earth. The immense spaces that the Greek imagination could roam in, where the sun flamed in splendour, and the moon waxed and waned in serener glory, and the stars shone out like "isles of light," are, when surveyed by the telescopic glass, found to be furnished with innumerable worlds. Nothing like a limit to creation can be discovered; far as man can penetrate he finds star upon star in compacted array. The distant star-dust has been resolved into densely-crowded orbs; and light from the remoter nebulæ must have been two million of years on its journey to us. The Lord of heaven has a kingdom which no imagination can measure in its vastness, nor depict in its variety and grandeur—the firmament thickly strewn with suns and planets. Surely such a one "dwelleth not in temples made with hands." The temples in front of the apostle, around him, and behind him, were the boast of Grecian taste and skill. The gods to whom they were dedicated were supposed, in some vague sense, to fill them. Their respective gods had shrines in them, and claimed them as their residence. They were, indeed, of unsurpassed magnificence. The Theseum was the earliest and most complete; the temple of Wingless Victory was "a thing of beauty;" and there was in front of him the Parthenon— virgin's house, or temple of Minerva—of majestic mass and outline, formed of Pentelican marble, with its forty-six

Doric columns adorned with sculptures and friezes, and its inner walls decorated with choicest paintings. But the Infinite can dwell in no such structure; nor needs He such a domicile. He fills space; infinitude is His temple. "Whither shall I go from thy Spirit? or whither shall I flee from thy presence? If I ascend up into heaven, thou art there: if I make my bed in hell, behold thou art there. If I take the wings of the morning, and dwell in the uttermost parts of the sea; even there shall thy hand lead me, and thy right hand shall hold me." This God whom Paul made known had no rival, no one like Him, no one second to Him; nor could He be supposed to inhabit any edifice built by the hands of man. Such a notion was unworthy of Him; it brought him down to the level of humanity, as if He were one of many tenants, and not the one proprietor. To localize Him would be to degrade Him.

"Neither is He worshipped with men's hands, as though He needed anything;" *worshipped*—served or cared for. The popular heathen idea was that the gods needed to be ministered unto, though the minds of a few thinking men, as Lucretius and Seneca, might rise above such a gross conception. Thus the priest of Apollo remonstrates:—

> "If e'er with wreaths I hung thy sacred fane,
> Or fed the flames with fat of oxen slain,
> God of the silver bow, thy shafts employ,
> Avenge thy servant, and the Greeks destroy."

The god was supposed to be placed under obligation by the service rendered to him, and was expected in equity to repay it. But this notion cannot apply to the Divine

Being, seeing He " giveth to all life, and breath, and all things "—the one universal benefactor. No one has anything which God has not given him; and the highest gift —*life*—conscious being, " life and *breath* "—life and that respiration on which life depends—are from Him; nay, life and *all things*—all that makes life desirable and happy.

He giveth " life," and none but He, the Living One. It is a rill from the Fountain of life. Growth and other qualities belong to plants, such as circulation of sap and respiration by their leaves; but life characterizes man — with its voluntary and involuntary functions, its enjoyments and capabilities, its appetites and instincts, its operations on the world without it, and its conscious possession of its powers within it. Pleasure, glory, and usefulness are bound up with its prolongation. So sweet is it that few choose to part with it, and the cessation of it was regarded by the apostle's hearers as the direst of calamities. He who is our life confers and supports it in His ineffable goodness—for " man liveth not by bread alone."

He giveth " breath," which, as the condition and means of life, is, therefore, singled out by the apostle. Even then the atmosphere was popularly valued as the first of necessary gifts, and, when scientifically examined, its preciousness is not only confirmed, but it becomes a powerful proof of divine unceasing goodness. For the air we breathe is endowed with many qualities, the loss or disturbance of which must be fatal to life. If it lose its gravity, or if its elasticity be changed or become changeable; if it thicken, and darken, and cease to be an invisible medium; if it be deprived of its compressibility, or if any amount of cold could condense it; if the gases composing it were to vary in their proportions; or if it were not universally present, and what is vitiated by respiration purified and restored—animal existence would be extinguished on the face of the earth.

And His bounty is immense, for He giveth " all things." Whatever we have He has given us—the food on our table, and the raiment on our persons, with ability to win them and health to enjoy them. Let there be a scanty harvest, and, when corn cannot be bought with money, there must be famine; let a worm gnaw the cotton plant, and the shadow of death would be cast over Britain—capital useless, gold without circulation, trades unemployed, machinery without motion, empty warehouses, ships without freights, and millions in want of work and bread. Nor let any man boast of being the architect of his own fortune; for the materials out of which he builds it, the skill with which he constructs it, and the propitious season which enables him to rear it without pause or discomfiture—are each of them the gift of the one sovereign benefactor. Discovery, invention, science, art, adventure, commercial shrewdness, literary power, mechanical skill, and political success; the sharp eye that is first to perceive the " tide in the affairs of men ;" and the wary enterprise that launches the vessel upon it—are not self-originated. " Every good gift and every perfect gift is from above, and cometh down from the Father of Lights."

Everything possessed by everyone, without exception of gift or person, is of God's bestowal. God is, therefore, independent of man for His happiness; it wells up from an

exhaustless fountain in His own bosom. Nor is He in need
of such services as are made in human temples—neither
the blood of sacrifices to support, nor the odour of incense
to refresh Him. For He is the one Giver, always giving
and never getting, still bestowing and never repaid—there
being a perpetual outflow, but no reflux. If, therefore,
all that man has be from God, and all he proposes to
supply his divinities with be from the same source, it is
plain that He who gives it, and has so freely parted with
it, is not in need of it. The wretched anthropomorphism
which had crept in among the Jews is thus reproved by
the psalmist—" I will not reprove thee for thy sacrifices,
or thy burnt-offerings, to have been continually before me.
I will take no bullock out of thy house, nor he-goats out
of thy folds: for every beast of the forest is mine, and the
cattle upon a thousand hills. I know all the fowls of the
mountains; and the wild beasts of the field are mine. If
I were hungry, I would not tell thee: for the world is
mine, and the fulness thereof. Will I eat the flesh of
bulls, or drink the blood of goats? Offer unto God
thanksgiving; and pay thy vows unto the most High;
and call upon me in the day of trouble; I will deliver thee,
and thou shalt glorify me." His service must correspond
to His nature, and must, therefore, be spiritual service.
Those who are so liberally provided for by Him, who live
by His bounty and breathe His air, and owe all things to
His goodness, will surely rejoice to bless Him; and when
they feel that they have no claim on His generosity, and
that yet it is so unceasing, will they not invoke their souls
and all within them " to bless His holy name?" " Can a

man be profitable to God as he that is wise may be profitable to himself?" "If thou be righteous, what givest thou Him, or what receiveth He of thine hand?" He is not worshipped with men's hands, but with men's hearts. The silent hymn of a grateful spirit rolls upward to His ear, though no music should be warbled from the lips. "God is a spirit, and they that worship Him must worship Him in spirit and in truth." When Solomon dedicated the temple, he exclaimed under this impression—"But will God in very deed dwell with men on the earth? Behold, heaven, and the heaven of heavens, cannot contain thee, how much less this house that I have built!" And, in his address before the council, Stephen had said in Paul's hearing—"Howbeit the Most High dwelleth not in temples made with hands; as saith the prophet, Heaven is my throne, and earth is my footstool; what house will ye build me, saith the Lord, or what is the place of my rest? hath not my hand made all these things?"

Part II.

Having shown them the divine independence and self-sufficiency, the apostle proceeds to assert the unity of the human race—as being of one origin, and—no matter how widely they may have been scattered—as being guided and controlled by the one God in their migrations and settlements; their history being but the record of His dealings with them, and His regulation of their movements. He adds —"And hath made of one blood all nations of men for to dwell on all the face of the earth, and hath determined the times before appointed, and the bounds of their habitation." All the nations are of one blood or race. The Athenians boasted that they were autochthones—self-produced, or sprung of the soil of Attica, and looked with contempt on surrounding barbarians. But all had a common origin, and none could vaunt themselves over their neighbours. The Greek with that lofty brow—"the dome of thought" —who lived on the idea of beauty, with whom the arts had found a home, and who had a history so grand from the days of Solon, was a brother of the rude Scythian with the low forehead and stolid visage, who wore a coarse vesture of sheepskin, and was as ignorant in .soul as degraded in life. For God "hath *made*—caused—*all nations for to dwell*—settle—on all the face of the earth." Whatever advantage any nation has in the country occupied by it, is due to God. It fills the realm which

God designed for it. Attica had not been chosen by the people on account of its superior qualities, but God chose it for them. It was not Hercules, Cecrops, Pelops, Theseus, or any other ancient mythical leader, that had selected Greece, but God had made the region, and made their forefathers to migrate into it. Bœotia, Sparta, Sicily, and Ionia, with many cities in which they had contended, were sprung of the same stock as themselves. And he who was now bespeaking their attention, whose dark eye and aquiline features showed him to be of a race which they despised, and whose annals they could not appreciate, stood, in point of lineage, on the same level with themselves.

Polytheism is bound up with the notion of distinct and different races. But if all nations be alike in bodily structure, and one blood be in all their veins, and they possess the same range of instinct and appetites, their oneness of origin is demonstrated. That man, no matter what his colour, or stature, or home, is but one species with many varieties, is a truth proved by ethnology, and confirmed by the results of comparative philology. Among the lower creation, the skull of the mastiff differs more from that of the Italian greyhound, than the skull of the European from the central African or the Hottentot, and dogs and horses carried to the hills in India lose their hair and become woolly, like the shawl-goats of the country. Complexion and features are soon altered by climate and physical condition. The third generation of educated and well-fed negroes loses the prognathous type, while filth and famine are known to reduce white victims to a dull and meaningless cast of countenance.

He that made the world and all things therein, is, therefore, God of all the nations. It is a fiction for them to have separate gods, as if each tribe had sprung from a different deity, and owed him homage as lord and guardian. The nations are all brethren, created by the one Divine Being—"Have we not all one Father; hath not one God created us?" It was imagined, too, that the various gods had separate and independent territories, beyond which their jurisdiction did not go, and which they were often obliged to defend against invasion. In the Homeric songs they espouse rival interests, and cabal and quarrel in petty jealousy and revenge. Juno will have her way for her favourites, Venus will not desert hers, Apollo sends a plague upon the Greeks because his priest is insulted, while Jupiter is at his wit's end amid the strifes and antipathies of Olympus. Nay, Minerva (Athené) had contended for the possession of Athens with Neptune, he appealing to a well which had sprung up at the stroke of his trident, and she to an olive which the king had seen her plant on the summit of the Acropolis. The deities of Greece were powerless in Italy, and had neither name nor residence in Persia. Every race had its mythology, and would fight for its idols as readily as for its acres, so that a war between two nations was usually a war between their gods, as well as between their soldiers. But the apostle tells them that the nations, no matter how distant in settlement, unlike in colour, civilization, or worship, descend from a common ancestry, and have a common origin in God. All the power and sovereignty which they assigned to numerous local divinities was, therefore, to be concentrated in one great Being—the Maker of the world, and the Lord of heaven and earth.

And this one Being also "hath determined the times before appointed, and the bounds of their habitations." This doctrine was also taught by Moses—"When the most High divided to the nations their inheritance, when he separated the sons of Adam, he set the bounds of the people according to the number of the children of Israel." The periods of their existence have been defined, and its limits mapped out by God. By the *periods* he means not simply their national duration, but also the crises or turning-points in their national experience. And they had many of them in their own history. Not to speak of such epochs as the return of the Heracleids, the religious mission of Epimenides, the deeds of the Alcmæonids, the despotism of Pisistratus, or the usurpation of the thirty tyrants, there had been the battle of Marathon, when Asiatic invasion was repelled by a gallant handful, and, ten years after, the victorious naval action at Salamis—both of them hairs-breadth escapes for Athens, and both securing against loss of liberty and degradation into a Persian satrapy. These momentous junctures were the fore-appointment of an unrecognized Protector, who settles the limits of nations; for there is a boundary which they can not pass, no matter what their ambition, and what the success of their arms. Their own defeats, and the ostracism of so many of their leaders, had shown this. Miltiades the patriot of Marathon, and Themistocles the hero of Salamis, had been sent into exile for misadventures by which the ambitious projects of Greece were limited, and similar had been the fate of Cimon and Alcibiades. Beyond certain termini Athens could not, with all her skill and valour, carry her arms; an unseen arm defined her bounds, and kept her within them. Minerva could not protect: Xerxes had burned her dwelling, and her spear and shield had neither repelled Philip from the north, nor beaten back the Roman warriors from the west. She stood immovable on that rock, defenceless against the invader. The sudden death of Alexander broke into four principalities the huge empire which he contemplated. But the divine providence is all-embracing, and all history proclaims it. The battle of Zama relieved Italy and civilization from all fears of Carthage. The Saracen power was thrown out of central Europe at a very critical period, and the tide of Turkish fanaticism was finally checked under the walls of Vienna. He blew with His winds and dispersed the Spanish armada. Borodino, Leipzig, Trafalgar, and Waterloo set bounds to France in recent times, and Blenheim and Ramillies in days gone by. Bunker's-hill put an end to British supremacy in the older American colonies. The fall of Sebastopol has retarded the southern march of Russia for a season. The congress of Vienna appointed bounds to the nations on selfish and political principles, but how long shall they last, and how soon may the map of Europe need to be remodelled? "God is the judge; He putteth down one and setteth up another." "He ruleth according to His will in the army of heaven and among the inhabitants of the earth; and none can stay His hand, or say unto him, What doest Thou?"

And the moral purpose of God in the allocation and

government of the different nations was a special one—
"That they should seek the Lord, if haply they might feel
after him, and find Him, though he be not far from every
one of us." To *seek* Him, is to acknowledge and worship
Him, to *feel after* is to grope, as if in darkness, in the dim
light of the gentile world, as he admits, but the last clause
shows that the search after Him might not have been in
vain. He was still within reach of discovery. There were
revelations, not, indeed, in clearness and expressness like
those given to the Jews, but still sufficient to have kept
the nations from atheism, polytheism, and idolatry. The
human race have been formed into nations, not to set up
exclusive national divinities, but that they should know and
adore the *Lord*—or God, as perhaps is the better text. The
finding of God should have been their chief concern; the
acknowledgment and worship of Him the business of their
lives. It might require anxiety and study—there might
be doubts to be overcome and difficulties to be removed—
but what intimations they had they should have followed,
and what surmises rose within them they should have
diligently pursued. They might occasionally blunder, but
they should not have abandoned the inquiry. He that
gropes may stumble, but he is not to desist; he may
weary himself, but still he should cast about for the object
of his search. For God was near to everyone, and therefore his duty was not so hard as the investigation of some
theorem, hopeless from its darkness and the distance of its
conclusion from the first step of its demonstration. God
was near them; their eyes saw the stately steps of His
majesty, and their ears heard the melody of His choirs.

God's great object, as he has thus shown, in organizing nations, in giving them duration, and in raising a mountain here and opening a channel there as their boundaries, is that Himself may be discovered and served. Nations forget this, and think of national greatness—armies, literature, commerce, colonies, and government. Mahometan tribes have at least the "form of godliness," as they begin their public documents with the word "Bismillah"— In the name of God. There is nothing, however, which a nation may legitimately covet that is incompatible with the homage due to God. For, what is science but the discovery of those laws which He has in His wisdom established? What is art but the embodiment of those ideas of beauty, symmetry, and power, which He has implanted in the soul? What is legislation but the human expression of His equity and benignity, which should reign supreme through all ranks and in all the occupations of society? What is commerce but the necessary interchange of the results of that labour which He enables men to perform? What is agriculture but the application of chemical skill to the agencies of the soil?—the skill that He imparts to the agencies which He has arranged and perpetuated; "for His God doth instruct the husbandman to discretion, and doth teach him." And what are manufactures but man's cunning manipulations of those products which He so bountifully provides from His sun and rain, and his versatile adaptation of them to his physical wants? God may be felt and adored in all, and ought to be felt and adored in all.

And why do nations cease to be, and why are their bounds

invaded and broken down? Simply because they do not
own or follow out this divine purpose. They deify themselves, and forget Him who is above them—live but for
themselves, and "feel after" aggrandisement, and not after
Him. The Canaanites were ripe for expulsion on the
invasion of Joshua, and so were the Jews themselves before
the Roman Titus. The liberties of Greece had been
struck down on the fatal field of Chæronea, and many a
nation has been dispossessed of its soil. No people have
an irrevocable charter to it; they possess it only so long
as they are worthy of it, and act in harmony with Him
who planted them in it. And they are displaced that the
new occupant may be put upon its trial, too. In this
light may be viewed those conquests which are establishing modern colonies—the conqueror in turn is judged,
and will, if God decrees it, be in turn exiled. The
Anglo-Saxon has driven back the Celt to the verge of the
Atlantic, but the Sclave may be commissioned to exercise
the same force upon the Anglo-Saxon if he do not service
as God's tenant of His lands. And thus God shall be for
Britain, so long as Britain is for God.

"He is not far from every one of us," says the orator;
"for in Him we live, and move, and have our being."
There seems to be neither climax nor anticlimax in the
expression. But our existence is viewed on all sides—life
and motion are *in Him*—as their sphere; in Him we live,
and move, and *are*—continue to be. This statement gives
no countenance to that mysticism which holds that every
thought and act is not ours, but God's; thus destroying
moral freedom and responsibility. But His existence

includes ours. As we are and walk in the atmosphere, so really are we in God, and in Him we live and move. Every pulsation of our hearts depends on His sovereign beneficence. The nerves have no sensibility, the muscles no motion, the eye no vision, the blood no circulation, the tongue no voice, and the brain no energy but from Him and in Him. Let a single organ be deranged, and death may follow; let some cerebral atoms be disturbed, and reason is destroyed. If "in Him we live, and move, and have our being," then surely He is not far from us. We touch Him on all sides of us, and at every moment. Men need not feel far or long after Him; for He envelopes them with continuous pressure. Nay, they sustain a close relationship to Him—such a relationship as should impress them with His nearness and glory—

For the apostle adds—"As certain also of your own poets have said, For we are also his offspring." The word "for" is a portion of the quotation, which belongs to more poets than one, showing that the doctrine was not unknown to the Grecian mind; and to this fact he gives prominence —"certain poets of your own." The sentiment occurs in two of them, especially in Aratus of Cilicia and in Cleanthes the Stoic. The first, a countryman of Paul's, in his "Phenomena"—an astronomical poem, extolled by Ovid and translated into Latin by Cicero—says—

> "From Jove begin we, whom we should never leave
> Uncelebrated. Of Jove the public walks are full,
> And all the councils of men; the sea is full of him,
> And the shore. All that we always enjoy is from Jove;
> For we are also his offspring;"

this last clause being the apostle's quotation, and forming

half a hexameter. The commencement of the famous
hymn of Cleanthes to Jupiter may be thus rendered—

> " Great Jove, most glorious of the immortal gods,
> Worshipped by many names, always almighty,
> Author of nature, governing by law the universe—
> Hail; for mortals all may lift their voice to thee,
> For we thine offspring are."

Both these poems acknowledge the apostle's doctrine—that
man springs from no idol, but from a superior power often
felt by the bards, if not excogitated by the philosophers
—perceived by the soul, if not always admitted by the
intellect. There had been, as was proved by the dedication
of an altar to an unknown god, a belief with thoughtful
men that there was some Essence or Power higher than all
collected in the Pantheon—a conviction which originated
such a sentiment as that quoted by the apostle. The
Hebrew stranger was not ignorant of their literature, and
could apply it to his purpose. Indeed, he was speaking
their current tongue, though it was not, in many respects,
that of their famous fathers.

The lesson is—that men are God's *offspring*—not His
creation simply, but His offspring. The argument turns on
this idea—the Fatherhood of God. Men are His offspring
—His children possessing the paternal likeness. Sheep
and oxen, the nightingale that warbled among the olives
by the Ilissus, and the bees that ranged among the flowers
on Mount Hymettus, were God's creatures, but not His
offspring. This is in fact the doctrine of the genealogy in
Luke, that Adam was " the son of God;" the doctrine of
the earliest record, that " God created man in His own

image— in the image of God created He him." Many features of that image have not been deleted. Holiness has been obliterated, and happiness has gone with it. But man yet preserves his capability of regaining this departed purity and felicity. And he still possesses his manhood though he is under sentence of death; still enjoys his erect mien, nor have reason and immortality been penally wrested from him. What belongs to his constitution he retains; what belongs to his character has been lost. Still has he those mental powers which fit him for speculation—for the attainment and application of knowledge. Conscious of his being, he can feel impressions from without, and perceive their cause; can think, and recall what he has seen, heard, or known, and can perform acts of mental abstraction and generalization. He can classify and decide, and can imagine and follow out long trains of thought and imagery under the influence of association. Nay, he can not only take cognizance of relations and differences, but ascend to ultimate and universal truths; and he is crowned with the gift of language through which his ideas and convictions are correctly expressed and conveyed. His heart can be stirred to emotion—to love or hatred, to joy or grief, to anger or gratitude, to fear what is to come or to hope for it, according to its character. And he is endowed with conscience—a witness and judge of his actions—God's vicegerent within him—while he is sensible of his moral freedom, that he is no series of sensational phenomena, no victim of impressions which he cannot control, or of mechanical laws which bind him in links of stern necessity.

These are features of God's image borne by His offspring —intelligence, liberty, personality, and conscience. Man, therefore, stands in a nearer and more tender relation to God than any other creature on earth—being to some extent still a shechinah—the Divinity resident within him. His life is sacred, because he bears the image of God. Mind in some sense belongs to the lower creation; but reason is not theirs, nor conscience, nor that higher spiritual nature by which man approaches and resembles God, and God by His Spirit works upon man. Look at that horse, he is strong, and "paweth in the valley," but he cannot rise in idea beyond his rider and his groom. "The ox knoweth his owner," and forms no higher conception; "and the ass his master's crib," with no apprehension of a world beyond.

> " The lamb thy riot dooms to bleed to-day,
> Had he thy reason, would he skip and play ?
> Pleased to the last he crops the flowery food,
> And licks the hand just raised to shed his blood."

Is it not godlike on the part of man to be lord of the lower creation, a divine representative to them? Is it not godlike for " the spirit of man" to know " the things of a man," even as " the Spirit of God knoweth the things of God?" Is it not godlike to be able to say as God says —" I know all the fowls of the mountains?" Is it not godlike to be able to do as God does, to " tell the number of the stars and call them all by their names?" to adapt nature for every purpose, even for the instantaneous transmission of thought? Is it not godlike for him, by his faculty of invention, to imitate God's power of creation ? Is it not godlike for him to have all things subservient to him, for he is an end to himself, at the same time as the means of glorifying his Creator? Certain of their own poets had said—"For we are also His offspring;" and one of their own philosophers had said—"On earth there is nothing great but man, in man there is nothing great but mind." So true it is, that even in fallen humanity, the divine image is still to be found—a protest against idolatry.

And man, as God's offspring, feels an instinctive impulse to recognize his Divine Father; has the means of knowing Him, of understanding this filial relationship, and profiting by it. The child calls for help when in danger, and presents its thanks when relief has been vouchsafed. It seeks to know the Divine will, as did the Greeks at Delphi; it is conscious of having offended, and devotes a victim. It hopes for some home nearer the Father when it leaves the world—some Elysian field, such as many could picture whom the apostle addressed. Idolatry is a confession of man's need that he must know his Father; the heart cannot be at rest without some deity to look up to and adore, to trust in and to obey. Polytheism may be irrational, but atheism is unnatural. To say that there are many gods is folly, but to say that there is no God is treason against man's own constitution, "for we are also His offspring"—not products simply, but children, formed, fed, and clothed; mentally and morally endowed by Him whose image we bear, though its brightness has been darkened by sin. What a blessed doctrine, then, that we are the divine offspring—children of one father. How high our dignity! how rich our patrimony! Wherever

we are, in whatever portion of His universe, we are still
in His house—our home.   We can never outstep our heri-
tage.   The Father has fitted nature not merely to supply
our wants, but also to minister to our delight—the glitter
of the star and of the dew-drop, the colour and scent of
the flower, freshness and beauty for the eye, and song and
melody for the ear.   Our Father's house is not barely
furnished, but richly ornamented.   Rocks are piled into
hoary mountains and picturesque heights; the woods are
budding forth into life in spring, laden with foliage in
summer, or swinging their great boughs to the tempest of
winter; the sky folds its curtains and trims its lamps; the
waters dance in torrents and leap in cascades, as well as
fill the seas; there is gold as well as iron, gems as well as
granites, the blush and fragrance of the blossom, as well
as the sweetness and abundance of the fruit.   The human
frame, too, has symmetry as well as strength—possesses
far more than is merely essential to life and work; the eye,
lip, and brow are rich in expression and power.   There is
not only the power of thought essential to business and
religion, but there is the garniture of imagination, poetry
as well as science, music in addition to speech, ode and
oracle as well as fact and doctrine in scripture, the lyre of the
bard no less than the pen of the apostle.   Above sensation
there rises the power of discovery—invention blends with
experience.   In man and around him there is not mere
provision for necessities; there are profuse luxuries.
"His offspring" walk in the lustre of His love.   It rejoices
them to know that the power which governs is no dark
phantom veiled in mystery; no majestic and all-controlling

force—a mighty and shadowless sceptre; no mere omniscience—an eye that never slumbers; no dim Spirit, having its only consciousness in the consciousness of man—but a Father with a father's heart to love us, and to the yearnings of which we may ever appeal—a father's ear to listen to us, and a father's hand to bless with kind and continued benefactions. And, as we have wandered, shall not each of us say—"I will arise and go unto my Father?" Will not He accept the returning child, giving us the adoption of sons, revealing Himself graciously through Christ the Elder Brother who leads us to cry in true filial devotion—"Our Father which art in heaven?"

In the next verse the apostle states his inference—"Forasmuch then as we are the offspring of God, we ought not to think that the Godhead is like unto gold, or silver, or stone, graven by art and man's device." At that moment the speaker stood in view of such idols and sculptures. Art had reached its perfection; device had exhausted itself in forms of sublimity and beauty. The market-place was thronged with the statues of the gods. The Acropolis before him had three statues of the great goddess, one of them the original image, which, like that of Diana at Ephesus, was believed to have fallen from Jupiter; another of them, in the shrine of the Parthenon, made of ivory and gold, the masterpiece of Phidias; and the third, the colossal image of the same divinity, towering in front of him, armed, and on guard—the top of whose spear might be seen by the mariner crossing the Saronic gulf. He was in the midst of a crowd of metal and marble deities, the like of which for symmetry and stateliness, for loveliness and majesty, no other nation had ever produced. But he does not denounce them and endanger himself; he appeals to his hearers, and presents an argument which their acute spirit could scarcely fail to appreciate. The neuter term rendered " Godhead," signifies the divine nature or essence; *graven by art and man's device*—means, " sculpture of the art and ingenuity of man."

The argument, then, is—being the offspring of God, we ought not to think that the Divine nature can ever be imaged in metal or stone, no matter what skill and art may be employed in the sculpture. Our filial relation to God should teach us this. It is a spiritual relation, and should convince us of the spirituality of the God-head. We cannot image ourselves, far less God. What is spiritual in us, what makes us the offspring of God, can neither be pencilled on canvas, or be carved by the chisel. The portrait, or the statue which flows from the furnace are not we, they are only an effigy of us, or rather only of our external appearance. Vital action, mental power, and spiritual susceptibility, cannot be so depicted. True a statue may be made, and it may resemble a man in form, attitude, and drapery. The likeness may be so vivid as to startle you; and as you gaze you almost expect it to move and speak. But it is chill and changeless—a lump of immobility—not even representing fully the shell or corporeal tabernacle of man. For much in it is beyond the reach of such vulgar delineation—the nerves conveying sensations and transmitting volitions; the lungs at work in their chemical laboratory; the heart in its dilatations, contractions, and propulsion of the vital fluid; the blood in its rapid arterial and venous courses, depositing tissues and clearing itself from impurities; the swelling and straining of the muscles and tendons; the motions and secretions of the joints; the secret functions of the skin; the optical wonders of the eye; the acoustic chambers of the ear; and the mighty and mysterious action of the brain—that complex process, in short, which we call life. Man's art and device cannot reproduce his living self in gold, silver, or stone.

Still more as those organs are his, but not he, therefore what he really is—his reason, soul, conscience, genius, and immortality—defy all representation. No power can shape them, Zeuxis could not paint them; Praxiteles could not figure them; gold, silver, and stone cannot body them forth. The apostle's thought then is—If as the offspring of one God, we cannot produce any likeness of ourselves, containing this relationship to Him, how can we imagine that we can produce any likeness of Him, containing His relationship to us. Spirituality is lost by being shadowed out to sense. How shall we depict His infinitude or omnipotence, His omniscience, His goodness and truth, or any of those qualities which have the reflection of themselves within us, and our possession of which proves us His offspring? If you cannot picture out the godlike in man, why attempt to picture out God Himself? If the image defy you to grasp and embody it, why dare to make trial upon the original? Idolatry is therefore false as well as foolish; his own likeness, far less the likeness of his Father, man cannot fabricate. Give the artist precious gold and silver, so ductile to his hand, and so brilliant in the polish which they take from it; or give him the pure and veinless marble of Pentelicus, out of which he can produce a shape so exquisite in limb and feature, and what is the result? The so-called likeness is only that of the outer form of a bold and graceful man, or a beautiful and lovely woman. The statues of their gods were quite the same as those of their heroes, sages, and orators, with the exception of some symbol—painted thunder or a crown of glory. The uninitiated eye could not tell the one from the other—the man from the god. Man's own dignity is a living argument against idolatry and polytheism. How absurd in him, therefore, so to limit and degrade his object of worship.

According to this report of his address, the apostle did not pursue farther his exposure of idolatry. He left his hearers to their own reflections—to follow out the lessons which their own poets had suggested. By knowing what they were themselves, they would come to know what God was. One, indeed, dares not gaze upwards on the sun as he pours out his burning radiance, but he may contemplate his image in the lake or river at his feet. Men may not pierce to the uncreated splendour, but they may see God in themselves—the likeness of the Father in His child. While we cannot believe with some modern philosophers that the physical creation is unable to prove to us the existence of God; while we differ from that notion of cause which those thinkers maintain, and believe it to be a reality, and not merely a logical form of thought—still we hold that man's mental and moral constitution presents the highest and fullest argument for the existence, personality, and character of the Supreme. Man knows God because he knows himself, or perceives the image of the All-Father within him. The revelations which God has made in scripture, he is enabled to understand in the same way, or with the same intuitional assistance. The terms employed to represent the character and attributes of God, I can understand only as they are descriptive of properties or processes in myself. If I am told that God possesses knowledge, I gather the meaning of the statement by a reference to my own mind and its information. Or, if I am told that God loves or hates, then, knowing what these emotions are within myself, I instinctively ascribe them to Him in infinite purity and degree.

Part III.

Changing his theme, the apostle advances—" And the times of this ignorance God *winked* at "—literally " overlooked." That is to say, He did not declare his special disapprobation of them, and sent no heralds with articulate denunciations of them. His oracles were given only to one nation. Man was left to the exercise of his own reason, and the results of his idolatry should have checked him. The argument had just concluded with this idea—that man's own nature should have taught him the spirituality of the divine nature. There was therefore no apology for " this ignorance." But still it was ignorance—lamentable ignorance, and the temples and statues of the Acropolis were a sad memorial and witness of it. The eye of Greece was sealed in spiritual gloom. It did not look within it to discover its own dignity, or above it to obtain a glimpse of the divine glories. There had been guesses at the truth, and crude and vicious idolatry with correspondent tales of mythology had sometimes been reprobated as a national scandal. But the mass of the people were never reached by such speculations; to them the idol was the god, and no mere symbol or representative of an unseen person or power. In fact the absence of faith produced idolatry. Man could not endure as " seeing Him who is invisible," and longed to have a palpable god, one that he could handle and carry about with him—one on his hearth as well as in his temple.

Actuated by this very principle, the Jews asked a king; losing faith in a divine, invisible Sovereign, the Lord of Hosts, their Guardian, they clamoured for a visible leader with helmet and sword to lead them forth to battle. And polytheism was the natural result of idolatry. The various powers of nature in operation around them could only be pictured by symbols, and each symbol soon rose to be an independent divinity. The omnipresence of the one God was lost sight of, or divided as a domain of numerous gods. His thousand modes of appearance and operation were deified. The tokens of His presence were hailed as indications of separate gods; the movements of His arm were personified, and temples were built on the prints of His feet. What higher knowledge and faith are possessed by us!

> " There's not a strain to memory dear,
>   Nor flower in sacred grove;
>   There's not a sweet note warbled there,
>   But minds us of thy love.
> O Lord, our Lord, and spoiler of our foes,
> There is no light but Thee, with Thee all beauty glows."

But the period of divine forbearance had expired. Such ignorance God had overlooked, " but now commandeth all men everywhere to repent"—chargeth this on everyone everywhere—to repent. " Now " is opposed to the past " times." He had overlooked such ignorance then, but his command is urgent now—no person is exempted, and no place is omitted. The men of Athens were under the injunction; with all their boasted wisdom, the proud Stoic, the light-hearted Epicurean, and the volatile populace were solemnly charged by the great God to repent. The command was new indeed, for it had been recently given, and it was to repent—to desist from those follies, to feel their guilt, and look to God for deliverance. A complete change of mind was implied; they were to unlearn their past creed and abandon their previous life, for Christianity proclaimed no truce, and admitted no. compromise. And the grand and solemn reason is affixed, that a period of judgment is coming and inquest would be made, for He who had issued the command would examine into the treatment it had met with. Unless they repented, they could not meet God in the judgment with hope of acceptance.

And that judgment-day was fixed—" Because He hath appointed a day in the which He will judge the world in righteousness." The judge is the great God, "Lord of heaven and earth." He simply changes His throne of majesty into a tribunal. He has the right to issue the command to repent, and He has the right to inquire if it be complied with. He is not, as those Epicureans thought, indifferent to or unobservant of the actions of men, for He legislates now, and He will judge hereafter. Nor is he, as those Stoics dreamed, so much identified with His universe as a portion of Himself that he cannot sever Himself from it, and sit in judgment upon it as responsible to Him. Nay, the period of the judgment is irrevocably set down —a period known only to the Judge Himself. It is not left to the course of events, but every day leads to and prepares for the "last day," when the human species shall have completed its cycle. It will not be antedated, and it cannot be postponed. And the world is to be judged—all its population—whatever their character or country. The judges of the Areopagus shall stand before a higher tribunal. No resistance will avail. No room is there for escape, for all must appear; the order of the judge cannot be set aside, and there is no moment for repentance, for time has been completed. Solemn thought for a human spirit to be arraigned before its Creator, whose eye sees at once its entire history—motive as well as action, wishes that may never have been expressed, desires that would have shuddered at their own gratification, and misdeeds which had long since faded into oblivion. Judgment implies omniscience, a perfect comprehension of the whole character of every man. If "in God we live and move, and have our being," He knows us, and each of us may say—" O Lord, Thou hast searched me, and known me. Thou knowest my down-sitting and mine uprising; Thou understandest my thought afar off. Thou compassest my path, and my lying down, and art acquainted with all my ways. For there is not a word in my tongue, but lo, O Lord, thou knowest it altogether. Thou hast beset me behind and before, and laid thine hand upon me."

Nor can the world object to be judged. Every man has been created by God for Himself, and all his mental and moral endowments have been conferred upon him with this view. Instinct may not bring along with it such a result, but the gift of reason and freedom implies responsibility. We have been made by God to live to God, and this is the standard of judgment; or, putting it into a more direct evangelical form, God has provided salvation for us, and may He not ask whether we have accepted it, or whether we have scorned His gift and destroyed ourselves? For all that God has made him, for all that God has done for him, for his belief as well as for his life, is man accountable to God.

While God, who creates, upholds, and governs us, has the right, and, from His omniscience, has the qualification to judge us, we are assured at the same time of His perfect rectitude. He will judge the world *in righteousness*—not only in the exercise of perfect equity, but His equity necessitates such a judgment. Justice belongs to His nature, and characterizes all his proceedings. Without it as the unchanging substratum, mercy might degenerate into weakness, and power stretch itself into tyranny. "Just and true are Thy ways, Thou King of saints;" "Thou only art holy." His laws are the expression of His rectitude, and His providence exemplifies it. In it Adam was expelled from Paradise, and the old world drowned—Israel sent into captivity, and ultimately dispersed. In it, and by its process of self-vindication, the drunkard undermines his health and shortens his life; nay, in the midst of many disturbing influences, vice is, in a true sense, its own punishment, and virtue its own reward. "Verily there is a reward for the righteous, verily He is a God that judgeth in the earth." "With righteousness shall He judge the world, and the people with equity."

For He cannot err, or be charged with unconscious injustice or partiality. A human judge may blunder, may fail to identify the criminal, or leave out of view some aggravating or some extenuating element in the evidence. His mind may be prejudiced insensibly by the face of the culprit, or swayed by the apparent candour of some hostile and unscrupulous witness. Even on that hill where the judges of the Areopagus had sat under night, that they might simply hear proof on either side and be unmoved by appearances, sentences at variance with equity had been pronounced, in spite of their rigid impartiality and severe and patient investigation; for they could not always get at the facts, or did not in every case give each fact its just weight in their deliberations. But the divine judge can never be imposed on. " All things are naked and open unto the eyes of Him with whom we have to do;" all motives and thoughts, all the complex elements that mould and make up character, are utterly known to Him. The scales of His justice are so delicate, that they vibrate under what would be utterly inappreciable before an earthly tribunal. As a man really is, so shall he appear before God, but man takes cognizance only of what appears, not what is.

For even the universe presents infallible witness. The following is the awful statement of one well qualified so to speak—" Whilst the atmosphere we breathe is the ever-living witness of the sentiments we have uttered, the waters and the more solid materials of the globe bear equally enduring testimony of the acts we have committed. If the Almighty stamped on the brow of the first murderer the indelible and visible mark of his guilt, He has also established laws by which every succeeding criminal is not less irrevocably chained to the testimony of his crime; for every atom of his mortal frame, through whatever changes its several particles may migrate, will still retain, adhering to it through every combination, some movement derived from that very muscular effort by which the crime itself was perpetrated. The soul of the negro whose fettered body, surviving the living charnel-house of his infected prison, was thrown into the sea to lighten the ship, that his Christian master might escape the limited justice at length assigned by civilized man to crimes whose profits had long gilded their atrocity, will need, at the last great day of human account, no living witness of his earthly agony. When man and all his race shall have disappeared from the face of our planet, ask every particle of air still floating over the unpeopled earth, and it will record the cruel mandate of the tyrant. Interrogate every wave which breaks unimpeded on ten thousand desolate shores, and it will give evidence of the last gurgle of the waters which closed over the head of his dying victim, confront the murderer with every corporeal atom of his immolated slave, and in its still quivering movements he will read the prophet's denunciation of the prophet-king—*Thou art the man.*" But even this strange and indelible record, legible only to the eye of omniscience, is imperfect; for there are many thoughts and purposes, hidden volitions and cravings, which belong solely to mind, and make no external impress. Yet these are not unknown, nor are they forgotten. They form the character, and that character meets with infallible judgment; or, according to the impressive figure, " the judgment is set, and the books are opened." Everything takes place in God, for " in Him we live and move, and have our being," and in God is it therefore laid up beyond possibility of error or oblivion. Nor can God pronounce any verdict not holy in the highest sense, and equitable to the fullest extent. "Every word of God is pure; He is a shield unto them that put their trust in Him." No sentence of His can be improved —"Add not thou unto His words, lest He reprove thee, and thou be found a liar."

Nor, perhaps, is it rash to say that our past history is so laid up also in ourselves, that God's touch can at any time evoke it into sudden consciousness. "Memory," said one of their own poets, "is the queen of things." Its storehouse is vast and secret, and what appears to be forgotten may in a moment start up under some impulse or association. The mind apparently never ceases to act, even in sleep, for a person suddenly roused wakes always out of a dream, and probably nothing ever really passes into absolute oblivion. Abnormal states of mind in somnambulism and in cerebral disease, prove the amazing power and compass of involuntary recollection—in repeating long arguments or pieces of poetry, in depicting scenes long ago visited, and in speaking languages unused since childhood—feats found to be utterly impossible in a sound and healthy condition. Innumerable instances of this nature show that, in all likelihood, no sensation received by the mind, no judgment formed, desire entertained, decision come to, acquisition made, or emotion felt by it, ever fades into nothing, as if it never had been; but that all is treasured up in it, and needs but a word from Him who made it to bring it into light, and to reproduce in a moment to a man all he ever was, or thought, or did, so that in a moment of intense and surprising consciousness he shall live over again the whole of his existence! May not he that stands before the tribunal be thus enabled to read himself in the light which God's eye flashes in upon him?

Thus every one at His awful tribunal will admit the justness of that decision pronounced upon him—not decision in the ordinary forensic sense, implying either previous ignorance or doubt before trial, but decision as the simple declaration of a living omniscience. Every one will feel that "God is justified when He speaks, and clear when He judges." For were any one even of those condemned to have doubts, or to feel that God had acted hardly towards him, such a sense of injury would nerve him to the endurance of all the agony which might be sent upon him. "He will judge the world in righteousness," and show it to be so. Believers are not justified by works, though they may be judged by them. Their character is declared to be, not the foundation of their acceptance, but the token or fruit of their union to Christ, and their love to Him; it is their service to Him by service to His, and their preparation for the kingdom prepared for them. Divine grace has so changed and blessed them, that they prove their meetness for heaven by their possession of its spirit—a spirit of love to Jesus and all who bear His image. The test is a sure one, and the rectitude of the judge cannot be impugned—"Inasmuch as ye have done it unto one of the least of these my brethren, ye have done it unto me."

But there is another and a special revelation. What the apostle had said might be admitted, for it is what the religion of nature could not deny. But he adds the startling peculiarity—"He will judge the world by that man whom He hath ordained"—*by that man*—in Him— as His representative and image. By a man? What would his audience now think? He had a few seconds ago been censuring their idolatry—telling them that statues can never be a likeness of Deity, and that He does not reside in hand-made shrines—and how then will He by a man do this solemn and divine work of judging the world? The apostle was not allowed to explain, or he could have easily solved the mystery as to the character and relations of the man whom He hath *ordained*—set apart to this high office. For that man is more than man. A man He is, and we rejoice to know it, but his manhood is a second and assumed nature. He is God—the Son of God—equal with God. That omniscience and equity which are requisite in a judge, meet in Him. "The Father judgeth no man, but hath committed all judgment unto the Son, and hath given Him authority to execute judgment also, because He is the Son of man." In His mediatorial position He is the Father's servant, and the judgment is the last great function of the mediatorial reign. Therefore the man Jesus is judge—He who loved us and died for us—and His question is, have you relied on my love, and accepted my atonement? Farther, man has been placed in a new position by Christ's incarnation. He has been allied to Divinity, that he might be brought back to the divine favour and image. Our nature had died under the penalty of the old covenant, but a new representative man has been given us, that a new spiritual life might be originated and developed within us. The Word was made flesh, that flesh might become divine. By Christ's becoming one of us another epoch commences, and a new path is opened up through our union with Him. God became man to win man back to Himself, and He who is the second Adam—"that man," man's Saviour and Brother—is to be judge.

And O what consolation in the thought that He is to be judge! How appalling the prospect of standing "before this holy Lord God"—of being enveloped and permeated with His brightness—of being conscious that every part of our naked nature is so filled with His presence and inspection! But He who is on that judgment-seat is Christ —the man Christ Jesus, with His heart of sympathy and tongue of comfort. And though He come in glory, surrounded by a dense and bright retinue—the armies of heaven following after Him; and though He seat Himself on the great white throne, amidst the wreck of elements and convulsions of nature, and other tokens of homage to His presence and majesty, yet He is our kinsman clothed in our nature—that very nature in which He lay on the Virgin's bosom, and died on the accursed tree.

And the proof is not lacking—"Whereof He hath given assurance unto all men in that He hath raised Him from the dead;" *given assurance*—literally afforded faith or the means of belief. How the apostle would have developed the proof we know not, for at this period he was rudely interrupted. Into the array of proof we do not enter, and we may find subsequent occasion to refer to it. But we may say, that the resurrection of Jesus proved His mission to be divine, and showed Him to be the head of humanity, and, therefore, entitled to be its judge. His resurrection is also the proof that all men are to be raised; not a token that they may be raised, but a pledge that they shall be raised. As by His resurrection He becomes judge, so they are raised in order to be judged. And thus assurance of judgment is given unto all men.

The apostle could easily have given them indubitable evidence that Christ had been raised from the dead; as, for example, that His tomb was guarded, and that the sentinels only befooled themselves and those who suborned them, by their contradictory announcement—" His disciples came and stole Him away while we slept." Roman soldiers asleep on special duty, and forward to confess it—asleep on a post which they were warned might be assailed—all of them asleep at the same instant, and when under orders of unusual strictness—asleep, and yet able to tell what happened, what was done, and who did it, too, when their eyes were shut in unanimous slumber—all of them asleep, and yet not one of them awakened by the noise and concussion of the earthquake which preceded the resurrection! Nor had these disciples any motive to do the act imputed to them. They had no idea that their Master should rise again, and all their hopes were buried along with Him. They could, therefore, never dream of such an attempt as stealing His body, it being of no use to them, as they had no romance to base upon its absence; and if they had, the eleven poltroons who " forsook Him and fled " at the sight

of the soldiers in the garden, would never have ventured
to attack a Roman guard of sixteen men under the bright
moonlight of the eastern heavens.   Farther, He who had
risen appeared to His former friends who could identify
Him, and on the spot, too, where He had been put to
death.   It was not as if one supposed to have risen in
Glasgow should be said to have appeared first in Inverness,
where he was a comparative stranger.   It was not as if it
were alleged that one had risen, but that the story was
only first heard of half a century after the imagined event.
At the time when, and in the place where He had died and
been buried, did the Lord appear, when full investigation
could be made into all the circumstances, and into the
testimony of crowds of living witnesses.   But those who
should have originated and conducted the inquiry shrank
from it under the impression that the result would not be
to their satisfaction, and resorted to the miserable refuge of
authority, "straitly threatening" the witnesses to say no
more on the matter; while they who were "witnesses of
these things" had no end to gain, and no worldly advantage to secure; on the contrary, proscription and death
resulted from the avowal of their belief in this momentous
tenet.   And the apostle might have referred, in conclusion,
to his own conversion, when the Lord appeared to him and
gave him that commission under which he was at that
moment speaking on the Areopagus.

But the simple mention of the "resurrection" led to
a burst of laughter on the part of some, and destroyed
all anxiety to hear any farther on the part of the whole.
They did not deem it worth their while to listen any

longer; and they felt so and said so, just when the argument had reached a crisis, and a chain of evidence was about to be woven—just when Christ was about to be specifically preached to them, they contemptuously shut the preacher's mouth, and told him that really they had heard enough, that their curiosity was satisfied, and that it would be a mere waste of time for him to proceed. The apostle must have felt this treatment very keenly; never had he had such an opportunity, and never had he failed so egregiously. He had made no general impression. The anxiety to hear him had been keen, but he could not even command attention to the close of his address. No wonder that after this severe disappointment he entered Corinth, the next Greek city he visited, as he says, " in weakness, and in fear, and in much trembling." Not that the preacher could blame himself, as if he had selected a wrong topic, or had not handled it with sufficient skill and power; but apprehensions of his success in southern Greece seem to have filled him with despondency. He was in a new scene, and the synagogue seems to have afforded no basis of operations. He had often battled with Jewish obstinacy, and to some purpose; had been in contact with Cyprian licentiousness, and had succeeded to a marvel; had mingled with the dissolute populations of Antioch, and gained hundreds of converts; had so impressed the rude men of Lycaonia that they took him for a god; had been the victim of Roman ferocity in Philippi, yet had formed a church; had preached in Thessalonica, and reaped compensatory fruit — but in Athens, the eye of Greece, where he first confronted " the wisdom of this world," he could not even succeed in stirring opposition or stimulating inquiry. He would rather have been persecuted than put off so gently in this way —would rather have been scourged as a peace-disturber than dismissed as a crazy enthusiast. What he had said had told so little upon his volatile audience that they affronted him by breaking up and leaving him in the midst of his harangue. Need we wonder that the apostle hasted to be off, or that we read—"So Paul departed from among them?" Though he was afterwards in Greece, nay, at Corinth, he never again visited Athens. But his work was not wholly fruitless: "Howbeit certain men clave unto him; among the which was Dionysius *the Areopagite*"— one of the judges of the Areopagus, and, therefore, of the best blood in the city—"and a woman named Damaris, and others with them." This woman must have been of some note that she is thus named. Possibly she belonged to the notorious class of Hetairai—mistresses—the class to which Aspasia, Lais, Phryne, and Lastheneia belonged— courtezans, indeed, and usually slaves or foreigners, though some of them, by superior education, boldness, and wit, rose to influence in the state, and held in their houses reunions of its chief statesmen, philosophers, and orators.

The Greek worship, with its magnificent architecture and sculpture, was a powerless institution. It had failed to lead men to true theology. The speculations of Thales, Pythagoras, and Zeno on the origin and phenomena of the universe, could not bring their disciples to this truth— "God made the world, and all things therein; He is Lord of heaven and earth." And though Socrates reclaimed many to the study of themselves, this self-knowledge made little or no impression on the masses. For their religion had a disastrous influence over their lives; the actions of their gods being a stimulus to depravity. Men became, like their objects of worship, sensual and debased, and gloried in pleading the example of the gods—examples we should blush to describe. As the mind did not arrive at truth, the conscience could not find repose. A veil lay upon the other world, and they scoffed at a resurrection. As the apostle was about to expatiate upon its certainty, they rose in their levity and bade him desist—they could not tolerate the mention of it. When " the man, the best of all his time, the most wise and just," stood on Mars-hill and received sentence of death as "a setter forth of strange gods," he is reported to have said—" To die is one of two things: for either the dead may be annihilated, and have no sensation of anything whatever; or, as it is said, there is a certain change and passage of the soul from one place to another. And if it is a privation of all sensation, as it were a sleep in which the sleeper has no dream, death would be a wonderful gain. For I think that if any one, having selected a night in which he slept so soundly as not to have had a dream, and having compared this night with all the other nights and days of his life, should be required on consideration to say how many days and nights he had passed better and more pleasantly than this night throughout his life, I think that not only a private person, but even the great king himself, would find them easy to number in comparison with other days and nights. If, therefore, death is a thing of this kind, I say it is a gain; for thus all futurity appears to be nothing more than one night. But if, on the other hand, death is a removal from hence to another place, and what is said be true, that all the dead are there, what greater blessing can there be than this, my judges? For if, on arriving at Hades, released from these who pretend to be judges, one shall find those who are true judges, and who are said to judge there, Minos and Rhadamanthus, Æacus and Triptolemus, and such others of the demigods as were just during their own life, would this be a sad removal? At what price would you not estimate a conference with Orpheus and Musæus, Hesiod and Homer? I indeed should be willing to die often if this be true." Thus doubt and fluctuation seem to have disturbed the mind of the sage, though he is depicted as arguing elsewhere the immortality of the soul as boldly and truly as unassisted reason ever could. But his philosophy had fallen so dead, that the Athenians, with all their love of news, declined to listen to a new appeal on the subject from a bold and eloquent stranger. What was speculation with Socrates is certainty with us. Our assurance is, that the spirit at death is conveyed to the bright spirit-world—the throne of God in its centre, and the Lamb the object of enraptured homage; that the true and the good are there; Abel and the martyrs; Enoch and the antediluvian witnesses; Abraham and the patriarchs; Aaron and the spiritual priesthood; David and the holy kingdom; Elijah and the prophets; the apostles and the early church; the saints of all ages and countries—all who have believed on Christ, done His work, and borne His image. What a glorious assembly to mingle with and enjoy, as we hold fellowship and offer worship with them—partakers all of us of the " common salvation."

But " the world by wisdom knew not God." Nay, in those degenerate days there was such indifference produced by this so-called wisdom, that "philosophers" did not deign to listen to what was highest philosophy. Pride of intellect has ever been the hardest barrier against the truth : " Seest thou a man wise in his own conceit? there is more hope of a fool than of him." " Simplicity and godly sincerity " were wanting at Athens, and the truth was rejected. Yes, even Athens, of which Lucretius sings—

> " Athens, of peerless name, to savage man
> First taught the blessings of the cultured field,
> His life remodelled, and with laws secured.
> She, too, the soul's sweet solaces first oped
> When erst the sage she reared, whose boundless breast
> Swelled with all science, and whose lips promulged "—

this Athens was indifferent to the noblest of blessings, which had brought down the "hidden manna" from heaven, with laws which are the expression of infinite love, and joys which spring from the fellowship of the soul with its Creator, as it becomes more intensely conscious of bearing His image and possessing His love. Yes; Athens, blinded by its wisdom and its worldliness, saw no truth nor beauty in the divine philosophy conveyed to it by a Jewish traveller in whose glance—

> " There lurked that nameless spell
> Which speaks, itself unspeakable."

May we not, in fine, fetch a lesson to ourselves? Are there no idols among us in this age of hero-worship? We allude not to the strange fact, that some months in our years are named from Roman idols, and that all the days of our week are named from Saxon idols. But is there no pride of reason nursed by intellectual ascendancy? In what does homage to force or genius, irrespective of the end to which they have been applied, and in oblivion of the One Giver, differ from idolatry or nature-worship—from that process which made a god of tutelar power, and a goddess of patriotic wisdom? Are there not those that bow the knee to Mammon in the exchange, who would not bow it to Jupiter in a temple? Are there not many who in boasted illumination cast aside the teaching of scripture, or who, in the enjoyment of wealth and power, feel not their need of it? This age is a strange one. There are open defenders of atheism, impugners of sabbatic obligation, and public revilers of Christianity, as if it were effete and worthless—denying God's existence and unhallowing God's day. One has written a book to show that religion is so feeble that it has had no influence on civilization; and another in a neighbouring nation, who is so proud as to believe and call himself a combination of Aristotle and Paul, proclaims that new gods should be introduced and adored—heroes and saints—Moses and Homer, Confucius and Shakspeare, Hercules and Frederick the Great. It is one hypothesis that man is but an elevated monkey, and that he and the universe around him are but developments out of the atoms of an ancient fire-mist; and it is another, quite in keeping, that the heavens, which of old declared the glory of God, now declare only the glory of Newton and Laplace. That God had become man, was once a faith to be gloried in, but with many the proposition has been reversed, and their creed is, that man has become God. Some maintain the grossest materialism—that there is no spirit in man; some, admitting that they are the "offspring of God," refuse to call Him Father, and unfilially style Him Nature; and others deny the responsibility of man for his belief even to that God who presents him with evidence, and has conferred upon him powers by which he can sift it and come to a right conclusion. Are not "wise men after the flesh" dealing with the gospel as the Epicureans and Stoics dealt with Paul? A resurrection to the one and the other sect was impossible in theory, and undesirable in hope; for with them the soul itself was supposed to sink into unconsciousness at death, either by being dissolved or being absorbed into the great sum of existence. So it is that philosophic minds still refuse the revelation of Christ, or strip it of all that is distinctive and remedial, before they profess to receive it. For some it is too simple, and for others too mysterious; one class objects that it takes too little notice of man's present interests; and another, that its morality is too transcendental. Inspiration is pared down, and the authority of scripture is lowered by this party; and by that party the truths of scripture are thought to be good enough for the age which produced them, but deficient in breadth and adaptation for the enlightened nineteenth century. By such seekers after wisdom, the gospel is dismissed as quietly and effectually as was its great apostle from Mars-hill.

O that all this wildness and passion were stilled by the remembrance that He "hath appointed a day in which He will judge the world in righteousness by that man whom He hath ordained—whereof He hath given assurance unto all men in that He hath raised Him from the dead." Is Christ risen—ay or no? The controversy turns on this— Is it fact or fable? If His resurrection be a demonstrable reality, then surely His voice must be listened to, and His warnings pondered. His gospel has a claim which no other form of truth presents—it is God's immediate and authentic revelation. It can be superseded by no dialectics, and rung out by no poetical peal. The light of science is unable to eclipse it, the treasures of art equal not its "pearl of great price." Legislation dares not displace it, for it gives law to the conscience, and without it civilization is but a whited sepulchre. Freedom rests upon it as a solid basis, because its disciples are not to be the "servants of men;" and national progress, true prosperity—greatest happiness to all—are measured by its development. For it gives nobility to the meanest, and the best of the graces to the highest—presents every one with an aim worthy of his nature—sanctifies every pursuit as a calling on which he may "abide with God"—sends a cheering influence through all the relations of life—relieves the poor and needy—visits the "fatherless and widows in their affliction"—sets its brightest jewel in the crown, and guards the purity of the ermine—breathes a just and generous spirit into legislation—opens up a widening circle of spiritual brotherhood, and blends earth with heaven: realizing the Saviour's natal anthem—"Glory to God in the highest, and on earth peace, goodwill toward men." Such a religion can have no rival, and admits of no substitute.

CHAPTER EIGHT

Athens,
What Paul Saw, Felt and Did

J.C. RYLE

ATHENS.[1]

"Now, while Paul waited for them at Athens, his spirit was stirred in him, when he saw the city wholly given to idolatry.

"Therefore disputed he in the synagogue with the Jews, and with the devout persons, and in the market daily with them that met with him."
—Acts xvii. 16, 17.

PERHAPS the reader of this paper lives in a town or city, and sees more of bricks and mortar than of green fields. Perhaps you have some relative or friend living in a town, about whom you naturally feel a deep interest. In either case, the verses of Scripture which head this page demand your best attention. Give me that attention for a few short minutes while I try to show you the lessons which the passage contains.

You see face to face, in the verses before you, no common city and no common man.

The city is the famous city Athens,—Athens, renowned to this very day for its statesmen, philosophers, historians, poets, painters, and architects,—Athens, the eye of ancient Greece, as ancient Greece was the eye of the heathen world.

The man is the great Apostle of the Gentiles, St. Paul,—St. Paul, the most laborious and successful minister and missionary the world has ever seen,—St. Paul, who by pen

---

[1] This paper contains the substance of a sermon preached at St. Mary's, Oxford, before the University, in 1880.

and tongue has left a deeper mark on mankind than any born of woman, except his Divine Master.

Athens and St. Paul—the great servant of Christ, and the great stronghold of old heathenism— are brought before us face to face. The result is told us: the interview is carefully described. The subject, I venture to think, is eminently suited to the times in which we live, and to the circumstances of many a dweller in London, Liverpool, Manchester, and other great English towns in the present day.

Without further preface, I ask you to observe three things in this passage :—

I. What St. Paul SAW at Athens.
II. What St. Paul FELT at Athens.
III. What St. Paul DID at Athens.

I. First, then, *What did St. Paul* SEE *at Athens?*

The answer of the text is clear and unmistakable. He saw a " city wholly given to idolatry." Idols met his eyes in every street. The temples of idol gods and goddesses occupied every prominent position. The magnificent statue of Minerva, at least forty feet high, according to Pliny, towered above the Acropolis, and caught the eye from every point. A vast system of idol-worship overspread the whole place, and thrust itself everywhere on his notice. The ancient writer Pausanias expressly says, that "the Athenians surpassed all states in the attention which they paid to the worship of the gods." In short, the city, as the marginal reading says, was "full of idols."

And yet this city, I would have you remember, was probably the most favourable specimen of a heathen city which St. Paul could have seen. In proportion to its size, it very likely contained the most learned, civilized, philosophical, highly educated, artistic, intellectual population on the face of the globe. But what was it in a religious point of view? The city of wise men like Socrates and Plato,—the city of Solon, and Pericles, and Demosthenes,—the city of Æschylus, Sophocles, Euripides, and Thucydides,—the city of mind, and intellect, and art, and taste,—this city was " wholly given to idolatry." If the true God was unknown at Athens, what must He have been in the darker places of the earth? If the eye of Greece was so spiritually dim, what must have been the condition of such places as Babylon, Ephesus, Tyre, Alexandria, Corinth, and even of Rome? If men were so far gone from the light in a green tree, what must they have been in the dry?

What shall we say to these things? What are the conclusions to which we are irresistibly drawn by them?

Ought we not to learn, for one thing, the *absolute need of a Divine revelation*, and of teaching from heaven? Leave man without a Bible, and he will have a religion of some kind, for human nature, corrupt as it is, must have a God. But it will be a religion without light, or peace, or hope. " The world by wisdom knew not God " (1 Cor. i. 21). Old Athens is a standing lesson which we shall do well to observe. It is vain to suppose that nature, unaided by revelation, will ever lead fallen man to nature's God. Without a Bible, the Athenian bowed down to stocks and stones, and worshipped the work of his own hands. Place a heathen philosopher,—a Stoic or an Epicurean,—by the side of an open grave, and ask him about a world to come, and he could have told you nothing certain, satisfactory, or peace-giving.

Ought we not to learn, for another thing, that the *highest intellectual training is no security against utter darkness in religion?* We cannot doubt that mind and reason were highly educated at Athens, if anywhere in the heathen world. The students of Greek philosophy were not unlearned and ignorant men. They were well versed in logic, ethics, rhetoric, history, and poetry. But all this mental discipline did not prevent their city being a "city wholly given to idolatry." And are we to be told in the nineteenth century, that reading, writing, arithmetic, mathematics, history, languages, and physical science, without a knowledge of the Scriptures, are sufficient to constitute *education?* God forbid! We have not so learned Christ. It may please some men to idolize intellectual power, and to speak highly of the debt which the world owes to the Greek mind. One thing, at any rate, is abundantly clear. Without the knowledge which the Holy Ghost revealed to the Hebrew nation, old Greece would have left the world buried in dark idolatry. A follower of Socrates or Plato might have talked well and eloquently on many subjects, but he could have never answered the jailor's question, "What must I do to be saved?" (Acts xvi. 30). He could never have said in his last hour, "O death, where is thy sting? O grave, where is thy victory?"

Ought we not to learn, for another thing, that the *highest excellence in the material arts is no preservative against the grossest superstition?* The perfection of Athenian architecture and sculpture is a great and undeniable fact. The eyes of St. Paul at Athens beheld many a "thing of beauty" which is still "a joy for ever" to artistic minds. And yet the men who conceived and executed the splendid buildings of Athens were utterly ignorant of the one true God. The world nowadays is well-nigh drunk with self-conceit about our so-called progress in arts and sciences. Men talk and write of machinery and manufactures, as if nothing were impossible. But let it never be forgotten that the highest art or mechanical skill is consistent with a state of spiritual death in religion. Athens, the city of Phidias, was a "city wholly given to idolatry." An Athenian sculptor might have designed a matchless tomb, but he could not have wiped a single tear from a mourner's eye.

These things ought not to be forgotten. They ought to be carefully pondered. They suit the times in which we live. We have fallen on a sceptical and an unbelieving age. We meet on every side with doubts and questionings about the truth and value of revelation. " Is not reason alone sufficient ? "—" Is the Bible really needful to make men wise unto salvation ? "—" Has not man a light within, a verifying power, able to guide him to truth and God ? " Such are the inquiries which fall thick as hail around us. Such are the speculations which disquiet many unstable minds.

One plain answer is an appeal to facts. The remains of heathen Egypt, Greece, and Rome shall speak for us. They are preserved by God's providence to this very day as monuments of what intellect and reason can do without revelation. The minds which designed the temples of Luxor and Carnac, or the Parthenon or Coliseum, were not the minds of fools. The builders who executed their designs did better and more lasting work than any contractor can do in modern times. The men who conceived the sculptured friezes, which we know as the Elgin Marbles, were trained and intellectual to the highest degree. And yet in religion these men were darkness itself (Eph. v. 8). The sight which St. Paul saw at Athens is an unanswerable proof that man knows nothing which can do his soul good without a Divine revelation.

II. I ask you to notice, in the second place, *what St. Paul* FELT *at Athens.* He saw a " city wholly given to idolatry." How did the sight affect him ? What did he feel ?

It is instructive to observe how the same sight affects different people. Place two men on the same spot; let them stand side by side; let the same objects be presented to their eyes. The emotions called forth in the one man will often be wholly different from those called forth in the other. The thoughts which will be wakened up and brought to birth will often be as far as the poles asunder.

A mere artist visiting Athens for the first time would doubtless have been absorbed in the beauty of its buildings. A statesman or orator would have called up the memory of Pericles or Demosthenes. A literary man would have thought of Thucydides and Sophocles and Plato. A merchant would have gazed on the Piræus, its harbour, and the sea. But an Apostle of Christ had far higher thoughts. One thing, above all others, swallowed up his attention, and made all else look small. That one thing was the spiritual condition of the Athenian people, the state of their souls. The great Apostle of the Gentiles was eminently a man of one thing. Like his Divine Master, he was always thinking of his "Father's business" (Luke ii. 49). He stood at Athens, and thought of nothing so much as Athenian souls. Like Moses, Phinehas, and Elijah, "his spirit was stirred within him when he saw the city wholly given to idolatry."

Of all sights on earth, I know none so impressive, none so calculated to arouse thought in a reflecting mind, as the sight of a great city. The daily intercourse of man with man, which a city naturally produces, seems to sharpen intellect, and stimulate mental activity to an extent which dwellers in rural parishes, or other solitary places, cannot realize. Rightly or wrongly, the inhabitant of a city thinks twice as much, and twice as quickly, as the inhabitant of a rural village. It is the city "where Satan's seat is" (Rev. ii. 13). It is the city where evil of every kind is most rapidly conceived, sown, ripened, and brought to maturity. — It is the city where the young man, leaving home, and launching into life, becomes soonest hardened, and conscience-seared by daily familiarity with the sight of sin.—It is the city where sensuality, intemperance, and worldly amusements of the vilest kind flourish most rankly, and find a congenial atmosphere.— It is the city where ungodliness and irreligion meet with the greatest encouragement, and the unhappy Sabbath-breaker, or neglecter of all means of grace, can fortify himself behind the example of others, and enjoy the miserable comfort of feeling that "he does not stand alone !"—It is the city which is the chosen home of every form of superstition, ceremonialism, enthusiasm, and fanaticism in religion.—It is the city which is the hotbed of every kind of false philosophy, of Stoicism, Epicureanism, Agnosticism, Secularism, Scepticism, Positivism, Infidelity, and Atheism.—It is the city where that greatest of modern inventions, the printing-press, that mighty power for good and evil, is ever working with unsleeping activity, and pouring forth new matter for thought.—It is the city where the daily newspapers are continually supplying food for minds, and moulding and guiding public opinion.—It is the city which is the centre of all national business. The banks, the law-courts, the Stock Exchange, the Parliament or Assembly, are all bound up with the city.—It is the city which, by magnetic influence, draws together the rank and fashion of the land, and gives the tone to the tastes and ways of society.—It is the city which practically controls the destiny of a nation. Scattered millions, in rural districts, without habitual concert or contact, are powerless before the thousands who dwell side by side and exchange thought every day. It is the towns which govern a land. I pity the man who could stand on the top of St. Paul's Cathedral, and look down on London without some emotion, and not reflect that he sees the heart whose pulsations are felt over the whole civilized globe. And shall I wonder for a moment that the sight of Athens "stirred the spirit" of such a man as the great Apostle of the Gentiles? I cannot wonder at all. It was just the sight which was likely to move the heart of the converted man of Tarsus, the man who wrote the Epistle to the Romans, and had seen Jesus Christ face to face.

He was stirred with holy *compassion*. It moved his heart to see so many myriads perishing for lack of knowledge, without God, without Christ, having no hope, travelling in the broad road which leadeth to destruction.

He was stirred with holy *sorrow*. It moved his heart to see so much talent misapplied. Here were hands capable of excellent works, and minds capable of noble conceptions. And yet the God who gave life and breath and power was not glorified.

He was stirred with holy *indignation* against sin and the devil. He saw the god of this world blinding the eyes of multitudes of his fellow-men, and leading them captive at his will. He saw the natural corruption of man infecting the population of a vast city like one common disease, and an utter absence of any spiritual medicine, antidote, or remedy.

He was stirred with holy *zeal* for His Master's glory. He saw the "strong man armed" keeping a house which was not lawfully his, and shutting out the rightful possessor. He saw his Divine Master unknown and unrecognised by His own creatures, and idols receiving the homage due to the King of kings.

Reader, these feelings which stirred the Apostle are a leading characteristic of a man born of the Spirit. Do you know anything of them? Where there is true grace, there will always be tender concern for the souls of others. Where there is true sonship to God, there will always be zeal for the Father's glory. It is written of the ungodly, that they not only commit things worthy of death, but "have pleasure in them that do them" (Rom. i. 32). It may be said with equal truth of the godly, that they not only mourn over sin in their own hearts, but mourn over sin in others.

Hear what is written of Lot in Sodom: "He vexed his soul from day to day with their unlawful deeds" (2 Pet. ii. 8). Hear what is written of David: "Rivers of water run down mine eyes, because they keep not Thy law" (Ps. cxix. 136). Hear what is written of the godly in Ezekiel's time: "They sigh and cry for all the abominations that be done in the midst of the land" (Ezek. ix. 4). Hear what is written of our Lord and Saviour Himself: "He beheld the city, and wept over it" (Luke xix. 41). Surely it may be laid down as one of the first principles of Scriptural religion, that he who can behold sin without sorrowful feelings has not the mind of the Spirit. This is one of those things in which the children of God are manifest, and are distinguished from the children of the devil.

I call the special attention of my readers to this point. The times demand that we look it fully in the face. The feelings with which we regard sin, heathenism, and irreligion are a subject of vast importance in the present day.

I ask you, first, to look outside our own country, and consider the state of the heathen world. At least six hundred millions of immortal beings are at this moment sunk in ignorance, superstition, and idolatry. They live and die without God, without Christ, and without hope. In sickness and sorrow they have no comfort. In old age and death they have no life beyond the grave. Of the true way of peace through a Redeemer, of God's love in Christ, of free grace, of complete absolution from guilt, of a resurrection to life eternal, they have no knowledge. For long weary centuries they have been waiting for the tardy movements of the Church of Christ, while Christians have been asleep, or wasting their energies on useless controversies, and squabbling and wrangling about forms and ceremonies. Is not this a sight which ought to " stir the spirit ? "

I ask you, next, to turn back to our own land, and consider the state of our great cities. There are districts in our great metropolis, in Liverpool, in Manchester, in Birmingham, in the Black Country, where Christianity seems practically unknown. Examine the religious condition of East London, or of Southwark, or Lambeth. Walk through the north end of Liverpool on Saturday evening, or Sunday, or on a Bank Holiday, and see how Sabbath-breaking, intemperance, and general ungodliness appear to rule and reign uncontrolled. " When the strong man armed keepeth his palace, his goods are in peace " (Luke xi. 21). And then remember that this state of things exists in a professedly Christian country, in a land where there is an Established Church, and within a few hours of Oxford and Cambridge ! Once more I say, ought not these things to " stir " our hearts ?

It is a sorrowful fact, that there is around us in the present day a generation of men who regard heathenism, infidelity, and irreligion with apathy, coolness, and indifference ? They care nothing for Christian missions either at home or abroad. They see no necessity for them. They take no interest in the Evangelistic work of any Church or society. They treat all alike with undisguised contempt. They despise Exeter Hall. They never give subscriptions. They never attend meetings. They never read a missionary report. They seem to think that every man shall be saved by his own law or sect, if he is only *sincere ;* and that one religion is as good as another, if

those who profess it are only *in earnest*. They are fond of
decrying and running down all spiritual machinery or
missionary operations. They are constantly asserting that
modern missions at home or abroad do nothing, and that
those who support them are little better than weak
enthusiasts. Judging by their language, they appear to
think that the world receives no benefit from missions and
aggressive Christian movements, and that it would be a
better way to leave the world alone !

What shall we say to these men ? They meet us on
every side. They are to be heard in every society. To
sit by, and sneer, and criticise, and do nothing,—this is
apparently their delight and vocation. What shall we say
to them ?

Let us tell them plainly, if they will only hear us, that
they are utterly opposed to the Apostle St. Paul. Let
us show them that mighty model of a Christian missionary
walking the streets of Athens, and " stirred " in spirit at
the sight of a " city wholly given to idolatry." Let us ask
them why they do not feel as he felt, about the idolatry of
China and Hindustan, of Africa and the South Seas, or
about the semi - heathen districts of London, Liverpool,
Manchester, Birmingham, and the Black Country. Let us
ask them whether 1800 years have made any difference in
the nature of God, the necessities of fallen man, the sinfulness of idol-worship, and the duty of Christians. We shall
ask in vain for a reasonable answer : we shall get none.
Sneers at our weakness are no argument against our
principles. Jests at our infirmities and failures are no
proof that our aims are wrong. Yes ; they may have the
wit and wisdom of this world upon their side ; but the
eternal principles of the New Testament are written clearly,
plainly, and unmistakably. So long as the Bible is the
Bible, charity to souls is one of the first of Christian graces,
and it is a solemn duty to feel for the souls of the heathen,

and of all unconverted people. He who knows nothing of this feeling has yet to become a learner in Christ's school. He who despises this feeling is not a successor of St. Paul, but a follower of him who said, "Am I my brother's keeper?"—even of Cain.

III. I ask my readers to observe, in the last place, *what St. Paul* DID *at Athens.* What he *saw* you have heard; what he *felt* you have been told; but how did he *act?*

He *did something.* He was not the man to stand still, and "confer with flesh and blood" in the face of a city full of idols. He might have reasoned with himself that he stood alone,—that he was a Jew by birth,—that he was a stranger in a strange land,—that he had to oppose the rooted prejudices and old associations of learned men,— that to attack the old religion of a whole city was to beard a lion in his den,—that the doctrines of the gospel were little likely to be effective on minds steeped in Greek philosophy. But none of these thoughts seem to have crossed the mind of St. Paul. He saw souls perishing; he felt that life was short, and time passing away; he had confidence in the power of his Master's message to meet every man's soul; he had received mercy himself, and knew not how to hold his peace. He acted at once; and what his hand found to do, he did with his might. Oh that we had more men of action in these days!

And he did what he did *with holy wisdom* as well as holy boldness. He commenced aggressive measures alone, and waited not for companions and helpers. But he commenced them with consummate skill, and in a manner most likely to obtain a footing for the gospel. First, we are told, he disputed "with the Jews" in the synagogue, and the "devout persons" or proselytes who attended the Jewish worship. Afterwards he went on to "*dispute,*" or hold discussions, "in the market daily with them that met with him." He advanced step by step like an experienced general. Here, as elsewhere, St. Paul is a model to us: he combined fiery zeal and boldness with judicious tact and sanctified common sense. Oh that we had more men of wisdom in these days!

But what did the Apostle teach? What was the grand subject which he argued, and reasoned out, and discussed, both with Jew and Greek, in synagogue and street? That he exposed the folly of idolatry to the ignorant multitudes, —that he showed the true nature of God to the worshippers of images made with hands,—that he asserted the nearness of God to us all, and the certainty of a solemn reckoning with God at the judgment day, to Epicureans and Stoics,— these are facts which we have recorded fully in his address on Mars' Hill.

But is there nothing more than this to be learnt about the Apostle's dealings with the idolatrous city? Is there nothing more distinctive and peculiar to Christianity which St. Paul brought forward at Athens? There is indeed more. There is a sentence in the 18th verse of the chapter we are looking at, which ought to be written in letters of gold,—a sentence which ought to silence for ever the impudent assertion, which some have dared to make, that the great Apostle of the Gentiles was sometimes content to be a mere teacher of deism or natural theology! We are told in the 18th verse that one thing which arrested the attention of the Athenians was the fact, that St. Paul "preached Jesus and the resurrection."

Jesus and the resurrection! What a mine of matter that sentence contained! What a complete summary of the Christian faith might be drawn from those words! That they are only meant to be a summary, I have no doubt. I pity those who would cramp and pare down their meaning, and interpret them as nothing more than Christ's prophetical office and example. I think it in-

credible that the very Apostle who a few days after went to
Corinth, "determined to know nothing but Christ crucified,"
or the doctrine of the cross, would keep back the cross from
Athenian ears. I believe that "Jesus and the resurrection" is a sentence which stands for the whole gospel.
The Founder's name, and one of the foundation facts of
the gospel, stand before us for the whole of Christianity.

What, then, does this sentence mean ? What are we to
understand St. Paul preached ?

(a) St. Paul at Athens preached the *person* of the Lord
Jesus,—His divinity, His incarnation, His mission into
the world to save sinners, His life, and death, and
ascension up to heaven, His character, His teaching, His
amazing love to the souls of men.

(b) St. Paul at Athens preached the *work* of the Lord
Jesus,—His sacrifice upon the cross, His vicarious satisfaction for sin, His substitution as the just for the unjust,
the full redemption He has procured for all, and specially
effected for all who believe, the complete victory He has
obtained for lost man over sin, death, and hell.

(c) St. Paul at Athens preached the *offices* of the Lord
Jesus,—as the one Mediator between God and all mankind, as the great Physician for all sin-sick souls, as the
Rest-giver and Peace-maker for all heavy-laden hearts,
as the Friend of the friendless, the High Priest and
Advocate of all who commit their souls into His hands,
the Ransom-payer of captives, the Light and Guide of all
wandering from God.

(d) St. Paul at Athens preached the *terms* which the
Lord Jesus had commanded His servants to proclaim to
all the world ;—His readiness and willingness to receive
at once the chief of sinners ; His ability to save to the
uttermost all who come unto God by Him ; the full,
present, and immediate forgiveness which He offers to all
who believe ; the complete cleansing in His blood from all

manner of sin ; faith, or simple trust of heart, the one
thing required of all who feel their sins and desire to be
saved ; entire justification without works, or doing, or
deeds of law for all who believe.

(*e*) Last, but not least, St. Paul preached at Athens
the *resurrection* of the Lord Jesus. He preached it as
the miraculous fact on which Jesus Himself staked the
whole credibility of His mission, and as a fact proved by
such abounding evidence that no caviller at miracles has
ever yet honestly dared to meet.——He preached it as a
fact, which was the very top-stone of the whole work of
redemption, proving that what Christ undertook He fully
accomplished, that the ransom was accepted, the atonement completed, and the prison doors thrown open for
ever.——He preached it as a fact, proving beyond doubt
the possibility and certainty of our own resurrection in
the flesh, and settling for ever the great question, " Can
God raise the dead ? "

These things and many like them, I cannot doubt, St.
Paul preached at Athens. I cannot for one moment
suppose that he taught one thing at one place and one at
another. The Holy Ghost supplies the substance of his
preaching in that rich sentence, " Jesus and the resurrection." The same Holy Ghost has told us fully how
he handled these subjects at Antioch in Pisidia, at
Philippi, at Corinth, and Ephesus. The Acts and the
Epistles speak out on this point with no uncertain sound.
I believe that " Jesus and the resurrection " means,——
Jesus and the redemption He effected by His death and
rising from the grave, His atoning blood, His cross, His
substitution, His mediation, His triumphant entrance into
heaven, and the consequent full and complete salvation
of all sinners who believe in Him. This is the doctrine
St. Paul preached. This is the work St. Paul did when
he was at Athens.

Now, have we nothing to learn from these doings of the great Apostle of the Gentiles ? There are lessons of deep importance to which I venture briefly to invite the attention of all who read this paper. I say briefly. I only throw them out, as seeds for private thought.

(*a*) Learn, for one thing, *a doctrinal lesson* from St. Paul's doings at Athens. The grand subject of our teaching, in every place, ought to be Jesus Christ. However learned or however unlearned, however high-born or however humble our audience, Christ crucified—Christ—Christ—Christ—crucified, rising, interceding, redeeming, pardoning, receiving, saving—Christ must be the grand theme of our teaching. We shall never mend this gospel. We shall never find any other subject which will do so much good. We must sow as St. Paul sowed, if we would reap as St. Paul reaped.

(*b*) Learn, for another thing, *a practical lesson* from St. Paul's doings at Athens. We must never be afraid to stand alone and be solitary witnesses for Christ, if need be,—alone in a vast ungodly parish, in our own land,—alone in East London, in Liverpool, in Manchester,—alone in Delhi, or Benares, or Pekin,—it matters not. We need not hold our peace, if God's truth be on our side. One Paul at Athens, one Athanasius against the world, one Wycliffe against a host of Romish prelates, one Luther at Worms,—these, these, are lighthouses before our eyes. God sees not as man sees. We must not stand still to count heads and number the people. One man, with Christ in his heart and the Bible in his hands, is stronger than a myriad of idolaters.

(*c*) Learn for another thing, the importance, let me rather say the necessity, of asserting boldly the *supernatural element* as an essential part of the Christian religion. I need not tell many who read these pages that unbelievers and sceptics abound in these days, who make a dead set at the miracles of the Bible, and are incessantly trying to throw them overboard as useless lumber, or to prove by ingenious explanations that they are fables and no miracles at all. Let us never be afraid to resist such teaching steadily, and to take our stand by the side of St. Paul. Like him, let us point to the resurrection of Christ, and confidently challenge all fair and reasonable men to refute the evidence by which it is supported. The enemies of supernatural religion have never refuted that evidence, and they never will. If Christ was not raised from the dead, the conduct and teaching of the Apostles after He left the world is an unsolved problem and a perfect mystery, which no man in his senses can account for. But if, as we believe, the resurrection of Christ is an undeniable fact which cannot be disproved, the whole fabric of sceptical arguments against supernatural religion is undermined, and must fall to the ground. The stupendous miracle of the resurrection of Christ once admitted, it is sheer nonsense to tell us that any other smaller miracle in the Bible is incredible or impossible.

(*d*) Learn, for one thing more, *a lesson of encouragement to faith* from St. Paul's doings at Athens. If we preach the gospel, we may preach with perfect confidence that it will do good. That solitary Jew of Tarsus who stood up alone on Mars' Hill appeared at the time to do little or nothing. He passed on his way, and seemed to have made a failure. The Stoics and Epicureans probably laughed and sneered as if the day was their own. But that solitary Jew was lighting a candle that has never since been put out. The Word that he proclaimed in Athens grew and multiplied, and became a great tree. That little leaven ultimately leavened the whole of Greece. The gospel that Paul preached triumphed over idolatry. The empty Parthenon stands, to this day, a proof that Athenian theology is dead and gone. Yes; if we sow good seed, we may sow it in tears, but we shall yet " come again with joy, bringing our sheaves with us " (Ps. cxxvi. 6).

I draw towards a conclusion. I pass from the consideration of what St. Paul *saw*, and *felt*, and *did* at Athens, to points of practical importance. I ask every reader of this paper what ought we to see, to feel, and to do ?

(1) *What ought we to see ?* It is an age of sight-seeing and excitement. " The eye is not satisfied with seeing " (Eccles. i. 8). The world is mad after running to and fro, and the increase of knowledge. The wealth, the arts, the inventions of man are continually gathering myriads into great Exhibitions. Thousands and tens of thousands are annually rushing about and gazing at the work of men's hands.

But ought not the Christian to look at the map of the world ? Ought not the man who believes the Bible to gaze with solemn thoughts on the vast spaces in that map which are yet spiritually black, dead, and without the gospel? Ought not our eyes to look at the fact that half the population of the earth is yet ignorant of God and Christ, and yet sitting still in sin and idolatry, and that myriads of our own fellow-countrymen in our great cities are practically little better than heathen, because Christians do so little for souls ?

The eyes of God see these things, and our eyes ought to see them too.

(2) *What ought we to feel ?* Our hearts, if they are right in the sight of God, ought to be affected by the sight of irreligion and heathenism. Many indeed are the feelings which the aspect of the world ought to call up in our hearts.

Thankfulness we ought to feel for our own countless privileges. Little indeed do the bulk of English people know the amount of their own daily unpaid debt to

Christianity. Well would it be for some if they could be compelled to dwell for a few weeks every year in a heathen land.

Shame and humiliation we ought to feel when we reflect how little the Church of England has done for the spread of Christianity hitherto. God has indeed done great things for us since the days when Cranmer, Ridley, and Latimer went to the stake,—has preserved us through many trials, has enriched us with many blessings. But how little return we have made Him! How few of our 15,000 parishes do anything worthy of the cause of missions at home or abroad! How little zeal some congregations show for the salvation of souls! These things ought not so to be!

Compassion we ought to feel when we think of the wretched state of unconverted souls, and the misery of all men and women who live and die without Christ. No poverty like this poverty! No disease like this disease! No slavery like this slavery! No death like this—death in idolatry, irreligion, and sin! Well may we ask ourselves, Where is the mind of Christ, if we do not feel for the lost? I lay it down boldly, as a great principle, that the Christianity which does not make a man feel for the state of unconverted people is not the Christianity which came down from heaven 1800 years ago, and is embalmed in the New Testament. It is a mere empty name. It is not the Christianity of St. Paul.

(3) Finally, *what ought we to do?* This, after all, is the point to which I want to bring your mind. Seeing and feeling are well; but doing is the life of religion. Passive impressions which do not lead to action have a tendency to harden the conscience, and do us positive harm. What ought we to do? We ought to do much more than we have ever done yet. We might all

probably do more. The honour of the gospel, the state
of the missionary field abroad, the condition of our
overgrown cities at home, all call upon us to do more.

Need we stand still, and be ashamed of the weapons of
our warfare ? Is the gospel, the old Evangelical creed,
unequal to the wants of our day ? I assert boldly that
we have no cause to be ashamed of the gospel at all. It
is not worn out. It is not effete. It is not behind the
times. We want nothing new, nothing added to the
gospel, nothing taken away. We want nothing but
" the old paths,"—the old truths fully, boldly, affection-
ately proclaimed. Only preach the gospel fully, the same
gospel which St. Paul preached, and it is still "the power
of God unto salvation to every one that believeth," and
nothing else called religion has any real power at all.
(Rom. i. 16.)

Need we stand still and be ashamed of the *results* of
preaching the gospel ? Shall we hang down our heads,
and complain that " the faith once delivered to the
saints" has lost its power, and does no good ? We have
no cause to be ashamed at all. I am bold to say that
no religious teaching on earth can point to any results
worth mentioning except that which is called doctrinal,
dogmatic theology. What deliverance on earth have all
the modern schools—which scorn dogmatic teaching—
what deliverance have they wrought ? What overgrown and semi-heathen parishes in the metropolis, in
our great seaports, our manufacturing towns, our colliery
districts, have they evangelized and civilized ? What
New Zealand, what Red River, what Sierra-Leone, what
Tinnevelly can the high-sounding systems of this latter
day point to as a fruit of their system ? No ! if the
question, " What is truth ? " is to be solved by reference
to results and fruits, the religion of the New Testament,
the religion whose principles are summarized, condensed,

and embalmed in our Articles, Creeds, and Prayer Book, has no cause to be ashamed.

What can we do now but humble ourselves for the past, and endeavour, by God's help, to do more for time to come? Let us open our eyes more, and *see*. Let us open our hearts more, and *feel*. Let us stir up ourselves to *do* more work — by self-denying gifts, by zealous co-operation, by bold advocacy, by fervent prayer. Let us do something worthy of our cause. The cause for which Jesus left heaven and came down to earth deserves the best that we can do.

And now, let me close this paper by returning to the thought with which it began. Perhaps your lot is cast in a city or town. The population of our rural districts is annually decreasing. The dwellers in towns are rapidly outnumbering the dwellers in country parishes. If you are a dweller in a town, accept the parting words of advice which I am about to offer. Give me your best attention while I speak to you about your soul.

(1) Remember, for one thing, that you are placed in a position of peculiar spiritual danger. From the days of Babel downwards, wherever Adam's children have been assembled in large numbers, they have always drawn one another to the utmost extremities of sin and wickedness. The great towns have always been Satan's seat. It is the town where the young man sees abounding examples of ungodliness; and, if he is determined to live in sin, will always find plenty of companions. It is the town where the theatre and the casino, the dancing room and the drinking bar, are continually crowded. It is the town where the love of money, or the love of amusement, or the love of sensual indulgence, lead captive myriads of slaves. It is the town where a man will always find hundreds to

encourage him in breaking the Sabbath, despising the means of grace, neglecting the Bible, leaving off the habit of prayer. Reader, consider these things. If you live in a town, take care. Know your danger. Feel your weakness and sinfulness. Flee to Christ, and commit your soul to His keeping. Ask Him to hold you up, and you will be safe. Stand on your guard. Resist the devil. Watch and pray.

(2) Remember, on the other hand, if you live in a town, you will probably have some special helps which you cannot always find in the country. There are few English towns in which you will not find a few faithful servants of Christ, who will gladly assist you and aid you in your journey towards heaven. Few indeed are the English towns in which you will not find some minister who preaches the gospel, and some pilgrims in the narrow way who are ready to welcome any addition to their number.

Reader, be of good courage, and never give way to the despairing thought that it is impossible to serve Christ in a town. Think rather that with God nothing is impossible. Think of the long list of witnesses who have carried the cross, and been faithful unto death in the midst of the greatest temptations. Think of Daniel and the three children in Babylon. Think of the saints in Nero's household at Rome. Think of the multitudes of believers at Corinth and Ephesus and Antioch in the days of the Apostles. It is not place but grace that makes the Christian. The holiest and most useful servants of God who have ever lived were not hermits in the wilderness but dwellers in towns.

Remember these things, and be of good cheer. Your lot may be cast in a city like Athens, " wholly given to idolatry." You may have to stand alone in the bank, the counting-house, the place of business, or the shop.

But you are not really alone, if Christ is with you. Be strong in the Lord, and in the power of His might. Be bold, thorough, decided, and patient. The day will come when you will find that even in a great city a man may be a happy, useful Christian, respected while he lives, and honoured when he dies.

CHAPTER NINE

False Religions and the True

B.B. WARFIELD

FALSE RELIGIONS AND THE TRUE[1]

"What therefore ye worship in ignorance, this set I forth unto you."—Acts xvii. 23. (R. V.)

These words give the gist of Paul's justly famous address at Athens before the court of the Areopagus. The substance of that address was, to be sure, just what the substance of all his primary proclamations to Gentile hearers was, namely, God and the judgment. The necessities of the case compelled him to approach the heathen along the avenue of an awakened conscience. They had not been prepared for the preaching of Jesus by a training under the old covenant, and no appeals to prophecy and its fulfillment could be made to them. God and the judgment necessarily constituted, therefore, the staple of his proclamation to them; and so typical an instance as this address to the Areopagus could not fail to exhibit the characteristics of its class with especial purity.

Nevertheless, the peculiar circumstances in which it was delivered have imprinted on this address also a particular character of its own. Paul spoke it under a specially poignant sense of the depths of heathen ignorance and of the greatness of heathen need. The whole address palpitates with his profound feeling of the darkness in which the heathen world is immersed, and his eager longing to communicate to it the light intrusted to his care. All that goes before the words selected for the text and all that comes after serve but to enhance their great declaration—build for it, as it were, but a lofty platform upon which it is raised to fix the gaze of men. Out of it all Paul fairly shouts this one essential message to the whole unbeliev-

[1] From the volume of sermons entitled *The Power of God Unto Salvation*, pp. 219-254.

ing world: "What therefore ye worship in ignorance, this set I forth unto you."

Let us consider for a little while the circumstances in which the address was delivered. Summoned by a supernatural vision, Paul had crossed the sea and brought the gospel into Europe. Landing in Macedonia, he had preached in its chief cities, meeting on the one hand with great acceptance, and arousing on the other the intensest opposition. He had been driven from city to city until the brethren had at last fled with him to the sea and, hurrying him upon a ship, had conveyed him far to the south and, at last, landed him at Athens. There they left him—alone but in safety—and returned to Macedonia to send his companions to him.

Meanwhile Paul awaited their coming at Athens. Athens! mother of wisdom, mistress of art; but famous, perhaps, above all its wisdom and above all its art for the intensity of its devotion to the gods. Paul had had a missionary's experience with idolatry, in its grosser and more refined forms alike; he had been forced into contact with it throughout his Asian work. Even so, Athens seems to have been a revelation to him—a revelation which brought him nothing less than a shock. Here he was literally in the thick of it. No other nation was so given over to idolatry as the Athenians. One writer tells us that it was easier to find a god in populous Athens than a man; another, scarcely exaggerating, declares that the whole city was one great altar, one great sacrifice, one great votive offering. The place seemed to Paul studded with idols, and the sight of it all brought him a paroxysm of grief and concern.

He was in Athens, as it were, in hiding. But he could not keep silence. He went to the synagogue on the Sabbath and there preached to the Jews and those devout inquirers who were accustomed to visit the synagogues of the Jews in every city. But this did not satisfy his aroused zeal. He went also to the market place—that agora which the public teachers of the city had been wont to frequent for the propagation of their views—and there, like them, every day, he argued with all whom he chanced to meet. Among these he very naturally encountered certain adherents of the types of philosophy then dominant—the Epicurean and Stoic—and in conflict with them he began to attract attention.

He was preaching, as was his wont, "Jesus" and the "resurrection"—doubtless much as he preached them in his recorded address, to which all this led up. Some turned with light contempt away from him and called him a mere smatterer; others, with perhaps no less contempt, nevertheless took him more seriously and anxiously asked if he were not "a proclaimer of alien divinities." This was an offense in Athens; and so they brought him to the Areopagus. He was not formally arraigned for trial—there was only set on foot something like a preliminary official inquiry; and the question put to him is oddly compounded of courteous suggestion and authoritative demand. They said: "May we be allowed to know what this new teaching is that is talked of by thee? For thou dost bring certain strange things to our ears; and it is our wish to know what these things may be." The hand is gloved, but you see the iron showing through. It was to Paul, however, only another opportunity; and in the conscious authority of his great mission he stood forth in the midst of the court and began to speak.

We must bear in mind that Paul was put to the question on the general charge that he was "a proclaimer of strange deities." He had no intention whatever of denying this general allegation. He was rather firmly determined to seize this opportunity yet once more to proclaim a Deity evidently unknown to the Athenians. And this, in fact, he proceeded at once to do. But he did it after a fashion which disarmed the complaint; which enlisted the Athenians themselves as unwilling indeed, but nevertheless real, worshipers of the God he proclaimed; and which powerfully pried at their consciences as well as appealed to their intelligences and even their national pride to give wings to his proclamation.

The hinge on which the whole speech turns is obviously Paul's deep sense of the darkness of heathen ignorance. As our

Saviour said to the Samaritan woman, so Paul, in effect, says
to the Athenian jurists and philosophers, "You worship you
know not what." The altar at Athens which he signalizes as
especially significant of heathen worship is precisely the altar
inscribed "To a Not-known God." The whole course of their
heathen development he characterizes as a seeking of God, if
by any chance—"in the possible hope at least that"—they may
touch Him as a blind man touches with his hands fumblingly
what he cannot see—and so doubtfully find Him; nay, shortly
and crisply, as "times of ignorance." The very purpose of his
proclamation of his gospel among them is to bring light into
this darkness, to make them to know the true nature and the
real modes of working, the all-inclusive plan and the decisive
purpose of the one true God. Therefore it is simply true to say
that the hinge on which the whole speech turns is the declaration that the heathen are steeped in ignorance and require,
above all things, the light of divine instruction.

But when we have said this we have not said all. After all,
it is not quite a blank ignorance that Paul ascribes to the
Athenians. He institutes a certain connection between what
they worship and the God he was commending to them. He
does not wholly scoff at their religion, though he certainly
sharply reprobates and deeply despises the modes in which
it expresses itself. He does not entirely condemn their worship
even of a not-known god; he rather makes it a point of attachment for proclaiming the higher worship of the known God of
heaven and earth which he is recommending to them. There is,
in a word, a certain amount of recognition accorded by him
to their religious feelings and aspirations.

It is accordingly not all a scoff when he tells them that he
perceives that they are apparently "very religious." The word
he employs is no doubt sometimes used in a bad sense, and
accordingly is frequently translated here by the ill-savored
word "superstitious." So our English version translates it: "I
perceive that in all things ye are too superstitious" or "somewhat superstitious," as the Revised Version puts it. But it is
scarcely possible to believe that Paul uses it in this evil sense

here. It means in itself nothing but "divinity-fearing"—not exactly "God-fearing," though generally equivalent to that, because it has a hint in it of the gods many and lords many of the heathen. It easily, therefore, lends itself to a bad sense, and is often, as we have seen, so used. But as often it is used in a perfectly good sense, as equivalent simply to "religious," and surely it is so used here. Paul is not charging his hearers with superstition; he is recognizing in them a religious disposition. He chooses a term, indeed, of somewhat non-committal character—which would not say too much—which might be taken perhaps as bearing a subtle implication of incomplete approval: but a word by which he expresses at least no active disapproval and even a certain measure of active approval. Paul, in fine, commends the religiousness of the Athenians.

The forms in which this religiousness expressed itself he does not commend. The sight of them, indeed, threw him into a paroxysm of distress, if not of indignation. He could not view without disgust and horror the degradation of their worship. In one sense we may say that it reached its lowest level in this altar, "To a Not-known God." For what could be worse than the superstitious dread which, after cramming every corner of the city with altars to every conceivable divinity, was not yet satisfied, but must needs feel blindly out after still some other power of earth or air or sky to which to immolate victims or before which to cringe in unintelligent fear? But in another aspect it may even have seemed to Paul that in this altar might rather be seen the least degraded expression of the religious aspirations of the Athenians. Where every definite trait given to their conceptions of divinity was but a new degradation of the idea of the divine, there is a certain advantage attaching to vagueness. At least no distinctive foulness was attributed to a god confessedly unknown. Perhaps just because of its undifferentiation and indefiniteness it might therefore seem a purer symbol of that seeking after God for which God had destined all nations when He appointed to them the ordained times and limits of their habitation, if by any chance they might feel

Him and so find Him. Surely the forms they gave to the gods they more definitely conceived, the characters they ascribed to them, the functions they assigned them, and the legendary stories of their activities which they wove around them, sufficiently evinced that in them the Athenians had not so much as fumblingly touched God, much less found Him. A worship offered to "an unknown god" was at least free from the horror of definitely conceiving God as corruptible men and birds and fourfooted beasts and creeping things.

In any event, behind the worship, however ill conceived, Paul sees and recognizes the working of that which he does not shame to call religion. Enshrined within his general condemnation of the heathenism of the Athenians there lies thus a recognition of something not to be condemned—something worthy of commendation rather—fit even on his lips to bear the name of "religion." All this is implied in the words we have chosen as our text, and it is therefore that we have said of them that they give us the gist of the whole address. "What ye thus not knowing adore," says Paul, "that it is that I am proclaiming to you." It will repay us, probably, to probe the matter a little in the way of its wider applications.

First, then, we say there is given in the apostolic teaching a certain recognition to the religion of the heathen.

We do not say, mark you, that a recognition is given to the heathen religions. That is something very different. The heathen religions are uniformly treated as degrading to man and insulting to God. The language of a recent writer which declares that man's "most unfortunate things" are his religions—nay, that man's religions are "among his worst crimes"—is thoroughly justified by the apostolic attitude toward them. Read but the account given at the end of the first chapter of Romans of the origin of these religions in the progressive degradation of man's thought of God, as man's repeated withdrawals from God and God's repeated judicial blindings of man interwork to the steady destruction of all religious insight and all moral perception alike, and from this observe how the writers of the New Testament conceived of the religions which men have in the procession of the ages formed for themselves.

Nor is it to be imagined that only the more degraded of the popular superstitions were in the apostle's mind when he painted this dreadful picture of the fruits of human religious thinking. In an almost contemporary epistle he calmly passes his similar judgment on all the philosophies of the world. Not by all its wisdom, he tells us, has the world come to know God, but in these higher elaborations also, becoming vain in its imaginations, its foolish heart has only become darkened. In a somewhat later epistle he sums up his terrible estimate of the religious condition of the Gentiles in that dreadful declaration that "they walk in the vanity of their mind, being darkened in their understanding, alienated from the life of God, because of the ignorance that is in them, because of the hardening of their heart."

This is what the apostle thought—not of some heathen, but of heathen as such, in their religious life—not of the degraded bushmen of Australia or Africa or New Guinea, but of the philosophic minds of Greece and Rome in the palmiest days of their intellectual development and ethical and æsthetic culture; of the Socrateses and Platos and Aristotles and Epictetuses and Marcus Aureliuses of that ancient world, which some would have us look upon as so fully to have found God as veritably to have taken heaven by storm and to have entered it by force of its own attainments. To him it was, on the contrary, in his briefest phrase, "without hope and without God."

Nevertheless, alongside of and in the very midst of this sweeping and unmitigated condemnation of the total religious manifestation of heathendom there exists an equally constant and distinct recognition of the reality and value of religion even among the heathen. It does not seem ever to have occurred to the writers of the New Testament to doubt that religion is as universal as intelligence itself; or to question the reality or value of this universal religiousness. To them man, as such, appears to be esteemed no more a reasonable creature than a religious animal; and they appeal to his religious instinct and build upon it expectations of a response to their appeal, with the same confidence which they show when they make their appeal to his logical faculty. They apparently no more expect to find a man without religion than they expect to find a man without understanding, and they seem to attach the same fundamental value to his inherent religiousness as to his inherent rationality.

In this the passage that is more particularly before us today is thoroughly representative of the whole New Testament. Paul, it is seen at once, does not here in any way question the fact that the Athenians are religious, any more than he questions that they are human beings. He notes, rather, with satisfaction that they are very especially religious. "I perceive that ye are in all things exceedingly divinity-fearing." There is a note of commendation in that which is unmistakable. Nor does he betray any impulse to denounce their religious sentiment as intrinsically evil. On the contrary, he takes it frankly as the basis of his appeal to them. In effect, he essays merely to direct and guide its functioning, and in so doing recognizes it as the foundation of all the religious life which he would, as the teacher of Christianity to them, fain see developed in and by them. In the same spirit he always deals with what we may call the inherent religiousness of humanity. Man, as such, in his view is truly and fundamentally religious.

Now this frank recognition, or, we might better say, this emphatic assertion of the inherent religiousness of humanity, constitutes a fact of the first importance in the biblical revelation. It puts the seal of divine revelation on the great fundamental doctrine that there exists in man a *notitia Dei insita*—a natural knowledge of God, which man can no more escape than he can escape from his own humanity. Endowed with an ineradicable sense of dependence and of responsibility, man knows that Other on which he depends and to whom he is responsible in the very same act by which he knows himself. As he can never know himself save as dependent and responsible, he can never know himself without a consciousness of that Other Not-self, on whom he is dependent and to whom he is responsible; and in this co-knowledge of self and Over-not-self is rooted the whole body of his religious conceptions, religious feelings, and religious actions—which are just as inevitable functionings of his intellect, sensibility, and will as any actions of those faculties, the most intimate and immediate we can conceive of. Thus man cannot help being religious; God is implicated in his very first act of self-consciousness, and he can avoid thinking of God, feeling toward Him, acting with respect to Him, only by avoiding thinking, feeling, and acting with respect to self.

How he shall conceive God—what notion he shall form, that is, of that Over-not-self in contrast with which he is conscious of dependence and responsibility; how he shall feel toward God—that is, toward that Over-not-self, conceived after this fashion or that; how he shall comport himself toward God—that is, over against that Over-not-self, so and not otherwise conceived, and so and not otherwise felt toward: these questions, it is obvious, raise additional problems, the solution of which must wait upon accurate knowledge of the whole body of conditions and circumstances in which the faculties of intellect, feeling, and will function in each given case. But that in his very first act of consciousness of self as a dependent and responsible and not as a self-centered and self-sufficient being, man is brought into contact with the Over-not-self on which he is dependent and to which he is responsible; and must therefore form some conception of it, feel in some way toward it, and act in some manner with respect to it, is as certain as that he will think and feel and act at all.

That man is a religious being, therefore, and will certainly have a religion, is rooted in his very nature, and is as inevitable as it is that man will everywhere and always be man. But what religion man will have is no more subject to exact *a priori* determination than is the product of the action of his faculties along any other line of their functioning. Religion exists and must exist everywhere where man lives and thinks and feels and acts; but the religions that exist will be as varied as the idiosyncrasies of men, the conditions in which their faculties work, the influences that play on them and determine the character of their thoughts and feelings and deeds.

Bearing this in mind, we shall not be surprised to note that along with the recognition of the religiousness of man embodied in the apostolic teaching, there is equally prominent in it, as we have said, the unwavering assertion of the absolute necessity of religious instruction for the proper religious development of man.

The whole mission of the apostle is founded upon, or, more properly speaking, is the appropriate expression of, this point of sight. Nor could he be untrue to it on an occasion like that which is more particularly engaging our attention today. We observe, then, as we have already pointed out, that though he commends the Athenians for their God-fearingness and finds in their altar to a "not-known god" a point of attachment for his proclamation of the true God; he does not for a moment suggest that their native religiousness could be left safely to itself to blossom into a fitting religious life; or that his proclamation of the known God of heaven and earth possessed only a relative necessity for them.

Clearly he presents the necessity rather as absolute. God had for a time, no doubt, left the nations of the world to the guidance of their own religious nature, that they might seek after Him in the possible expectation at least of finding Him. But on God's part this was intended rather as a demonstration of their incapacity than as a hopeful opportunity afforded them; and in its results it provides an empirical proof of the absolute necessity of His interference with direct guidance. Accordingly the apostle roundly characterizes the issue of all heathen religious development, inclusive of that in Athens itself, the seat of the highest heathen thinking on divine things, as just bald ignorance. That the world by its wisdom knows not God and lies perishing in its ignorance is the most fixed element of his whole religious philosophy.

What is involved here is, of course, the whole question of the necessity of "special revelation." It is a question which has been repeatedly fought out during the course of Christian history. In the eighteenth century, for example, it was this very issue that was raised in the sharpest possible form by the deistic controversy. A coterie of religious philosophers, possessing an eye for little in man beyond his logical understanding, undertook to formulate what they called the "natural religion." This they then set over against the supernatural religion, which Christianity professed to be, as the religion of nature in contrast with the religion of authority—authority being prejudged to be in this sphere altogether illegitimate. The result was certainly instructive. Bernard Pünger is not a jot too severe when he remarks of this boasted "natural religion" of the Deists, that it deserves neither element of its designation. "It is," he declares, "neither religion nor natural, but only an extremely artificial abstraction of theologians and philosophers. It is no religion, for nowhere, in no spot, in either the old or new world, has there ever existed even the smallest community which recognized this 'natural religion.' And it is not natural; for no simple man ever arrived of himself at the ideas of this 'natural religion.'"

And when it was thus at last formulated by the philosophers of the eighteenth century, it proved no religion even to them. A meager body of primary abstract truth concerning God and His necessary relations to man was the entire result. This formed, indeed, an admirable witness to the rational rooting of these special truths concerning God and our relations to Him in the very nature of man as a dependent and responsible being; and this the Christian thinker may well view with satisfaction. It may be taken as supplying him also with a demonstration, once for all, that an adequate body of religious truth can never be obtained by the artificial process of abstracting from all the religions of the world the elements held in common by them all, and labeling this "natural religion." Neither in religion nor in any other sphere of life can the maxim be safely adopted that the least well-endowed member of a coterie shall be crowned king over all. Yet obviously that is the result of proceeding by what is called "the consensus method" in seeking a norm of religious truth.

Taught wisdom by experience like this, our more modern world has found a new method of ridding itself of the necessity of revelation. The way was pointed out to it by no less a genius than Friedrich Schleiermacher himself. Led no doubt by the laudable motive of seeking a place for religion unassailable on the shallow ground of intellectualistic criticism, he relegated it in its origin exclusively to the region of feeling. In essence he said, religion is the immediate feeling of absolute dependence.

He calls it an "immediate feeling" or an "immediate self-consciousness" just in order to eliminate from it every intellectual element. That is to say, he wishes to distinguish between two forms of self-consciousness or feeling, the one mediated by the perception of an object and the other not so mediated, but consisting in an immediate and direct sensation, abstracted from every intellectual representation or idea; and in this latter class of feelings he places that feeling of absolute dependence with which he identifies religion. Religion, therefore, it is argued, is entirely independent of every intellectual conception; it is rooted in a pure feeling or immediate consciousness which enters into and affects all of our intellectual exercises, but is itself absolutely independent of them all, and persists the same through whatever intellectual conceptions we may form of the object of our worship or through whatever actions we may judge appropriate to the service of that object thus or otherwise conceived.

Upon the basis of this mode of conceiving religion we have been treated of late to innumerable pæans to religion as a primal force running through all the religions; and are being constantly exhorted to recognize as absolutely immaterial what forms it takes in its several manifestations, and to greet it as subsisting equally valid and equally noble beneath all its forms of manifestation indifferently, because in itself independent of them all. It is thus only the common cry that echoes all around us which Père Hyacinthe repeats in his passionate declaration: "It is not true that all religions are false except one only."

Only a few years ago when a professor was being inducted into a new chair of the History of Religion established in one of the oldest of the Reformed schools, he took up the same cry with much the same passion, and professed himself able to feel brotherhood with every form of religion—except that perhaps which arrogated to itself to be the only legitimate form. "When the history of religions," he eloquently said, "places in our hands the religious archives of humanity it is surely our duty rather to garner these treasures than to proclaim Christianity the only good, the only true one among the religions of men. 'We also, we also are the offspring of God,' the poet Aratus cried three centuries before Christ. Let us pause before this cry of the human soul and let us contemplate with attention the luminous web in which the history of this divine sonship has been woven by universal worship. When we have opened, with the same respect which we demand for our own, the sacred books of other peoples, when we have observed them clinging, as to their most holy possessions, to their sublime traditions, in which are enshrined the mother-thoughts of all true religion—lavishing their genius in exalting them, sacrificing their fortunes in defending them, exiling themselves to the most distant lands and sinking into the burning sands in propagating them, accepting death itself in order to preserve them— our hearts, moved with surprise and brotherly sympathy, will repudiate for ever the Pharisaic pride which treats as heathen or as uncircumcised all God's creatures which are without the sacred pale of the elect." "Men of all nations," he tells us, "and of all tongues—whether savage or civilized, whether ignorant or instructed, whether Parsi or Christian—though God may have been revealed to them diversely, though they may be looking up to Him through variously-colored glasses—are yet all looking nevertheless up to the same God, by whatever liturgical name He may be known to them—and it is to Him that all their prayers alike are ascending. And to all of them," he adds, "I feel myself a brother—except to the hypocrite."

"No one," he concludes, "who has ever felt echoing in his heart the murmur of this universal worship will ever be able to return to the sectarian apologetics with which the unhappiness of the times inspired the Jews after the exile, and which from Judaism has passed into the Church of Christ."

I have not thus adverted to this eloquent address because it is especially extreme in its assertions. It is not. Rather, let it be said, it enunciates with unusual balance and moderation views common to a large part of the modern world. It is on this very account that I have adduced its presentation of this very widespread conception—because it affords us a very favorable opportunity to observe it at its best, touched with fervor and announced with winning eloquence of speech. Even in it, however, we may perceive the portentous results to which the whole conception of religion as an "immediate feeling" may take us—nay, must inevitably carry us. If what it tells us be true, it obviously is of no importance whatever with what conceptions religion may be connected. So only the religious sentiment be present, all that enters into the essence of religion is there; and one may call himself Brahmin or Mohammedan, Parsi or Christian, and may see God through whatever spectacles and name Him by whatever designation he will, and yet be and remain alike, and alike, validly, religious. We may justly look upon this inevitable result of the identification of religion with an "immediate feeling" as its sufficient refutation.

In no event could it be thought difficult, however, to exhibit the untenability of this entire conception. We should probably only need to ask, How could an abstract feeling of dependence, with no implication whatever of the object on which the dependence leans, possess any distinctively religious quality whatever? It would appear too clear to require arguing that the whole religious quality of a feeling of dependence, recognized as religious, must be derived necessarily from the nature of the object depended upon—viz., God. If we conceive that object as something other than God, then the feeling of dependence ceases to be in any intelligible sense religious. It is assuredly only on God that a specifically religious feeling can rest.

Schleiermacher himself appears to have felt this. And accordingly he distinguished between the feeling of dependence in general and the feeling of absolute dependence in particular; and on the supposition that absolute dependence can be felt only toward the Absolute, confined the religious feeling to it. Here there appears to be a subintroduction of the idea of God; and therefore a veiled admission that we have in this "feeling of absolute dependence" not an "immediate feeling," but a feeling mediated by an idea, to wit, the idea of God. Thus the whole contention is, in principle, yielded; and we revert to the more natural and only valid ground—that all their quality is supplied to feelings by the objects to which they are directed, and that, therefore, the nature of our conceptions so far from having nothing, has everything, to do with religion.

I recall with great vividness of memory a striking picture I once saw, painted by that weird Russo-German genius Sasha Schneider, in order to illustrate religion conceived as the feeling of absolute dependence, and at the same time to express the artist's repugnance to it and scorn of it. It has seemed to me to provide us with a most striking parable. He figures a man stripped naked and laden down with chains, head bowed, in every trait dejection, every fiber of every muscle relaxed, every line a line of hopelessness and despair. The ground on which he stands is the earth itself, fashioned, however, into the hideous presentment of a monstrous form, so painted as to give it the texture of hard, black, iron-like stone. The horizon that stretches around the figure and seems to bend in upon him consists of two great iron-like arms ending in dreadfully protuberant fingers, which appear about to close in on his limbs; while just before him heavy shoulders rise slightly into a low forbidding hillock, and between them thrusts forward the hard mound of a scarce-distinguishable head, lit by two malevolent eyes, like low volcano-fires glaring up upon their victim. Thus is set forth the artist's conception of religious sentiment as the "feeling of absolute dependence."

Yes—but we then must add, there are two points that require criticism in the conception presented. First, in this figure of a despondent man, the artist has, after all, painted not the feeling of dependence, but rather the feeling of helplessness. These are very different things. And in their difference we touch, as I think, the very heart of the error we are seeking to unmask. A feeling of dependence, properly so-called, necessarily implies an object: helplessness—yes, that may exist without an object, but not dependence. He that depends must needs have somewhat on which to depend. A feeling of dependence is unthinkable apart from the object on which the dependence rests. In picturing for us abject "helplessness," then, the artist has not at all pictured for us "dependence." The former is passive, the latter is active, and the abjectness that belongs to the one is not at all inherent in the other. Secondly, even so, the artist has not been able to get along without an object. He has painted this dejected man: there he stands before us the very picture of helplessness. But the artistic sense is not satisfied: and so he throws around him these hideous encircling arms; he sets upon him this baleful gaze. He must suggest, after all, an object toward which the feeling of dependence he is endeavoring to depict turns. But why this hideous object? Only to justify the abjectness of the figure he has painted. From which we may learn at once that the character of the feeling—all that gives quality and meaning to it—is, after all, necessarily dependent on the nature of the object to which it is referred.

And so, if we mistake not, Sasha Schneider's picture is itself the sufficient refutation of the whole conception of religion we are discussing. Given no object, the figure of helplessness remains inexplicable and meaningless and will result in nothing. Given a monstrous object, it develops at once into a figure of abject misery. Given a glorious object—a God of righteousness and goodness—and only then does it develop into a figure of that dependence which we call religion. And if we require an earthly image of this feeling of dependence, let us find it in an infant on its mother's bosom, looking up in confidence and trust into a face on which it perceives the smiles of goodness and love. Even the heathen poet tells us that the happy infant laughs as it sees the smile of love on the mother's countenance. It is in such scenes as this that the true earthly portrait of the absolute dependence, which is religion is to be found.

But it is neither to logical analysis nor to the artistic instinct of a Sasha Schneider that we need to turn today to assure ourselves that this whole construction of religion as independent of knowledge is impossible. For surely it is obvious that it is the very antipodes of Paul's view of the matter. This we have already sufficiently pointed out, and need only now to remind ourselves of it.

Perhaps it is enough for this purpose simply to ask afresh how Paul dealt with the religiousness of the Athenians, notable as they were among all nations for their religiousness. Assuredly he did not withhold due recognition from it. "O men of Athens," he cried, "I perceive that in all things ye are exceedingly religious." But did he account this exceeding religiousness enough for their needs? As he went about the streets of Athens and beheld the great city studded with idols—one great sanctuary, as it were—did he reason within himself that the forms of manifestation were of no importance, that through and beneath them we should rather perceive that pure impulse to worship which sustained and gave vitality and value to them all; and, observing in it the essence of all religions alike, recognize it as enough?

Our text gives us the emphatic answer: "What ye, thus, in ignorance adore, that it is that I declare unto you." The whole justification of his mission hangs on the value he attaches to knowledge as the informing principle of all right, of all valid, of all availing religion. And if we care to follow Paul we must for our part also, once and for all, renounce with the strongest emphasis all attempts to conceive the native religious impulse as capable in sinful man of producing religious phenomena which can be recognized as well pleasing in the sight of God.

No doubt we shall be under manifold temptations to do otherwise. Our modern atmosphere is charged to saturation

with temptations to do otherwise. Let us all the more carefully
arm ourselves against them. In warning us against this over-
estimate of natural religions Paul may perhaps be allowed to
give us also a name for it, by the employment of which we
may possibly be able to put a new point on our self-admoni-
tions. He calls it, as we have seen, in the case of the Athenians,
by a term of somewhat peculiar flavor. "Divinity-fearing" we
bunglingly translate it—that is, so to say, "generally Divinity-
fearing," without too close inquisition into which divinity it is
that we fear or what is the character of the service that we
render it. "Deisidaimonism" is the Greek term he makes use of.
It is an uncouth term. But, then, it is not a very lovely thing it
designates. And perhaps, in the absence of a good translation,
we may profitably adopt the Greek term today, with all its
uncouthness of sound and its unlovely association, and so enable ourselves to make a recognizable distinction between that
general natural religiosity and its fruits which we may call
"deisidaimonism" and true religion, which is the product of
the saving truth of God operating upon our native religious
instincts and producing through them phenomena which owe
all their value to the truth that gives them form.

Ah, brethren, let us avoid "deisidaimonism" in all its manifestations! As you look out over the heathen world with its
lords many and gods many, and see working in every form of
faith the same religious impulses, the same religious aspirations,
producing in varying measure indeed, but yet everywhere, to
some extent, the same civilizing and moralizing effects—are
you perhaps sometimes tempted to pronounce it enough; possibly adding something about the special adaptation of the
several faiths to the several peoples, or even something about
the essential truth underlying all religions? This is "deisidaimonism." And on its basis the whole missionary work of the
Church is an impertinence, the whole history of the Church
a gigantic error; the great commission itself a crime against
humanity—launching the Christian world upon a fool's errand,
every step of which has dripped with wasted blood. Surely the
proclamation of the gospel is made, then, mere folly and the

blood of the martyrs becomes only the measure of the narrow fanaticism of earlier and less enlightened times.

It is possible, however, that your temptation does not come to you in such a crass shape. Perhaps it may whisper to you only something about the narrowness of sectarianism within the limits of Christianity—of the folly of contentions over what we may at the moment be happening to call "the truth." Look, it may say—do you not see that under every faith the religious life flourishes? Why lay stress then on creed? Creeds are divisive things; away with them! Or at least let us prune all their distinctive features away, and give ourselves a genial and unpolemic Christianity, a Christianity in which all the stress is laid on life, not dogma, the life of the spirit in its aspirations toward God, or perchance, even the life of external activities in the busy fulfillment of the duties of life. This too, you observe, is "deisidaimonism." Embark once on that pathway and there is no logical and—oh, the misfortune of it!—no practical stopping-point until you have evaporated all recognizable Christianity away altogether and reduced all religion to the level of man's natural religiosity. A really "undogmatic Christianity" is just no Christianity at all.

Let us not for an instant suppose, to be sure, that religion is a matter of the intellect alone or chiefly. But in avoiding the Scylla of intellectualism let us not run into the Charybdis of mere naturalism. All that makes the religion we profess distinctively Christian is enshrined in its doctrinal system. It is therefore that it is a religion that can be taught, and is to be taught—that is propagated by what otherwise would be surely, in the most literal sense, the foolishness of preaching. Mere knowledge, indeed, does not edify; it only puffs up. But neither without knowledge can there be any edification; and the purer the knowledge that is propagated by any church the purer, the deeper, the more vital and the more vitalizing will be the Christianity that is built up under that church's teaching. Let us renounce, then, in this sphere, too, all "deisidaimonism," and demand that our church shall be the church of a creed and that that creed shall be the pure truth of God—all of it and nothing but it. Only so can we be truly, purely, and vitally Christian.

And what shall we say of "deisidaimonism" in the personal religious life? Ah, brethren, there is where its temptations are the most subtle and its assaults the most destructive! How easy it is to mistake the currents of mere natural religious feeling, that flow up and down in the soul, for signs that it is well with us in the sight of God! Happy the man who is born with a deep and sensitive religious nature! But shall that purely natural endowment save him? There are many who have cried, Lord, Lord, who shall never enter into the kingdom of heaven. Not because you are sensitive and easily moved to devotion; not because your sense of divine things is profound or lofty; not because you are like the Athenians, by nature "divinity-fearing"; but because, when the word of the Lord is brought to you, and Jesus Christ is revealed in your soul, under the prevailing influence of the Holy Ghost, you embrace Him with a hearty faith—cast yourself upon His almighty grace for salvation, and turning from your sins, enter into a life of obedience to Him— can you judge yourself a Christian. Religious you may be, and deeply religious, and yet not a Christian. How instructive that when Paul himself preached in "deisidaimonistic" Athens, where religiosity ran riot, no church seems to have been founded. We have only the meager result recorded that "there were some men that clave unto him and believed, among whom also was Dionysius, the Areopagite, and a woman named Damaris, and others along with them." The natively religious are not, therefore, nearer to the kingdom of God.

But, thank God, the contrary is also true. Those who have no special native religious endowments are not, therefore, excluded from the kingdom of God. We may rightly bewail our coldness: we may rightly blame ourselves that there is so little response in our hearts to the sight of the glory of God in the face of Jesus Christ, or even to the manifestation of His unspeakable love in the death of His Son. Oh, wretched men that we are to see that bleeding love and not be set on fire with a flame of devotion! But we may be all the more thankful that it is not in our frames and feelings that we are to put our trust. Let us abase ourselves that we so little respond to these great spectacles of the everlasting and unspeakable love of God. But let us ever remember that it is on the love of God and not on our appreciation of it that we are to build our confidence. Jesus our Priest and our Sacrifice, let us keep our eyes set on Him! And though our poor sinful hearts so little know how to yield to that great spectacle the homage of a suitable response, His blood will yet avail even for us.

> "Nothing in my hand I bring,
> Simply to Thy cross I cling"—

here—and let us bless God for it—here is the essence of Christianity. It is all of God and nothing of ourselves.

CHAPTER TEN

The Areopagus Address

NED B. STONEHOUSE

CONTENTS

THE
AREOPAGUS ADDRESS

INTRODUCTION

IN venturing upon a discussion of the address of the apostle Paul at Athens, recorded in Acts xvii. 22-31, I am mindful that I am not entering upon a largely neglected field of investigation. The passage is so replete with exceptional and arresting features that the commentators and the historians of early Christianity have been stimulated to treat it at considerable length. Moreover, a remarkable number of learned monographs have been devoted to its interpretation.

Much as one may learn from what others have written, my impression is that the last word has by no means been spoken, and that the Areopagus address will continue to challenge the Biblical interpreter to press forward to his goal, both because of the variety and intricacy of problems which it presents and because of its far-reaching implications for the understanding of early Christianity. Many modern discussions, moreover, have been absorbed with certain restricted aspects of the narrative such as linguistic or archaeological features. Such studies are indispensable to a proper evaluation of the problems; at certain points account is taken of them here, at others they are presupposed. But they have, perhaps unavoidably, left rather undeveloped the broader questions of the historical and theological significance of the *Areopagitica,* and my purpose is to try, if only in small measure, to improve that situation.

A further impression is that many influential treatises

proceed upon the basis of a wrong exegetical method. This appears to be particularly true of representatives of the *religions-geschichtliche methode.* While they have the merit of struggling with the basic questions of the place occupied by this address within the context of the history of religion in the Hellenistic Age, it is ironical that in seeking to integrate the narrative with contemporaneous thought and action they end up by displaying sharply divisive tendencies. For tensions and discrepancies are alleged to exist, not only between the Paul of the Athens story and the earliest Christianity, and between this Paul and the Paul of the Epistles, and between this Paul and the Paul of the rest of Acts, but even within the testimony of Acts xvii.

Albert Schweitzer gives brief but pungent expression to this general approach in his book, *The Mysticism of Paul the Apostle.*[1] On the background of Norden's learned and challenging work, *Agnostos Theos* (1913), he regards certain features of the address, and especially the quotation, 'In Him we live and move and have our being' (xvii. 28), as expressing a God-mysticism which is Stoic rather than Christian, and as having in view an immanentistic and natural view of the world rather than one that conceives of God as transcendent and of history in supernatural terms. This pantheistic God-mysticism is declared to be utterly antithetical to the particularistic, predestinarian Christ-mysticism of the genuine Paul. For this basic reason, as well as for the reason that he judges that there 'can never have been such an inscription' as is reported in Acts xvii. 23, Schweitzer concludes that the speech is unhistorical.

Far more elaborate is the treatment of Martin Dibelius in a monograph published in 1939,[2] which is perhaps the most important study of its kind since Norden's monu-

---

[1] *Die Mystik des Apostels Paulus* (1930) ; E.T., 1931.

[2] *Paulus auf dem Areopag* (Sitzungsberichte der Heidelberger Akademie der Wissenschaften, Phil.-hist. Klasse, 1938-39, 2. Abhandlung).

mental treatise. The body of the address Dibelius regards as distinctly Hellenistic; its general theme the true knowledge of God, a knowledge which is viewed as being accessible to every man inasmuch as his place within the world and the affinity of God must lead thereto. Three principal divisions of the address are distinguished: (a) God, Creator and Lord of the world, requires no temple because He is without needs (verses 24, 25); (b) God made man with the destiny that he should seek Him (verses 26, 27); (c) the affinity of man with God (for we are ' His offspring ') should preclude all worship of images (verses 28, 29). All three divisions are thought to betray Hellenistic motifs and the address as a whole is viewed as representing a significant development of theology in the soil of Greek culture. The author of Acts is regarded as dealing so freely with the facts that he presents a largely imaginative picture of the manner in which, according to his conception, Paul would have sought to commend Christianity to the heathen. The only Christian feature of the address, according to Dibelius, is the concluding sentence which presents a call to repentance in connection with a declaration of the eschatological judgment, but even this conclusion is thought not to be wholly consistent with the teaching of Paul in the Epistles. The introduction to the address, moreover, is regarded as inconsistent with the mood of the address itself, although not sufficiently to disallow that it could be the work of the author of Acts.

Evaluations such as those of Schweitzer and Dibelius underscore the propriety of seeking to gauge anew what the account actually represents Paul as saying—what the disposition and motif of the address really are. And in treating these matters one is compelled to explore to some extent the larger questions as to the place of this message within the total witness of the New Testament to the teaching of Paul and even within the compass of the still larger question as to the essence of Christianity.

The question of the *Anknüpfungspunkt* is in the foreground of interest. Wherever there is a grappling with the
Christian doctrine of revelation and the Christian doctrine
of man it will necessarily have to be faced with all earnestness. How can the divine Word, without losing its divine
character, be communicated to and apprehended by a finite
creature, and especially a creature who, as the consequence
of the noetic effects of sin, is viewed as darkened in his
understanding to the point where he cannot know the
things of the Spirit of God? This urgent theological problem confronts the reader of Acts xvii in a most arresting
manner, and though the systematic discussion of the problem would take us far afield, the interpretation of the passage will require some reflection upon it.

The immediate reaction of Paul's hearers indeed does
not suggest that *they* recognized that the respective religions had much in common or that the Pauline message
found an echo in their own experience. Paul seemed to
them to be a setter forth of *strange gods,* to be bringing
certain *strange things* into their ears, to be speaking *a new
teaching;* and their interest in hearing further concerning
it is associated with their characteristic interest as Athenians
in something *new* (verses 18-21). It is Paul rather than his
pagan hearers who may appear to stress the element of religious commonness especially at the beginning of his address in his observations concerning the altar, and later in
his quotations from the heathen poets. Plainly he is at these
points doing far more than cleverly applying so-called practical psychology calculated 'to win friends and influence
people.' Paul does show himself to be a masterful public
speaker in his ability to arrest attention by linking his message with features of his listeners' own experience, but his
apparently favourable judgments concerning their religious
beliefs and practices obviously transcend barely formal
aspects. The question remains, however, exactly how the
element of commonness is conceived. Does the evidence

support the conclusion that Paul tones down the antithesis between Christianity and paganism, or at least that the author of Acts represents him as doing so at Athens? Or is perhaps the situation rather that the intolerance of paganism is as unrelieved here as anywhere in the Scriptures, but that the point of contact is found basically to be concerned with judgments regarding the nature of man and his religious responses to the divine revelation?

I.   HISTORICAL SETTING AND OCCASION

Although my interest in this study centres upon the Areopagus address itself and it is therefore beyond the scope of this paper to treat all the questions which emerge in connection with the examination of the fascinating context in which Luke presents the address, there are features of the context which are so basically significant for our understanding of the discourse that they must be evaluated, however briefly. The consequences of the address, including especially the intimation that it did not meet with general favour, bear pointedly upon one's final evaluation of it. But no less does the introduction to the discourse in the midst of the Areopagus help towards the understanding of Paul's aim and method as preacher and apologist.

Paul had come to Athens with the purpose of finding a brief respite from the arduous experiences and the perils of his activity in Macedonia rather than to carry forward his apostolic mission. Almost from the beginning of his European ministry he had been harassed by hostile men; in Philippi he and Silas had been severely beaten and imprisoned; at Thessalonica the unbelieving Jews incited a tumult which made further activity impracticable and dangerous; in Berea the advantage of a favourable reception was offset when the Thessalonian Jews arrived once more to stir up the multitudes against Paul and imperilled his

mission and person. To relieve this situation Paul was constrained to go to Athens, but evidently it was regarded as
a mere stopping place on his way to Corinth. For Silas and
Timothy were enjoined to catch up with him as speedily as
possible, and, as Acts reports (xviii. 5), the reunion was
realized in Corinth, where he remained for a year and a
half.[3] Paul accordingly was taking a brief holiday in Athens
and did not anticipate the activity which he actually carried on in this brief interlude. An unforeseen circumstance
constrained him to speak, and once having made himself
heard he came soon to encounter the quite novel situation
of giving an account of his Christian faith in the midst of
the Areopagus.

Like many men of today on holiday in an historic and
illustrious city, Paul had gone to see the sights of Athens.
Though it was no longer in its golden age, the splendour
of that age was still in evidence. The beautiful setting of
the city in the midst of hills on a great bay of the Aegean
was quite as stirring as ever, and the magnificent temples
and public works added lustre to the munificence of nature.
To conclude that Paul had no eye whatsoever for the
beauty that surrounded him as he strode about the city
would be rash and gratuitous. Nevertheless, his philosophy
of life was not such as would permit him to evaluate nature
and civilization in detachment from his religious faith. The
gigantic gold and ivory statue of Athena in the Parthenon
on the Acropolis, for example, could not be viewed by Paul
simply as a thing of beauty. The fact that it was an idol
stirred Paul far more profoundly than its aesthetic merits.

3 1 Thes. iii. 1, 6 implies indeed that Timothy must have joined Paul in
Athens and returned to Thessalonica before rejoining Paul, presumably at
Corinth. Lake and Cadbury, in *The Beginnings of Christianity,* Part I, Vol. IV,
in their note on Acts xviii. 5, among others, find a discrepancy here on the
ground that ' we . . . alone ' in 1 Thes. iii. 1 must include Silas whose name
is joined with Paul's and Timothy's in the salutation. Although the Pauline
language allows for this interpretation, it does not require it. As the usage
in 1 Corinthians, for example, discloses, the inclusion of others besides Paul
in the salutation does not govern the decision as to the use of the singular
or plural in the Epistles themselves.

Paul was struck, moreover, by the fact that Athens was 'full of idols' (verse 16). Luke can hardly mean to suggest that now for the first time Paul had come face to face with the prevalence of idolatry in a pagan city, for Luke had reported his residence in Syrian Antioch and he himself probably knew from first-hand knowledge how typically pagan was that city also. Still less can Luke intend to imply that Paul was ordinarily rather complacent towards idolatry. Perhaps the excessive zeal of Athens in this regard, which indeed had become proverbial in the ancient world— especially when considered in the perspective of the intellectual and cultural achievements and pretensions of Athens —contributed to the sharply negative reaction of Paul. But Paul's irritation is referred to not so much that we should dwell upon the novelty or relative novelty of his psychological state as he was confronted with the idolatry of Athens, but in order to explain why Paul could not remain silent in Athens and felt compelled to preach the gospel in spite of his original intention to secure a brief period of relief from the tensions attendant upon his apostolic mission. The special circumstances in Athens merely provided the occasion for Paul's deep indignation; his fervent monotheism was the actual cause of it. And it is not without significance that the word which Luke employs to indicate Paul's feeling is frequently used in the LXX where the Lord is described as being provoked to anger at the idolatry of His people.[4] The zeal of the Lord was eating up His servant Paul, and he was constrained to break his silence in the presence of the presumption of pagan worship.

Another significant feature of the Lucan introduction to the Areopagus address is the intimation that Paul's preaching in Athens was by no means confined to the address reported at some length. Even in Athens Paul did not fail to take advantage of the liberty of the synagogue.

[4] See the use of παροξύνομαι in Dt. ix. 18; Psalm cvi. 29; Is. lxv. 3; Ho. viii. 5: cf. Dt. xxix. 25ff., 28).

Evidently, in view of what is to come, Luke treats the ministry there quite summarily, but he can hardly have much less in view than what he has reported, also somewhat summarily, concerning Paul's activity in Thessalonica, when he states that 'as his custom was' he went into the synagogue of the Jews, 'and for three sabbath days reasoned with them from the scriptures, opening and alleging, that it behoved the Christ to suffer, and to rise again from the dead; and that this Jesus, whom, said he, I proclaim unto you, is the Christ' (xvii. 2-4, R.V.).[5] His reasoning with the Jews in Athens, as in Thessalonica, must have involved a fairly comprehensive presentation of his apostolic message.

Perhaps Luke deals so summarily with the ministry in the synagogue because of his interest in informing his readers of what developed as Paul, taking advantage of the liberty of the market-place, confronted the devotees of pagan religion with the Christian evangel. In contrast with the weekly contact with the Jews, Paul reasoned every day with those who encountered him in the *agora*. But the message during the week was the same as that on the sabbath, for Luke declares that, however novel or trifling the Stoics and Epicureans judged it to be, actually 'he preached Jesus and the resurrection' (verse 18). Although perhaps they so far misunderstood that message as to suppose that he was actually proclaiming two divinities,[6] there can be no doubt that Luke himself regards this phrase as a summary characterization of the apostolic preaching. So indeed all of the sermons previously recorded in Acts might well be designated; so rather precisely Luke has spoken of the apostolic

5 It is of significance that the verb διαλέγομαι is used in both instances (Acts xvii. 2, 17). See also Acts xviii. 4, 19, xix. 8, 9, xx. 7, 9, xxiv. 12, 25. Of further interest is the fact that, while the aorist tense is employed in referring to the activity covering three sabbaths in Thessalonica, the imperfect tense is used in speaking of his ministry in the synagogue in Athens. While the imperfect form may not involve an extensive period, it underscores the impression that Luke by no means restricts his preaching in the synagogue to a single sabbath.

6 So most expositors suppose. Jake and Cadbury form an exception.

kerygma in Acts iv. 2 when, in telling of the opposition of the Sadducees to Peter and John, he declares that they were vexed because the apostles 'taught the people and proclaimed in Jesus the resurrection from the dead.'

It was in the course of this preaching of 'Jesus and the resurrection' in the *agora* that the stage was set for the Areopagus address. The question whether Paul was led away from the market-place to the Hill of Ares (the 'Mars' Hill' of A.V.) near the Acropolis, or was haled before the supreme council of Athens, known as the Areopagus in view of its former custom of convening upon that hill, is not of decisive significance for the determination of the disposition and meaning of the address itself. For even in the latter case, a broader audience than the constituency of the council would appear to be in view. Nevertheless, the question is of such intrinsic interest and positive bearing upon one's understanding of the historical setting that it may not fairly be passed over in this discussion. My own judgment is that, although perhaps the view that the hill rather than the council is in mind cannot be finally discarded as being beyond the realm of possibility, there are preponderant reasons for concluding that Paul is represented as appearing before the council of the Areopagus. That indeed the philosophers should have desired to take Paul away from the busy market-place to the somewhat isolated hill with a view to a more quiet and leisurely inquiry may well be allowed. But this explanation is not compelling since no adequate reason appears why the inquiry should not have continued there in the *agora* where they were wont to carry on their disputations. If, however, Paul is taken before the Areopagus, probably in the *Stoa Basileios* in the market-place itself, all is intelligible. The absence of intimation of arrest and of distinctly judicial examination disallows the possibility of a formal trial, and if that were the sole prerogative of the supreme council of Athens, the position favoured here would have to be rejected. But since the council evidently enjoyed some general prerogatives, including the exercise of some control of lecturing in the market-place, full justice is done to the data of Acts if one understands that Paul was compelled to face the council to demonstrate that his appearance among the public lecturers of Athens was unobjectionable.

The most specific confirmation of this view is found, in my judgment, in the manner in which references to the Areopagus are introduced. Paul is said to have stood 'in the midst of the Areopagus' (verse 22), and following the conclusion of his address to have gone out 'from their midst' (verse 33). The prepositional phrase 'in the midst of' may be used with reference to places as well as persons: Lk. xxi. 28 refers to those who are in the midst of Judæa; Mk. vi. 47 to the boat of the disciples as being in the midst of the sea. But it is exceedingly doubtful that a person or group of persons would be described as being in the midst of a hill. On the other hand, Luke repeatedly speaks of persons as being in the midst of other persons (Acts i. 15, ii. 22, iv. 7, xxvii. 21 ; Lk. ii. 46, xxii. 27, 55, xxiv. 36). And the utmost continuity is preserved on this view since Paul is said to have gone forth from *their* midst.[7]

That Paul's address was delivered before the supreme council of Athens emphasizes accordingly the uniqueness of the occasion of its delivery and underscores the necessity of making due allowance for its distinctive contents. Apart from the brief summary of the discourse at Lystra (Acts

---

[7] See especially Ramsay, *St. Paul the Traveller and Roman Citizen* (1903), pp. 243ff.; *The Bearing of Recent Discovery on the Trustworthiness of the New Testament* (1915), pp. 102ff.; Lake and Cadbury *ad loc.* Dibelius, *op. cit.*, p. 9, argues that the hill is favoured by the consideration that in Acts xvii. 19 a change of scene is indicated ; and since Paul has been viewed as active in the *agora* he must now be thought of as being taken away from the *agora* to the hill. However, he may quite well be conceived of as being taken from a certain point within the *agora* to the particular place where the Areopagus convened. Moreover, the preposition ἐπί may quite possibly mean 'before' rather than 'to' at this point; cf. the usage in Acts xvi. 19, xvii. 6 ; and the designation of Dionysius as the Areopagite, that is, as a member of the council, is most intelligible on the understanding that the council has been referred to in the preceding context.

xiv. 15 ff.) and such intimations as are provided in Paul's Epistles, the address at Athens provides our only evidence of the apostle's direct approach to a pagan audience. And even this address, though not presented as unrepresentative of his preaching to unconverted Gentiles, is likewise not included as completely typical of such preaching.[8]

II. THE ALTAR TO AN UNKNOWN GOD

At the commencement of Paul's address the attention is unmistakably centred upon the religious devotion of the Athenians. Recalling his tour of the city in which he had been aroused to indignation at the prevalence of idolatry, he singles out for special attention one altar among the many 'objects of worship' upon which was inscribed the words ΑΓΝΩΣΤΩ ΘΕΩ ('To an unknown God'). A basic problem facing the interpreter is that of Paul's evaluation of the worship of the unknown God. But a prior question is what such an altar discloses as to the religiosity of the Athenians in the context of their own religious history and outlook, a question which cannot be dissociated from that of the historicity of the book of Acts at this point.

Baur and Zeller as exponents of the Tübingen criticism of Acts, and Schweitzer and Dibelius as representatives of a contemporaneous point of view which retains certain basic evaluations of that school, may be mentioned among the many modern writers who have flatly rejected the testimony of Acts regarding the existence of such an altar. Schweitzer, whose position on this matter is fairly representative, sets forth his view as follows :

That the speech is unhistorical is at once portrayed by the

[8] In passing one may observe how Luke gives evidence of being completely at home in describing the Athenian scene, a fact which is left unaccounted for on certain evaluations of his competence. Lake and Cadbury remark on verse 19 : ' According to Acts, therefore, just as Paul is brought before the στρατηγοί at Philippi, the πολιτάρχαι at Thessalonica, the ἀνθύπατος at Corinth, so at Athens he faces the Areopagus. The local name for the supreme authority is in each case different and accurate.'

fact that Paul takes for his starting-point an inscription dedicating an Athenian altar ' to an unknown God.' There can never have been such an inscription. There is evidence in current literature only for altars to 'unknown Gods' in the plural, not to *an* unknown God in the singular.[9]

Appealing to the often-quoted allusions in the writings of Pausanias and Philostratus, and recalling Jerome's judgment that Paul had altered the inscription to serve the purposes of his address, he concludes that it was the author of Acts rather than Paul 'who transposed the inscription from the plural to the singular, in order to provide Paul with a starting-point for his discourse on monotheism.' 'Such alterations of traditions and citations,' he goes on to say, 'were practised without scruple by the religious propaganda of antiquity in its literary forms.'[10]

Several critical observations are in order here:

(1) We must challenge the propriety of the assumption that Luke would have felt free to take liberties with historical fact simply because there are evidences that ancient historians sometimes accommodated their facts to their practical purposes. This unscientifically disallows of exceptions to what is said to be characteristic of that age; it begs the question whether the Christian Luke may not have had higher standards; it demands that his specific claim to write accurately and with a view to providing certainty concerning what had actually taken place be set aside as being merely conventional and rhetorical.

(2) This position is most rash, further, in its declaration that 'there can never have been such an inscription' on the basis of nothing more than an argument from silence. For even if there were many instead of a very few declarations extant concerning altars to unknown gods, they could never demonstrate that an altar to an unknown god never existed; silence concerning such an altar could prove only that, for one reason or another, allusion to it had not been

[9] *Op. cit.,* E.T. p. 6.
[10] *Op. cit.,* p. 7.

preserved. Actually, of course, the consideration rests on even less than an argument from silence since the Acts itself, even if doubt were cast upon the Lucan authorship, remains a contemporaneous witness of the first rank. And as it is the testimony of Luke, an intimate associate of Paul, it would be rash to set it aside merely because no confirmation of its historicity has been discovered. Schweitzer's dogmatism may be happily contrasted with the statement of Foakes-Jackson in the Moffatt Commentary that 'Paul implies that on close inspection he found a single altar thus dedicated, which may have escaped the notice of those who had written about Athens.'

(3) It is not as conclusive as many modern critics of the Acts claim that no confirmatory evidence has been forthcoming. While I should certainly not challenge the conclusion that there were in Athens altars dedicated to unknown *gods,* it remains possible to construe the language of Pausanias and Philostratus so as to allow for knowledge of an altar to an unknown god as well, although certainly it was not pertinent to their purpose to distinguish between them. When Pausanias says, for example, that on this visit to Athens (about the middle of the second century of the Christian era) he noticed on the road from the Phaleron Bay harbour to the city 'altars of the gods named unknown ' (βωμοὶ δὲ θεῶν τε ὀνομαξομένων ἀγνώστων), who can insist that there was not among them one inscribed Ἀγνώστῳ Θεῷ ? Likewise the statement Philostratus ascribes to Apollonius, that it is the part of wisdom 'to speak well of all the gods, especially in Athens where altars are set up in honour even of unknown gods' (τὸ περὶ πάντων θεῶν εὖ λέγειν καὶ ταῦτα Ἀθήνησιν, οὗ καὶ ἀγνώστων δαιμόνων βωμοὶ ἵδρυνται), though no doubt applying to altars inscribed with the plural designation, is sufficiently general to comprehend one with the singular form.[11]

[11] Pausanias, *Description of Greece*, i. 1. 4 ; Philostratus, *Life of Apollonius*, vi. 3. 5.

(4) Moreover, even if these historical allusions to the religious life of Greece and Athens were exclusive of the Lucan report, there would be powerful confirmation of the credibility of Acts from the well-known story of Diogenes Laertius concerning Epimenides the Cretan, who, when summoned during a plague, advised that white and black sheep should be driven from the Areopagus and that where they came to rest the Athenians should sacrifice 'to the appropriate god' (τῷ προσήκοντι θεῷ). As a result the plague was stayed, and Diogenes reports that even in his day (in the third century A.D.) 'anonymous altars' (βωμοὺς ἀνωνύμους) were found in the vicinity of Athens.[12]

Norden and Dibelius, to be sure, know this story and discuss it in relation to their view that the author of Acts must have altered the plural to the singular in the interest of presenting Paul as an exponent of monotheism, and thus actually invented the altar with the inscription Agnosto Theo. They point out that the story of Diogenes Laertius says nothing concerning an *inscription* upon the altars erected to the appropriate deity.[13] It must indeed be admitted that no precise confirmation of the inscription as reported in Acts is provided by it. This conclusion fails, however, to face the issue in the sharpest terms. It fails to observe that the narrative sheds no light whatever upon the origin of an altar to unknown *gods*. Polytheists might fear that their pantheon was not complete and that there were *gods* who were being deprived of their rightful service because they remained unknown, and thus one may conceive of the erection of altars to unknown *gods*. But the story of Epimenides has in view an essentially different type of situation, in which on a particular historical

---

12 Diogenes Laertius, *Lives of the Philosophers*, i, 110 ; cf. Wetstein, *Novum Testamentum*, II (1752), *ad loc.* Among modern commentators who have utilized this story as a background for the understanding of the narrative mention may be made of Joseph Addison Alexander (1858), Knowling. and Lake and Cadbury.

13 Norden. *Agnostos Theos*, p. 57, n. 1 ; Dibelius, *op. cit.*, pp. 16f.

occasion sacrifice was offered to a specific, though unknown, *god*. Accordingly, though this story does not establish the existence of an altar or altars with the precise inscription found in Acts xvii, it furnishes the very background which is required to make it intelligible and bears witness to the prevalence in Athens of the very kind of piety upon which Paul reflects.[14]

The question as to the religious motif which came to expression in the offering of sacrifices 'to the appropriate god,' and which could have taken the form of worship of an unknown god, needs to be analysed more specifically. Knowling is representative of the view that 'in such an inscription Paul wisely recognized that there was in the heart of Athens a witness to the deep unsatisfied yearning of humanity for a clearer and closer knowledge of the unseen power which men worshipped dimly and imperfectly, a yearning expression in the sacred Vedic hymns of an old world, or in the crude religions of a new.'[15] Such a formulation reads much more of positive religious significance into the Athenian piety than is suggested either by the story of Epimenides or by Paul's allusion to the altar to the unknown god. Knowling seems to imply that Paul regarded the polytheistic religion of Athens as a kind of imperfect monotheism, a 'knowledge of the unseen power' which needed only to become clearer and more intimate. But how can the readiness to include still another god in their pantheon constitute an approach towards monotheism? The idea of an open pantheon, like that of an open universe in which anything can happen, points to an under-

14 Lake, *Beginnings*, V, p. 242, says: 'There is no evidence for an altar to any one god who was specially called "the unknown," but the story in Diogenes Laertius suggests that the singular may have been used in the formula τῷ προσήκοντι θεῷ meaning " to the unknown god who is concerned in the matter " ; ἀγνώστῳ θεῷ would be a loose but not very inaccurate paraphrase.'

15 In the *Expositor's Greek Testament*, II, on v. 23. See also Dibelius, *op. cit.*, p. 19: 'Für den Areopagredner aber ist einzig der singularische Text der Inschrift brauchbar, denn ihm gilt sie als Zeugnis für das unbewusste Ahnen des wahren Gottes bei den Athenern.'

lying scepticism and irrationalism rather than to a movement towards the one living and true God.

On the other hand, it may not be overlooked that a measure of awareness of the inadequacy of their own religion is indicated. For the erection of the altar manifested an acknowledgment on a particular occasion that they had to do with a god not previously worshipped, one whom they had neglected and offended, and whose disfavour had to be appeased, and who, for all that, yet remained unknown.[16] The worship of an unknown god, coming to expression within the framework of polytheism, remains the idolatrous worship of one god among many. But the singular expression of idolatry exhibited by the altar which attracted Paul's special attention, intimating as it did its own defectiveness, provided a starting point for Paul's proclamation of the living God who was unknown to them.

III. PAUL'S CHARACTERIZATION OF THEIR WORSHIP

Paul's own characterizations of the religion of the Athenians serve most immediately to introduce his positive proclamation. They bear pointedly upon one's evaluation of its disposition and thrust, since the question whether he assumes a relatively complacent attitude toward their idolatry, or maintains a mood of indignation, or adopts some other attitude towards it, is in the foreground of interest.

One's attention centres, first of all, upon the fact that he classifies the altar in the focal point of interest among 'the objects of your worship' (τὰ σεβάσματα). This word is used on only one other occasion in the New Testament, namely in 2 Thes. ii. 4, where Paul speaks of the man of lawlessness

16 J. H. Bavinck, *Alzoo Wies het Woord* (Baarn, Holland, n.d.), p. 175, presents basically this view when he says that the maker of this altar apparently, ‘hetzij vanwege bijzonderen nood of vanwege bijzonderen zegen, genoopt gevoeld heeft een bepaalden god aan te roepen, maar dat hij niet geweten heeft tot welken god hij zich wenden moest.’ It is doubtful, however, that he is on equally solid ground in his conclusion that Paul viewed the altar as symptomatic of heathen religion generally.

as 'he that opposeth and exalteth himself against all that is called God or is an object of worship.' While the anti-religious and blasphemous pretensions of the one who sets himself forth as God are thought of as a most direct assault upon the worship of the living God, the use of the compound 'God or object of worship' is best explained as having in view the comprehensiveness and absoluteness of his religious claims. Accordingly, Paul appears to be using the term in 2 Thessalonians at best in a neutral sense and more probably in the unfavourable sense of the idolatrous worship of his day, and there is therefore no hint from the Biblical usage of the term that commendation in the slightest degree is in his mind.[17]

The single instance of the use of the cognate verb 'worship' (σεβάѕομαι) in the New Testament does not lead to a different result. In fact it does quite the contrary, for in that instance Paul is characterizing the pagan religious outlook with the strongest tones of condemnation : 'they exchanged the truth of God for a lie, and worshipped (ἐσεβάσθησαν) and served (ἐλάτρευσαν) the creature rather than the Creator, who is blessed for ever ' (Rom. i. 25). Although the terms 'idol' and 'objects of worship' as used by Paul in Acts xvii. 23 would not necessarily have disclosed to the Athenians Paul's considered judgment concerning such worship, there is, on the other hand, no reason to suppose that his employment of these terms signifies any relaxation of the mood of indignation which Luke attributes to Paul.[18]

Nor is the situation altered by the consideration that Paul uses the verb εὐσεβεῖν to describe their worship of an unknown God when he says, 'That which ye worship . . . I declare unto you ' (verse 23). For this verb with its cognate forms, while frequently employed to express the piety which

---

[17] Considering the usage here and in certain apocryphal writings, Frame, *Thessalonians* (I.C.C.), p. 256, says that it 'indicates not a divinity (*numen*) but any sacred object of worship.'

[18] The verb σέβομαι is used several times in the Acts, usually apparently of the worship of God-fearers, but in xix. 27 of the pagan worship of Diana.

merits divine approval, was widely used in the Hellenistic world as descriptive of religious loyalty demanded by or offered to the Roman emperors.[19] In the context of Acts the εὐσεβεῖν is the worship of one idol among the many heathen objects of worship.

More significant for our understanding of Paul's evaluation of pagan religion is his general characterization of their cultic piety which resulted from his observations concerning their worship: 'I perceive that ye are very religious' (verse 22). The interpretation of the adjective δεισιδαιμονεστέρους reflected in the translation 'very religious' is widely accepted today. It is the translation of both the A.S.V. and the new R.S.V. McGiffert suggested the rendering 'uncommonly religious.' On the other hand, the rendering in the unfavourable sense 'superstitious' cannot be ruled out of court in advance. Although the translation of the A.V. 'too superstitious' is unacceptable from a linguistic and contextual viewpoint, the same cannot be as dogmatically asserted of the rendering of the R.V. 'somewhat superstitious,' which is also supported in the margin of the A.S.V. And the support which the *Commentary* of Lake and Cadbury gives to the rendering 'very superstitious' is indicative of the standing which this evaluation of the word still enjoys.

No good service would be rendered by embarking here upon a survey of the usage of this word with a view to determining its precise meaning, since this has been done in a thorough way, and it has become clear that the word is sufficiently ambiguous and comprehensive to bear both connotations.[20] That this might turn out to be the case is quite understandable when one keeps in view the difference of subjective evaluation of religions, according as a religion may be one's own cherished faith or another's alleged aberration or defection from a standard of piety. The question

19 Cf. Moulton and Milligan, *Vocabulary of the Greek New Testament.*
20 See especially Foerster in *Theologisches Wörterbuch z. N.T.* and Lake and Cadbury in *Beginnings,* IV, on *v.* 22, and their references to the literature.

whether Paul means that they were uncommonly religious or uncommonly superstitious (allowing for some ambiguity in the term and accordingly for differences of interpretation) will have to be determined, in so far as that is possible, by the evaluation of the context.

Although, in my judgment, there is no evidence within the address or outside of it to suggest that Paul is in the slightest degree complacent towards idolatry, and much that demonstrates his thoroughgoing repudiation of it, it does appear definitely more satisfactory in the present connection to conclude that Paul is underscoring their religiosity rather than their superstition. The observation that their worship of idols included even the veneration of an unknown god provides a ground for calling attention to their extraordinary religiousness, a religiousness which went so far as to include even worship of an unknown god. Such worship, however, would not plausibly be regarded, within the context of polytheism, as an evidence of unusual superstition. On the other hand, to affirm that their religiosity rather than their superstition is prominently in view in Paul's opening observation is not to imply commendation on Paul's part of their religiosity. As has been observed, the very flexibility and ambiguity of the word makes it ill-suited to designate a piety which is favourably regarded; and there is nothing in the present context to warrant the conclusion that Paul's purpose is to compliment them on their worship.

On this analysis of the Pauline language, his marked interest in the religion and worship of the Athenians may be of profound significance for the understanding of Paul's approach to the heathen. So far as the analysis has proceeded, there is nothing to suggest that Paul acted on the assumption that he needed only to supplement what the heathen already knew or to build upon a common foundation. However, the occupation with the religiosity of the Athenians can plausibly be explained as due to reflection upon the nature of man as created in the image of God and as therefore made to respond religiously to the Creator. However inadequate and even false the religion of the pagan might be judged to be as a consequence of sin, it would still be a fact of profound significance for the proclamation of the gospel that man retained his fundamental character as a religious being, that, as Calvin taught, he possesses as man, inseparable from his very constitution, an indelible *sensus divinitatis,* which the wicked seek to extinguish, but which is still strong and frequently discovers itself.[21]

That the apostle Paul actually held such a view regarding the constitution and nature of men, and therefore of wicked men too, is demonstrated in Romans i. 19 and its immediate context where he teaches that, in addition to and evidently actually prior to the revelation of God with which all men are confronted in nature round about them, there is a revelation of God 'in them.' In profound agreement with this thought is his further teaching that the heathen have the law of God 'written in their hearts' (Rom. ii. 15). The explicit teaching of Paul therefore provides a background which, rather than setting up tensions or contradictions with the address at Athens, sheds welcome light upon his interest in the religion and worship of the natural man.

IV. THE CHARGE OF IGNORANCE

Although, therefore, the reflections upon the worship of the heathen Athenians in Acts xvii. 22, 23 contain observations concerning the religious state and activity of the natural man rather than evidences of positive agreement as to, or of common ground concerning, what true religion is and requires, one nevertheless encounters in this very context one feature which expresses a basic judgment as to the

[21] *Institutes,* I, iii, 1-3.

character of their religion. This is found in the indictment that their religion was one of ignorance.

The full impact of the charge is easily obscured in translation. The rendering of the King James' Version: 'Whom therefore ye ignorantly worship, him declare I unto you' is particularly unhappy. For besides presupposing an inferior text in the masculine forms 'whom' and 'him' (for 'what' and 'this'), it is quite unsatisfactory in translating the participle ἀγνοοῦντες by the adverb 'ignorantly,' a rendering which lacks precision and, moreover, seems to reflect an emotional reaction not definitely established by the language employed. These defects are overcome in the r.v. and a.s.v. which read: 'What therefore ye worship in ignorance, this I set forth unto you.' Nevertheless, one feature that is still missed is the clear allusion of the participle ἀγνοοῦντες to the adjective ἀγνώστῳ in the inscription which gives real point to the Pauline evaluation. Paul makes the most of their public profession of lack of knowledge concerning the objects of worship by virtually reading it back to them as a characterization of their religion. He says in effect, 'That which ye worship *acknowledging openly your ignorance*, I proclaim unto you.' The ignorance rather than the worship is thus underscored, and Paul is indicating that he will inform them with regard to that concerning which they acknowledge ignorance. The r.s.v. perhaps reflects the point made here when it translates: 'What therefore you worship as unknown, this I proclaim to you.' The words, 'as unknown,' at any rate serve to reflect the inscription 'To an unknown god.' But even this translation fails to make clear that Paul is characterizing the *worshippers* as without knowledge rather than the object of worship as being, from his own point of view, as such unknown. The original, in any case, demonstrates that Paul, though not censorious, takes advantage of their confession to pronounce censure upon the Athenians and describes their religion bluntly as one of ignorance.

But how seriously and absolutely is this indictment of ignorance to be taken ? Does Paul maintain a sharp antithesis between the Christian religion and pagan idolatry? Or is he represented here as softening his polemic, accommodating his point of view to the Hellenistic religiosity of his day, and even acknowledging significant common aspects in Christianity and paganism? The latter viewpoint is widely maintained. Dibelius, for example, argues that an attitude towards idol worship quite different from that in Rom. i appears in Acts xvii. Whereas in Rom. i. 23, 25 Paul is recognized as condemning the pagan entanglement in idolatry with indignation (' *in empörtem Ton* ') he is thought in Acts xvii to be represented as correcting their idolatry in a merely admonishing and reproving tone.[22] On this approach the indictment of ignorance could not be regarded as intended very earnestly.

To advance the clarification of this point it seems advisable to take account immediately of a statement near the close of the address which uses similar language. In verse 30 Paul says that ' the times of ignorance God therefore overlooked, but now he commandeth men that they should all everywhere repent.' This declaration appears to some, especially in view of the use of the verb ' overlook,' to express an exceedingly moderate conception of the culpability of the heathen. Thus Percy Gardner states that, while idolatry was for Paul ' an utter abomination,' to the author of this address ' it is only an unworthy way of regarding their Heavenly Father, for men who are the offspring of God who however in past time tolerated such materialism, until a fresh revelation came in the fulness of time.'[23] But has the thrust of Paul's language in Acts xvii. 30 been correctly understood when he is said to have declared merely that God tolerated their materialism?[24]

[22] *Op. cit.*, p. 39.
[23] ' The Speeches of St. Paul in Acts ' in *Cambridge Biblical Essays* (London, 1909), p. 400.
[24] A. C. McGiffert expresses a quite different view : ' The " overlooking " of ignorance which is here referred to does not imply that in pre-Christian days

Is what Paul states here any different from his utterance concerning 'the passing over of the sins done aforetime, in the forbearance of God' (Rom. iii. 25)? The overlooking of ignorance, like the passing over of sins, properly signifies an attitude of forbearance, a failure to enter into final judgment with the guilty, but is by no means to be identified with complacency towards, or tolerance of, idolatry.

Those who find a discrepancy between the Paul of the Acts and the Paul of the Epistles at this point should have been forewarned against their divisive conclusions by a consideration of the tone of the Lystra episode where Paul's reproof of paganism is plainly not moderate or restrained! Paul was hardly undisturbed when with Barnabas, following the effort of the people to sacrifice to them, he rent his garments, and sprang forth among the multitude, crying out, 'Sirs, why do ye these things?' (Acts xiv. 14f.). In this narrative there is a close parallel to Rom. iii. 25 as well as to Acts xvii. 30, for in verse 16 he says that God 'in past generations permitted all the nations to walk in their own ways,' words which likewise are associated with a call to repentance, that they 'should turn from these vain things unto the living God who made the heaven and the earth . . .' (verse 15). Here clearly there is no tolerance of idolatry; the idols are 'vain things' which are to be repudiated. Paul does not condemn idolatry more emphatically when he writes that the Galatians had been 'in bondage to them that by nature are no gods' (Gal. iv. 8; cf. Rom. i. 21, viii. 20; 1 Cor. xii. 2).[25]

His permitting the nations to walk in their ways, while perhaps not quite the equivalent of saying, as W. L. Knox has recently stated, that God 'handed them over to a repro-

God regarded the idolatry of the heathen with indifference or saved them from the consequences of their sins, denounced so vigorously in Romans i, but simply that the time for the final judgment had not come until now, and that they were, therefore, summoned now to prepare for it as they had not been before' (*The Apostolic Age* [New York, 1903], p. 260, n. 1).

[25] K. J. Popma, *De Oudheid en Wij* (Kampen, 1948), pp. 96ff., has effectively pointed out the significance of the Lystra address.

bate mind,'[26] gives expression to the long-suffering of God who postpones decisive judgment upon sin although men have been deserving of His wrath. In the light of this plain disclosure of how Paul, the Paul of Acts if any one pleases, contemplated the state of the heathen prior to the dawn of the Gentile mission in the new dispensation, it is indefensible to force upon his declaration that God overlooked the times of ignorance the interpretation that God was relatively complacent towards idolatry.

The heathen in Athens were accordingly held responsible, according to Paul, for their state of ignorance as they were for their worship of vain things in Lystra. Their ignorance was a sinful ignorance which if persevered in could lead only to imminent judgment; hence the urgency of the call to repentance both at Lystra and at Athens.

The connection established between Paul's characterizations of the state of the heathen in verses 23 and 30 raises the question of the broad disposition and thrust of the address, for that also bears upon the more specific question of the attitude taken towards idolatry. Dibelius' analysis of the address, which has been mentioned, appears to fail in particular to do justice to its coherence. In dissociating Paul's mood of indignation as described in Acts xvii. 16 from the rest of the address, in isolating likewise the conclusion of Acts xvii. 30, 31 as a Christian appendage to a basically Hellenistic address (as is supposed), and in formulating the theme of the address proper as concerned with the true knowledge of God accessible to the natural man, the antithesis drawn throughout between the idolatrous religion of the heathen and the true worship of God represented by Christianity is not recognized. The facts are, however, that idolatry was the occasion of Paul's activity in Athens, a particular form of idolatry formed the starting-point for his address before the Areopagus, and the proclamation of God as the sovereign Creator and Ruler of all was

26 *The Acts of the Apostles* (Cambridge, 1948), p. 70.

directed against idolatry. It established the impropriety of the worship which makes its gods dependent upon men's handiwork, and showed rather that man, owing his life, breath and all things to God, 'ought not to think that the Godhead is like unto gold, or silver, or stone, graven by art and device of man.' All of this then forms the background for the call to repentance in view of the coming judgment. There are indeed certain features of the address which remain unaccounted for on this analysis, especially the introduction of quotations from the heathen poets in an apparently sympathetic manner. The problems raised by this feature are weighty and they will need to be faced with all earnestness. But it may be observed at once that even these quotations are obviously introduced by Paul to support his principal argument as to the untenability of idolatry, and therefore do not impinge upon the judgment as to the disposition of the address. Paul roundly condemns what he observed as a religion of ignorance.

V. THE APOSTOLIC AUTHORITY

Another fact of fundamental import for the understanding of Paul's approach to the heathen is that he claims that he alone is immediately able to supply their real need, that he alone is able to provide them with a knowledge of the true and living God: 'That which ye worship acknowledging your ignorance, I declare unto you' (ἐγὼ καταγγέλλω ὑμῖν). How bold, if not presumptuous and bigoted, his claim must have appeared to his hearers who had already found occasion to ridicule him as a babbler, or at best conceived of him as proclaiming a deity or deities besides those already worshipped among them! But the note of authority to proclaim the true God, however strange and offensive it may have been to his Athenian hearers, is not a novelty. The Christian proclamation thoughout the New Testament is never viewed as mere human observations concerning the message of the Old Testament and least of all as human reflections upon the religions of the age, but rather as a divine message, true and authoritative as coming from God Himself. Paul declares that the gospel which he preached 'is not after man; for neither did I receive it from man, nor was I taught it, but it came to me through revelation of Jesus Christ' (Gal. i. 11f.). Faith, Paul taught, is of hearing, and hearing 'through the Word of Christ,' and this Word of faith in Christ and His resurrection was proclaimed by Paul and others commissioned by God (Rom. x. 8ff.). And throughout the Acts attention is centred upon the apostolic preaching as carried on by those who were appointed to, and qualified from above for, this task (i. 15ff., ii. 42, vi. 2, 4 and *passim*). Paul in particular is singled out as having received his apostolic commission by an extraordinary divine intervention: he was a chosen vessel to whom the exalted Christ had appeared to appoint him as a minister and witness both of the things wherein he had seen Christ and of the things wherein Christ would appear to him.[27]

Special interest in this connection attaches to the verb which Paul employs in verse 23 in introducing his proclamation. The verb καταγγέλλειν is used frequently in the Acts and the Pauline Epistles of the official apostolic proclamation of the gospel. 'The word of God' is proclaimed by Paul and Barnabas (Acts xiii. 5, xv. 36, xvii. 13); 'the testimony of God' was proclaimed to the Corinthians (1 Cor. ii. 1); 'the gospel' is that which is proclaimed by divine appointment (1 Cor. ix. 14); 'Jesus' (Acts iv. 2, xvii. 3) and 'Christ' (Phil. i. 17, 18; Col. i. 28) likewise sum up the divine message (cf. also Acts iii. 8; 1 Cor. xi. 26). That the publication of the apostolic message was viewed as claiming direct divine authority is furthermore confirmed by the use of the same verb in describing the proclamation beforehand of Christ by the prophets (Acts iii. 24; cf. iii. 18, 52).

When therefore Paul undertakes to inform the Athenians

[27] Cf. Acts ix. 15, 16, xx. 24, xxii. 14f., xxvi. 16ff.

concerning the sovereign Creator and Judge, and declares that he is proclaiming to them that with regard to which they had in a measure acknowledged ignorance, he sounds the characteristic apostolic note of divine authority. How far he is therefore from stressing supposedly common ground between himself and his pagan hearers! When he says that the state of the heathen was characterized by ignorance of the true God, and he himself boldly asserts his qualifications to provide them with true knowledge, he is accenting, rather than toning down, the antithesis between the pagan religiosity and the Christian religion. When Paul's claim to inform them truly and authoritatively concerning God is taken earnestly, there is no place for the judgment that the thrust of the address is concerned with the knowledge of God and the affinity with God of the natural man, as Dibelius contends, and especially for his asseveration that nothing is said of the claim of the Christian message that the true knowledge of God can be possessed and communicated only by way of revelation.[28] Although the word 'revelation' does not appear, Paul's claim does not fall short of that of the Christian message generally, whether published by the prophets or apostles or by Jesus Christ Himself.

VI.   THE SOVEREIGN CREATOR AND LORD

Perhaps the most controversial terrain in the entire narrative lies before us in the study of verses 24-29. The proclamation of God as Creator and Ruler of the world, as has been observed, is often viewed as an affirmation of monotheism, which is thought of as being not distinctively Christian and even as occupying to a large extent common ground with the religious outlook of non-Christians in the

28 *Op. cit.,* pp. 36ff. and passim. He says : ' Von dem Anspruch der christlichen Botschaft die wahre Gotteserkenntnis erst durch Offenbarung zu besitzen und mitteilen zu koennen wird nichts gesagt ' (p. 36). The revelational note appears also with particular force in verses 30, 31.

Hellenistic age. Although it will not be practicable to consider all the data in detail, certain observations can be made with regard to the main problem. I wish here especially to raise the question as to whether Paul remains on distinctly Christian ground in his positive affirmations and to gauge the implications of his utilization of quotations from heathen poets.

The first observation is that the God whom Paul proclaims the Creator and Lord of heaven and earth, who is self-sufficient, and therefore ought not to be thought of as dependent upon man and worshipped as an idol, is not presented as a matter of fact *in this address* as one whose knowledge may be taken for granted or presupposed or even inferred from a study of the world and history. As has been stressed, Paul proclaims this God as one who is basically unknown to his hearers. Moreover, the appeal is not, at least not in verses 24-26, to natural revelation which would yield these conclusions if properly interpreted. There is nothing, for example, even parallel to the teaching of Paul in Romans i. 20 that 'the invisible things of him since the creation of the world are clearly seen, being perceived through the things that are made, even his everlasting power and divinity, that they may be without excuse.' Rather the mood is the quite dogmatic one of special revelation associated with Paul's own authoritative claims and reinforced by a direct dependence upon the teaching of the Old Testament. Paul may have thought it inappropriate to appeal specifically to the authority of the Old Testament, but the reflection of its language and thought is none the less in evidence throughout. For example, he is on thoroughly Biblical ground in speaking of God as the one 'that made the world and all things therein,' for this language is a virtual quotation from Ex. xx. 11 and has found expression repeatedly in both the Old and New Testaments (cf. Ps. cxlvi. 6; Is. xxxvii. 16; Acts iv. 24, xiv. 15). Likewise the declaration that God is 'Lord' of heaven and earth and 'dwelleth not in temples made with hands' is an echo of 1 Ki. viii. 27 and was previously affirmed in the address of Stephen (Acts vii. 48 ; cf. Is. xlvi. 1f.).[29] The entire statement concerning God as Creator and Ruler is so obviously a reflection of Biblical perspectives that the argument as to supposedly Hellenistic motifs at most establishes points of contact with the contemporaneous religious vocabulary. Only in the Bible does the doctrine of the sovereign Creator and Ruler, without compromise with immanentistic ideas, come to expression, and this is conspicuously in evidence in verses 24-26.

Paul may perhaps have in the background of his thought his teaching regarding the revelation through nature concerning which he spoke at Lystra in affirming that they had not been left without witness (Acts xiv. 17), and in Rom. i. 20, where he writes concerning the witness to the everlasting power and divinity in the things that are clearly seen. In so far as the testimony of nature may be in mind, however, Paul would have to be understood as concerned to interpret the natural revelation in terms of special revelation.

Nor is the supposedly common ground of natural religion reached when Paul intimates that God had created the world and ordained its affairs that men 'should seek God, if haply they might feel after him and find him' (verse 27). For there is no hint that the heathen are conceived of as having found God as the result of a groping after Him or as yearning after Him in a manner which had gained the divine approbation. There is no suggestion of a recognition of a kind of 'unconscious Christianity.' Paul is not describing contemporaneous pagan religion but rather is disclosing the divine purpose regarding man's religious

---

[29] Other evidences of agreement with Biblical perspectives concerning the divine self-sufficiency, sovereign ordering of events, and the impropriety of idol worship have often been pointed out. Cf. especially Dt. xxxii. 8 ; Is. xlii. 5 ; Ps. l. 12. Even Norden, *op. cit.*, pp. 8ff., admits the influence of such passages as these, and declares that the 'Grundmotiv' is 'jüdisch-christlich.'

response which was grounded in the creation of man and the divine rule over him. To man was appointed the privilege of religious fellowship with his Creator, and this was to be attained by way of a conscious seeking after God in response to the divine revelation. That goal had always remained, but in 'the times of ignorance' it evidently remained distant and had not been reached.

When now Paul adds the concession, 'though he is not far from each one of us,' he appears to present a new perspective. The concessive character of this statement indeed confirms the conclusion that the goal of finding God had not been attained, but it also reflects positively on an actual relationship of God to all men in the present situation. And what Paul has in mind in characterizing God as being near to all men is apparently regarded as illumined and supported by the more specific affirmations that 'in him we live and move and have our being' and that 'we are also his offspring.' Since the latter quotation is derived from a work of the Stoic Aratus, and the former is almost certainly from Epimenides the Cretan,[30] there emerges most acutely the problem of the propriety of appealing to pagan teaching with the apparent intent of confirming Christian doctrine.

The problem is formidable because the quotations in their proper pagan contexts express points of view which were undoubtedly quite repugnant to Paul. How far removed from the Christian theism of Paul, with its doctrine of the sovereignty of the Creator and Lord and of man as created and fallen, were the heathen deification of man or the humanizing of a god, and the pantheistic mysticism of the Stoics, not to dwell on the irreligious scepticism of the Epicureans! Moreover, Paul would appear to be contradicting his evaluation of the Gentiles, which must have included the poets who are quoted as belonging to the 'times of ignorance,' and his judgment upon the

---

[30] On these questions see Lake and Cadbury *ad loc.*; Lake, *Beginnings*, V. pp. 246ff.; and F. F. Bruce, *The Speeches in Acts* (London, 1942), pp. 16ff.

religion of Athens as one of ignorance. In spite of the antithesis which in fact existed, and which Paul insists upon, can there be a finding of common ground between him and his pagan audience?

A tempting and rather facile solution might be found if Paul could be regarded as virtually Christianizing the quotations in incorporating them into his proclamation. Their language as such indeed would not necessarily compromise the Christian theism enunciated by Paul. In the context of the thought of the preceding verses, the immanence of God expressed in the former quotation could be viewed as deriving its significance from the fact that God is acknowledged by the apostle with full earnestness as the Creator and Lord of all men. That 'we live and move and have our being' in God would then be a corollary of the doctrine of the absolute dependence of the creature upon the Creator for life and breath and all things. Similarly, the recognition that man is the offspring of God might enunciate a doctrine which lies at the basis of Paul's reflections in the narrative upon the original constitution of man and his retention of his creaturehood in the midst of his present idolatrous and blameworthy state and acts. Paul then might be regarded as arguing that, if only man had taken due account of his creation in the divine image, he might have recognized the error of his idolatry which conceived of God in terms of dependence upon man's reflection and handiwork.

But is not this approach much too simple? To maintain that Paul has Christianized pagan ideas suggests that propositions which subjectively considered are the antithesis of Christianity might be viewed as being objectively true. K. J. Popma has effectively shown that such a distinction between thought and word, as well as an approach which would allow that the quotations are materially untrue but formally true, sets up dualisms in mind and in history which are intolerable.

When, however, the same writer, on the background of a salutary recognition of the antithesis of Christianity and paganism, argues that the quotations are introduced only with a view to shaking his hearers loose from the apostate religious convictions which the quotations express, it appears that he has not done full justice to all the evidence.[31] This viewpoint overlooks, in particular, the manner in which Paul introduces one quotation, and perhaps both, with the words, 'as certain even of your own poets have said' (verse 28). In arguing from the quotations to his Christian conclusions Paul appears unmistakably to be attaching validity to them even while he is taking serious account of their presence within the structure of pagan thought. The formula confirms indeed an observation made previously: it intimates that the quotations are not offered as foundation features of the Pauline proclamation, but only quite subordinately and even incidentally to the main thrust of his address, which stands on strong Biblical ground. The fact remains, however, that, at least momentarily, he appears to occupy common ground with his pagan hearers to the extent of admitting a measure of validity to their observations concerning religion.

This question remains a pressing one, therefore: how can the argument supported by appeal to the quotations of pagan poets be valid even while their pagan origin and character were fully recognized? One will be in an impasse here, I believe, unless account is taken of other teaching of Paul, teaching in the Epistles as well as in the Acts, which provides a broader and richer content of truth. Paul maintained that even pagans remained confronted with the revelation of God in nature, and that this contact with revelation rendered them inexcusable (Acts xiv. 17; Rom. i. 19ff.). This confrontation with the divine revelation had not been without effect upon their minds since it brought them into contact with the truth, but their basic antipathy

31 *Evangelie contra Evangelie* (Franeker, Holland, n.d.), pp. 47ff.

to the truth was such that they suppressed it in unrighteousness (Rom. i. 18).[32] Thus while maintaining the antithesis between the knowledge of God enjoyed by His redeemed children and the state of ignorance which characterized all others, Paul could allow consistently and fully for the thought that pagan men, in spite of themselves and contrary to the controlling disposition of their minds, as creatures of God confronted with the divine revelation were capable of responses which were valid so long as and to the extent that they stood in isolation from their pagan systems. Thus, thoughts which in their pagan contexts were quite un-Christian and anti-Christian, could be acknowledged as up to a point involving an actual apprehension of revealed truth. As creatures of God, retaining a *sensus divinitatis* in spite of their sin, their ignorance of God and their suppression of the truth, they were not without a certain awareness of God and of their creaturehood. Their ignorance of, and hostility to, the truth was such that their awareness of God and of creaturehood could not come into its own to give direction to their thought and life or to serve as a principle of interpretation of the world of which they were a part. But the apostle Paul, reflecting upon their creaturehood, and upon their religious faith and practice, could discover within their pagan religiosity evidences that the pagan poets in the very act of suppressing and perverting the truth presupposed a measure of awareness of it. Thus while conceiving of his task as basically a proclamation of One of whom they were in ignorance, he could appeal even to the reflections of pagans as pointing to the true relation between the sovereign Creator and His creatures.[33]

[32] Cf. also γνόντες τὸν Θεὸν in Rom. i. 21 with οὐ δύναται γνῶναι in 1 Cor. ii. 14.

[33] Cornelius Van Til has recently stressed, in connection with a salutary emphasis upon the significance and meaning of history, that the wicked within history, for all of their ignorance of and hostility to God, are kept from being fully satanic. See his ' Introduction' to B. B. Warfield, *The Inspiration and Authority of the Bible* (Philadelphia, 1948), especially pp. 24, 32, 38f. Cf. also his *Common Grace* (Philadelphia, 1947).

One aspect of the criticism of the message attributed to Paul in Acts xvii. 24-29 remains to be considered. The charge that Paul is represented as introducing an expression of pantheistic mysticism in verse 28 in contrast to a particularistic conception of sonship in his Epistles is presented on the background of the judgment that the body of the address is occupied with a presentation of monotheism which has little or nothing to do with specific Christianity. Assuredly a monotheism which knows nothing of the particularism of divine grace forfeits its right to the name Christian, and hence if living in God and being the offspring of God were intended by Paul in Acts to indicate the sufficiency and validity of a religion of nature, there would be the most violent antithesis to the Christian gospel. However, as has been observed, there is no good reason to conclude that Paul means to characterize true religion in these terms. And to come to my main point in this connection, in my judgment a basic fault of modern criticism of Acts xvii is that it supposes that Christianity may exist as a message of grace and judgment apart from monotheism, or from what I should prefer to call a Christian theistic view of the world. This raises a profoundly controversial issue of the modern day which the limits of this paper do not permit me to discuss, an issue so basic as to involve the total question of what Christianity really is. I must be satisfied here with the observation that the message of Paul at Athens, taken in its grand sweep as a message which integrates creation and providence with the teaching concerning Jesus, sin, repentance, the resurrection and the day of judgment, is not confined to this chapter or to the Acts. It certainly may not fairly be ruled out of the thought of Paul of the Epistles.

It is astonishing that Dibelius and Schweitzer apparently fail to take into account the far-reaching implications of 1 Thes. i. 8, 9, a most precious record of Paul's early preaching in Thessalonica, in which as at Lystra and at

Athens he regards as essential to conversion to Christianity a turning unto God from idols to serve the living and true God. However this silence may be explained, one fears that there is at work here, and in much of the modern exegesis, an arbitrary and divisive approach which has disastrous consequences. The modern effort to detach the specific Christian message from the Biblical theism of the Scriptures involves a radical transformation of the Christian doctrines of creation, sin, salvation and consummation, and also the substitution of a modern world view for the one that has been rejected. Hence it represents a thoroughgoing modernization of Christianity rather than a scientific interpretation of it.

VII. THE CONSEQUENCES OF THE ADDRESS

The conclusion that the apostle Paul remains on solid Christian ground, in complete consistency with his teaching in his Epistles, and yet effectively takes advantage of the religious faith and practice of his pagan hearers in calling upon men to turn from idols to serve the living and true God, is challenged from still another point of view. One might maintain that the narrative is quite trustworthy as a record of Paul's ministry in Athens, but if the apostle himself, as the consequence of the paucity of converts, or because of a revaluation of the propriety or wisdom of his particular approach before the Areopagus, became disillusioned and later determined to follow a different evangelistic method, the address would possess virtually as little relevance for the understanding of the authoritative apostolic proclamation of the New Testament as it would if we held the view that the address is largely imaginative. Such an evaluation of the consequences of the address has enjoyed considerable vogue in recent decades, perhaps as a result of the influence of Sir William M. Ramsay, who summed up his judgment as follows:

> It would appear that Paul was disappointed and perhaps disillusioned by his experience in Athens. He felt that he had gone at least as far as was right in the way of presenting his doctrine in a form suited to the current philosophy; and the result had been little more than naught. When he went on from Athens to Corinth, he no longer spoke in the philosophic style. In replying afterwards to the unfavourable comparison between his preaching and the more philosophical style of Apollos, he told the Corinthians that, when he came among them, he 'determined not to know anything save Jesus Christ, and Him crucified' (1 Cor. ii. 2); and nowhere throughout his writings is he so hard on the wise, the philosophers, and the dialecticians, as when he defends the way in which he had presented Christianity at Corinth. Apparently the greater concentration of purpose and simplicity of method in his preaching at Corinth is referred to by Luke, when he says, xviii. 5, that when Silas and Timothy rejoined him there, they found him wholly possessed by and engrossed in the word. This strong expression, so unlike anything else in Acts, must, on our hypothesis, be taken to indicate some specifically marked character in the Corinthian preaching.[34]

The argument no doubt is plausible, and enjoys a measure of popular appeal because of its apparent readiness to be content with the simple gospel rather than with philosophical argument. But my own judgment is that it is quite untenable when the pertinent data are evaluated at their true worth.

In the first place, it is essential to take due account of the Lucan methods and aims in the Acts as the proper background for the estimate of his purpose in introducing this

---

34 *St. Paul the Traveller and Roman Citizen*, p. 252. Recent expressions of this viewpoint are found in Foakes-Jackson *ad loc.* and Finegan, *Light from the Ancient Past* (Princeton, 1946), p. 247. Even G. T. Purves, *Christianity in the Apostolic Age* (New York, 1900), p. 193, though regarding the contents of the address as being of 'the highest value, because it presented aspects of truth which were to be of fundamental importance in the coming conflict between Christianity and paganism,' speaks of the results as 'disappointing' and says that 'Paul finally moved on to Corinth resolved to know nothing but Jesus Christ and Him crucified (1 Cor. ii. 1, 2).'

address. In pursuance of his goal to exhibit the manner in which the ascended Lord brought His word to men and established His Church in the face of many obstacles, Luke presents many examples of the apostolic preaching and especially that of Peter and Paul. Without specific evidence to support such a conclusion it is incredible that he should have reported apostolic preaching, which was intended to demonstrate how the gospel was *not* to be preached, and it is particularly incomprehensible that the Areopagus address should be regarded in that light when one contemplates the pains which Luke takes to portray the exceptional historical situation in which Paul found himself and the impressiveness with which the address itself is reported. Luke gives every impression of presenting Paul as a masterful orator who knew exactly how to suit his message to a distinctive and challenging situation. That Paul can have been thought of as in reality a failure can be accepted only if the most decisive proofs can be mustered in support of that hypothesis.

When one measures the consequences of the preaching, one must admit that they may not appear impressive. There was the repetition of the ridicule which had been expressed earlier; others continued to show the curiosity that had led to his being taken before the Areopagus (verse 32; cf. verse 18), and thus there is no change in the general situation. There is added, however, the report that certain men joined him and believed, and that among these converts there was a Dionysius who was a member of the supreme council, and a woman named Damaris. Though the number of believers was evidently not great, Luke does not underscore their paucity. It is even possible to suppose that he regarded it as remarkable in the circumstances, with all of the unfavourable religious and philosophical commitments which characterized the Athenians, that there should have been some who were prepared to make a break with views which were in good standing in Athens and to share the ignominy or disdain attached to Paul's faith.

Moreover, even if the results were actually more meagre than Luke shows them to have been, and even if Luke had directed special attention to the paucity of converts, it still would not follow that any blame would be attached to the message of Paul for the failure of a larger company of Athenians to turn to belief in Christ. To the extent that historical factors may have influenced the results, one is on far sounder ground if note is taken of the original purpose of Paul to enjoy a period of rest rather than to preach in Athens, and of the apparent brevity of his activity there.[35] Actually, however, it is most precarious to engage in rationalizing from the number of converts to the correctness of the message. That there were converts at all should be sufficient proof, within the context of the Acts, that the message was regarded as the Christian message. Luke did not share the pragmatism of our day which judges the truth of the message by the criterion of outward success.

Another decisive reason for rejecting the judgment that a casual connection exists between the character of Paul's message at Athens and the meagre results is that the Areopagus address by no means constitutes the only preaching Paul undertook there. As I have previously observed, his activity there included preaching in the Jewish synagogue and in the market-place, and his apostolic message was summed up in the terms 'Jesus and the resurrection,' a most apt and succinct characterization of the preaching of Paul and Peter as reported in Acts.[36] It is quite unjustifiable, accordingly, to insist that there were few converts in Athens because Paul preached somewhat distinctively before the Areopagus. Even if this address were quite at

---

[35] Ramsay, *St. Paul*, p. 239, himself says that 'the lack of results at this stage is . . . fully explained by the shortness of time. Paul's stay in Athens can hardly have been longer than six weeks, and was probably less than four ; and the process described in verse 17 was brought to a premature close by the great event of his visit, which the historian describes very fully.'

[36] See pp. 11f. above.

variance with Paul's usual message, one would still have to reckon with the fact that in his general approach to the Athenians he had evidently followed a fairly stereotyped pattern.

Although, accordingly, the narrative affords no hint that Paul was on the wrong track at Athens, it is averred that a contrary impression is given by other data in the Acts and in 1 Corinthians. Paul himself is thought in 1 Cor. ii. 2 to reflect upon his ministry in Athens and to be expressing a new determination to know only 'Christ and him crucified' in contrast to a philosophically oriented message. And in Acts xviii. 5 Luke is viewed as likewise indicating that at Corinth Paul adopted a different, simpler approach. In the latter passage Luke indeed characterizes the early phase of Paul's preaching in Corinth in a somewhat unusual manner when he says that 'when Silas and Timothy came down from Macedonia, Paul was engrossed in the word, testifying to the Jews that Jesus was the Christ.'[37] And it is possible that a contrast of some kind is being drawn with the description of his activity in the preceding verse where, following a reference to his labour with Aquila and Priscilla at his trade as a tentmaker, the narrative reports that 'he was reasoning in the synagogue every sabbath and persuading Jews and Greeks.' If a contrast between two phases of his preaching to the Jews is actually in view, it would be completely gratuitous to explain this development in terms of a simpler, less philosophical approach in the second phase. There is not a trace of a suggestion that this was in mind, and it would furthermore imply that at Corinth, in the beginning, Paul was preaching to the Jews in a form suited to the current philosophy! It would be far more in point to suppose, as Lake and Cadbury do, for example, that the coming of Silas and Timothy somehow

[37] The R.V. and A.S.V. translate the phrase 'was constrained by the word,' but most commentators more satisfactorily render it substantially as given above. The new R.S.V. reads : 'was occupied with preaching.' The A.V. ' was pressed in the spirit' is based upon an inferior text.

relieved Paul of the necessity of engaging in earning his living and that he began to be engrossed in the word in the sense that he gave all of his time to preaching. Even the latter view, however, is largely inferential and rather forced, since Luke does not qualify his reference to the preaching activity by stating that he could now engage in it *every day*. Inasmuch as Luke says that Paul was occupied with preaching to the Jews when Silas and Timothy came to Corinth, and thus may be understood as virtually repeating the description of Paul's activity among the Jews in xviii. 5, it is more satisfactory to conclude that xviii. 5 is a résumé of xviii. 4 introduced in order to indicate that, as xviii. 6 immediately goes on to disclose, soon after the arrival of these men, the Jews turned so sharply against his mission that he turned to the Gentiles (cf. Acts xiv. 44ff.). At any rate, there is no foundation whatsoever for the interpretation that Paul's being engrossed in preaching to the Jews reflects a rejection or modification of his message and method in preaching to the pagans in Athens.

Nor does the appeal to 1 Cor. ii. 2 rest upon a firm basis. Paul does not say that, when he came to Corinth, he adopted a new evangelistic approach, and there is no suggestion that he had accommodated his message of 'Christ and Him crucified' to his hearers at Athens and now regretted it. There is no hint even that he ever preached any differently than he did at Corinth, but Paul takes pains to remind the Corinthians that he had not come with 'excellency of speech or of wisdom'; his gospel was not one that commended itself to the wise in Corinth, but was foolishness unto them. And so indeed his message had largely proved to be to the Athenians.[38]

There remains the consideration, however, that the

---

[38] This interpretation is even more emphatically supported by the original, for Paul does not say, 'I determined not to know . . .' (A.V., R.V.), or 'I decided to know nothing . . .' (R.S.V.), but 'I did not determine to know . . .' See also Lightfoot, *Notes on Epistles of St. Paul* (1895), p. 171, who renders it, 'I had no intent, no mind to know anything.'

message says nothing concerning Christ crucified or of salvation by faith in Him. Does not the address, therefore, even if its content is quite unobjectionable, appear to stop short of being a well-rounded Christian proclamation of the gospel? In considering this question, one may reckon with the distinct possibility that Luke intends to intimate that Paul was interrupted before he had reached his real conclusion. When his hearers heard mention of the resurrection, some mocked while others indicated an interest in hearing Paul at a later time, and Paul thereupon departed out of their midst (xvii. 23f.). Moreover, when a comparison is made between the address and Paul's summary of his message to the Gentile world in 1 Thes. i. 9, 10, it may plausibly be argued that there is agreement in the declarations concerning conversion from idols to the true God, the return of Christ, and the resurrection of Christ but that the feature of deliverance by Christ from the wrath to come alone fails of mention at Athens. On this approach one might well maintain that Paul had preached Christ and Him crucified, and deliverance through Him from the wrath to come, in his earlier preaching in Athens, but that in the instance of the Areopagus address the offence taken at the doctrine of the resurrection, disclosing as it did the chasm that separated their thinking from Paul's, was so profound that they precipitately and impatiently closed their ears, as it were, to the proclamation of salvation through Christ.[39]

There are weighty reasons, however, for judging that this evaluation of the conclusion of the address, for all of its plausibility and attractiveness, is not firmly established. In the first place, Luke clearly does not say that Paul's hearers interrupted his address before he had finished.

[39] On this point and the argument that the Athenian audience definitely broke off his address before it was completed, see Bavinck, *op. cit.*, pp. 126ff., 139f., 122ff., 183. Bavinck goes so far as to say, ' Als Paulus over de opstanding der dooden begint te handelen, roepen de intellectueele fijnproevers van Athene hem tot orde en breken zijn rede af ' (p. 183).

The reactions of his audience may be fully understood as being expressed following the completion of his message, just as similar reactions developed after Paul's earlier proclamation of Jesus and the resurrection (xvii. 18). Secondly, one is not on incontestable ground in assuming that all of Paul's preaching would have conformed to a stereotyped pattern, and especially that the address on the extraordinary occasion of his appearance before the Areopagus would not have expressed a certain formal and material individuality.[40]

Another approach to the problem which escapes these particular difficulties appears to be definitely tenable, one which, rather than inferring that the address was abruptly terminated by his hearers, takes account of the exceedingly compressed character of the reports of the speeches in Acts.[41] If one once recognizes that the addresses must be regarded as condensed accounts of speeches that lasted considerably longer than the time it takes us to read them through, one may be prepared to face the question whether the several reports, while indicating accurately the disposition and contents of the addresses in summary form, do not imply as much as they actually state. As applied to the situation confronting us here, this observation suggests that Luke means to imply that the message of salvation through Christ is being intimated in epitome in Paul's proclamation of the divine command that all men everywhere should repent. 'The times of ignorance therefore God overlooked; but now he commandeth men that they should all everywhere repent; inasmuch as he hath appointed a day in which he will judge the world in righteousness by

40 It is necessary to guard against exaggerating the stereotyped character of Paul's preaching in general. ' To await his son from heaven ' (1 Thes. i. 10) strikes the eschatological note, but it has a somewhat different orientation from that in Acts xvii. 31 which centres upon the coming judgment. The preaching of Paul in Pisidian Antioch (xiii. 16ff.), while stressing the resurrection of Christ and declaring remission of sins through Him, appears to omit the distinctively eschatological feature.

41 Bruce, *op. cit.*, p. 27, takes note of this characteristic of the speeches of Acts in its bearing upon their trustworthiness.

the man whom he hath ordained; whereof he hath given assurance unto all men, in that he hath raised him from the dead ' (verses 30, 31).

There can surely be no doubt that Paul is proclaiming here the wrath to come. The day of judgment is announced on the authority of an apostle of Christ as a day when God will judge the world in righteousness. The One through whom the divine judgment will be executed has already been designated. And not only has the commission to execute judgment been bestowed upon One especially chosen, but there has also already been a sign of the coming of that day and of that Judge. For in raising Christ from the dead God had revealed with sufficient clearness that the age to come had begun to be realized and that the One who had gained pre-eminence by the divine power which raised Him from the dead was One with whom men were compelled to reckon as a unique servant of God.

But the proclamation of the *dies irae* also brings to Paul's hearers a message of grace. Favour had been expressed in overlooking their ignorance; now there was manifested the goodness of God which confronted the Gentiles with the revelation of the day of judgment and urgently warned them—'all men everywhere'—of the necessity of repentance. But this command to repent expresses more than the thought of the inevitability of divine judgment upon men who fail to repent. It discloses also that the days before the dread day of judgment would come are days of grace and salvation, when men may still repent for their sins and escape the wrath to come.

That the proclamation of the divine command to repent may be understood as a preaching of the glad tidings of salvation is confirmed by the manner in which it is introduced in the apostolic preaching generally. Peter, for example, declares: 'Repent ye therefore, and turn again, that your sins may be blotted out . . .' (iii. 19; cf. ii. 38). And Paul informs Agrippa that he was not disobedient to the heavenly vision, but declared to Jews 'and to Gentiles that they should repent and turn to God, doing works worthy of repentance' (xxvi. 20; cf. xiv. 15). Repentance is described not only as a turning unto God, but also as a 'repentance unto life' which God granted to the Gentiles (Acts xi. 18), and also as giving assurance of the forgiveness of sins (v. 31; cf. xxiv. 47).

And since Paul points to Christ as the One whose resurrection establishes His credentials to judge among men as to their acceptance with God, one may at least read between the lines that those who are to share with Christ the blessedness of the world to come are faced with the necessity of being assured of a favourable relationship to Him who guards the portals of eternal life.

The gospel of Jesus Christ, according to Luke, as disclosed in both his Gospel and the Acts, is the gospel of the crucified One. But since the divine action of salvation is viewed as reaching its consummation in the exaltation of Christ, there is a profound occupation with the resurrection of Christ as serving to sum up even more pointedly than the cross the decisive saving work of God. This accounts for the prominence given to the resurrection in Luke's record of that which Jesus did before His ascension; it also explains the emphasis which falls upon it in the records of the apostolic preaching. In the Areopagus address the declaration concerning the profound significance of the resurrection of Christ appropriately subsumes the fact of the cross. Thus also in the Epistles Paul, who wished to know only Christ and Him crucified, preaches Christ as the one 'that died, yea rather, that was raised from the dead' (Rom. viii. 34).

CHAPTER ELEVEN

Paul at Athens

CORNELIUS VAN TIL

Paul at Athens

When Paul and Barnabas came to Lystra and performed the miracle of the healing of the man unable to walk from birth, the inhabitants wanted to worship them as gods. They called Barnabas Jupiter and Paul Hermes because he was the chief speaker. Then Paul and Barnabas "rent their clothes and ran in among the people saying, Sirs why do ye these things? We also are men of like passion with you and preach unto you that ye should turn from these vanities unto the living God, which made heaven and earth and the sea and all the things that are therein: Who in times past suffered all nations to walk in their own ways. Nevertheless he left not himself without witness in that he did good and gave us rain from heaven, and fruitful seasons, filling our hearts with food and gladness. And with these sayings scarce restrained they the people, that they had not done sacrifice unto them. And there came thither certain Jews from Antioch and Iconium who persuaded the people, and having stoned Paul, drew him out of the city, supposing he had been dead" (Acts 14:14-19).

Quite a contrast this, between being sacrificed to as a god, and then being stoned as it were to death. Which would you rather be? Paul chose rather to be stoned to death if need be. He was willing at least to take whatever might follow rather than be sacrificed to as a god.

Paul knows only two classes of people, those who worship and serve the Creator and those who worship and serve the creature more than the Creator. He had once upon a time worshiped and served the creature; then on the way to Damascus he had learned to worship and serve the Creator. Therein lay his conversion. To get men to worship and serve the Creator rather than the creature, therein lay his mission after his conversion. He knew the hatred of those who worshiped and served the creature against those who worshiped and served the Creator. It was that hatred that had impelled him to go to Damascus to find and bind those that were of "that Way," that served the Creator. He was prepared now to be the victim, if need be, rather than the persecutor. Men must at all costs be shown the folly of worshiping the creature; the issue between the two types of worshipers must never be blurred.

In a sense, this story of Paul's preaching at Lystra may be taken as typical of his entire method and ·attitude when preaching the gospel to those who worshiped the creature. Creature worshipers he found everywhere he went, in the synagogues, in the market place, in the temples; among the religious and among the irreligious; among the educated and among the non-educated; among the Epicureans and Stoics as well as among the men of the street; among the naturalists and the supernaturalists alike.

Paul appealed to the heart of the natural man, whatever mask he might wear, and required of him that he repent from the vanity of creature worship to the fruitfulness of the worship of the "living God." That living God had appeared to him on the way to Damascus. He had appeared as the second person of the Trinity through whom the world had been created and was still sustained. He had appeared to Paul, this living God, as the one who had come down into this world to die for the sins of men, for their worship of the creature rather than the Creator. No one could now, he had learned, worship and serve the Creator except he worship and serve this Jesus Christ as Lord. This Jesus was God. He was the Creator and the great benefactor in giving men forgiveness of their sin of worshiping the creature. So Paul was determined to know nothing among men save Jesus Christ and Him crucified. And this Jesus Christ as crucified had been raised from the dead by the power of God the Creator. Being God He had power to lay down His life and also had power to take it to Himself again. In

His resurrection through the power of the Creator there
stood before men the clearest evidence that could be given
that they who would still continue to serve and worship the
creature would at last be condemned by the Creator then
become their Judge (Acts 17:31). Will men deny and defy
the work of the Son of God in His death and in His resurrection? If they do, they will meet Him as their Judge.
Will they refuse to repent from their sin of creature worship
when called to repentance? Then let them know that the
judgment and their condemnation is coming as surely as
their own consciences condemn them when they serve the
creature. No one can be confronted with the fact of the
Christ and of His resurrection and fail to have his own
conscience tell him that he is face to face with his Judge.

Having meditated on all this in the long period of his
preparation for his apostolic work, the Apostle Paul was
fully determined never to have his message subtly inter-
woven with that of those who worshiped and served the
creature. He would rather be stoned to death than flat-
tered. He would rend his clothes and call upon men not to
confuse his message with that of the priests of Jupiter, with
the highest being of Plato, or the "thought thinking itself"
of Aristotle.

But where did Paul say anything about the god of Plato
or the god of Aristotle? Was he not from all we know more
favorable to the "monotheism" of the Greeks than he was
to the polytheism of the popular religions? At any rate
was he not favorably disposed to the "monotheism" of the
Stoics whom he met in Athens? Is there not a mildness of
speech on the part of Paul that does not look as though he
is even inwardly rending his clothes and calling on men not
to do such things? Was his message in the Areopagus
milder than that which he had given to the common people
in the market place? Or was he somewhat afraid of the
authorities who might forbid his preaching or possibly even
cast him into prison?

The answer must be that the attitude of Paul with respect to creature worshipers was the same in Athens as that which it had been in Lystra. Moreover, for him the "monotheism" of the Greek philosophers, even that of the Stoics, was still for him the worship of the creature more than the Creator.

Paul saw the many vanities in Athens, the city of the philosophers. He was stirred in his spirit because the city was wholly given to idolatry. And when asked to speak before the intelligentsia of the city, he did not say that he saw how the common people of the city, the people who had never heard of the Porch, or the Academy, who knew nothing of "the rational principle" which according to the Stoics pervaded all of the world, were very religious or very superstitious. He knew that all men are by virtue of creation by God very religious, and that all men are by virtue of sin very superstitious. He knew that this is true of the learned and of the unlearned alike. He knew that even the Epicureans who professed to believe in no gods and who likely spurned the idea of building any altar to any god, whether to a supposedly known or to an admittedly unknown god, could nevertheless fitly be represented by that altar to the unknown god.

Whatever his reason may have been for singling out the altar to the unknown God rather than the altars to supposedly known gods as evidence that they were religious, it surely was not that he attached himself to the system of thought that any of them professed to hold.

In particular it would be no more possible, from Paul's point of view, to attach himself to their doctrine of the unknown god than to their doctrine of their known gods. And this for the reason that their doctrine of the unknown god was involved in their doctrines of their known gods.

ALL IS ONE

Basic to all the thinking of the Greeks was the assumption that all being is at bottom one, that all change comes by way of some form of emanation from that one being and is therefore ultimate as the One, and that somehow all the ultimate multiplicity that exists as due to ultimate change again ultimately returns to the One. They were therefore all of them monists; they spoke of the reality as a whole without making the distinction between the Creator and the creature. *All* is water, *all* is air, *all* is change or *nothing* changes. Whatever is true of the world was for them also true of the god or gods above the world. But they were at the same time also ultimate pluralists. To the extent that they allowed for change at all, this change was ultimate. If there was freedom anywhere, this freedom was the same sort of freedom for gods and for men; if there was accident, gods and men were alike subject to it.

There was therefore in their way of thinking no place for the supernatural in Paul's sense of the term at all. Theirs was an exclusively immanentistic way of thinking; following Adam and Eve they sought to do without God; they had no place for God, the Creator, in their system of thought. They were sure that such a God as Paul preached did not and could not exist. They were therefore sure that Paul could not "declare" this God to them. No one could know such a God as Paul believed in.

But Paul knew that on the contrary, all men at bottom know God, the Creator. All men know that they are creatures of God, that they are law breakers. At bottom they know that their own systems, according to which God cannot exist, are rationalizations by means of which they seek to suppress the fact of their responsibility as creatures of God. Their own systems therefore could not satisfy them. Yet they would not, and as sinners could not, do without these systems. These systems were like masks which they had put on their faces not merely for "stunt night," but which they had put on so as never to be able to remove them. So they tried over and again to polish up and restyle these masks; there were face-liftings of various sorts. And the particular style of masks in vogue at the time of Paul when he came to Athens, as best we can make it out from secular historians of philosophy, was a nice blend of all previous schools of philosophy. In this blend there was a generous allowance made for what was thought to be "the divine" and "the supernatural." Men were very religious. There were the Epicureans, to be sure, but they were considered to be rather extreme. Even among the cultured it was in good style to recognize the fact that there was more in heaven and on earth than they had yet dreamed of in their philosophy. They believed in "the mysterious universe"; they were perfectly willing therefore to leave open a place for "the unknown." But this "unknown" must be thought of as the utterly unknowable and indeterminate.

THE SUPERNATURAL

There were according to these Greeks two ideas of "the supernatural," one of which they would gladly recognize, which it was custom and style at the time to recognize, and another which they would not and could not recognize. They were glad to recognize the fact that the universe is mysterious, that "science" does not cover the whole of reality. They were even willing to recognize that it is so mysterious that no one knows what it is. They had come to the conclusion that man as finite cannot know the universe (including man) which is infinite. The infinite, they had concluded, was "wholly other" than anything they had so far known. The infinite was without quality. If it was not without quality it was no longer infinite. The idea of the infinite as *apeiron*, as wholly without quality, was the necessary concomitant of their idea of the universe as known by man in terms of man.

AUTHORITY

There were therefore also two kinds of authority, one of which they would gladly recognize and one of which they could not and would not, on their basis, have anything to do with at all. They would gladly recognize the authority of experts, in whatever field, the authority of those who had had special experiences and had made special researches in one region or another; they would be glad to hear Paul too on the subject of religion as they might have been glad to hear Einstein on relativity. If he wanted to speak to them about some experience that he had had with the "noumenal realm," or if he wanted to tell them of some *Einfuhlung* that he enjoyed for *Das Heilige*, they were perfectly willing to hear of it; they were tired anyway and had no hopes of anything really new coming forth. But they would not listen to Paul if he came to them with absolute authority and if he claimed to tell them about that which they knew was inherently unknowable. Who did he think he was? Was he not a human being like themselves? Was he not subject to the same limitation as they?

THE RESURRECTION

They were a bit suspicious, shall we say, because of what they had heard Paul say about Jesus and the resurrection in the market place. But he is no common revivalist; so let us hear him out. Let us take him away from the rabble and ask him to make clear to us what he means by Jesus and the resurrection. Maybe there are such things as resurrections. Aristotle has told us about monstrosities has he not? Reality seems to have a measure of the accidental in it. And if anywhere, history is the realm where the accidental appears. So maybe he has something strange to tell us.   We have an Odditorium in which there is some vacant space.

But Paul speaks to them about Jesus and the resurrection in a way not expected by them.   He was determined to know nothing among them save Jesus Christ and Him crucified.   He wanted to speak to them of the living God, the Creator and Ruler of the Universe and of mankind.   He wanted them to be converted from the service of man to the service of God; he wanted them to become covenant-keepers instead of covenant-breakers.   So he did the equivalent of what he did in the presence of the men of Lystra. Again he tore his garments, this time figuratively.   Again he said in effect, "Sirs why do ye these things?   Why are you seeking to weave the resurrection of Jesus Christ into the pattern of your immanentistic way of thinking?   I am come to preach unto you that ye should turn from these vanities to the living God.   You yourself admit that reality is mysterious.   You have many altars to gods you think you know and then you have an altar to a god you say you do not know.   Will you show me how you make this sort of view intelligible to yourself?   What is the relation between the gods you say you know and the god or gods you say you do not know?   Is it not the same reality, the same universe of which in one breath you say that it is wholly unknown and also that it is wholly known?   If there is that in the universe which, on your system, is wholly unknown, and if this which is wholly unknown has an influence for good or for evil on that which you say you know, do you then really know anything at all?   Why not destroy all the altars to the gods you say cannot be known?   On your basis it is impossible to know anything unless you know everything, and since by admission you do not know everything you should admit that the whole of your religious activity is an irrational procedure.   And what is true of your religion is true of your science.   You do not know what water, earth, air and fire are.   You appeal to some common principle above them all from which as a common source they spring. But then this common source has, as Anaximander said, no positive quality at all. It must be without quality to be truly beyond and thus truly common, and when truly beyond and therefore without quality, it cannot serve as the explanation of anything that has quality in the world that you claim to know.

Your worship is therefore one of ignorance, of ignorance far deeper than you are willing and able on your assumptions to own. On your basis there is no knowledge at all; there is nothing but ignorance.

CULPABLE IGNORANCE

But worse than that, your ignorance is not only much deeper than you own; it is of a wholly different character than you think it is. It is ethical, not metaphysical in character. You are making excuse for your ignorance on the ground that you are finite and that the world is infinite. And you make an altar to a god whom you speak of as unknown. Well, God the true God, is not unknown to man at all. He is not unknown to you. It is but sham modesty when you speak of reverently bowing before the mysterious universe. To be sure, finite man cannot know all the wondrous works of God. But man can and does know that God, his Creator, exists. Man can and does know that God is the living God who is not only the original Creator but also the controller and bountiful benefactor of mankind. He is not far from any of us, His creatures. Has He not made us aware of ourselves only as we are aware of Him as our God and as our Judge? Your own conscience answers "Yes" to what I say. You must admit that it is only because you are seeking to hide the true state of affairs about yourself that you have erected this altar to the unknown god. You are trying to make yourself believe that you have done justice to the demands of God if only you faintly recognize that there is something that is higher than yourself, that God is bigger and better than yourself. But when you thus recognize God as bigger and better you are still bringing Him down to the level of the creature. You are still worshiping and serving the creature more than the Creator. The God you are worshiping is Himself involved in the cosmos and therefore dependent upon its laws. He is in need of your worship; He is not sovereign over all but dependent upon all. What ignorance, what *guilty* ignorance, what unbelievable ignorance for those who call themselves philosophers and pretend to know what the people do not know.

REPENTANCE AND HOPE

But there is hope; there is hope through repentance. I am here to tell you of the way of escape; I am not a philosopher. I am not telling about monstrosities and wondrous things when I speak of the resurrection. I speak of the Creator God who in Jesus of Nazareth came down to earth to die for the sins of men, and was raised for their justification. Through Him there is pardon for your sins, for men of all classes, for common men, for philosophers and wise men, too. But to receive this pardon you must accept this message on the authority of God Himself. I am come to tell you that of which by your system you could never know. I am come to tell you that your systems are not merely inadequate in the sense that they do not cover all the questions that men must ask, but that they are sinful because they leave out God. The wrath of God is upon you philosophers, upon you scientists, you men who are monotheists as well as upon you who are pluralists, upon you who recognize the supernatural as well as upon you who do not recognize the supernatural, upon you who make the altar to the unknown gods and upon you who make the altars to the known gods. You heard me preach Jesus and the resurrection in the marketplace. I am now, at your request, giving you the setting for such preaching.

And the setting is all-important. It is that which gives meaning to the fact of the resurrection. *Without this setting the resurrection would be a monstrosity that you could weave into the pattern of your immanentistic views.* Please do not so interpret the resurrection. I am teaching you of a philosophy of history in which there are no monstrosities. The Jesus who died and rose again from the dead died to remove the sins of men that believe and trust in Him. Naturally those who do not so believe and trust in Him will finally be punished. For He is God, He is the Creator and Controller of the laws of the universe. He is the ever living God. He will appear again in a special way to judge as He has once come in the past to redeem. He came into the world that they that should believe in Him should be saved and that they who should not believe in Him should be damned; He will therefore come again as He promised His apostles when He left for heaven; He will come again, the second time as the Judge of men, to judge men by the truth which He himself is.

Will you not then repent and bow to him now? Kiss the Son lest He be angry with you in the judgment day.

By this time the men that heard him knew that Paul did not mean the same thing that their poets had meant when they too said that men live and move and have their being in God and that they are the offspring of God. The Stoics meant by such expressions to assert that men were essentially of a piece with God: men are by virtue of their intellects participant in deity, they said. The intellect of man as participant in deity cannot sin. Man's intellect may make mistakes because it is finite, but it cannot be wrong in its purposes.

THE FRAME OF REFERENCE

So Paul tells them that if their poets have said what is right as far as the words are concerned they should have placed a different meaning in these words than they did. If they said what was true and right, they said what is right because their systems are not right. They could say what is right not in accord with, but only in spite of their systems. It is because the framework of the universe is what Paul spoke of when he proclaimed to them the God whom in their consciences they knew, but whom according to their professed systems they did not know, the Creator and Controller of the universe, that they could say what is true about parts of that world or about the whole world. They could say this adventitiously only. That is, it would be in accord with what they deep down in their hearts knew to be true in spite of their systems. It was that truth which they sought to cover up by means of their professed systems, which enabled them to discover truth as philosophers and scientists. Would Paul for a moment attach himself to what Stoics meant when they spoke of man as the offspring of God? No more than he would attach himself to what they meant who had built the altar to the unknown God. If he attached himself to the one he could also attach himself to the other. But he could not and did not attach himself to either. Both were involved in one another, and if Paul had attached himself to either he could no longer have preached Jesus and the resurrection.

Jesus and the resurrection presupposed the doctrine of creation. Jesus and the resurrection implied the doctrine of judgment to come. It was the Son of God who had made the world and who was to come as judge of men at the end of the history of the world, who died and rose again from the dead in His human nature. It would not be this Jesus nor this resurrection that Paul would be preaching if he preached Him as consistent with the system of origin or destiny as held to by any of the forms of Hellenistic philosophy of the day. How could the resurrection be preached as evidence of the coming of the judgment and therefore as evidence of the coming condemnation of those that did not believe and trust in Him, if the universe is all of one piece and gods and men are both subject to its laws? How could Paul communicate to the Greeks about the resurrection of Christ if he did not place this resurrection before them in the theistic frame of reference given in the Bible in order thus to distinguish it from the "monstrosities" of Greek philosophy?

So then we conclude that even at Athens Paul did virtually the same thing that he had done in Lystra; he challenged the wisdom of the world. He did what later he did in his letter to the Corinthinians when he said: "Where is the wise? where is the scribe? where is the disputer of this world? hath not God made foolish the wisdom of this world? For after that the world by wisdom knew not God, it pleased God through the foolishness of preaching to save them that believe" (I Cor. 1:20,21).

Is the church of Christ doing this thing today, and are we doing this today? Are we really desirous of knowing nothing save Jesus Christ and Him crucified? Are we really anxious to preach Jesus and the resurrection and the living God to men? Do we want to ask all men everywhere to repent and to see in the resurrection the evidence of their own eternal condemnation unless they do repent?

Then we must surely do what Paul did, tear our garments when men would weave our message into the systems of thought which men have themselves devised. We must set the message of the cross into the framework into which Paul set it. If we do not do so, then we are not really and fully preaching Jesus and the resurrection. The facts of Jesus and the resurrection are what they are only in the framework of the doctrines of creation, providence and the consummation of history in the final judgment. No man has found this framework unless he has been converted from the other framework through the very fact of the death and resurrection of Jesus as applied to him by the

Holy Spirit and His regenerating power. It takes the fact of the resurrection to see its proper framework and it takes the framework to see the fact of the resurrection; the two are accepted on the authority of Scripture alone and by the regenerating work of the Spirit. Half-way measures therefore will not suffice; the only method that will suffce is that of challenge of the wisdom of the world by the wisdom of God.

Let us look at some of those who claim to believe or bring the Christian message to men today but who still want to attach this message of Jesus and the resurrection to the framework of philosophical speculation that does not fit with it.

CHRISTIANITY AND REASON [1]

The recent little book entitled *Christianity and Reason* is similar to that other little book of a few years ago called *The Christian Answer*. The aim of both books is to make Christianity acceptable to its cultured despisers. One of those cultured despisers, thinks Dr. Theodore M. Greene, was Professor Walter Stace who wrote an article in the *Atlantic Monthly* of September 1948 under the title *Man Against Darkness*. According to Stace the universe has been shown to have no meaning. Science has shown that man need no longer build any altars to the unknown god. He knows that there are no gods, at least no gods that are good and will reward the good. Against this thesis Greene would prove that "science, in its strict sense, can neither prove nor disprove God or goodness or beauty. It simply has nothing to say on these subjects" (p. 9). If Stace's assumption, that all experience is of a sensory nature, were true, then his conclusion would be right. "But what is to prevent us from being really empirical and believing that man's moral and religious experiences, which are no less coercive, vivid, sharable, and rationally interpretable than

[1] Ed. D. Myers, Oxford University Press, 1951

are his sensory experiences, provide further contacts with reality and further clues to its nature?" (p. 11). Greene is contending that it is quite possible to reach a "moral and religious dimension of reality" by a truly scientific method. He thinks it is possible to hold intelligently that "man can in some measure know God" (p. 12). He would also justify the idea of authority in religion as wholly proper for the subject. But in all this he is very careful to keep his feet on the ground as he thinks. He agrees wholly with Stace that science says nothing about God. He insists very carefully that whatever any minister of religion might ever want to say about God and religion must be in accord with what has already been said about the universe by science even if this science has said nothing about God. "Not only, therefore, is the position I would defend not anti-scientific, it is committed to reliance upon scientific evidence and to the full incorporation of accepted scientifically supported interpretations of nature" (p. 9). It is thus that the would-be defender of religion makes sure that there shall never be any preaching of Jesus and the resurrection after the manner of Paul as far as he can help it. Even if the fact of the resurrection should be preached, it would have to be reduced, according to Greene, to a repeatable instance of a law that the scientist can deal with on his exclusively immanentistic principles. Here a lay preacher of religion, though he says that "Man in the twilight need not falter" yet leaves him without any call to repentance, without any confrontation with Jesus and the resurrection. The worshiper of the creature is left without a challenge.

John Wild speaks in the same book on *The Present Relevance of Catholic Theology* as maintained by theologians of the Anglican communion. He speaks of a "keen sense of transcendent reality" (p. 34). He would speak of the *Deus absconditus*, but again this *Deus absconditus* must be sure that he does not affirm anything that is out of accord with the realism that has been developed by the natural man in accord with the method of Aristotle. Jesus and the resurrection, surely we ought by all means to have it, but by all means only as a monstrosity, not as something that requires conversion on the part of those who are confronted with it.

George F. Thomas, Professor of Religious Thought at Princeton University, wants to defend the idea of religion and the knowledge of God. But he wants to do it by means of an empiricism that is somewhat milder and more modest in its claims than was the theism of Thomas Aquinas. He wants to build an altar to the unknown God but insists, as does Greene and as does Wild, that this God must never presume to speak with absolute authority to men. At most he must use the authority of the expert.

In each case the writers of this volume, as were the writers of *The Christian Answer*, are careful to maintain that what they assert about Jesus and the resurrection must be seen in the non-theistic framework that destroys its very significance and challenge to conversion. No one, in hearing what these men say, will feel compelled to ask himself whether he is ready to meet his judge.

DIALECTICAL THEOLOGY

But what then of the dialectical theologians? Do they not present the fact of Jesus and the resurrection as a challenge to conversion? Did not Barth vigorously reject Brunner's idea when he suggested that the Christian must make his religion understandable to the consciousness of the time? Did he not write his pamphlet *Nein* and assert that it is the first commandment by which we as Christians are to live?

Strange as it may seem, it is precisely Barth who exhibits best of all how one cannot present Jesus and the resurrection at all unless one does it in the framework in which Paul presented it. For what has happened? Barth seems to proclaim Jesus and the resurrection as a fact and on the absolute authority of that Christ Himself. And he tells men that there is no condemnation for them that are in Christ Jesus who walk not after the flesh but after the Spirit. But he adds that all men are in Christ Jesus and that all men do walk after the Spirit. How else could they be men? No man can be conscious of himself without being conscious of forgiveness of his sins in Christ. Self-consciousness and Christ-consciousness are involved in one another. The *No* of God, the condemnation by God of the unrighteous, cannot in any case be the last word of God. His *Yes* is the final word. The negation of God, that is the sin of man against God, is an "impossible possibility." Man sins against God, of course he sins against God, all men sin against God, but in sinning against God they are in God; how else could they be present to God? How else can a child disobey the parent that gives it orders unless it be in the house of the parent? How else can the little child slap its father in the face unless it sit on the knee of the father?

It is the resurrection of Jesus Christ which, according to Barth, guarantees this fact that all men, to be men, must be in Him. Thus for him the resurrection is witness of the fact that there is *no* judgment coming in the sense that Paul used the word judgment. He uses the facts of Jesus and the resurrection as evidence that men need *no* conversion in the sense that Paul spoke of conversion; men are already converted when they are aware of themselves as men. And all this because Barth is once more trying to fit the fact of Jesus and the resurrection into the framework that is accepted by an immanentist philosophy. Those who worship and serve the creature are thus not asked to serve and worship the Creator; they are rather told that what they are worshiping is the proper object of worship.

EVANGELICAL THEOLOGY

How then shall the Reformed minister set off his preaching of Christ and the resurrection from that of the old and the new modernism of which mention has just been made? Can he join the "evangelical" in this matter? Is not the deity and the resurrection of Christ one doctrine on which all evangelicals and all Reformed Christians agree?

To answer this question let us first assert that all true Christians believe in the resurrection in their hearts. But it is not true that all true Christian preachers preach the resurrection of Christ in the same way.

In particular there is a great difference between the "evangelical" and the Reformed way of preaching the resurrection. The "evangelical" will silently grant that the non-Christian scientist and philosopher have interpreted the "phenomenal realm" correctly with their exclusively immanentistic principles. He does this by saying in effect that those who believe the resurrection of Christ see *more* than the scientist and the philosopher can discover. The resurrection is just said to open "great vistas of truth" not falling within the field of science.

Secondly the "evangelical" will preach the resurrection not as an indisputable fact but as something that Christians believe in and bet their lives on for reasons that are not objective.

In both of these points the "evangelical," as is his wont, makes concession to natural man's sense of autonomy. In both of these cases the "evangelical" seeks "common ground" with the unbeliever in order to win him. In both of these cases the evangelical compromises the gospel and to an extent frustrates his own efforts. There can be no full preaching or speaking of the resurrection unless the entire framework of non-Christian thought be challenged.

Reformed Christians are bound to be tempted toward cooperation with evangelicals in the presentation of doctrines that all Protestants are said to have in common. Yet their own system of theology ought to lead them to follow Paul at whatever cost.

CHAPTER TWELVE

The Encounter of Jerusalem with Athens

GREG BAHNSEN

APPENDIX:

THE ENCOUNTER OF JERUSALEM WITH ATHENS

What indeed has Athens to do with Jerusalem? What concord is there between the Academy and the Church?... Our instructions come from "the porch of Solomon".... Away with all attempts to produce a mottled Christianity of Stoic, Platonic, and dialectic composition! We want no curious disputation after possessing Christ Jesus...!

So said Tertullian in his *Prescription against Heretics* (VII). Tertullian's question, what does Athens have to do with Jerusalem?, dramatically expresses one of the perennial issues in Christian thought—a problem which cannot be escaped by any Biblical interpreter, theologian, or apologist. We all operate on the basis of *some* answer to that question, whether we give it explicit and thoughtful attention or not. It is not a matter of *whether* we will answer the question, but only of *how well* we will do so.

What does Tertullian's question ask? It inquires into the proper relation between Athens, the prime example of secular learning, and Jerusalem, the symbol of Christian commitment and thought. How does the proclamation of the Church relate to the teaching of the philosophical Academy? In one way or another, this question has constantly been before the mind of the church. How should faith and philosophy interact? Which has controlling authority over the other? How should the

This chapter was first published in the *Ashland Theological Bulletin* XIII:1 (spring, 1980).

believer respond to alleged conflicts between revealed truth and extrabiblical instruction (in history, science, or what have you)? What is the proper relation between reason and revelation, between secular opinion and faith, between what is taught outside the church and what is preached inside?

This issue is particularly acute for the Christian apologist. When a believer offers a reasoned defense of the Christian hope that is within him (in obedience to 1 Peter 3:15), it is more often than not set forth in the face of some conflicting perspective. As we evangelize unbelievers in our culture, they rarely hold to the authority of the Bible and submit to it from the outset. The very reason most of our friends and neighbors *need* an evangelistic witness is that they hold a different outlook on life, a different philosophy, a different authority for their thinking. How, then, does the apologist respond to the *conflicting* viewpoints and sources of truth given adherence by those to whom he witnesses? What should he think "Athens" has to do with "Jerusalem" just here?

Christians have long disagreed over the proper strategy to be assumed by a believer in the face of unbelieving opinions or scholarship. Some renounce extrabiblical learning altogether ("Jerusalem versus Athens"). Others reject Biblical teaching when it conflicts with secular thought ("Athens versus Jerusalem"). Some try to appease both sides, saying that the Bible and reason have their own separate domains ("Jerusalem segregated from Athens"). Others attempt a mingling of the two, holding that we can find isolated elements of supportive truth in extrabiblical learning ("Jerusalem integrated with Athens"). Still others maintain that extrabiblical reasoning can properly proceed only upon the foundation of Biblical truth ("Jerusalem the capital of Athens").

The Biblical Exemplar

Now it turns out that the Bible has not left us in the dark in answering Tertullian's important question. Luke's account of the early church, The Acts of the Apostles, offers a classic encounter between Biblical commitment and secular thought. And appropriately enough, this encounter takes place between a superb representative of "Jerusalem"—the apostle Paul—and the intellectuals of Athens. The exemplary meeting between the two is presented in Acts 17.

Throughout the book of Acts Luke shows us how the ascended Christ established His church through the apostles. We are given a selective recounting of main events and sermons which exhibit the powerful and model work of Christ's servants. They have left us a *pattern* to follow with respect to both our message *and* method today. Thus, it is highly instructive for contemporary apologists to study the way the apostles, like Paul, reasoned and supported their message of hope (cf. 1 Peter 3:15). Paul was an expert at suiting his approach to each unique challenge, and so the manner in which he confronted the Athenian unbelievers who did not profess submission to the Old Testament Scriptures—like most unbelievers in our own culture—will be noteworthy for us.

We know that Paul's approach to such pagans—for instance, those at Thessalonica, where he had been shortly before coming to Athens—was to call them to turn from idols to serve the living and true God and to wait for His resurrected Son who would judge the world at the consummation (cf. 1 Thess. 1:1-10). In preaching to those who were dedicated to *idols* Paul naturally had to engage in *apologetical* reasoning. Proclamation was inseparable from defense, as F. F. Bruce observes:

> The apostolic preaching was obliged to include an apologetic element if the stumbling-block of the cross was to be overcome; the *kerygma*... must in some degree be *apologia*. And the *apologia* was not the invention of the apostles; they had all "received" it—received it from the Lord.[1]

The currently popular tendency of distinguishing witness from defense, or theology from apologetics, would have been preposterous to the apostles. The two require each other and have a common principle and source: Christ's authority. Paul's Christ-directed and apologetical preaching to pagans, especially those who were philosophically inclined (as in Acts 17), then, is paradigmatic for apologists, theologians, and preachers alike today.

Although the report in Acts 17 is condensed, Luke has summarized the main points of Paul's message and method.

But is this Paul at His Best?

Some biblical interpreters have not granted that Acts 17 is an exemplar for the proper encounter of Jerusalem with Athens. Among them there are some who doubt that Paul was genuinely the author of the speech recorded in this chapter, while others think that Paul actually delivered this speech but repudiated its approach when he went on to minister at Corinth. Both groups, it turns out, rest their opinions on insufficient grounds.

A non-evangelical attitude toward the Scripture allows some scholars a supposed liberty to criticize the authenticity or accuracy of its contents, despite the Bible's own claim to flawless perfection as to the truth. In Acts 17:22 Luke identifies the speaker of the Areopagus address as the apostle Paul, and Luke's customary historical accuracy is by now well known among scholars of the New Testament. (Interestingly, classicists have been more generally satisfied with the Pauline authenticity of this speech than have modernist theologians.) Nevertheless, some writers claim to discern a radical difference between the Paul of Areopagus and the Paul of the New Testament epistles. According to the critical view, the Areopagus focuses on world-history rather than the salvation history of Paul's letters, and the speaker at Areopagus teaches that all men are in God by nature, in contrast to the Pauline emphasis on men being in Christ by grace.[2]

These judgments rest upon an excessively narrow perception of the writings and theology of Paul. The Apostle understood his audience at Athens: they would have needed to learn of God as the Creator and of His divine retribution against sin (even as the Jews knew these things from the Old Testament) before the message of grace could have meaning. Thus the scope of Paul's theological discussion would necessarily be broader than that normally found in his epistles to Christian churches. Moreover, as we will see as this study progresses, there are conspicuous similarities between the themes of the Areopagus address and what Paul wrote elsewhere in his letters (especially the opening chapters of Romans). Johannes Munch said of the sermon: "its doctrine is a reworking of thoughts in Romans transformed into missionary impulse."[3] Finally, even given the broader perspective on history found in the address of Acts 17, we cannot overlook the fact that it, in perfect harmony with Paul's more restricted salvation-history elsewhere, is bracketed by creation and final judgment, and that it finds its climax in the resurrected Christ. The speech before the Areopagus was a "plea for the Jewish doctrine of God, and for the specifically Christian emphasis on a 'Son of Man' doctrine of judgment"⁴ (*not* an "idealized scene" printing a message about man's [alleged] "dialectical relation to God").⁵ The Paul on Areopagus is clearly the same Paul who writes in the New Testament epistles.

Did Paul suddenly shift his apologetical strategy after leaving Athens though? It has sometimes been thought that when Paul went on from Athens to Corinth and there determined to know nothing among the people except Christ crucified, repudiating the excellency of wisdom (1 Cor. 2:1-2), he confessed that his philosophical tactics in Athens had been unwise. Disillusioned with his small results in Athens, Paul prematurely departed the city, we are told, and then came to Corinth and became engrossed in the word of God (Acts 18:5), never to use philosophical style again.⁶ This outlook, while intriguing, consists of more speculation and jumping to conclusions than hard evidence.

In the first place, Paul is herein portrayed as a novice in Gentile evangelism at Athens, experimenting with this and that tactic in order to find an effective method. This does not square with the facts. For several years Paul had already been a successful evangelist in the world of pagan thought; moreover, he was not of an experimental mindset, and elsewhere he made plain that favorable results were not the barometer of faithful preaching. Besides, in Athens his results were *not* completely discouraging (17:34). And of a *premature* departure from Athens the text says nothing. After leaving Athens, Paul can hardly be said to have abandoned the disputing or "dialogue" for which he became known at Athens (cf 17:17); it continued in Corinth (18:4), Ephesus (18:19), and Troas (20:6-7)—being a daily exercise for two years in the school of Tyrannus (19:8-9). It is further inaccurate to project a *contrast* between post-Athens Paul, engrossed in the word, and Athenian Paul, absorbed in extrabiblical thought. Some Greek texts of Acts 17:24-29 (e.g., Nestle's) list up to 22 Old Testament allusions in the margin, thus showing *anything but* a neglect of the Scriptural word in Paul's Athenian preaching!

Mention can again be made of the enlightening harmony that exists between Paul's writings, say in Romans 1 and 1 Corinthians 1, and his speech in Acts 17. The passages in the epistles help us understand the apologetical thrust of the Areopagus address, rather than clashing with it—as the subsequent study will indicate. Finally, it is quite difficult to imagine that Paul, who had previously declared "Far be it from me to glory save in the cross of our Lord Jesus Christ" (Gal. 6:14), and who incisively taught the inter-significance of the death and resurrection of Christ (e.g., Rom. 4:25), would proclaim Christ as the resurrected one at Athens *without* explaining that He was also the crucified one—only later (in Corinth) to determine not to neglect the crucifixion again. We must conclude that solid evidence of a dramatic shift in Paul's apologetic mentality simply does not exist.

What Luke portrays for us by way of summary in Acts 17:16-34 can confidently be taken as a speech of the Apostle Paul, a speech which reflected his inspired approach to Gentiles without the Bible, a speech consistent with his earlier and later teachings in the epistles. His approach is indeed an exemplar to us. It was specially selected by Luke for inclusion in his summary history of the early apostolic church. "Apart from the brief summary of the discourse at Lystra..., the address at Athens provides our only evidence of the apostle's direct approach to a pagan audience."[7] With respect to the author's composition of Acts, Martin Dibelius argues: "In giving only one sermon addressed to Gentiles by the great apostle to the Gentiles, namely the Areopagus speech in Athens, his primary purpose is to give an example of how the Christian missionary should approach cultured Gentiles."[8] And in his lengthy study, *The Areopagus Speech and Natural Revelation*, Gartner correctly asks this rhetorical question: "How are we to explain the many similarities between the Areopagus speech and the Epistles if the speech did not exemplify Paul's customary sermons to the Gentiles?"[9] In the encounter of Jerusalem with Athens as found in Paul's Areopagus address, we thus find that it was genuinely Paul who was speaking, and that Paul was at his best. Scripture would have us, then, strive to emulate his method.

Intellectual Backgrounds

Before looking at Acts 17 itself, a short historical and philosophical background for the speaker of and listeners to, the Areopagus address would be helpful.

Paul was a citizen of Tarsus, which was not an obscure or insignificant city (Acts 21:39). It was the leading city of Cilicia and famed as a city of learning. In addition to general education, Tarsus was noted for its schools devoted to rhetoric and philosophy. Some of its philosophers gained significant reputations, especially the Stoic leaders Zeno of Tarsus (who cast doubt on the idea of a universal conflagration), Antipater of

Tarsus (who addressed a famous argument against Carneade's skepticism), Heraclides of Tarsus (who abandoned the view that "all mistakes are equal"), and Athenodorus the Stoic (who was a teacher of Augustus); Nestor the Academic followed Athenodorus, evidencing thereby the *variety* of philosophic perspectives in Tarsus. The city surely exercised an academic influence on Paul, an influence which would have been broadened later in Paul's life when he came into contact with its culture again for some eight years or so, three years following his conversion. In his early years Paul was also educated by Gamaliel in Jerusalem (Acts 22:3), where he excelled as a student (Gal. 1:14). His course of study would have included critical courses in Greek culture and philosophy (as evidence from the Talmud indicates). When we add to this the extensive knowledge of Greek literature and culture which is reflected in his letters, it is manifest that Paul was neither naive nor obscurantist when it came to a knowledge of philosophy and Gentile thought. Given his background, training, and expertise in Scriptural theology, Paul was the ideal representative for the classic confrontation of Jerusalem with Athens.

Athens, the philosophical center of the ancient world, was renowned for its four major schools: The Academy (founded ca. 287 B.C.) of Plato, the Lyceum (335 B.C.) of Aristotle, the Garden (306 B.C.) of Epicurus, and the Painted Porch (300 B.C.) of Zeno.

The outlook of the Academy was radically altered by Arcesilaus and Carneades in the third and second centuries before Christ; respectively, they moved the school into utter skepticism and then probabilism. Carneades relegated the notion of god to impenetrable mystery. When Antiochus of Ascalon claimed to restore the "old Academy" in the first century B.C., in actuality he introduced a syncretistic dogmatism which viewed Stoicism as the true successor to Plato. The Platonic tradition is remembered for the view that man's soul is imprisoned in the body; at death man is healed, as his soul is released from its tomb.

This anti-materialist emphasis was somewhat challenged by Aristotle's Peripatetic school, which denied the possibility of immortality and invested much time in specialized empirical study and classification of the departments of knowledge. The influence of this school had greatly weakened by the time of the New Testament. However, its materialistic proclivity was paralleled in the atomism of Epicureanism.

Democritus had earlier taught that the universe consisted of eternal atoms of matter, ever falling through space; the changing of combinations and configurations of these falling atoms was explained by reference to chance (an irrational "swerve" in the fall of certain atoms). This metaphysic, in combination with an epistemology which maintained that all knowledge stemmed from sense perception, led the Epicurean followers of atomism to believe that a naturalistic explanation of all events could and should be given. By their doctrine of self-explanatory naturalism the Epicureans denied immortality thereby declaring that there was no need to fear death. Moreover, whatever gods there may be would make no difference to men and their affairs. Epicurus taught that long-lasting pleasure was the goal of human behavior and life. Since no after-life was expected (at death a person's atoms disperse into infinite space), human desires should focus on this life alone. And in this life the only genuine long-term pleasure was that of tranquility—being freed from disturbing passions, pains, or fears. To gain such tranquility one must become insulated from disturbances in his life (e.g., interpersonal strife, disease), concentrating on simple pleasures (e.g., a modicum of cheese and wine, conversations with friends) and achieving serenity through the belief that gods never intervene in the world to punish disobedient behavior. Indeed, whatever celestial beings there are, they were taken merely as dreamlike images who—in deistic fashion—care nothing about the lives of men. Thus Philodemus wrote: "There is nothing to fear in god. There is nothing to be alarmed at in death." The Epicureans were, as is evident here, antagonistic to theology. Epicurus had taught them to appeal to right reason against superstition. Accordingly Lucretius denied any need for recourse to "unknown gods" in order to explain the plague at Athens or its alleviation.

Zeno, the founder of the Stoic school, agreed that sensation was the sole origin of knowledge, and that the mind of man was a *tabula rasa* at birth. However, against Epicurean materialism, he taught that reason governs matter in both man and the world, thus making man a microcosm of the universal macrocosm. Man was viewed as integrated with nature—man's reason seen as being of a piece with the ever-living fire which permeates the world order. This was the "Logos" for the Stoics. As a kind of refined matter that actively permeates all things and determines what will happen, the Logos was the unchanging rational plan of historical change. Nature's highest expression, then, was reason or the world-soul, being personified eventually as god. In addition to this pantheistic thrust, Zeno expounded a cyclic view of history (moving through conflagration-regeneration sequences) which precluded individual immortality. Being subordinated to immanent forces (the divine world-soul and historical determinism) the individual was exhorted to "live in harmony with nature," not concerning himself with matters which were beyond his control. If life was to be conducted "conformably to nature," and reason was nature's basic expression, then virtue for man was to live in harmony with reason. The rational element in man was to be superior to the emotional. Epictetus wrote that men cannot control events, but they can control their attitude toward events. So everything outside reason, whether it be pleasure, pain, or even death, was to be viewed as indifferent. Stoicism gave rise to a serious attitude, resignation in suffering, stern individualism, and social self-sufficiency. In turn, these achievements produced pride. Aratus and Cleanthes, two pantheistic Stoics of the mid-third century B.C., viewed Zeus as a personification of the unavoidable fate which governs man's life. Later Stoics either abandoned or modified much of Zeno's teaching. For instance, a century after Cleanthes, Panaetius essentially became a humanist who saw theology as idle chatter; and a century after Panaetius another Stoic leader, Posidonius (Cicero's instructor), opted for a Platonic view of the soul, the eternality of the world (contrary to the idea of conflagration), and the dynamic continuity of nature under fate. The famous Roman Stoic, Seneca, was a contemporary of Paul.

A final line of thinking which was influential in Athens in Paul's day (mid-first century A.D.) was that of the neopythagoreans. In the late sixth century B.C. Pythagoras had taught a mathematical basis for the cosmos, the transmigration of souls, and a regime of purity. Mixed with the thought of Plato, the Peripatetics, and Stoicism, his thought reappeared in the first century B.C. with the *neo*pythagoreans, who emphasized an exoteric and mystical theology which took a keen interest in numbers and the stars. The neophythagoreans influenced the Essene community as well as Philo—Paul's other philosophical contemporary[10]

In Paul's day Athenian intellectual life had come to be characterized by turmoil and uncertainty. Skepticism had made heavy inroads, which in turn fostered various reactions—notably: interaction between the major schools of thought, widespread eclecticism, nostalgic interest in the past founders of the schools, religious mysticism, and resignation to hedonism. Men were turning every which way in search for the truth and for security. On the other hand, over four hundred years of philosophical dispute with its conflicts, repetitions, and inadequacies had left many Athenians bored and thirsty for novel schemes of thought. Thus one can understand Luke's accurate and insightful aside to the reader in Acts 17:21, "Now all the Athenians and the strangers sojourning there spent time in nothing else, but either to tell or to hear some new thing." The curiosity of the Athenians was indeed proverbial. Earlier, Demosthenes had reproached the Athenians for being consumed with a craving for "fresh news". The Greek historian, Thucydides, tells us that Cleon once declared, "You are the best people for being deceived by something new which is said." With this background let us now examine Paul's apologetic to secular intellectuals.

Paul's Encounter with the Philosophers
Acts 17:16-21 (American Standard Version)

(16) NOW WHILE PAUL WAITED FOR THEM AT ATHENS, HIS SPIRIT WAS PROVOKED WITHIN HIM AS HE BEHELD THE CITY FULL OF IDOLS.

(17) SO HE REASONED IN THE SYNAGOGUE WITH THE JEWS AND THE DEVOUT PERSONS, AND IN THE MARKETPLACE EVERY DAY WITH THEM THAT MET HIM.

(18) AND CERTAIN ALSO OF THE EPICUREAN AND STOIC PHILOSOPHERS ENCOUNTERED HIM. AND SOME SAID, WHAT WOULD THIS BABBLER SAY? OTHERS, HE SEEMETH TO BE A SETTER FORTH OF STRANGE GODS: BECAUSE HE PREACHED JESUS AND THE RESURRECTION.

(19) AND THEY TOOK HOLD OF HIM, AND BROUGHT HIM UNTO THE AREOPAGUS, SAYING, MAY WE KNOW WHAT THIS NEW TEACHING IS, WHICH IS SPOKEN BY THEE?

(20) FOR THOU BRINGEST CERTAIN STRANGE THINGS TO OUR EARS: WE WOULD KNOW THEREFORE WHAT THESE THINGS MEAN.

(21) (NOW ALL THE ATHENIANS AND THE STRANGERS SOJOURNING THERE SPENT THEIR TIME IN NOTHING ELSE, BUT EITHER TO TELL OR TO HEAR SOME NEW THING.)

In the early 50's of the first century Paul was on something of a "missionary furlough," waiting in Athens for Silas and Timothy. (Luke's rehearsal of this situation, Acts 17:14-16, is confirmed by Paul's own account in 1 Thess. 3: 1-2). However, his brief relief was broken when he became internally provoked at the idolatry of the city, being reminded anew of the perversity of the unbeliever who suppresses God's clear truth and worships the creature rather than the Creator (Acts 17:16; cf. Rom. 1:25). Paul's love for God and His standards meant he had a corresponding hatred for that which was offensive to the Lord. The idolatry of Athens produced a strong and sharp emotional disturbance within him, one of exasperated indignation. The Greek word for "provoked" is the same as that used in the Greek Old Testament for God's anger at Israel's idolatry (e.g., at Sinai). The Mosaic law's prohibition against idolatry was obviously *binding* outside of Old Testament Israel, judging from Paul's attitude toward the idolatrous society of Athens. Paul was thinking God's thoughts after Him, and strong emotion was generated by the fact that this "city full of idols" was "without excuse" for its rebellion (Rom. 1:20)— as also had been Israel of old.

The profligate Roman satirist, Petronius, once said that it was easier to find a god in Athens than a man; the city simply teemed with idols. Visitors to Athens and writers (e.g., Sophocles, Livy, Pausanius, Strabo, Josephus) frequently remarked upon the abundance of religious statues in Athens. According to one, Athens had more idols than all of the remainder of Greece combined. There was the altar of Eumenides (dark goddesses who avenge murder) and the hermes (statues with phallic attributes, standing at every entrance to the city as protective talismans). There was the altar of the Twelve Gods, the Temple of Ares (or "Mars," god of war), the Temple of Apollo Patroos. Paul saw the image of Neptune on horseback, the sanctuary of Bacchus, the forty foot high statue of Athena, the mother goddess of the city. Sculptured forms of the Muses and the gods of Greek mythology presented themselves everywhere around Paul.[11] What is today taken by tourists as a fertile field of aesthetic appreciation—the artifacts left from the ancient Athenian worship of pagan deities—represented to Paul not art but despicable and crude religion. Religious loyalty and moral considerations precluded artistic compliments. These idols were not "merely an academic question" to Paul. They provoked him. As Paul gazed upon the Doric Temple of the patron goddess Athena, the Parthenon, standing atop the Acropolis, and as he scrutinized the Temple of Mars on the Areopagus, he was not only struck with

the inalienable religious nature of man (v.22), but also outraged at how
fallen man exchanges the glory of the incorruptible God for idols (Rom.
1:23).

Thus Paul could not keep silent. He began daily to reason with the
Jews in the synagogue, and with anybody who would hear him in the
agora, at the bottom of the Acropolis, the center of Athenian life and
business (where years before, Socrates had met men with whom to discuss philosophical questions) (v.17). Paul's evangelistic method was always suited to the local conditions—and portrayed with historical accuracy by Luke. In Ephesus Paul taught in the "school of Tyrannus," but in
Athens his direct approach to the heathen was made in the marketplace.
Paul had already approached the unbelieving Jews and God-fearing Gentiles at the synagogue in Athens. Now he entered the marketplace of
ideas to "reason with" those who met him there. The Greek word for
Paul's activity recalls the "dialogues" of Plato wherein Socrates discusses
issues of philosophical importance; it is the same word used by Plutarch
for the teaching methods of a peripatetic philosopher. Paul did not simply announce his viewpoint; he discussed it openly and gave it a reasonable defense. He aimed to educate his audience, not to make common
religious cause with their sinful ignorance.

Paul was well aware of the philosophical climate of his day. Accordingly he did *not* attempt to use premises agreed upon with the philosophers, and then pursue a "neutral" method of argumentation to move
them from the circle of their beliefs into the circle of his own convictions. When he disputed with the philosophers *they* did not find any
grounds for agreement with Paul at any level of their conversations. Rather,
they utterly disdained him as a "seed-picker," a slang term (originally
applied to gutter-sparrows) for a peddler of second-hand bits of pseudo-
philosophy—an intellectual scavenger (v. 18). The word of the cross was
to them foolish (1 Cor. 1:18), and in their pseudo-wisdom they knew not
God (1 Cor. 1:20-21). Hence Paul would not consent to use their verbal
"wisdom" in his apologetic, lest the cross of Christ be made void (1 Cor.
1:17).

Paul rejected the assumptions of the philosophers in order that he
might educate them in the truth of God. He did not attempt to find
common beliefs which would serve as starting points for an uncommit-
ted search for "whatever gods there may be." His hearers certainly did not

recognize *commonness* with Paul's reasoning; *they* could not discern an echo of their own thinking in Paul's argumentation. Instead, they viewed Paul as bringing *strange, new* teaching to them (vv. 18-20). They apparently viewed Paul as proclaiming a new divine couple: "Jesus" (a masculine form that sounds like the greek *iasis*) and "Resurrection" (a feminine form), being the personified powers of "healing" and "restoration." These "strange deities" amounted to "new teaching" in the eyes of the Athenians. Accusing Paul of being a propagandist for new deities was an echo of the nearly identical charge brought against Socrates four and a half centuries earlier.[12] It surely turned out to be a more menacing accusation than the name "seed-picker." As introducing foreign gods, Paul could not simply be disdained; he was also a threat to Athenian well-being. And that is precisely why Paul ended up before the Areopagus council.

In the marketplace Paul had apologetically proclaimed the fundamental, apostolic *kerygma* which entered on Jesus and the resurrection (Acts 17:18; cf. Acts 4:2). This summed up God's decisive saving work in history for His people: Christ had been delivered up for their sins, but God raised Him for their *justification* (Rom. 4:25) and thereby constituted Him the Son of God *with power* (i.e. exalted Lord; Rom. 1:4). As mentioned previously, Paul's approach to those who were without the Scriptures was to challenge them to turn from their idolatry and serve the living God, whose *resurrected* Son would finally *judge* the world (cf. 1 Thess. 1:9-10). This was the burden of Paul's message at Athens.

> Paul was determined to know nothing among men save Jesus Christ and Him crucified....in His resurrection through the power of the Creator there stood before men the clearest evidence that could be given that they who would still continue to serve and worship the creature would at last be condemned by the Creator then become their Judge (Acts 17:31)....No one can be confronted with the fact of Christ and of His resurrection and fail to have his own conscience tell him that he is face to face with his Judge.[13]

It was specifically the aspect of Christ's resurrection in Paul's gospel that elicited a challenge from the philosophers. At this they hauled him before the Areopagus Council for an explanation and reasoned defense of the hope that was in him (cf. 1 Peter 1:3; 3:15).

Luke tells us that Paul was "brought before the Areopagus" (v.19). The *Areios pagos* literally means "'the hill of Ares" (or "Mars' hill"); however, his referent is not likely a geographical feature in the local surrounding of the agora. The *Council of the Areopagus* was a venerable commission of the ex-magistrates which took its name from the hill where it originally convened. In popular parlance its title was shortened simply to "the Areopagus," and in the first century it had transferred its location to the Stoa Basileios (or "Royal Portico") in the city marketplace—where the Platonic dialogues tell us that Euthyphro went to try his father for impiety and where Socrates had been tried for corrupting the youth with foreign deities. Apparently the Council convened on Mars' hill in Paul's day only for trying cases of homicide. That Paul "stood in the midst of the Areopagus" (v.22) and "went out from their midst" (v. 33) is much easier understood in terms of his appearance before the Council than his standing on the hill (cf. Acts 4:7).[14]

The Council was a small but powerful body (probably about thirty members) whose membership was taken from those who had formerly held offices in Athens which (due to the expenses involved) were open only to aristocratic Athenians. This Council was presently the dominating factor in Athenian politics, and it had a reputation far and wide. Cicero wrote that the Areopagus assembly governed the Athenian affairs of state. They exercised jurisdiction over matters of religion and morals, taking concern for teachers and public lecturers in Athens (and thus Cicero once induced the Areopagus to invite a peripatetic philosopher to lecture in Athens). A dispute exists over the question of whether the Areopagus had an educational subcommittee before which Paul likely would have appeared.[15] But one way or another, the Council would have found it necessary to keep order and exercise some control over lecturers in the agora. Since Paul was creating something of a disturbance, he was "brought before the Areopagus" for an explanation (even if not for a specific examination toward the issuance of a teaching license). The mention of "the Areopagus" is one of many indicators of Luke's accuracy as a historian. "According to Acts, therefore, just as Paul is brought before the *strategoi* at Philippi, the *politarchai* at Thessalonica, the *anthupatos* at Corinth, so at Athens he faces the Areopagus. The local name for the supreme authority is in each case different and accurate."[16]

Paul appeared before the Areopagus Council for a reason that probably lies somewhere between that of merely supplying requested information and that of answering to formal charges. After indicating the questions and requests addressed to Paul before the Areopagus, Luke seems to offer the motivation for this line of interrogation in verse 21—the proverbial curiosity of the Athenians. And yet the language used when Luke says in verse 19 that "they took hold of him" is more often than not in Acts used in the sense of *arresting* someone (cf. 16:19; 18:17; 21:30—although not always, as in 9:27, 23:19). We must remember that Luke wrote the book of Acts while Paul had been awaiting trial in Rome for two years (Acts 28:30-31). His hope regarding the Roman verdict was surely given expression in the closing words of his book—that Paul continued to preach Christ, "none forbidding him." An important theme pursued by Luke in the book of Acts is that Paul was continually appearing before a court, but never with a guilty verdict against him. Quite likely, in Acts 17 Paul is portrayed by Luke as *again* appearing before a court without sentencing. Had there been the legal formality of charges against Paul, it is inconceivable that Luke would not have mentioned them or the formal verdict at the end of the trial. Therefore, Paul's appearance before the Areopagus Council is best understood as an informal exploratory hearing for the purpose of determining whether formal charges ought to be formulated and pressed against him. Eventually none were.

In the same city which had tried Anaxagoras, Protagoras, and Socrates for introducing "new deities," Paul was under examination for setting forth "strange gods" (vv. 18-20). The kind of apologetic for the resurrection which he presented is a paradigm for all Christian apologists. It will soon be apparent that he recognized that the *fact* of the resurrection needed to be accepted and interpreted in a *wider philosophical* context, and that the unregenerate's *system* of thought had to be placed in *antithetic contrast* with that of the Christian. Although the philosophers had used disdainful name-calling while considering Paul in the marketplace (v. 18), verses 19-20 show them expressing themselves in more refined language before the Council. They politely requested *clarification* of a message which had been apparently incomprehensible to them. They asked to be made acquainted with Paul's strange new teaching and to have its meaning explained. Given their philosophical presuppositions and mindset, Paul's teaching could not even be integrated sufficiently into their thinking to be understood. This in itself reveals the underlying fact that a conceptual paradigm clash had been taking place between them and Paul. Given their own worldviews, the philosophers did not think that Paul's outlook *made sense*. As Paul stood in the midst of the prestigious Council of the Areopagus, with a large audience gathered around from the marketplace, he set himself for a defense of his faith. Let us turn to examine his address itself.

Paul's Presuppositional Procedure

Acts 17:22-31 (American Standard Version)

(22) AND PAUL STOOD IN THE MIDST OF THE AREOPAGUS, AND SAID, YE MEN OF ATHENS, IN ALL THINGS I PERCEIVE THAT YE ARE VERY RELIGIOUS (MARGIN: SOMEWHAT SUPERSTITIOUS).

(23) FOR AS I PASSED ALONG, AND OBSERVED THE OBJECTS OF YOUR WORSHIP, I FOUND ALSO AN ALTAR WITH THIS INSCRIPTION, TO AN UNKNOWN GOD. WHAT THEREFORE YE WORSHIP IN IGNORANCE, THIS I SET FORTH UNTO YOU.

(24) THE GOD THAT MADE THE WORLD AND ALL THINGS THEREIN, HE, BEING LORD OF HEAVEN AND EARTH, DWELLETH NOT IN TEMPLES MADE WITH HANDS;

(25) NEITHER IS HE SERVED BY MEN'S HANDS, AS THOUGH HE NEEDED ANYTHING, SEEING HE HIMSELF GIVETH TO ALL LIFE, AND BREATH, AND ALL THINGS;

(26) AND HE MADE OF ONE EVERY NATION OF MEN TO DWELL ON THE FACE OF THE EARTH, HAVING DETERMINED THEIR APPOINTED SEASONS, AND THE BOUNDS OF THEIR HABITATION;

(27) THAT THEY SHOULD SEEK GOD, IF HAPLY THEY MIGHT FEEL AFTER HIM AND FIND HIM, THOUGH HE IS NOT FAR FROM EACH ONE OF US:

(28) FOR IN HIM WE LIVE, AND MOVE, AND HAVE OUR BEING; AS CERTAIN EVEN OF YOUR OWN POETS HAVE SAID, FOR WE ARE ALSO HIS OFFSPRING.

(29) BEING THEN THE OFFSPRING OF GOD, WE OUGHT NOT TO THINK THAT THE GODHEAD IS LIKE UNTO GOLD, OR SILVER, OR STONE, GRAVEN BY ART AND DEVICE OF MAN.

(30) THE TIMES OF IGNORANCE THEREFORE GOD OVERLOOKED; BUT NOW HE COMMANDETH MEN THAT THEY SHOULD ALL EVERYWHERE REPENT:

(31) INASMUCH AS HE HATH APPOINTED A DAY IN WHICH HE WILL JUDGE THE WORLD IN RIGHTEOUSNESS BY THE MAN WHOM HE HATH ORDAINED; WHEREOF HE HATH GIVEN ASSURANCE UNTO ALL MEN, IN THAT HE

HATH RAISED HIM FROM THE DEAD.

It must first be noted that Paul's manner of addressing his audience was *respectful* and gentle. The boldness of his apologetic did not become arrogance. Paul "stood" in the midst of the Council, which would have been the customary attitude of an orator. And he began his address formally, with a polite manner of expression: "You men of Athens." The *magna carta* of Christian apologetics, 1 Peter 3:15, reminds us that when we offer a reasoned defense of the hope within us, we must do so "with meekness and respect." Ridicule, anger, sarcasm, and name-calling are inappropriate weapons of apologetical defense. A Spirit-filled apologist will evidence the fruits of the Spirit in his approach to others.

Next we see that Paul's approach was to speak in terms of *basic philosophical perspectives*. The Athenians had specifically asked about the resurrection, but we have no hint that Paul replied by examining various alternative theories (e.g., Jesus merely swooned on the cross, the disciples stole the body, etc.) and then by countering them with various evidences (e.g., a weak victim of crucifixion could not have moved the stone; liars do not become martyrs; etc.) in order to conclude that "very probably" Jesus arose. No, nothing of the sort appears here. Instead, Paul laid the presuppositional groundwork for accepting the authoritative word from God, which was the source and context of the good news about Christ's resurrection. Van Til comments:

> It takes the fact of the resurrection to see its proper framework and it takes the framework to see the fact of the resurrection; the two are accepted on the authority of Scripture alone and by the regenerating work of the Spirit.[17]

Without the proper theological context, the resurrection would simply be a monstrosity or freak of nature, a surd resuscitation of a corpse. Such an *interpretation* would be the best that the Athenian philosophers could make of the fact. However, given the monism, or determinism, or materialism, or the philosophy of history entertained by the philosophers in Athens, they could intellectually find sufficient grounds, if they wished, for disputing even the *fact* of the resurrection. It would have been futile for Paul to argue about the facts, then, without challenging the unbelievers' *philosophy of fact.*[18]

Verses 24-31 of Acts 17 indicate Paul's recognition that between his hearers and himself two complete *systems of thought* were in conflict. Any alleged fact or particular evidence which was introduced into the discussion would be variously seen in the light of the differing systems of thought. Consequently, the Apostle's apologetic had to be suited to a philosophical critique of the unbeliever's perspective and a philosophical defense of the believer's position. He was called upon to conduct his apologetic with respect to *worldviews* which were in collision. The Athenians had to be challenged, not simply to add a bit more information (say, about a historical event) to their previous thinking, but to renounce their previous thoughts and undergo a thorough change of mind. They needed to be converted in their total outlook on life, man, the world, and God. Hence Paul reasoned with them in a presuppositional fashion.

The basic contours of a Biblically guided, presuppositional approach to apologetical reasoning can be sketched from scriptures outside of Acts 17. Such a summary will give us sensitivity and insight into Paul's argumentation before the Areopagus.

(1) Paul understood that the unbeliever's mindset and philosophy would be systemically contrary to that of the believer—that the two represent *in principle a clash of total attitude and basic presuppositions.* He taught in Ephesians 4:17-24 that the Gentiles "walk in the vanity of their mind, being darkened in their understanding" because of their "ignorance and hardened hearts," while a completely different epistemic condition characterizes the Christian, one who has been "renewed in the spirit of your mind" and has "learned Christ" (for "the truth is in Jesus"). The "wisdom of the world" evaluates God's wisdom as foolishness, while the believer understands that worldly wisdom "has been made foolish" (1 Cor. 1:17-25; 3:18-20). The basic commitments of the believer and unbeliever are fundamentally opposed to each other.

(2) Paul further understood that the basic commitments of the unbeliever produced only ignorance and foolishness, allowing an effective internal critique of his hostile worldview. The *ignorance of the non-Christian's presuppositions* should be exposed. Thus Paul refers to thought which opposes the faith as "vain babblings of knowledge falsely so called" (1 Tim. 6:20), and he insists that the wise disputers of this age have been made foolish and put to shame by those called "foolish" (1 Cor. 1:20, 27).

Unbelievers become "vain in their reasonings"; "professing themselves to be wise, they became fools" (Rom. 1:21, 22).

(3) By contrast, the Christian takes *revelational authority* as his *starting point and controlling factor* in all reasoning. In Colossians 2:3 Paul explains that "all the treasures of wisdom and knowledge" are deposited in Christ—in which case we must be on the alert against philosophy which is "not after Christ," lest it rob us of this epistemic treasure (v. 8). The Old Testament proverb had put it this way: "The fear of Jehovah is the beginning of knowledge, but fools despise wisdom and instruction" (Prov. 1:7). Accordingly, if the apologist is going to cast down "reasonings and every high thing exalted against the knowledge of God" he must first bring "every thought into captivity to the obedience of Christ" (2 Cor. 10:5), making Christ pre-eminent in *all* things (Col. 1:18). Upon the platform of God's revealed truth, the believer can authoritatively declare the riches of knowledge unto believers.

(4) Paul's writings also establish that, because all men have a clear knowledge of God from general revelation, the unbeliever's *suppression of the truth* results in *culpable ignorance.* Men have a natural and inescapable knowledge of God, for He has made it manifest unto them, making his divine nature perceived through the created order, so that all men are "without excuse" (Rom. 1:19-20). This knowledge is "suppressed in unrighteousness" (v. 18), placing men under the wrath of God, for "knowing God, they glorified Him not as God" (v. 21). The ignorance which characterizes unbelieving thought is something for which the unbeliever is morally responsible.

(5) Given the preceding conditions, the appropriate thing for the apologist to do is to set his worldview with its *scriptural presuppositions* and authority in *antithetical contrast* to the worldview(s) of the unbeliever, explaining that in principle the latter destroys the possibility of knowledge (that is, doing an internal critique of the system to demonstrate its foolishness and ignorance) and indicating how the Biblical perspective alone accounts for the knowledge which the unbeliever sinfully uses. By placing the two perspectives in contrast and showing "the impossibility of the contrary" to the Christian outlook, the apologist seeks to expose the unbeliever's suppression of his knowledge of God and thereby call him to *repentance,* a change in his mindset and convictions. Reasoning in this presuppositional manner—refusing to become intellec-

tually neutral and to argue on the unbeliever's autonomous grounds—prevents having our "minds corrupted from the simplicity and purity that is toward Christ" and counteracts the beguiling philosophy used by the serpent to ensnare Eve (2 Cor. 11:3). In the face of the fool's challenges to the Christian faith, Paul would have believers meekly "correct those who are opposing themselves"—setting Biblical instruction over against the self-vitiating perspective of unbelief—and showing the need for "repentance unto the knowledge of the truth" (2 Tim. 2:25).[19]

As we look further now at Paul's address before the Areopagus philosophers, we will find that his line of thought incorporated the preceding elements of Biblically presuppositional reasoning. He pursued a pattern of argument which was completely congruous with his other relevant New Testament teachings. They virtually dictated his method to him.

The Unbeliever's Ignorance

As Paul began his Areopagus apologetic, he began by drawing attention to the *nature of man* as inherently a religious being (Acts 17:22; cf. Rom. 1:19; 2:15). The term used to describe the Athenians in verse 22 (literally "fearers of the supernatural spirits") is sometimes translated "very religious" and sometimes "somewhat superstitious." There is no satisfactory English equivalent. "Very religious" is too complimentary; Paul was not prone to flattery, and according to Lucian, it was forbidden to use compliments before the Areopagus in an effort to gain its goodwill. "Somewhat superstitious" is perhaps a bit too critical in thrust. Although the term could sometimes be used among pagans as a compliment, it usually denoted an excess of strange piety. Accordingly, in Acts 25:19 Festus refers to Judaism, using this term as a mild reproach for its religiosity. It is not beyond possibility that Paul cleverly chose this term precisely for the sake of its ambiguity. His readers would wonder whether the good or bad sense was being stressed by Paul, and Paul would be striking a double blow: men cannot eradicate a religious impulse within themselves (as the Athenians demonstrate), and yet this good impulse has been degraded by rebellion against the living and true God (as the Athenians also demonstrate). Although men do not acknowledge it, they are aware of their relation and accountability to the living and true God who created them. But rather than come to terms with Him and His wrath against their sin (cf. Rom. 1:18), they pervert the truth. And in this they become ignorant and foolish (Rom. 1:21-22).

Thus Paul could present his point by making an illustration of the altar dedicated "To an Unknown God." Paul testified that as he "observed" the Athenian "objects of worship" he found an altar with an appropriate inscription. The verb used of Paul's activity does not connote a mere looking at things, but a systematic inspection and purposeful scrutiny (the English term 'theorize' is cognate). Among their "objects of religious devotion"' (language referring to idol worship without any approbation) Paul finally found one which contained "a text for what he had to say."[20] Building upon the admission of the Athenians themselves, Paul could easily indict them for the ignorance of their worship—that is, any worship which is contrary to the word of God (cf. John 4:22). The Athenians had brought Paul before the Areopagus with a desire to "know" what they were missing in religious philosophy (vv. 19, 20), and Paul immediately points out that heretofore their worship was admittedly of the "unknown" (v. 23). Paul did not attempt to supplement or build upon a common foundation of natural theology with the Greek philosophers here. He began, rather, with their own expression of theological inadequacy and defectiveness. He underscored their *ignorance* and proceeded from that significant epistemological point.

The presence of altars "to unknown gods" in Athens was attested by writers such as Pausanias and Philostratus. According to Diogenes Laertius, such altars were erected to an anonymous source of blessing. For instance, once (ca. 550 B.C.), when a plague afflicted Athens without warning and could not be mitigated by medicine or sacrifice, Epimenides counseled the Athenians to set white and black sheep loose on the Areopagus, and then to erect altars wherever the sheep came to rest. Not knowing the specific source of the plague's elimination, the Athenians built various altars to *unknown* gods. This sort of thing was apparently common in the ancient world. The 1910 excavation at Pergamum unearthed evidence that a torchbearer who felt under some obligation to gods whose names were unknown to him expressed his gratitude by erecting an anonymous altar for them. Deissmann's conclusion bears repeating:

> In Greek antiquity cases were not altogether rare in which "anonymous" altars "to unknown gods" or "to the god whom

it may concern" were erected when people were convinced, for example after experiencing some deliverance, that a deity had been gracious to them, but were not certain of the deity's name.[21]

The Athenians had a number of such altars on Mars' hill alone. This was testimony to the Athenian conviction that they were lorded over by mysterious, *unknown* forces.

Yet these altars were also evidence that they assumed enough *knowledge* of these forces to worship them, and worship them in a particular manner. There was thus an element of subtle, internal critique in Paul's mention of the Athenian worship of that which they acknowledged as unknown (v. 23). Moreover, Paul was noting the basic schizophrenia in unbelieving thought when he described in the Athenians *both* an awareness of God (v. 22) and an ignorance of God (v. 23). The same condition is expounded in Romans 1:18-25. Berkouwer notes, "There is full agreement between Paul's characterization of heathendom as ignorant of God and his speech on the Areopagus. Ever with Paul, the call to faith is a matter of radical conversion from ignorance of God."[22] Knowing God, the unregenerate nevertheless suppresses the truth and follows a lie instead, thereby gaining a darkened mind. Commenting on our passage in Acts 17, Munck said:

> What follows reveals that God was unknown only because the Athenians had not wanted to know him. So Paul was not introducing foreign gods, but God who was both known, as this altar shows, and yet unknown.[23]

The unbeliever is fully responsible for his mental state, and this is a state of *culpable ignorance*. That explains why Paul issued a call for *repentance* to the Athenians (v. 30); their ignorant mindset was immoral.

The Authority of Revelational Knowledge

Having alluded to an altar to an unknown god, Paul said, "That which you worship, acknowledging openly your ignorance, *I proclaim* unto you." There are two crucial elements of his apologetic approach to be discerned here. Paul started with an emphasis upon his hearers' ignorance and from there went on to declare with authority the truth of God. Their *ignorance* was made to stand over against his unique *authority* and ability to expound the truth. Paul set forth Christianity as *alone* reasonable and true, and his *ultimate starting point* was the authority of Christ's revelation. It was not uncommon for Paul to stress that the Gentiles were ignorant, knowing not God. (e.g., 1 Cor. 1:20; Gal. 4:8; Eph. 4:18; 1 Thess. 4:5; 2 Thess. 1:8). In diametric contrast to them was the believer who possessed a knowledge of God (e.g., Gal. 4:9; Eph. 4:20). This antithesis was fundamental to Paul's thought, and it was clearly elaborated at Athens.

The Greek word for "proclaim" ("set forth") in verse 23 refers to a solemn declaration which is made with authority. For instance, in the Greek papyri it is used for an announcement of the appointment of one's legal representative.[24] It might seem that such an authoritative declaration by Paul would be appropriate only when he dealt with Jews who already accepted the scriptures; however, whether dealing with Jews or secular philosophers, Paul's epistemological platform remained the same, so that even in Athens he "proclaimed" the word of God. The verb is frequently used in Acts and the Pauline epistles for the apostolic proclamation of the gospel, which had direct divine authority (e.g., Acts 3:18; 1 Cor. 9:14; cf. Gal. 1:11-12). Therefore, we see that Paul, although ridiculed as a philosophical charlatan, presumed unique authority to provide the Athenian philosophers with that knowledge which they lacked about God. This was far from stressing common ideas and beliefs. How offensive the Pauline antithesis between their ignorance and his God-given authority must have been to them!

> They were sure that such a God as Paul preached did not and could not exist. They were therefore sure that Paul could not "declare" this God to them. No one could know such a God as Paul believed in.[25]

Paul aimed to show his audience that their *ignorance* would no longer be tolerated; instead, God *commanded* all men to undergo a radical *change of mind* (v. 30). From beginning to end the unbeliever's ignorance was stressed in Paul's apologetic, being set over against the revelational knowledge of God.

Culpable Suppression of the Truth

Paul reasoned on the basis of antithetical presuppositions, a different starting point and authority. He also stressed the *culpability* of his hearers for that ignorance which resulted from their unbelief. Natural *revelation* certainly played a part in his convicting them of this truth. However, there is no hint in Paul's words that this revelation had been handled properly or that it established a common *interpretation* between the believer and unbeliever. Rather, Paul's references to natural revelation were made for the very purpose of *indicting* the espoused beliefs of his audience.

His allusion to their religious nature has already been discussed. In addition, verses 26-27 show that Paul taught that God's providential government of history was calculated to bring men to Him; they should have known Him from His works. Paul's appeal to providence was conspicuous at Lystra as well (Acts 14:17). The goodness of God *should* lead men to repentance (cf. Rom. 2:4). Acts 17:27 indicates that God's providential governance of history should bring men to seek God, "if perhaps" they might feel after Him. The subordinate clause here expresses an unlikely contingency[26] The natural man's seeking and finding God cannot be taken for granted. Citing Psalm 14:2-3 in Romans 3:11-12, Paul clearly said: "There is none that seeks after God; they have all turned aside and together become unprofitable." Returning to Acts 17:27, even if the unregenerate should attempt to find God, he would at best "feel after" Him. This verb is the same as that used by Homer for the groping about of the blinded Cyclops. Plato used the word for amateur guess at the truth. Far from showing what Lightfoot thought was "a clear appreciation of the elements of truth contained in their philosophy"[27] at Athens, Paul taught that the eyes of the unbeliever had been blinded to the light of God's revelation. Pagans do not interpret natural revelation correctly, coming to the light of the truth here and there; they grope about in darkness. Hence Paul viewed men as blameworthy for not holding fast to the knowledge of God which came to them in creation and providence. The rebellious are left without an excuse due to God's general revelation (Rom. 1:19-23).

Paul's perspective in Acts 17 is quite evidently identical with that in

Romans 1. In both places he teaches that unbelievers have a knowledge of God which they suppress, thereby meriting condemnation; their salvation requires a radical conversion from the ignorance of heathendom. G. C. Berkouwer puts it this way:

> The antithesis looms large in every encounter with heathendom. It is directed, however, against the maligning that heathendom does to the revealed truth of God in nature and it calls for conversion to the revelation of God in Christ.[28]

So it is that Paul's appeals to general revelation function to point out the guilt of the unbeliever as he mishandles the truth of God. He is *responsible* because he possesses the truth, but he is *guilty* for what he does to the truth. *Both* aspects of the unbeliever's relation to natural revelation must be kept in mind. When evidence is found of the unbeliever's awareness of the truth of God's revelation around and within him, Paul uses it as an indicator of the unbeliever's culpability, and the apostle shows that it needs to be understood and interpreted in terms of the special revelation which is brought by Christ's commissioned representative. Where natural revelation plays a part in Christian apologetics, that revelation must be "read through the glasses" of special revelation.

In Acts 17:27, heathen philosophers are said at best to grope in darkness after God. This inept groping is not due to any deficiency in God or His revelation. The philosophers grope, "even though God is not far from each one of us." Verse 28 begins with the word, "for," and thereby offers a clarification or illustration of the statement that God is quite near at hand even for blinded pagan thinkers. The unbeliever's failure to find God and his acknowledged ignorance is not an innocent matter, and Paul demonstrates this by quoting two pagan poets. The strange idea that these quotations stand "as proof in the same way as biblical quotations in the other speeches of Acts"[29] is not only contrary to Paul's decided emphasis in his theology upon the unique authority of God's word, but it simply will not comport with the context of the Areopagus address wherein the groping, unrepentant ignorance of pagan religiosity is declared forcefully. Paul quotes the pagan writers to manifest their guilt. Since God is near at hand to all men, since His revelation impinges on them continually, they *cannot escape* a knowledge of their Creator and

Sustainer. They are without excuse for their perversion of the truth. Paul makes the point that *even* pagans, contrary to their spiritual disposition (1 Cor. 2:14), possess a knowledge of God which, though suppressed, renders them guilty before the Lord (Rom. 1:18ff.).

Paul supports this point before the Areopagus by showing that even pantheistic Stoics are aware of, and obliquely express, God's nearness and man's dependence upon Him. Epimenides the Cretan is quoted from a quatrain in an address to Zeus: "in him we live and move and have our being" (Acts 17:28a; interestingly, Paul quotes another line from this same quatrain in Titus 1:12). The phrase "in him" would have denoted in idiomatic Greek of the first century (especially in Jewish circles) the thought of "in his power" or "by him." This declaration—"By him we live..."—is not at all parallel to Paul's theology of the believer's mystical union with Christ, often expressed in terms of our being "in Christ." Rather, Acts 17:28 is closer to the teaching of Colossians 1:15-17, "in him were all things created...and in him all things consist." The stress falls on "man's absolute dependence on God for his existence,"[30] even though the original writing which Paul quoted had aimed to prove that Zeus was not dead from the fact that *men* live—the *order* of which thought is fully reversed in Paul's thinking (viz., men live because *God* lives). Paul's second quotation is introduced with the words, "as certain of your own poets have said." His use of the plural is further evidence of his educated familiarity with Greek thought, for as a matter of fact the statement which is quoted can be found in more than one writer. Paul quotes his fellow Cilician, Aratus, as saying "for we are also his offspring" (from the poem on "Natural Phenomena," which is also echoed in Cleanthes' "Hymn to Zeus"). Paul could agree to the formal statement that we are God's "offspring". However, he would certainly have said by way of qualification what the Stoics did not say, namely that we are children of God merely in a natural sense and not a supernatural sense (John 1:12), and even at that we are quite naturally "children of wrath" (Eph. 2:3). Yes, we can be called the offspring of God, but certainly *not* in the intended pantheistic sense of Aratus or Cleanthes! Knowing the historical and philosophical context in which Paul spoke, and noting the polemical thrusts of the Areopagus address, we cannot accept any interpreter's hasty pronouncement to the effect that Paul "cites these teachings with approval unqualified by allusion to a 'totally different frame of reference.'"[31] Those who make such remarks eventually are forced to acknowledge the qualification anyway: e.g., "Paul is not commending their Stoic doctrine," and he "did not reduce his categories to theirs."[32]

Berkouwer is correct when he says "There is no hint here of a point of contact in the sense of a preparation for grace, as though the Athenians were already on the way to true knowledge of God."[33] Paul was well enough informed to know, and able enough to read statements in context to see, that he did *not* agree with the *intended* meaning of these poets. He was certainly not saying that these philosophers had somehow arrived at unqualified, isolated, elements of the truth—that the Zeus of Stoic pantheism was a conceptual step toward the true God!

> This is to be explained only in connection with the fact that the heathen poets have distorted the truth of God.... Without this truth there would be no false religiousness. This should not be confused with the idea that false religion contains *elements* of the truth and gets its strength from those elements. This kind of quantitative analysis neglects the nature of the distortion carried on by false religion. Pseudo-religion witnesses to the truth of God in its apostasy.[34]

Within the ideological context of Stoicism and pantheism, of course, the declarations of the pagan philosophers about God were not true. And Paul was surely not committing the logical fallacy of equivocation by using pantheistically conceived premises to support a Biblically theistic conclusion. Rather, Paul appealed to the distorted teachings of the pagan authors as evidence that the process of theological distortion cannot fully rid men of their natural knowledge of God. Certain expressions of the pagans manifest this knowledge *as suppressed*. Within the philosophical context *espoused* by the ungodly writer, the expressions were put to a false use. Within the framework of God's revelation—a revelation clearly *received* by all men *but hindered* in unrighteousness, a revelation renewed in writing in the Scriptures possessed by Paul—these expressions properly expressed a truth of God. Paul did not utilize pagan ideas in his Areopagus address. He used pagan expressions to demonstrate that ungodly thinkers have not eradicated all idea, albeit suppressed and distorted, of the living and true God. F. F. Bruce remarks:

Epimenides and Aratus are not invoked as authorities in their own right; certain things which they said, however, can be understood as pointing to the knowledge of God. But the knowledge of God presented in the speech is not rationalistically conceived or established; it is the knowledge of God taught by Hebrew prophets and sages. It is rooted in the fear of God; it belongs to the same order as truth, goodness, and covenant-love; for lack of it men and women perish; in the coming day of God it will fill the earth 'as the waters cover the sea' (Is. 11:9). The 'delicately suited allusions' to Stoic and Epicurean tenets which have been discerned in the speech, like the quotations from pagan poets, have their place as points of contact with the audience, but they do not commit the speaker to acquiescence in the realm of ideas to which they originally belong.[35]

Paul demonstrated that even in their abuse of the truth pagans cannot avoid the truth of God; they must first *have* it in order that they might then distort it. As Ned B. Stonehouse observed,

The apostle Paul, reflecting upon their creaturehood, and upon their religious faith and practice, could discover within their pagan religiosity evidences that the pagan poets in the very act of suppressing and perverting the truth presupposed a measure of awareness of it.[36]

Their own statements unwittingly convicted the pagans of their knowledge of God, suppressed in unrighteousness. About the pagan quotations Van Til observes:

They could say this adventitiously only. That is, it would be in accord with what they deep down in their hearts knew to be true in spite of their systems. It was that truth which they sought to cover up by means of their professed systems, which enabled them to discover truth as philosophers and scientists.[37]

Men are engulfed by God's clear revelation; try as they may, the truth which they possess in their heart of hearts cannot be escaped, and inadvertently it comes to expression. They do not explicitly understand it properly; yet these expressions are a witness to their inward conviction and culpability. Consequently Paul could take advantage of pagan quotations, not as an agreed upon ground for erecting the message of the gospel, but as a basis for calling unbelievers to repentance for their flight from God. "Paul appealed to the heart of the natural man, whatever mask he might wear."[38]

Scriptural Presuppositions

In Acts 17:24-31 Paul's language is principally based on the Old Testament. There is little justification for the remark of Lake and Cadbury that this discourse used a secular style of speech, omitting quotations from the Old Testament.[39] Paul's utilization of Old Testament materials is rather conspicuous. For instance, we can clearly see Isaiah 42:5 coming to expression in Acts 17:24-25, as this comparison indicates:

> Thus saith God Jehovah, he that created the heavens and stretched them forth; he that spread abroad the earth and that which cometh out of it; he that giveth breath unto the people upon it...(Isaiah 42:5). The God that made the world and all thing therein, he, being Lord of heaven and earth...giveth to all life, and breath, and all things (Acts 17:24, 25).

In the Isaiah pericope, the prophet goes on to indicate that the Gentiles can be likened to men with eyes blinded by a dark dungeon (42:7), and in the Areopagus address Paul goes on to say that if men seek after God, it is as though they are groping in darkness (i.e., the sense for the Greek phrase "feel after Him," 17:27). Isaiah's development of thought continues on to the declaration that God's praise ought not to be given to graven images (42:8), while Paul's address advances to the statement that "we ought not to think that the Godhead is like unto gold, or silver, or stone, graven by the art and device of men (17:29). It surely seems as though the prophetic pattern of thought is in the back of the apostle's mind. F. F. Bruce correctly comments on Paul's method of argumentation before the Areopagus:

He does not argue from the sort of "first principles" which formed the basis of the various schools of Greek philosophy; his exposition and defense of his message are founded on the biblical revelation of God.... Unlike some later apologists who followed in his steps, Paul does not cease to be fundamentally biblical in his approach to the Greeks, even when (as on this occasion) his biblical emphasis might appear to destroy his chances of success.[40]

Those who have been trained to think that the apologist must adjust his epistemological authority or method in terms of the mindset of his hearers as he finds them will find the Areopagus address quite surprising in this respect. Although Paul is addressing an audience which is not committed or even predisposed to the revealed Scriptures, namely educated Gentiles, his speech is nevertheless a *typically Jewish* polemic regarding God, idolatry, and judgment! Using Old Testament language and concepts, Paul declared that God is the Creator, a Spirit who does not reside in man-made houses (v. 24). God is self-sufficient, and all men are dependent upon Him (v. 25). He created all men from a common ancestor and is the Lord of history (v. 26). Paul continued to teach God's disapprobation for idolatry (v. 29), His demand for repentance (v. 30), and His appointment of a final day of judgment (v. 31). In these respects Paul did not say anything that an Old Testament prophet could not have addressed to the Jews. As the Lord Creator (cf. Isa. 42:5), God does not dwell in temples made by hand—the very same point spoken before the Jews by Stephen in his defense regarding statements about the Jerusalem temple which God himself commanded to be built (Acts 7:48). Both Paul and Stephen harkened back to the Old Testament, where it was taught that the heavens cannot contain God, and so neither could a man-made house (1 Kings 8:27; Isa. 66:1). And if God is not limited by a house erected by men, neither is He served by the sacrifices brought to such temples (Acts 17:25). Paul undoubtedly recalled the words of God through the Psalmist, "If I were hungry, I would not tell thee; For the world is mine, and the fullness thereof. Will I eat the flesh of bulls, or drink the blood of goats?" (Ps. 50:12-13). The Areopagus address stresses the fact that "life"' comes from God (v. 25), in whom "we live" (v. 28); such statements may have been subtle allusions to the etymology of the name of Zeus (*zao* in Greek, meaning 'to live')—the god exalted in the poetry of Aratus and Epimenides. The genuine Lord of life was Jehovah, the Creator, who in many ways was self-sufficient and very different from the Zeus of popular mythology or of pantheistic speculation. God has appointed the various seasons (or epochs) and boundaries of men (Acts 17:26)—even as the Psalmist wrote, "Thou hast set all the borders of the earth; Thou hast made summer and winter" (Ps. 74:17). Paul's mention of "appointed seasons" referred either to the regular seasons of the year (as in Acts 14:17, "fruitful seasons") or to the appointed periods for each nation's existence and prominence.[41] Either way, his doctrine was rooted in the Old Testament—the Noahic covenant (Gen. 8:22) or Daniel's interpretation of dreams (Dan. 2:36-45). Another point of contact between the Areopagus apologetic and the Old Testament is obvious in Acts 17:29. Paul indicated that nothing which is produced *by* man (i.e., any work of art) can be thought of as the producer *of* man. Here Paul's polemic is taken right out of the Old Testament prophets (e.g., Isa. 40:18-20). No idol can be likened to God or thought of as His image. God's image is found elsewhere, in the work of His own hands (cf. Gen. 1:27), and He thus prohibited the making of other pseudo-images of Himself ("Thou shalt not make unto thee a graven image...," Ex. 20:4). Paul's reasoning was steeped in God's special revelation.

Consistent with his teaching in the epistles, then, Paul remained on solid Christian ground when he disputed with the philosophers. He reasoned from the Scripture, thereby refuting any supposed dichotomy in his apologetic method between his approach to the Jews and his approach to the Gentiles. In any and all apologetic encounters Paul began and ended with God. "He was himself for no instant neutral."[42] "Like the biblical revelation itself, his speech begins with God the creator of all, continues with God the sustainer of all, and concludes with God the judge of all."[43] He had previously established his hearers' ignorance; so they were in no position to generate knowledgeable refutations of Paul's position. He had also indicated his authority to declare the truth; this was now reinforced by his appeal to the self-evidencing authority of God's revelation in the Old Testament Scriptures. Finally, he had established his audience's awareness and accountability to the truth of God in natural revelation. Paul now provides the interpretive context of special rev-

elation to rectify the distorted handling of previous natural revelation
and to supplement its teaching with the way of redemption.

Pressing the Antithesis

The themes of Paul's address in Acts 17 parallel those of Romans 1:
creation, providence, man's dependence, man's sin, future judgment. Paul
boldly sets the revelational perspective over against the themes of Athenian philosophy. The statements of Paul's Areopagus address could hardly
have been better calculated to reflect Biblical theology while contradicting the doctrines of pagan philosophy. Paul did not appeal to Stoic doctrines in order to divide his audience (a ploy used in Acts 23:6).[44] Rather
he philosophically offended both the Epicurean and Stoic philosophers
in his audience, pressing teaching which was directly antithetical to their
distinctives.

Against the monism of the philosophers, Paul taught that God had
created all things (v. 24; cf. Ex. 20:11; Ps. 146:6; Isa 37:16; 42:5). This
precluded the materialism of the Epicureans and the pantheism of the
Stoics. Against naturalistic and immanentistic views Paul proclaimed supernatural transcendence. As his listeners looked upon the Parthenon,
Paul declared that God does not dwell in temples made with hands (1
Kings 8:27; Isa 66:1-2).

God needs nothing from man; on the contrary man depends on
God for everything (v. 25; cf. Ps. 50:9-12; Isa 42:5). The philosophers of
Athens should thus do all things to God's glory—which is inclusive of
bringing every thought captive to Him, and thereby renouncing their
putative autonomy. Paul's teaching of the unity of the human race (v.
26a) was quite a blow to the Athenians' pride in their being indigenous to
the soil of Attica, and it assaulted their felt superiority over "barbarians."
Paul's insistence that God was not far from any would deflate the Stoic's
pride in his elitist knowledge of God (v. 27b). Over against a uniform
commitment to the concept of fate Paul set forth the Biblical doctrine of
God's providence (v. 26b; cf. Deut. 32:8); God is not remote from or
indifferent to the world of men.

Upon the legendary founding by Athena of the Areopagus court,
Apollo had declared (according to Aeschylus): "When the dust drinks up
a man's blood, Once he has died, there is no resurrection." However, the
apostle Paul forcefully announced the resurrection of Jesus Christ, a fact

which assures all men that He will judge the world at the consummation (Ps. 9:8; 96:13; 98:9; Dan. 7:13; John 5:27; Rom. 2:16)—a doctrine which contravened the Greek views of both cyclic and eternal history. The Epicureans were deceived to think that at death man's body simply decomposed, and that thus there was no fear of judgment; the resurrection refuted their ideas, just as it disproved the notion that the body is a disdainful prison. Throughout Paul's address the common skepticism about theological knowledge found in the philosophic schools was obviously challenged by Paul's pronounced authority and ability to openly proclaim the final truth about God.

Calling for Repentance and Change of Mindset

One can hardly avoid the conclusion that Paul was *not* seeking areas of agreement or common notions with his hearers. At every point he set his Biblical position in *antithetical contrast* to their philosophical beliefs, undermining their assumptions and exposing their ignorance. He did not seek to add further truths to a pagan foundation of elementary truth. Paul rather challenged the foundations of pagan philosophy and called the philosophers to full *repentance* (v. 30).

The new era which has commenced with the advent and ministry of Jesus Christ has put an end to God's historical overlooking of nations which lived in unbelief. At Lystra Paul declared that in past generations God "allowed all nations to walk in their own ways" (Acts 14:16), although now He was calling them to turn from their vanities to the living God (14:15). Previously, God had shown forbearance toward the sins of the Jews as well (cf. Rom. 3:25). However, with the advent of Christ, there has been a new beginning. Sins once committed in culpable ignorance have been made even *less* excusable by the redemptive realities of the gospel. Even in the past God's forbearance ought to have led men to repentance (Rom. 2:4). How much more, then, should men *now* respond to their guilt by repenting before God for their sins. The lenience of God demonstrates that His concentration of effort is toward the salvation rather than judgment of men (cf. John 3:17). This mercy and patience must not be spurned. Men everywhere are now *required* to repent. In Paul's perspective on redemptive history, he can simply say by way of summary: "*Now* is the acceptable time" (2 Cor. 6:2). As guilty as men had been in the past, God had passed over confrontation with them. Unlike in Israel, messengers had not come to upbraid the Gentiles and declare the punishment they deserved. God had "overlooked" (not "winked at"' with its inappropriate connotations) the former times of ignorance (Acts 17:30). Whereas in the past He had allowed the pagans to walk in their own ways, *now* with the perfect revelation which has come in Jesus Christ, God commands repentance (a "change of mind") of all men and sends messengers to them toward that end. Paul wanted the philosophers at Athens to not simply refine their thinking a bit further and add some missing information to it; but rather to abandon their presuppositions and have a complete change of mind, submitting to the clear and authoritative revelation of God. If they would not repent, it would be an indication of their love for *ignorance* and hatred of genuine knowledge.

Paul's appeal to them to repent was grounded not in autonomous argumentation but the presupposed authority of God's Son (v. 31), an authority for which there was none more ultimate in Paul's reasoning. Paul's hearers were told that they must repent, for God had appointed a day of final judgment; if the philosophers did not undergo a radical shift in their mindset and confess their sinfulness before God, they would have to face the wrath of God on the day of final accounting.

To whom would they have to give account? At this point Paul introduced the "Son of Man eschatology" of the gospels. The judgment would take place by a man (literally, a 'male') who had been ordained to this function by God. This man is the "Son of Man" mentioned in Daniel 7:13. In John 5:27, Christ spoke of himself, saying that the Father "gave him authority to execute judgment, because he is the Son of Man." After His resurrection Christ charged the apostles "to preach unto the people and to testify that this is He who is ordained of God to be the Judge of the living and the dead" (Acts 10:42). Paul declared this truth in his Areopagus apologetic, going on to indicate that God had given "assurance"' or proof of the fact that Christ would be mankind's final Judge. This proof was provided by the resurrection of Jesus Christ from the dead.

To be accurate, it is important for us to note that the resurrection was evidence in Paul's argumentation, it was *not* the conclusion of his argumentation. He was arguing, *not* for the resurrection, but for final judgment by Christ. The misleading *assumption* made by many popular evangelical apologists is that Paul here engaged in an attempted proof of the resurrection—although nothing of the sort is mentioned by Luke. Proof *by means* of the resurrection is mistakenly seen in verse 31 as proof *of* the resurrection.[45] Others know better than to read such an argument *into* the text and hold that detailed proof of the resurrection was *cut short* in Paul's address.[46] He *would* have proceeded to this line of reasoning, we are told, if he had not been interrupted by his mocking hearers. Once again, however, such an interpretation gains whatever plausibility it has with an interpreter in terms of preconceived notions, rather than in terms of textual support. F. F. Bruce remarks, "There is no ground for supposing that the ridicule with which some of his hearers received his reference to Jesus' rising from the dead seriously curtailed the speech he intended to make."[47] Haenchen says, "There is no hint that Paul is interrupted"; the speech as it appears in Acts 17 "is inherently quite complete."[48] Paul proclaimed that Christ had been appointed the final Judge of mankind, as His resurrection from the dead evidenced. The Apostle did not supply an empirical argument for the resurrection, but argued theologically from the fact of the resurrection to the final judgment. For Paul, even in apologetical disputes before unbelieving philosophers, there was no authority more ultimate than that of Christ. This epistemological attitude was most appropriate in light of the fact that Christ would be the ultimate Judge of man's every thought and belief.

The Outcome of Paul's Apologetic

Acts 17:32-34 (American Standard Version)

(32) Now when they heard of the resurrection of the dead, some mocked; but others said, We will hear thee concerning this yet again.

(33) Thus Paul went out from among them.

(34) But certain men clave unto him, and believed: among whom also was Dionysius the Areopagite, and a woman named Damaris, and others with them.

Had Paul spoken of the immortality of the soul, his message might have appeared plausible to at least some of the philosophers in his audience. However all disdained the idea of the resuscitation of a corpse. When Paul concluded his discourse with reference to the resurrection of

Christ, such an apparent absurdity led some hearers to "sneer" in open mockery of Paul. There is some question as to what should be made of another reaction mentioned by Luke—namely, that some said they would hear Paul again on this matter. This may have been a polite procrastination serving as a brush-off,[49] an indication that this segment of the audience was confused or bewildered with the message,[50] or evidence that some wistfully hoped that Paul's proclamation might prove to be true.[51] One way or another, it should not have been thought impossible by anybody in Paul's audience that God could raise the dead (cf. Acts 26:8), but as long as this philosophical assumption controlled their thinking, the philosophers would never be induced to accept the fact of the resurrection or allow it to make a difference in their outlook.

Until the Holy Spirit regenerates the sinner and brings him to repentance, his presuppositions will remain unaltered. And as long as the unbeliever's presuppositions are unchanged a proper acceptance and understanding of the good news of Christ's historical resurrection will be impossible. The Athenian philosophers had originally asked Paul for an account of his doctrine of resurrection. After his reasoned defense of the hope within him and his challenge to the philosopher's presuppositions, a few were turned around in their thinking. But many refused to correct their presuppositions, so that when Paul concluded with Christ's resurrection they ridiculed and mocked.

Acceptance of the facts is governed by one's most ultimate assumptions, as Paul was well aware. Paul began his apologetic with God and His revelation; he concluded his apologetic with God and His revelation. The Athenian philosophers began their dispute with Paul in an attitude of cynical unbelief about Christ's resurrection; they concluded the dispute in cynical unbelief about Christ's resurrection. However, Paul knew and demonstrated that the "closed system" of the philosophers was a matter of dialectical pseudo-wisdom and ignorance. Their view that God dwelt in impenetrable mystery undermined their detailed teaching about Him. Their view that historical eventuation was a matter of irrational fate was contravened by their conviction that all things are mechanistically determined, and so on. In their "wisdom" they had become utterly ignorant of the ultimate truth.

Paul knew that the explanation of their hostility to God's revelation (even though they evidenced an inability to escape its forcefulness) was to be found in their desire to exercise control over God (e.g., v. 29) and to avoid facing up to the fact of their deserved punishment before the judgment seat of God (v. 30). They secretly hoped that ignorance would be bliss, and so preferred darkness to light (John 3:19-20). So Paul "went out from among them" (v. 33)—a statement which expresses nothing about his apologetic being cut short, and which gives no evidence that Paul was somehow disappointed with his effort. Such thoughts must be read into the verse.

The minds of the Athenian philosophers could not be changed simply by appealing to a few disputed, particular facts, for their philosophical presuppositions determined what they would make of the facts. Nor could their minds be altered by reasoning with them on the basis of their own fundamental assumptions; to make common cause with their philosophy would simply have been to confirm their commitment to it. Their minds could be changed only by challenging their whole way of thought with the completely different worldview of the gospel, calling them to renounce the inherent foolishness of their own philosophical perspectives and to repent for their suppression of the truth about God.

Such a complete mental revolution, allowing for a well-grounded and philosophically defensible knowledge of the truth, can be accomplished by the grace of God (cf. 2 Tim. 2:25). Thus Luke informs us that as Paul left the Areopagus meeting, "certain men clave unto him and believed" (v. 34). There is a note of triumph in Luke's observation that some within Paul's audience became believers as a result of his apologetic presentation. He mentions conspicuously that a member of the Areopagus Counsel, Dionysius, became a Christian, as well as a woman who was well enough known to be mentioned by name, Damaris. These were but some converts "among others." Ecclesiastical tradition dating from around 170 A.D. says that Dionysius was appointed by Paul as the first elder in Athens. (In the fifth century certain pseudepigraphical works of a neoplatonic character made use of his name.) However Luke himself mentions no church having been planted in Athens, as we would have expected an educated Gentile to mention if a church had been started in Athens. Indeed, a family residing in Corinth was taken by Paul as the ecclesiastical "firstfruits of Achaia" (1 Cor. 16:15). Apparently no church was immediately developed in the city of Athens, even though patristic writers (especially Origen) mention a church being in Athens—eventually getting under way sometime after Paul's ministry there, so it seems. The earliest post-apostolic apologists, Quadratus and Aristides, wrote during the time of Emperor Hadrian, and both were from Athens. However we choose to reconstruct the ecclesiastical history of the city, it is plain that Paul's work there was not futile. By God's grace it did see success, and his apologetic method can be a guide and goad for us today. Would that we had the boldness in a proud university setting, enjoying the highest level of culture of the day, to proclaim clearly to the learned philosophers, with their great minds, that they are in fact ignorant idolaters who must repent in light of the coming judgment by God's resurrected Son.

Observations in Retrospect

(1) Paul's Areopagus address in Acts 17 has been found to set forth a classic and exemplary encounter between Christian commitment and secular thinking—between "Jerusalem and Athens." The Apostle's apologetical method for reasoning with educated unbelievers who did not acknowledge scriptural authority turns out to be a suitable pattern for our defending the faith today.

(2) Judging from Paul's treatment of the Athenian philosophers, he was not prepared to dismiss their learning, but neither would he let it exercise corrective control over his Christian perspective. The two realms of thought were obviously dealing with common questions, but Paul did not work to integrate apparently supportive elements from pagan philosophy into his system of Christian thought. Because of the truth-distorting and ignorance-engendering character of unbelieving thought, Paul's challenge was that *all reasoning* be placed within the presuppositional context of revelational truth and Christian commitment. The relation "Athens" should sustain to "Jerusalem" was one of necessary dependence.

(3) Rather than trying to construct a natural theology upon the philosophical platform of his opponents—assimilating autonomous thought wherever possible—Paul's approach was to accentuate the antithesis between himself and the philosophers. He never assumed a neutral stance, knowing that the natural theology of the Athenian philosophers was inherently a natural idolatry. He could not argue from their unbelieving premises to Biblical conclusions without equivocation in understanding. Thus his own distinctive outlook was throughout placed over against the

philosophical commitments of his hearers.

(4) Nothing remotely similar to what is called in our day the historical argument for Christ's resurrection plays a part in Paul's reasoning with the philosophers. The declaration of Christ's historical resurrection was crucial, of course, to his presentation. However he did not argue for it independently on empirical grounds as a brute historical—yet miraculous—event, given then an apostolic interpretation. Argumentation about a particular fact would not force a shift in the unbeliever's presuppositional framework of thought. Paul's concern was with this basic and controlling perspective or web of central convictions by which the particulars of history would be weighed and interpreted.

(5) In pursuing the presuppositional antithesis between Christian commitment and secular philosophy, Paul consistently took as his ultimate authority Christ and God's word—not independent speculation and reasoning, not allegedly indisputable eyeball facts of experience, not the satisfaction or peace felt within his heart. God's revelational truth—learned through his senses, understood with his mind, comforting his heart, and providing the context for all life and thought—was his self-evidencing starting point. It was the presuppositional platform for authoritatively declaring the truth, and it was presented as the sole reasonable option for men to choose.

(6) Paul's appeal was to the inescapable knowledge of God which all men have in virtue of being God's image and in virtue of His revelation through nature and history. A point of contact could be found even in pagan philosophers due to their inalienable religious nature. Paul indicated that unbelievers are conspicuously guilty for distorting and suppressing the truth of God.

(7) In motivation and direction Paul's argumentation with the Athenian philosophers was presuppositional. He set two fundamental worldviews in contrast, exhibiting the ignorance which results from the unbeliever's commitments, and presenting the precondition of all knowledge—God's revelation—as the only reasonable alternative. His aim was to effect an *overall* change in outlook and mindset, to call the unbeliever

to repentance, by following the two-fold procedure of internally critiquing the unbeliever's position and presenting the necessity of the Scripture's truth. Through it all, it should also be observed, Paul remained yet earnest. His manner was one of humble boldness.

Notes:

[1] F.F. Bruce, *The Defence of the Gospel in the New Testament* (Grand Rapids: Wm. B. Eerdmans, 1959), p.18.

[2] E.g., H. Conzelmann, "The Address of Paul on the Areopagus," *Studies in Luke-Acts*, ed. L. E. Keck and J. L. Martyn (Nashville: Abingdon, 1966), pp. 217ff. A. Schweitzer, *The Mysticism of Paul the Apostle* (New York: H. Holt, 1931), pp. 6ff.

[3] Johannes Munck, *The Anchor Bible: The Acts of the Apostles*, revised by W. F. Albright and C. S. Mann (Garden City, New York: Doubleday & Co., 1967), p. 173; cf. Adolf Harnack, *The Mission and Expansion of Christianity* (New York: Harper and Brothers, 1961), p. 383.

[4] Kirsopp Lake and Henry J. Cadbury, *The Acts of the Apostles*, vol. 4 (Translation and Commentary) in *The Beginnings of Christianity*, Part 1, ed. F. J. Roakes Jackson and Kirsopp Lake (Grand Rapids: Baker Book House, 1965 [1932]), pp. 208-209.

[5] Ernst Haenchen, *The Acts of the Apostles, a Commentary* (Philadelphia: Westminster Press, 1971 [German, 1965]), pp. 528, 529.

[6] E.g., W. M. Ramsay, *St. Paul the Traveller and the Roman Citizen* (New York: G. P. Putnam's Sons, 1896), p. 252; cf. P. Vielhauer, "On the 'Paulinism' of Acts," *Studies in Luke-Acts*, ed. Keck and Martyn, pp. 36-37.

[7] Ned B. Stonehouse, *Paul Before the Areopagus and Other New Testament Studies* (Grand Rapids: Wm. B. Eerdmans, 1957), pp. 9-10.

[8] Martin Dielius, *Studies in the Acts of the Apostles* (New York: Charles Scribner's Sons, 1956), p. 79.

[9] Bertil Gartner, *The Areopagus Speech and Natural Revelation* (Uppsala: C. W. K. Gleerup, 1955), p. 52.

[10] For further details on the philosophical schools of the Hellenic and Roman periods the reader can consult with profit the standard historical studies of Guthrie, Brehier, and Copleston.

[11] Cf. Oscar Broneer, "Athens: City of Idol Worship," *The Biblical Archaeologist* 21 (February, 1958):4-6.

[12] For a comparison of the apologetical methods of Socrates and Paul see G. L. Bahnsen, "Socrates or Christ: The Reformation of Christian Apologetics," in *Foundations of Christian Scholarship*, ed. Gary North (Vallecito, CA: Ross House Books, 1976).

[13] Cornelius Van Til, *Paul at Athens* (Phillipsburg, New Jersey: L. J. Grotenhuis, n.d.), pp. 2, 3.

[14] Contrary to Haenchen, *Acts Commentary*, pp. 518-519, 520.

[15] For the affirmative position see Gartner, *Areopagus Speech*, pp. 64-65; for the negative see Haenchen, *Acts Commentary*, p. 519.

[16] Lake and Cadbury, *Acts of the Apostles*, p. 213.

[17] Van Til, *Paul at Athens*, p. 14.

[18] Cornelius Van Til, *A Christian Theory of Knowledge* (Nutley, New Jersey: Presbyterian and Reformed, 1969), p. 293.

[19] For further discussion of the presuppositional method, refer to the earlier chapters of this book.

[20] F. F. Bruce, *Commentary on the Book of Acts*, in the New International Commentary on the New Testament (Grand Rapids: Wm. B. Eerdmans, 1955), p. 356.

[21] Adolf Deissman, *Paul: A Study in Social and Religious History* (London: Hodder and Stroughton, 1926), pp. 287-291.

[22] G. C. Berkouwer, *General Revelation* (Grand Rapids: Wm. B. Eerdmans, 1955), p. 145.

[23] Munck, *Anchor Bible: Acts*, p. 171.

[24] J. H. Moulton and George Milligan, *The Vocabulary of the Greek New Testament* (Grand Rapids: Wm. B. Eerdmans, 1950), p. 324.

[25] Van Til, *Paul at Athens*, p. 5.

[26] Henry Alford, *The Greek New Testament* (Boston: Lee and Shepherd Publishers, 1872), 2:198.

[27] J. B. Lightfoot, "St. Paul and Seneca," *St. Paul's Epistle to the Phillipians* (Grand Rapids: Zondervan Publishing House, 1953), p. 304.

[28] Berkouwer, *General Revelation*, p. 145.

[29] Haenchen, *Acts Commentary*, p. 525.

[30] Gartner, *Areopagus Speech*, p. 188.

[31] Gordon R. Lewis, "Mission to the Athenians" part IV, Seminary Study Series (Denver: Conservative Baptist Theological Seminary, November, 1964), p. 7; cf. pp. 1, 6, 8, and part III, p. 5.

[32] Ibid., part III, p. 2; part IV, p. 6.

[33] Berkouwer, *General Revelation*, p. 143.

[34] Ibid., p. 144.

[35] F. F. Bruce, "Paul and the Athenians," *The Expository Times* 88 (October, 1976): 11.

[36] Stonehouse, *Paul Before the Areopagus*, p. 30.

[37] Van Til, *Paul at Athens*, p. 12.

[38] Ibid., p. 2.

[39] Lake and Cadbury, *Acts of the Apostles*, p. 209.

[40] F. F. Bruce, *The Defense of the Gospel in the New Testament*, pp. 38, 46-47.

[41] Compare Gartner, *Areopagus Speech*, pp. 147-152, with Haenchen, *Acts Commentary*, p. 523.

[42] Berkouwer, *General Revelation*, pp. 142-143.

[43] F. F. Bruce, *"Paul and the Athenians,"* p. 9.

[44] Contrary to E. M. Blaiklock, *The Acts of the Apostles, An Historical Commentary*, in the Tyndale New Testament Commentaries, ed. R. V. G. Tasker (Grand Rapids: Wm. B. Eerdmans, 1959), pp. 140-141.

[45] E.g., R. C. Sproul, tape "Paul at Mars' Hill," in the series Exegetical Bible

Studies: Acts (Pennsylvania: Ligonier Valley Study Center), tape AX-13.

[46] E.g., Blaiklock, *Acts, Historical Commentary*, p. 142; Everett F. Harrison, *Acts: The Expanding Church* (Chicago: Moody Press, 1975), p. 272.

[47] F. F. Bruce, *Book of Acts*, p. 362.

[48] Haenchen, *Acts Commentary*, p. 526.

[49] Harrison, *Acts*, p. 273.

[50] Lake and Cadbury, *Acts of the Apostles*, p. 219.

[51] J. S. Steward, *A Faith to Proclaim* (New York: Charles Scribner's Sons, 1953), p. 117.